DATE DUE		

East European Fault Lines

East European Fault Lines

Dissent, Opposition, and Social Activism

Janusz Bugajski
and Maxine Pollack

Westview Press
BOULDER, SAN FRANCISCO, & LONDON

Westview Special Studies on the Soviet Union and Eastern Europe

This Westview softcover edition is printed on acid-free paper and bound in softcovers that carry the highest rating of the National Association of State Textbook Administrators, in consultation with the Association of American Publishers and the Book Manufacturers' Institute.

Published in 1989 in the United States of America by Westview Press, Inc., 5500 Central Avenue, Boulder, Colorado 80301, and in the United Kingdom by Westview Press, Inc., 13 Brunswick Centre, London WC1N 1AF, England

Library of Congress Cataloging-in-Publication Data
Bugajski, Janusz, 1954–
    East European fault lines : dissent, opposition, and social
activism / Janusz Bugajski and Maxine Pollack.
    p. cm.—(Westview special studies on the Soviet Union and
Eastern Europe)
    Bibliography: p.
    Includes index.
    ISBN 0-8133-7714-5
    1. Europe, Eastern—Politics and government—1945-   . 2. Dissenters—
Europe, Eastern. 3. Social action—Europe, Eastern. I. Pollack,
Maxine. II. Title. III. Series.
DJK50.B84 1989
947—dc19   89-5647
                                                                    CIP

Printed and bound in the United States of America

⊗ The paper used in this publication meets the requirements of the American National
    Standard for Permanence of Paper for Printed Library Materials Z39.48-1984.

10   9   8   7   6   5   4   3   2

To Winifred, Arthur, Jadwiga, and Piotr

Contents

Acknowledgments

During the course of our research for this book, the following libraries, institutions, and organizations proved particularly valuable: Radio Free Europe/Radio Liberty (Munich, West Germany); Library of Congress (Washington, DC); Hoover Institution (Stanford University, California); London School of Slavonic and East European Studies; Solidarity Information Office (London); Hungarian October Freepress Information Centre (London); Palach Press Ltd (London); and the Helsinki Watch Committee (New York).

Rewarding research assistance during various parts of the project was provided by: Monika Michejda, Alina Zyszkowski, Catherine Murray, Pamela Rein, Heidi Liszka, Ilinca Popescu, Jeanette Besemer, Lisa Gibney, Adriana Ercolano, Andrea Doromby, Ellen Stroud, Jasmin Kosovic, Michael Uster, Peter O'Brien, John Gutbezahl, David Perry, Robert Scott, Torben Christiansen, Frank Watanabe, and Jean Carlo Rivera.

We would also like to thank the Earhart Foundation for their generous financial support enabling us to complete the project.

Janusz Bugajski
Maxine Pollack

Introduction

An extensive submerged network of social and political fault lines snakes across the Communist states of Eastern Europe, deepening where dissent and opposition are most trenchant. These areas of independent activity, which by definition challenge the Communist Party stranglehold on freedom of expression and public self-organization, indicate a corresponding systemic vulnerability. Though it would be premature to predict an imminent "earthquake" of revolutionary proportions resulting from these fault lines, the latter do constitute definite long-term weaknesses in the Leninist political bedrock. A comprehensive "seismological" study of this phenomenon is overdue. This work endeavors to provide a comparative analysis of oppositionist trends in the Soviet satellite states of contemporary Eastern Europe: Bulgaria, Czechoslovakia, the German Democratic Republic, Hungary, Poland, and Romania. It gauges, describes, and evaluates the extent and objectives of independent social activism in these countries, and explores both the causes and effects of public dissent. Limited space precludes a full assessment or even a complete listing of every dissident group, oppositionist trend, and independent public initiative in the East bloc. We principally single out movements and campaigns which serve as pertinent examples of distinct independent currents and strategies in the region. The study also provides an overview of the major literature on Soviet bloc dissent, and draws attention to less well known sources of unofficial ideas and actions.

Chapter 1 examines the main cycles of repression and resistance that have enveloped Eastern Europe since the post-World War II Communist takeovers. The Soviet-directed seizures of power in each state are chronicled, as are the more consequent instances of rebellion, resistance, and political opposition. In order to understand the severe limitations placed on dissent and autonomous social activism throughout the region, an interpretation of the essential structures and features of the Leninist Party-state is offered. Thereafter, the bloc-wide process of de-Stalinization is described, with special attention paid to the resultant upsurge of popular resistance to Communist rule. Subsequent sections explore more recent developments in Czechoslovakia and Poland respectively—the reformist "Prague Spring" in 1968 and the "normalization" that vanquished it; the flowering of the Solidarity movement in 1980–81 and the imposition of martial law that outlawed it.

Chapter 2 explores categories of dissent and opposition, placing them in historical context, defining them, and assessing their objectives. Some notable comparisons and contrasts are drawn between dissent and opposition, and reformism and revisionism. Official government responses to organized dissent, involving various forms of repression, co-optation, manipulation, and neutralization of organized opposition are also discussed. Chapter 3 is a thematic continuation of the preceding chapter that focuses on various forms of extra-systemic social activism. Whereas revisionism and reformism attempt to change the system from within, social activism during the past decade in particular, emphasizes transforming the existing social, political, and economic order from outside the Communist power structure. One major dichotomy proposed here is that between revolutionism and evolutionism; the latter can in turn be subdivided into a predominantly social and an explicitly political strategy of change. In addition, manifestations of individual non-conformism, unorganized dissent, and non-violent protest are explored. Social movements of self-defense and public resistance are documented, as are more substantial independent mass movements and embryonic "alternative societies." A concluding section on dissident foreign policy highlights international cooperation between oppositionists within the Soviet bloc, as well as their points of contact with the West.

A country-by-country analysis of political movements and human rights campaigns is presented in Chapter 4. The first section deals with Solidarity's Poland, focusing on underground and above-ground structures of the free trade union movement and on the avowedly political groupings it has helped to spawn. A second part looks at the Charter 77 human rights campaign in Czechoslovakia, sketching distinctions between the diverse political currents subsumed under the Charter umbrella. From there, the discussion turns to contemporary Hungary and the dissident, largely intellectual activism therein which styles itself as the "democratic opposition." Also covered are the more traditionalist, rural-based Magyar "populists" opposition. Nascent human rights movements and political resistance in the GDR, Romania, and Bulgaria are enumerated in the last section.

An analytic overview of independent and institutional religious activities throughout the bloc is provided in Chapter 5. Special emphasis is accorded to dissident and oppositionist trends that are religious in origin or aim. Against a backdrop of official hostility to organized religious life, the assessment is primarily multi-denominational, with each significant faith examined in turn. The study focuses on Roman Catholicism in each country; on Protestant denominations in the GDR,

Hungary, Czechoslovakia, Romania, and Poland; and on independent currents in the Orthodox Churches of Romania and Bulgaria. Finally, an assortment of minority religions throughout Eastern Europe are considered, such as the Uniate Catholics, small Protestant sects, Islam, and Judaism.

In Chapter 6, economic initiatives outside or on the periphery of the Party-state system are explored. The first section examines the parameters of government-sponsored economic reforms, and assesses the extent of privatization and free enterprise in agriculture and industry. The latter includes numerous small-scale manufacturers, "cottage industries," and a legion of self-employed petty entrepreneurs. A second section concentrates on parallel economies and informal distribution networks that supply a considerable volume of services and goods on the "black" and "grey" markets. Also considered are the extensive, self-serving bribery networks on the one hand, and charitable aid initiatives on the other. The nature, extent, and impact of free labor unionism and autonomous industrial self-management are also scrutinized in a concluding section.

In Chapter 7 independent social campaigns and cultural trends are covered in some detail. Peace and disarmament movements are documented, with particular attention given to the protests of conscientious objectors, nuclear disarmers, and anti-Warsaw Pact groups. Ecological campaigns against the unchecked degradation of the natural environment are then chronicled. The few organized human rights initiatives of several national and ethnic minorities are also explored. In addition, the growing number of autonomous youth currents and student movements is highlighted. On the cultural scene, alternative education programs and independent publishing in the region are examined, as are the political acts of graphic and dramatic artists who work outside official circles.

Emerging prospects for reform, dissent, opposition, and social activism in Eastern Europe are elaborated in the concluding Chapter 8. The impact throughout the bloc of recent developments, such as the accession to power of Soviet leader Mikhail Gorbachev, is analysed, with special focus on official East bloc reactions and dissident responses to the reformist winds blowing from Moscow. Plausible scenarios for economic and political change are considered, including government restructuring initiatives, and the prospects for any emerging independent public life. Appropriate and contingent Western policies are also discussed within a historical framework, and the potential for Western influence during the coming years is subsequently assessed.

1

Historical Dimensions

The historical context of contemporary dissent, opposition, and independent social activism in Eastern Europe will be assessed here by surveying the major political developments since the post-World War II Communist Party takeovers. Native Communist organizations obedient to Moscow's will imposed Marxist-Leninist dictatorships over those areas of Central-Eastern Europe that had been designated by the Allied powers as part of the Soviet "sphere of influence." "Revolutions from above" were engineered after the war in Bulgaria, Czechoslovakia, East Germany, Hungary, Poland, and Romania. At the outset, pseudo-democratic coalition governments and falsified national elections helped to reduce internal resistance and to deceive the West as to the ultimate political objective—unchallenged monoparty rule.[1] We will focus on the manner in which domestic opposition was eliminated during the capture of state power and the consolidation of Communist rule. The main characteristics of the sociopolitical systems thereby established will then be outlined and examined.

After the death of Soviet leader Jozef Stalin in 1953, a prolonged and often fitful process of "de-Stalinization" was set in motion throughout the bloc. It consisted of diverse currents of reform and retrenchment, liberalization and orthodoxy, rebellion and "normalization." Each Party-state endeavored to survive the ensuing internal and external political storms, while Moscow sought to maintain Communist control and overall Warsaw Pact cohesion. The contradictions and antagonisms between Communist supremacy and popular aspirations for political and economic freedoms continued to surface throughout the Khrushchev and Brezhnev eras. The Hungarian Revolution, Polish October, Prague Spring, and Poland's Solidarity were the mainsprings of opposition in post-Stalin Eastern Europe; the significance of each phenomenon will be assessed in turn. This evaluation will then serve as an historical introduction to dissent, opposition, and social activism in the Soviet bloc during the past decade.

4

Communist Takeovers and Public Resistance

Communist Party takeovers in all East European states, except Yugoslavia (expelled from the bloc in 1948) and Albania (which broke with Moscow in 1961), would not have been possible without a Red Army presence after their liberation from Nazi occupation in 1944–45.[2] Under the cover of Soviet military control and close political supervision, minority Communist Parties, which in most cases could claim little public support, imposed Leninist dictatorships and launched programs of "socialist construction" between 1945 and 1948. Having largely abandoned the idea of simply incorporating the East European countries into the Soviet Union, Stalin sought to establish stable and fully subservient Communist regimes to project and protect Soviet power, to undermine Western security, and to promote the eventual neutralization of Western Europe.[3]

Seton-Watson has outlined three distinct stages in the Communist takeover process.[4] First, each local Party entered into temporary coalition governments with non-Communist political organizations while excluding those parties and groups that were denounced as "undemocratic" or "reactionary." Second, the semi-genuine "coalitions" were replaced with completely bogus "alliances" while political rivals were banned and eliminated. In many instances, the fiction of genuine cooperation between independent political organizations was upheld during the further strengthening of Communist control. Third, absolute one-party rule was established with the abolition of all oppositionist groups, or through forced mergers with the ruling Party. Communist-controlled "front organizations" were created to elicit and channel public activism in the desired direction. The length of the first two stages varied significantly between states. In Poland the first period was practically bypassed; in Romania and Bulgaria the first stage lasted for only a few months; in Hungary it was completed by the spring of 1947; in Czechoslovakia stage three was achieved only in February 1948.[5]

The omnipresence of Soviet forces and the widespread use of police terror generally dissuaded anti-Communist forces from undertaking open revolts against the Party administration.[6] Though the context of each takeover varied, several common factors helped to account for the absence of more widespread resistance during the consolidation of power. The wartime devastation played an important role in exhausting local propensities for armed opposition, and decimating the ranks of the intelligentsia as potential leaders for a postwar non-Communist political revival. The Soviet proxies exploited to their advantage the massive territorial adjustments, economic dislocations, and extensive population transfers. Early Western disengagement, and the limited military and political leverage of the West in the Soviet "sphere of influence," both aided the Communist augmentation of power and defused local willingness to resist actively. Skilled Kremlin diplomacy during and after the war—particularly at the Tehran, Yalta, and Potsdam conferences—helped to seal Moscow's control over the region and precluded any substantive Allied assistance to non-Communist forces.

Growing numbers of East Europeans began to view Communist Party rule and Soviet domination as inevitable and irreversible, and adjusted their expectations accordingly.[7] The governing Parties embarked on a gradual process of Communization, with an initial appearance of pluralism and promises of well-being and democracy to pacify wide sectors of the population. The overall popularity of some of the programs espoused and policies initially adopted by the Communists must not be discounted. These were frequently appropriated from the more popular political parties and included the nationalization of industry, banking, and commerce, and redistribution of land to private small farmers. Promises of rapid economic development and a steady rise in living standards also played a part in subduing potential discontent. Nevertheless, though the postwar "reconstruction" programs clearly had a widespread resonance, the subsequent radicalization of state control in all sectors of public life began to breed fresh resentments among both the urban and rural masses.

The Communists also exploited patriotic and nationalist sentiments to promote their authority and legitimacy. In Poland, for example, the reclamation and resettlement of the formerly German "Western territories" and the Baltic Coast areas were manipulated by the regime to capture public support and divert attention from Poland's territorial losses in the East to the USSR. Among the politically active, some left-wing socialists and radical agrarians calculated that by cooperating with the Communists they could help moderate the latter's platform and prevent the imposition of a Soviet-type political system. The ruling Parties themselves encouraged and exploited such sentiments to gain recruits and defuse opposition. Large Communist-controlled bureaucracies were formed in each state, bestowing material benefits on loyal and obedient functionaries; millions of citizens were thereby enticed into the service of the Party-state.

Despite overall Soviet supervision, the early postwar period was characterized by considerable latitude for the local Parties. Decisions about the pace and content of Communization, the pattern of reconstruction, and the elimination of resistance was left largely to local leaders. However, after the supranational Cominform was created in September 1947 and Communist consolidation in each country was completed, Stalin sought to eradicate national divergencies and impose monocentrism and ideological uniformity while accelerating the "construction of socialism." This second phase of the Communist stranglehold between 1948 and 1953 enforced Stalinism throughout the bloc. It involved the elimination of non-Communists from all influential posts— through imprisonment, exile, or execution. Totalitarian controls were extended to all spheres of social life. A vehement antireligious campaign was launched alongside extensive political and cultural repression and ideological-educational indoctrination. In the economic realm, the full-scale collectivization of agriculture was undertaken, and the nationalization program embraced all medium and small-scale enterprises aside from some marginal private trading.

To ensure Moscow's overall control and supervision, Soviet advisers were installed in key slots throughout the Party, government, military, police, and security apparatus. Each state was placed in a relationship of economic as well as political and military dependence on the Soviet Union. Ultimate Party control rested in the hands of reliable "Muscovite" cadres, who until about 1948 had shared power with the "native" Communists in each country.[8] The immediate postwar emphasis on "domestic peculiarities" was reversed during the "anti-nationalist" and "anti-rightist" drive in the late 1940s, especially after the "national deviation" and excommunication of Tito's Yugoslavia. Between 1948 and 1952 Kremlin controls over each Party were tightened. Real and suspected "national Communists" were hounded down, silenced, and liquidated in each satellite.[9] The sweeping purges of revisionists, "rightist deviationists," and "nationalists" were followed by campaigns against "cosmopolitans" between 1951 and 1953. A principal objective was to construct a monolithic political system in each state by eliminating Party divisions and eradicating disruptive frictions between competing interest groups. Though the degree of police terror varied—with the German Democratic Republic and Bulgaria at one extreme, and Poland at the other—all effective resistance to the Stalinist model was quashed both inside and outside each governing Party.[10]

It is useful at this point to summarize the chief highlights in the six Soviet bloc states during the Communist seizure of power and consolidation of Party rule, with particular emphasis on the elimination of political opposition. Though the Bulgarian Communist Party (*Bulgarskata Komunisticheska Partiia*, BCP) was active during World War Two in the armed underground resistance against the pro-Nazi regime, it was small and largely ineffectual.[11] Soon after the Soviet military occupation, the Fatherland Front coalition, established clandestinely in 1942, emerged from hiding and assumed power after a coup on 9 September 1944.[12] Several thousand actual and potential opponents of the new regime were branded as "fascists," "traitors," and "war criminals," summarily tried, and promptly executed.[13] The Fatherland Front itself encompassed some left-wing agrarians and socialists, in addition to the Communist members who held the two key government positions—the Ministry of the Interior and the Ministry of Justice. From this vantage point, the BCP proceeded to root out non-Communist leaders and supporters, and undermined the position of its purported allies. The Fatherland Front was steadily brought under full Communist control.

Georgi Dimitrov, a seasoned Comintern agent and diehard Stalinist, returned to Bulgaria from Moscow in late 1945 to take over the Party leadership and assume the premiership. With his arrival, the Communization process gathered steam. In September 1946 the monarchy was formally abolished and Bulgaria was proclaimed a "peoples' republic." The rigged elections to the National Assembly in October 1946 placed the BCP firmly in control, with the Fatherland Front allegedly receiving 70.8% of the vote. The regime temporarily tolerated a viable political opposition in the shape of the independent Agrarian Union. But following the adoption of the new "Dimitrov" constitution in December 1947, the Party initiated a reign of terror which swept aside the autonomous agrarians, absorbed the remnants of the Social Democrats into the BCP, liquidated the remaining political bodies that had desisted from joining the Fatherland Front, and rearranged the political system according to "Leninist norms." During the renewed Stalinization drive in 1948–49, the "native" faction of the BCP was purged by the "Muscovites," and many Bulgarian Communists were imprisoned or executed. Dimitrov died in July 1949 and was replaced by another staunch "Muscovite" Vulko Chervenkov who became both Prime Minister and Secretary-General of the BCP. Chervenkov tightened Party control in all areas in strict imitation of the Soviet system and eliminated all remaining "nationalist deviationists." During Chervenkov's six-year tenure, approximately 100,000 BCP members were expelled or demoted. Stalin's economic model was imposed, with full-scale nationalization, heavy industrialization, and comprehensive agricultural collectivization. By 1960, 97.4% of all land was either collectivized under Party supervision or placed under the control of agricultural enterprises operated by the state.

In Czechoslovakia, the first post-war National Front government, established in April 1945, consisted of a system of power sharing between Communists, Social Democrats, Socialists, and Catholics in Bohemia and Moravia, and between Communists and Democrats in Slovakia.[14] All conservative and rightist political parties were swiftly banned, including the powerful pre-war Republican (Agrarian) Party. The Communist Party of Czechoslovakia (*Komunisticka Strana Ceskoslovenska*, CPCS) obtained several key ministries in the coalition administration, including those of the Interior, Agriculture, Information, Education, and Social Welfare. The CPCS also successfully maneuvered to gain control of the country's labor unions, youth groups, and various other mass organizations in order to build up its power base. During relatively free parliamentary elections in May 1946, the Communists gained a narrow majority, and Party leader Klement Gottwald became Prime Minister.

The CPCS delayed its seizure of absolute power until 1948, partly to correspond with Soviet interests in lulling the West and promoting Communist parliamentary victories in Western Europe, and partly because of its apparent conviction that the Party could obtain full control through legalistic means. But even though the CPCS was traditionally fairly strong and claimed to have substantial support among the working class, particularly in comparison to other East European Communist Parties, there were growing indications after 1946 of a steady decline in its popularity. Public opinion polls preceding the national elections scheduled for May 1948 revealed a sharp drop in public backing for the Communists. Growing domestic hostility to its policies, and fading chances for the CPCS in any genuinely democratic election, coupled with Stalin's growing impatience with the slow pace of Czechoslovak communization, compelled the Party to seize power and dispense with the electoral process altogether.[15]

The CPCS *coup d'état* was instigated during a cabinet crisis in February 1948. The ministers of three non-Communist parties resigned in protest when the CPCS Minister of the Interior packed the police force with his supporters despite official instructions to the contrary from a clear government majority. The CPCS pressurized President Eduard Beneš to form a new government containing a Communist majority. Both constitutional and illegal means were employed in the bloodless takeover, with the ever-present threat of force by armed, Communist directed workers' detachments. Several non-Communist leaders fled to the West, while others were arrested by the police. The Minister of Foreign Affairs, Jan Masaryk, was discovered dead under suspicious circumstances, and President Beneš resigned in June 1948 and died three months later. All "bourgeois" political parties were now prohibited and their property confiscated by the state, while parliament was transformed into a pliant instrument of one-party rule.

Klement Gottwald, the new Czechoslovak President and Secretary-General of the CPCS, was instructed by Moscow to resolutely impose a Stalinist political and economic model. The Party itself was reorganized and extended its control networks over all state bodies and bureaucracies, using the National Front as a convenient vehicle for building its monopoly of power. During the closely supervised national elections, staged in May 1948, the single list of Communist and pro-Communist candidates received almost 90% of the vote. This veneer of legality was supplemented soon afterwards by the passing of a new national constitution based on the Stalinist prototype. The ruling Party was expanded with the creation of a loyal core of cadres; between 200,000 and 300,000 politically reliable people from proletarian and peasant backgrounds were elevated to high posts to serve CPCS aims. At the height of the Stalinization drive, "bourgeois elements," "national deviationists," "opportunists," and other non-conformists were purged from the Party; former CPCS Secretary-General Rudolf Slansky was hanged in 1952 as an "enemy of the people." In the early 1950s about 100,000 political prisoners were believed to be incarcerated in jails and concentration camps, and numerous political trials were held to root out any remaining opposition to Stalinism. By this time, resistance to Sovietization both within and outside the Party was scant among all sectors of the population; it was further extinguished by the mid-1950s.

After the entry of the Red Army on German territory, the "Ulbricht group" of German Communists arrived from Moscow in April 1945 to implement Soviet instructions.[16] Independent anti-fascist political groups and voluntarily formed citizens' aid committees, which sprung up in various cities in the wake of the Nazi defeat, were swiftly disbanded and suppressed by Soviet occupation forces in the Russian sector of Germany. Stalin was initially hesitant to establish a Communist state but tended to treat Germany as a single entity in order to extend Soviet influence, neutralize the entire country, and prepare the groundwork for a possible pro-Soviet united Germany in the years ahead. In June 1945, the German Communist Party was formally reorganized, and three other parties were founded in the Soviet Zone—the Social Democrats, Christian Democrats, and Liberal Democrats—under overall Communist supervision. This "Anti-Fascist Democratic Bloc," later renamed the "Democratic Bloc of Parties and Mass Organizations," formed a provisional German government until the creation of the German Democratic Republic (GDR) in October 1949, when the Bloc became the National Front.

The Communist Party, in close cooperation with the Soviet Military Administration in Germany, placed its members in key administrative posts. In April 1946, the Communists and Social Democrats were amalgamated to form a Socialist Unity Party (*Sozialistische Einheitspartei Deutschlands*, SUP) in which the Communists were clearly in a dominant position. Meanwhile, the ranks of the Christian and Liberal Democrats were decimated and their political influence substantially diminished.[17] In late 1947, the SUP formed a People's Congress that established the new government for the GDR ("a socialist state of the German nation") and formulated a new constitution. National elections were held in May 1949 for representation in the Peoples' Congress; all candidates were meticulously screened by the SUP. The Third Party Congress in 1950 officially transformed the SUP into a Leninist organization and accelerated the thrust toward totalitarianism. Party leader Walter Ulbricht imposed an austere, orthodox regime, overseen by Soviet forces and political "advisors," under the facade of "anti-fascism" and "peoples' democracy." The East German Communists became the principal executors of Stalin's will, while most of the regime's political opponents fled to the West during the mass migration of Germans in the 1940s and 1950s.

A provisional government was established in Budapest in December 1944, with a Hungarian Communist Party minority in addition to representatives of other parties—the Smallholders, Social Democrats, and National Peasants.[18] The Communists took command of the police, security service, army, and civil service with NKVD (Soviet security service) assistance. They proceeded to create and control various local and national mass organizations while penetrating the labor unions and other existing bodies. The process of attrition against rival political parties culminated in the elimination of democrats, socialists, and agrarians from decision-making.[19] The People's Courts, established in February 1945 to purge "reactionaries," alleged fascists and war criminals with assistance from Russian troops, summarily tried and deported about 150,000 people. Several thousand of the accused were executed or simply disappeared. Despite the Communist defeat in the elections of October 1945, a national "coalition" government remained in place, dominated by the Party which retained control over the police and security organs.

Within the Communist Party itself, the "Muscovite" and "native" factions were merged under the leadership of Moscow stalwart Mátyás Rákosi. Hungary was proclaimed a "peoples' republic" in January 1946 after which the Communists sharpened their drive for total power.[20] Rákosi's infamous "salami tactics" were employed to sow dissension within and between rival parties, to weaken their influence, and absorb their enfeebled remnants. Various "extra-institutional" measures and official prohibitions were also activated to disperse and eliminate the opposition. Following the Third Party Congress in September 1946, the program of eradicating the capitalist sectors of the economy was stepped up. The main offensive was launched against the Smallholders Party, especially after the national elections in August 1947 in which the weakened Smallholders still received the majority of the vote much to the chagrin of the regime. Subsequently, Prime Minister Ferenc Nagy was exiled, while other Smallholders leaders were imprisoned or executed. By early 1948, the Communists were preponderant in the state apparatus and had penetrated every government department. The Smallholders organization was dismembered, and in June 1948 the forced merger of the Hungarian Communist Party and the Social Democrats into a new Hungarian Socialist Workers Party (*Magyar Szocialista Munkaspart*, HSWP) signalled "unity among the working class" under firm Communist control.

During the fraudulent elections staged in May 1949 the newly created Peoples' Independence Front obtained 95.6% of the vote. In August the constitution of the Hungarian Peoples' Republic was adopted which formalized the country's subordination to the Soviet Union. Full blown Stalinization involved a major purge of the Party between 1949 and 1953, when more than 350,000 "revisionists" and "national deviationists" were expelled amid massive police terror. More Communists were executed during this period than under the prewar authoritarian regime of Admiral Horthy; they included the potential "Hungarian Tito," Interior Minister László Rajk. As in neighboring states, the Party also launched a collectivization campaign in the countryside in order to eradicate rural opposition to Communist rule.

With the arrival of Soviet forces on Polish territory, Moscow helped to establish the Polish Committee of National Liberation (or Lublin Committee) in July 1944 as a provisional Communist-controlled administration.[21] The initial coalition government proceeded to emasculate the mass-based peasant and socialist movements while ensuring its political stranglehold. The opposition was systematically undermined through hostile propaganda, disruption, harassment, and press censorship. Notwithstanding the overwhelming unpopularity of Soviet-imposed Communism, the Polish Workers Party was steadily built up through a vigorous recruitment drive and the offering of various privileges to new members. The remaining contingents of the war-time anti-Nazi resistance movement, the Home Army (AK), were liquidated by Polish Communist and Soviet forces, including detachments which refused to surrender their arms and disband their units.[22] About 200,000 AK troops voluntarily came out into the open during 1945, while about 30,000 to 35,000 continued fighting against Communist militia and military units. In some regions of the country this internal war continued until mid-1948.[23] The Warsaw regime claimed that nearly 15,000 of their troops died in sporadic clashes with the underground during this period; the latter reportedly suffered 7,500 killed and over 2,000 wounded. Thousands more were arrested and placed in former German concentration camps, while thousands of others were executed.

The political arm of the opposition was also eliminated by the Warsaw regime. The chief delegate of the legal wartime Polish government-in-exile was arrested by the NKVD, together with the commander-in-chief of the Home Army and fourteen other AK leaders; they were taken to Moscow, secretly tried and imprisoned. As in other states, after the liquidation of organized political opposition the peasants were neutralized through the initial land redistribution program, and much of the intelligentsia withdrew from public life into an "internal emigration" where silence usually signified passive resistance. A rigged referendum in June

1946 was followed by a fraudulent general election in January 1947, in which the government bloc purportedly obtained 78.9% of the vote. The ballot was marked by voter intimidation, the gerrymandering of electoral districts, the exclusion of independent socialists, and the repression of other parties and non-Communist candidates. Over one million voters were deprived of the right to cast their ballots, many Peasant Party candidates were arrested, and vituperative anti-Peasant propaganda was unleashed in the official media. The election result itself was falsified in favor of the Communist-controlled "Democratic Bloc" which reportedly received about 80% of the vote. The actual total was believed to be substantially lower, though officials prohibited any independent monitoring of the balloting.

After the elections the independent Peasant Party was finally eliminated; its branches were closed, its active members arrested, and its leader Stanisław Mikołajczyk escaped into exile. December 1948 marked the forced merger of the Polish Workers Party and the crippled Polish Socialist Party, at the first Polish United Workers Party (*Polska Zjednoczona Partia Robotnicza*, PUWP) Congress. With the onset of Stalinization, Władysław Gomułka, the Communist First Secretary between 1945 and 1948, was replaced by Moscow loyalist Bolesław Bierut; other "native Communists" were also removed from leadership positions.[24] A farm collectivization campaign was inaugurated in 1949, leading to widespread passive resistance by the peasantry and a serious decline in agricultural productivity. A crackdown against the Catholic Church was also launched in the late 1940s to neutralize religious influence, the authority of the clergy, and the breadth of the anti-Communist opposition.

Following a multi-party *coup d'état* in Romania in August 1944 against the wartime Antonescu government, the Romanian Communist Party strengthened its position in the country.[25] With assistance from the Soviet High Command and Red Army, the Party achieved a predominant role in the coalition government by March 1945 following three major reshuffles of the Bucharest administration.[26] Severe repression against wartime political leaders and postwar political allies aided the Party in neutralizing any credible non-Communist opposition and stymied the reactivation of viable peasant and liberal party organizations. The security organs under firm Communist control thwarted active resistance and arrested, tried, incarcerated, and executed the leaders of competing parties. During 1945 the Party captured control of most local government bodies, purged their political opponents from leading positions, and assumed a dominant central role. Falsified elections in the fall of 1946 sealed the Communist victory. King Michael was formally deposed in December 1947 and the largest independent political body, the National Peasant Party, was outlawed the same year. A new constitution was adopted in April 1948 and Romania was declared a "people's republic."[27] Tens of thousands of Peasant and Liberal Party activists and members were imprisoned during the next few years: the survivors were not released until 1964.

In February 1948, the Communist Party was transformed into the Romanian Workers Party (*Partidul Muncitoresc Român*, RCP) through fusion with the leftwing of the dismembered Social Democratic Party. With the last source of organized opposition quashed, the Communist regime embarked on its own Stalinization program which included the nationalization of industry, central economic planning, and a reinvigorated collectivization campaign that swallowed up about 96% of arable land by 1962. At the height of Communist consolidation, the "native" Party Secretary-General Gheorghe Gheorghiu-Dej won the factional struggle against the "Muscovites," purged his rivals, and gained full control. By 1952 he was *de facto* leader of both state and Party. Despite his more independent stance toward Moscow, in comparison to other Soviet bloc heads, Gheorghiu-Dej was a doctrinaire Stalinist intent on rapidly Communizing Romania. As a result, his differences with the Kremlin did not reach breaking point, though they laid the foundations for Bucharest's semi-autonomous foreign policy after Stalin's death.

In order to understand the limitations placed on dissent, opposition, and independent social activism in Eastern Europe, it is important to examine the structure of Communist Party-states and enumerate the features common both to the original Lenin-Stalin model and its post-Stalin variants.[28] The ruling Parties claim and practice a monopoly of political activity and determine the objectives of state and society. The Communist Party itself is an organization standing above all domestic bureaucracies but closely intertwined with all of them. It formulates policy goals and monitors their implementation through its supervisory organs at each administrative level.

Each Leninist Party is governed internally by the principles of "democratic centralism," which guarantee strict inner-Party discipline and hierarchical control. A specialized political apparatus manipulates all internal Party elections, this is in turn subordinate to the self-appointed ruling Politburo. Following "open discussion" in the Central Committee and some input from lower Party echelons, the Politburo makes binding decisions and sets policy goals. These decisions are implemented by the Secretariat through its control over the Party apparatus and its numerous functionaries at each regional, institutional, and occupational tier. The executive committees of all lower-level Party bodies are nominated and vetted by higher Party organs. All such nominations are closely monitored by the central bureaucracy, which ultimately approves the composition of all dependent bodies. This *nomenklatura* system of appointments extends to all national bureaucracies; it assures that only politically reliable cadres are selected for positions of authority and responsibility, and it helps guarantee elite oligarchic control. Political reliability is often more important than technical ability for ensuring job appointments through the *nomenklatura* network. In most cases all non-Party people are excluded from key positions in management and public administration. The entire Party apparatus is thereby sealed off from the masses, while the majority of members tend to join the Party for the material prospects or career opportunities it bestows, rather than from ideological or political convictions.

The Communist power apparatus embraces all governmental, military, judicial, police, economic, and other pyramidical bureaucracies. The Party supervises all state and local government activities. The parliamentary structure presents a facade of democratic participation by all social strata, political interests, and occupational groupings. The token representation of avowedly non-Communist parties and associations is a pluralistic smokescreen for single-Party control. There is little actual debate or dissension over state policies, particularly as all candidates are screened, selected, and scrutinized by the Communist apparatus. A multi-party fiction is maintained to create the appearance of genuine pluralism among "non-antagonistic" political groups.

The central government selected by the Party Secretariat controls parliament and passes executive decisions and ministerial orders which the national assembly duly approves. In effect, the legislature endorses, formalizes, and legitimizes Party decisions. It also selects the Head of State, whether an individual or a presidium; in some instances, the posts of Head of State and Communist Party First Secretary (or General Secretary) are filled by one individual. "National" or "Peoples' Front" umbrella organizations help to buttress Party control by channelling the interests of various affiliated public organizations in the desired direction. National fronts also have the exclusive right to nominate candidates for parliamentary and local government councils. Each local council, acting upon Party instructions, selects its Executive Committee and President; this pattern is replicated at all territorial-administrative levels up to the national tier. The population at large does not freely nominate or select either the local or central government members. Even where election ballots contain more than one nominee for each council or parliamentary seat, the candidates are first approved by Communist-controlled electoral colleges and commissions.

In Communist Party states political control is extended into spheres that are normally the province of non-political organizations in democratic countries. All public mass organizations, including occupational, cultural, youth, women's, war veterans', and pensioners' groups, are subject to political regulation so that any independent social activities are effectively precluded.[29] All employees are supervised through a network of professional organizations. Official labor unions undertake all decisions pertaining to relations between workers and management; they dispense sizeable funds for health care, vacation and recreational facilities, or other welfare benefits, and help keep employees in check. For intellectuals such as writers and artists, the professional unions decide on the allocation of scholarships, royalties, and publishing rights. Occupational unions, often identified as "transmission belts," function as supportive organs by exercising control over the workforce through Party-appointed officials and staff. Rather than defending the interests of workers *vis-à-vis* management, the chief role of union officials is to enforce discipline, promote production, monitor the mood on the shop floor, and defuse worker discontent.

The legal system in Leninist states is wielded to pacify society and subdue political deviance. All courts and their personnel are selected by the Party or its client organizations. The "procuracy" system combines the role of public prosecutor with that of defending "socialist legality" as interpreted by Communist officials. The law thereby enshrines the interests of the state against the atomized and virtually undefended society. The police and security apparatus further assist in protecting Party rule by neutralizing nonconformists and potential political opponents. In addition, an extensive network of police agents and informers permeates practically every sphere of society to forestall the crystallization of organized opposition and to keep the Party informed about the activities of dissidents.

The all-embracing web of political, administrative, judicial, and police controls is supplemented by powerful economic levers at the Party's disposal. The country's economic bureaucracy sets the national economic plan and supervises its implementation, controls national investments, the money supply, and foreign and domestic trade, sets wages and prices, manages all financial institutions, work enterprises, state farms, and wholesale and retail outlets. The bulk of society, including practically every economic unit, is organized into a vast productive enterprise controlled by the state apparatus. All crucial economic decisions are made by the Communist elites, whereby free market principles have been largely replaced by administrative directives and state plans. Since the mid-1950s, the ruling Parties have sought to eliminate the worst anomalies of central planning by incorporating more "scientific" management methods and catering for "consumerism" to avoid serious economic crisis and social turmoil. Some leeway has been allowed in the more "liberalized" post-Stalin systems for privatization in certain sectors of the economy, such as agriculture, small-scale manufacturing, and services. In addition, a shadow "second economy" or "black market" is commonly tolerated to help meet the grossly unsatisfied popular demands for goods and services.

De-Stalinization, Rebellion, and Normalization

Domestic and international developments in the years following Stalin's death in 1953 did not fundamentally alter the principle and practice of Leninist hegemony in Eastern Europe. However, they did herald a period of political conflict, internal power struggles, and in some instances, popular opposition to Communist Party rule. Moscow's "New Course" meant some economic and cultural concessions within the bloc, while preserving Party control over the most significant aspects of public life. For example, forced heavy industrialization was muted in favor of a more pronounced consumer orientation; police ubiquitousness was somewhat curtailed, state arbitrariness refined, and some cultural liberalization tolerated. In the Soviet Union and most East bloc states, the "cult of personality" was replaced by a "collective leadership," with the Party First Secretary made more accountable to the Politburo. The relaxation of Kremlin controls, ideological inconsistency, political instability, and leadership divisions in the immediate post-Stalin era also set in motion various political initiatives and public opposition in Eastern Europe. In some cases, domestic confusion as to the limits of Soviet tolerance and attempts at Party democratization led to profound political crises and sparked popular rebellion against some or all features of Communist rule. Moscow in turn tried to immunize itself against open revolt and ensure bloc-wide cohesion during this "thaw" period, and sought to delineate the parameters of reform and political freedom.[30]

Despite the dissolution of the Cominform in April 1956, and the greater leeway for East European regimes in their pursuit of "national roads to communism," no extensive diminution of Party control was envisioned. Restrictions were placed on economic experimentation and the Warsaw Pact alliance system was deemed sacrosanct. Particularly after danger signals began to surface in Hungary, Poland, and elsewhere, Moscow shifted the emphasis from reformism to retrenchment and the preservation and protection of the Communist system throughout the bloc. The creation of the Warsaw Pact in May 1955 had formalized Soviet military domination over Eastern Europe and provided a legalistic justification for maintaining Red Army troops in these states. The Warsaw Treaty of Mutual Assistance was in fact an immediate precursor to the "Brezhnev Doctrine," which "legitimized" direct Soviet intervention in the internal affairs of East European states.

Government relaxation in the mid-1950s spurred opposition movements of variable strength, scope, and duration in a number of countries. This phenomenon was in several instances seriously underestimated by the Kremlin. We shall examine the two most important and extensive rebellions against the Party-state during this period—the Hungarian Revolution and the "Polish October"—and also survey post-Stalin dissent and opposition in the remaining East European states. Hungary's Stalinist leader Rákosi was reluctant to implement Moscow's "New Course" and allow for a measure of power-sharing with less hard line comrades. As a result, the leadership was riddled with conflict for several years. Unable to pursue vigorously any one political program, the Party's authority was measurably undermined and eventually endangered. In 1953, Rákosi was forced by Kremlin pressures to relinquish the premiership; he was replaced by Imre Nagy who sought to limit repression and restrain the forced collectivization program. After two years, Nagy himself was ousted for "right-wing deviation" and expelled from the Party. Rákosi's return in February 1955 reversed the liberalization process, but failed to stem rising popular aspirations for democratization. Khrushchev's "secret speech" in 1956 against Stalin's policies breathed new life into Hungarian reformers and helped to increase dissent among students, intellectuals, and workers demanding Nagy's reinstatement as well as the implementation of numerous civil liberties. Paradoxically, according to Griffith, Communist revisionists

> unwittingly paved the way for their own loss of political leadership. For the more they succeeded in arousing latent popular forces of opposition, the more they tended to be displaced in popular favor by 'legitimate' spokesmen of the older political and social trends—i.e. peasant, worker, and religious leaders deriving their popular support from past positions of influence and their adherence to traditional patterns of national patriotism and social and parliamentary democracy.[31]

De-Stalinization increased popular restlessness in Hungary amid demands for lessened Party control over all aspects of social life. Brzezinski points out that in such a potentially revolutionary situation, halfway measures by Rákosi and Ernö Gerö, his replacement as Party First Secretary in July 1956, "could not satisfy the masses which were by then craving a political reform."[32] Hungarian intellectuals, both Communist and non-Communist, became increasingly vociferous in their campaign to restore democracy; they became more radicalized by Rákosi's dogmatism and intransigence. Gerö proved to be an equally doctrinaire Communist unable to forestall mounting discontent through relatively minor concessions such as wage increases. Even the reappearance of

Nagy as Prime Minister in October 1956 failed to stop the escalation of protest actions and political demands among various social groups.

A mass demonstration in Budapest on 23 October 1956, organized by the dissident Petofi Circle, triggered the Hungarian Revolution after the Secret Security Police (AVO) intervened by firing at the demonstrators. The initial deployment of Soviet troops did not succeed in "restoring order." Instead, the rebellion swiftly spread, and the number of armed revolutionaries rapidly increased. They were joined by units of the Hungarian army and by sympathetic policemen who supplied weapons and ammunition, and fought alongside the insurgents against Soviet forces; the rest of the Hungarian army disintegrated. During the fighting, the rebels put forward a program for extensive political, economic, and social change, including full pluralism, civil liberties, free elections, independent labor unions and workers' councils, the abolition of the security police and collective farms, and the restoration of parliamentary democracy and a mixed economy. Their demands exceeded the policies proposed by revisionist Communists such as Nagy, who was eventually swept along in the popular tide and bowed to public pressure for national independence and the termination of Leninist dictatorship. Following the temporary Soviet withdrawal Nagy announced the abolition of the one-party system. This was to involve the recreation of independent political parties including the Smallholders Party, and the establishment of an authentic coalition government in which the Communists would occupy a minority position in line with their actual support in the country. Local self-government councils were formed in various parts of Hungary to represent various social and occupational strata, and workers' councils effectively took over factory management. As the Party structure disintegrated under democratic pressures, the government surrendered its monopolistic central controls.

The Kremlin increasingly feared that the Hungarian Communists would permanently lose power if free elections were allowed to take place. The gathering pace of democracy was interrupted by the second Soviet armed intervention on 4 November 1956. Moscow relied on the massive use of force to crush the rebellion and install a pro-Soviet single-party regime; about 200,000 Soviet troops were employed.[33] Aside from fierce clashes in Budapest, the fighting quickly spread to several major cities, including Gyor, Szeged, Pecs, Miskolc, and Szolnok. An estimated 25,000 to 50,000 Magyar insurgents were killed in the fighting, together with about 7,000 Soviet soldiers. Over 200,000 people fled the country, while several thousand were arrested, imprisoned, executed, or deported to Soviet labor camps.[34] Most armed resistance was subdued by 8 November, and the remaining rebels surrendered by 14 November. The Russian invasion was followed by Nagy's declaration of Hungarian neutrality and cessation from the Warsaw Pact. Simultaneously, a general strike was proclaimed by the independent trade unions in the midst of the fighting. In fact, during the uprising the real centers of authority were the revolutionary workers' councils established spontaneously when Party control and police supervision collapsed.

The Soviet authorities dissolved Nagy's government and assembled a group of loyal pro-Moscow Hungarian Communists to form a new administration under the leadership of First Secretary Janos Kádár; Nagy was later executed. Further clashes erupted in various parts of the country until Kádár declared martial law on 9 December 1956. The workers' councils were officially dissolved; the responses to calls for a general strike were mostly sporadic. A wave of mass arrests and dismissals swept the country, and about 5,000 people were executed by the regime during the post-revolutionary reprisals. Kádár's "normalization" program banned all autonomous organizations and re-established Communist controlled bodies in all areas of public life. Once the resistance had been crushed and order restored, Kádár endeavored to gain the trust if not the loyalty of citizens through an unwritten "social contract" in which society would forsake political involvement in exchange for economic security and rising living standards. Kádár's solution did not envisage a return to Stalinist measures once political opposition had been eliminated; it also precluded any replication of Nagyist liberalization. A mass Party recruitment drive was launched in 1957, and the Eighth HSWP Congress in November 1962 declared the country to be embarking upon the construction of a fully socialist society. In 1968, Budapest launched its New Economic Mechanism, combining some market elements with decentralized planning, and greater enterprise autonomy with regard to production and investment. This loosened some state economic controls and allowed for a modicum of private and cooperative enterprise, but did not undermine the Communist political and economic monopoly.

In Poland, PUWP leaders were initially extremely cautious de-Stalinizers and managed to contain any liberalizing trends until mid-1956. The system then lost some of its most obvious oppressive features and social protests gained in strength. However, the bulk of the emerging opposition was not centered among Party revisionists or any organized political movement. It was largely an amorphous expression of frustration, devoid of any singular political platform and susceptible to state disruption. The major eruption of public protests by workers in Poznań on 28 June 1956 was put down within three days by police and army units. The strikes and demonstrations were provoked by the introduction of an unfair bonus system requiring an increase in productivity that effectively diminished the already low wages. The regime estimated that 48 people were killed in the clashes, but unofficial sources claim the figure was closer to 300, with over 1,000 subsequent arrests.[35] The authorities displayed sufficient tactical skill following the Poznań riots to defuse a potentially explosive situation—through leadership changes and promises of reform—while keeping the anxious Soviets at bay. Warsaw publicly admitted to policy mistakes as one justification for the workers' grievances, but warned about "provocateurs" and "agitators" whose attempts to detach Poland from "socialism" would be mercilessly crushed.

One repercussion of the widespread popular ferment and discontent, of which Poznań was the most dramatic manifestation, was the replacement of Party First Secretary Edward Ochab by the "native" Communist Władysław Gomułka in October 1956. The threat of direct Soviet military intervention subsided once Moscow was assured that Gomułka's "Polish road to socialism" would run parallel with the Kremlin's main avenue, and that Warsaw's policies posed no threat to Moscow in the international Communist movement. The leadership changes in the PUWP evidently took some account of popular feelings, as Gomułka purportedly represented an anti-Stalinist, "national-focused" brand of Communism not responsible for the Stalinist terror. Gomułka gained the support of many critical students and non-Party intellectuals who believed that he could provide a significant spur to the budding liberalization movement; but their initial hopes proved to be misplaced.[36] The new Party leadership also pacified the bulk of the workforce through concessions to industrial workers, farmers, and the Church, amid promises of greater rewards in the future. Constant appeals were made to patriotism, while direct Soviet control over Polish internal affairs visibly lessened. The blatantly uneconomic collective farms were largely dissolved, leading to a re-privatization of the bulk of agriculture.[37] Religious freedoms were restored following the release of Cardinal Stefan Wyszyński from prison. Gomułka aimed to bolster the legitimacy of his regime through a guarded reconciliation with the Catholic Church, but the honeymoon proved to be short-lived.

Soon after acceeding to power, Gomułka embarked on a "middle course" between the harder-line Stalinist elements within the Party and potential liberalizers; after dealing with Stalin's "old guard" he turned his offensive against the reformers. Once Gomułka had consolidated his position within the PUWP, ideological revisionists were purged and the screws were tightened on dissenting intellectuals and non-conformist students. The "Polish October," which bloomed fleetingly in the late 1950s, was both a social revolt by wide sectors of the populace against dictatorial rule, and a moderately revisionist movement within the Party itself. Both strands of opposition were extinguished, preventing the creation of any organized counterforce to "democratic centralism." The liberalizing Polish "October" was converted into the "little stabilization" of the post-Stalin turmoil. The Hungarian episode was not repeated in Poland because of overall policy continuity and gradualism within the Party despite leadership reshuffles; firm brakes were placed on any national democratic revolution. There was no unification of any organized opposition forces, and no tangible all-encompassing program of action emerged either among intellectuals or workers. The upper echelon of the Party did not undergo any major political split, nor did it lose control over the situation at the grassroots.[38] The leadership was also able to reassure the Soviets that socialism would be strengthened by Gomułka's program. Moscow's latitude toward Polish developments showed that the USSR was willing to make some allowances for national diversity in the process of domestic political stabilization. Aside from Hungary, each East European regime was able to adjust to changing circumstances without provoking Soviet intervention by reassuring the Kremlin that Party rule was not under threat.

The significant democratizing gains of the "Polish October" were gradually eroded. The workers' councils that emerged in 1956 were rendered powerless as their authority was never clearly defined and they displayed little real autonomy in decision-making. By the close of the decade they became fully subordinate to the Party and the management controlled factory committees. Unlike in Hungary, the Warsaw regime was unable to register any dramatic economic improvements, as the command system was not substantially relaxed to allow for individual enterprise, decentralization, and marketization. In local and national elections, voting rights were not greatly extended as all candidates remained Communist Party nominees. Liberalizing elements within the PUWP were purged and condemned for weakening Leninist discipline and leadership. The independent and influential student weekly *Po Prostu* was banned in 1957, leading to student disturbances and clashes with police in which several hundred people were detained. The *Krzywe Koło* and other autonomous discussion clubs were outlawed as they threatened to exceed the bounds of permissible de-Stalinization. Strict censorship was restored throughout the mass media by October 1957, and the ice age of Gomułkaism persisted for more than a decade over the Polish political landscape.

In the German Democratic Republic, the initial shock waves following Stalin's death led to programmatical divisions within the Party leadership and disruptions in the functioning of the political apparatus. These developments were in turn fanned by serious workers' revolts on 17 June 1953, incited by 10% increases in work norms and unrealistically high state plans that would have drastically cut basic wages. About 25,000 to 50,000 workers staged protests in East Berlin, spurring dem-

onstrations in about 270 different locations throughout the Soviet zone
of occupation. The embryonic insurrection, in which workers demanded
economic improvements, free elections, and the release of political
prisoners, was violently suppressed by the Red Army as the local Party
militia stood by, powerless. According to independent estimates, about
400 German workers were killed in the clashes and dozens were later
executed under the cover of martial law. Soviet military courts also
sentenced several thousand protest organizers to long prison terms.[39]
The regime combined repression with promises of leniency, hasty supplies
of food to placate disgruntled employees, and the rescinding of increases
in work norms. Though further sporadic strikes were reported in several
cities between July and September 1953, the security forces eventually
quashed all active resistance.

After the Hungarian Revolution, Soviet forces in East Germany were
reinforced to prevent any repetition of rebellion. The East Berlin regime
remained one of the most rigid and illiberal in the bloc, even though
the Soviet occupation administration was formally dissolved in March
1954 and GDR sovereignty recognized. Stalinist stalwart Walter Ulbricht
remained in power and on guard against any liberalizing trends among
intellectuals or Party members. Moscow backed Ulbricht in his purge
of revisionists and reformers within the SUP and the persecution of
non-Party dissidents. Renewed student unrest in 1957 in East Berlin,
Leipzig, Dresden, and other cities was resolutely suppressed. The construction of the Berlin Wall and the general fortification of the border
between East and West Germany in August 1961 constituted a major
move against internal opposition. It also sealed off an important escape
hatch for skilled workers, technicians, and other professionals whose
exodus had gravely weakened the GDR economy.[40] The collectivization
of German agriculture was accelerated, so that by 1961 84% of arable
land was under "cooperative control," as compared to only 50% in
1959. The "New Economic System" (NES), announced in 1963, modified
the central planning model and instituted certain alterations in Party
organization. Greater emphasis was placed on "economic levers," enterprise profitability and cost effectiveness, with personal incentives and
rewards for managers and workers. By 1968 the "leading role" of the
SUP had been re-emphasized, and the importance of centralized state
planning underscored. Ulbricht was replaced in May 1971 after the NES
was finally abandoned in the wake of mounting economic strain. Erich
Honecker took over as General Secretary in a fairly smooth leadership
transition. He successfully kept the lid on dissent within and outside
the Party, while steadily improving economic performance and living
standards.

In Czechoslovakia, de-Stalinization did not gather significant momentum until the mid-1960s; it merely consisted of small-scale modifications of the existing structure.[41] Antoni Zapotocky succeeded Gottwald after the latter's death in March 1953. His initial attempts to liberalize the system were quickly checked and he was soon replaced as the party's first secretary by the more orthodox Antonin Novotny, who was also named President after Zapotocky's death in 1957. Novotny resisted pressures for change and delayed the political and social shock waves of de-Stalinization. Events in Hungary and Poland in 1956 strengthened his hand to tighten Party discipline and oust reformist elements. Czechoslovakia also experienced workers' protests in May 1953, due to a "currency reform" which confiscated the savings of skilled workers and lowered the purchasing power of the entire workforce. For several hours workers in Plzen took over the entire city and demanded better economic conditions and political liberties. The demonstrations were suppressed by militia units brought in from Prague; at least six workers were shot dead and a number of organizers and participants were later excluded from benefits disbursed by the official labor unions. Further workers' protests in Ostrava and Brno in May and June 1953 were also speedily quelled by security troops.

From 1955 Czechoslovak writers and students began to voice demands for greater cultural freedom. In October and November 1956, some intellectuals and workers demonstrated in support of the Hungarian Revolution, but were dispersed by the police. Prague tightened censorship and police surveillance, while several political trials were staged to root out alleged spies and saboteurs. Yugoslav, Hungarian, and Polish forms of "national Communism" were condemned as serious nationalist or "rightist deviations." The political turbulence in neighboring states was used as a pretext for maintaining repression, even though the centralized economic reins were loosened somewhat with less prority given to heavy industry after 1958. A new constitution was adopted in 1960, ending the "peoples' democracy" phase and declaring Czechoslovakia a "socialist republic." Czech centralism was also reinforced to the detriment of any remaining Slovak self-determination.

The populations of Bulgaria and Romania were effectively shielded from post-Stalin political turbulence and the regimes were not faced with any serious domestic disturbances. Any liberalizing trends were suppressed in Bulgaria while some changes were introduced in the Party leadership. After Stalin's death Chervenkov fell from grace and was removed from Party leadership; his replacement Todor Zhivkov also became premier in 1962, succeeding Anton Yugor. Chervenkov still remained a force within the government, and as Minister of Culture in 1957 he helped to silence those intellectuals who were pressing for democratization. The majority of Zhivkov's ruling associates were closely involved in the Stalinist tyranny and were slow to soften their methods of political and social control. Police terror was somewhat relaxed, pressures on collective farmers were loosened, and some improvements were registered in working conditions to forestall proletarian disquiet. Some small-scale protests were speedily dispersed, such as the tobacco workers' strike in Plovdiv in 1953. After 1962 Zhivkov proceeded to eliminate any factional divisions within the Party and reinforced Sofia's highly "conservative" ideological and political line. According to Fejto, Bulgarian de-Stalinization was largely limited to theoretical denunciations of "dogmatism" and the "cult of the personality," and some minor personnel shake-ups in the Party.[42]

De-Stalinization in Romania was equally subdued, with a few curbs placed on police brutality and the release of some political prisoners. Through a mixture of concessions to workers, the threat of reprisals, and selective repression, no serious challenges to the government materialized. Unrest in Hungary and Poland gave the green light to a crackdown against student and intellectual critics. Bucharest's version of de-Stalinization consisted of a more forthright pursuit of national identity in foreign affairs, and a "New Course" for economic development, while rigid political controls remained intact.[43] A nominal "collective leadership" was inaugurated while Gheorghiu-Dej tightened his hold on the Party apparatus, purged potential liberalizers and neo-Stalinists, handpicked loyal cadres at central and regional levels, and disallowed any political flexibility in domestic affairs. The small student and worker demonstrations during 1956, in Cluj, Tirgu Mures, Timisoara, and Bucharest, which reflected dissatisfaction with economic conditions, were rapidly repressed. In 1958 the Party purged from its ranks Hungarian intellectuals who were pressing for national and cultural autonomy in Transylvania.

Gheorghiu-Dej resisted Khrushchev's efforts at Comecon integration and seemed determined to uphold a more independent economic course in opposition to Moscow's search for an international division of labor among its satellites. A Central Committee plenum in November 1958 formalized Gheorghiu-Dej's "Romanian road to socialism." It was followed by a withdrawal of Russian troops at a time when the Kremlin was pursuing "peaceful co-existence" with the West. During this circumscribed "de-satellization" process, Moscow was guaranteed stringent Communist Party controls in Romania and no revisionist deviations. Bucharest's "declaration of independence" in April 1964 underscored Romania's right to "build socialism" according to Party plans, alongside a posture of international "neutrality." In actual fact, Romanian independence remained severely limited by the regime's ultimate dependence on Moscow for its economic and political survival. Gheorghiu-Dej died in March

1965 and was replaced as Party chief by Nicolai Ceausescu, who consolidated his position as President of the State Council, or head of state. At its Ninth Congress in July 1965, the Party's name was changed back to the Romanian Communist Party (*Partidul Communist Roman*, RCP), a new constitution was adopted, and Romania was proclaimed a "socialist republic." In March 1974 the constitution was altered once again and Ceausescu was "elected" President.

Revolution in Hungary, political conflict in Poland, and sporadic public protests in the GDR and Czechoslovakia spurred East Europe's leaders to reaffirm their loyalty to Moscow while opposing those variants of "revisionism," "liberalism," or "national communism" which jeopardized full Party control. After the rebellions and crises of 1953–56, the Soviet bloc regimes developed their own "new deals" with the population. They combined a reduction in overt repression, unwritten "social compacts" based on the loosening of some economic constraints, greater emphasis on consumerism, and higher living standards. But no substantive political, social, or economic powers were surrendered. The Kremlin allowed some leeway for internal divergencies, as long as the central tenets of Party rule and Warsaw Pact unity were maintained. The Soviets also intensified economic pressures to integrate more fully the CMEA under Russian direction. Their efforts have at no point proved fully successful even though each state is dependent on the USSR—particularly with regard to supplies of crucial raw materials. Moscow retained significant political and military levers to keep potentially unruly dominions in line.[44] The fall of Khrushchev in 1964 and the dawn of Brezhnevism reinforced the process of Soviet consolidation throughout Eastern Europe. In the estimation of most observers, developments from the mid-1960s onward represented a retreat from the liberalizing trends of the late 1950s and early 1960s, but an advance over the cruder Stalinist techniques of coercion and manipulation.[45]

Steadily rising living standards in Czechoslovakia during the 1950s and early 1960s contributed to limiting the potential for mass unrest and political instability. However, by the mid-1960s the forces of reform both inside and outside the Party had gathered momentum, and the delayed effects of de-Stalinization began to be felt.[46] Party First Secretary Novotny was ousted in January 1968 and replaced by Alexander Dubček. Though the latter was not an enthusiastic reformer, he was thrust into this role due to considerable pressure from assorted "liberal," "reformist," and "radical" CPCS factions, and despite strong resistance to liberalization from the Party's more conservative lobbies. Dubček in fact represented the "centrist" group within the Party leadership, while Communists such as Ota Sik, Josef Spacek, and Josef Smrkovsky headed the more "radical" currents. These factions united to drive out Novotny's neo-

Stalinist forces in early 1968. Dubček wanted to strengthen the Party's position and public legitimacy through far-reaching reforms, and not usher in its ultimate demise as Moscow later claimed. When much of the Stalinist system was modified or dismantled during 1968, the Soviets were clearly fearful of the slippery slope toward political pluralism and "counter-revolution."

The "anti-dogmatist" drive within the CPCS re-awakened demands among non-Communist intellectuals, workers, students, and farmers. Factional fighting within the Party helped spark influential movements for democratization outside the power structure. Embryonic and largely autonomous political parties began to function and recruit members; some of their proposals and demands were subsequently adopted in Party programs. Practically the entire mass media came under reformist control and buttressed the campaign for liberalization. The eight month long "Prague Spring," during which police repression visibly decreased, witnessed the release of previously stifled political diversity. Ideological and programmatic differences soon became apparent between staunch anti-reformers, restrained reformers, radical reformers, and revolutionaries, as various organizations and lobbies pressed for lasting change. The democratic awakening outside the Communist Party was constrained by Prague, as the political elite sought to initiate and direct the reform process, preserve the CPCS's supremacy, and preclude any repetition of the Hungarian uprising with its loss of Party control. Indeed, Prague's program of liberalization did not advocate outright political pluralism or any institutionalized opposition parties, but focused on the separation of the Party apparatus from the government administration, economic decentralization, a greater public input in decision-making, the abolition of censorship, and improved relations between Church and state.[47]

The "Action Program" of the CPCS Central Committee, issued in April 1968, called for greater internal democratization, but rejected the more "radical" position of political pluralism. It also approved of wide-ranging social initiatives outside the Party, as well as other limitations on state control—though within the general parameters of "socialist democracy." Dubček's reform platform included the separation of the state from economic management, the segregation of Party from government, and a more pronounced role for intellectuals and experts outside the *nomenklatura* system. During the heady reformist months, organizations which were previously simply transmission belts for the CPCS, such as the labor unions, were transformed into independent bodies. Horizontal channels of information were established at various levels, and contacts between intellectuals and workers were extended and often bypassed the Party structure. Even though censorship was largely abolished, the media tried to defuse any manifest public resentment against

Communist rule and Soviet domination, thus hoping to avoid charges of "anti-socialism" and "anti-Sovietism" from Moscow. The campaign against the Stalinist "old guard" gathered momentum. A 2,000-word appeal signed by about 40,000 people from across the country, including several CPCS Central Committee members and many prominent intellectuals, demanded a purge of all Stalinist forces. These developments were later seized upon by the Kremlin as a pretext for military intervention. The Soviets were equally perturbed by the upcoming Extraordinary Party Congress, scheduled for 9 September 1968, which was designed to eliminate any remaining "dogmatist" elements from leading positions in the Party-state apparatus.[48]

Soviet leaders grew increasingly impatient with the Czechoslovak reforms and ultimately proved unwilling to tolerate the democratic renaissance. They feared that the CPCS could rapidly lose political control even though no specific demands had been lodged for national neutrality or withdrawal from the Warsaw Pact. They were also concerned to preclude any "spillover" of reformist currents to other bloc states.[49] Economic reform in itself did not create serious consternation in Moscow, but there was apprehension that such reforms would have serious political repercussions.[50] Warsaw Pact forces led by the Red Army invaded Czechoslovakia on 20–21 August, before the convocation of the 14th CPCS Congress which seemed set to approve a remodelled Party statute and select a new Politburo and Central Committee. The Czechoslovak army was swiftly immobilized without firing a shot, while the unarmed population resisted as best they could—through strikes, demonstrations, and various forms of civil disobedience and passive resistance.[51] The opposition movement, which attempted to hamper the invading troops and disrupt their communications, was spearheaded by students and young workers. Though some further protests were staged after the self-immolation of Jan Palach in January 1969, the wave of protest in the weeks following the Soviet intervention soon subsided. The dispersal of protest was accompanied by the imposition of severe police controls and a program of constrictive political "normalization."

The Russian occupation reversed the democratization process, and restored "Leninist norms" within the CPCS and Party domination of all public institutions.[52] The Dubček leadership was only decisively defeated by April 1969, when most reformers were eliminated through expulsion or forced resignation. Dubček himself was compelled to resign while Moscow strengthened the position of its designated successors under the leadership of the new Party chief Gustáv Husák. It took more than two years for the Prague regime to fully "normalize" the political situation and stage an anti-reformist Party congress following a massive CPCS purge. One-third of the 1,500,000 strong Party were expelled, including many prewar Communist veterans and assorted groups of reformers.[53] Soviet-sponsored collaborators were welded into the ruling clique, all non-Party organizations such as the "Club 231" were banned, and strict censorship was re-imposed. "Normalization" signalled the eradication of all traces of "reform Communism," the rebuilding of a Party monopoly over all social activities, and the enforcement of internal Party discipline.[54]

The population was pacified through a mixture of direct police repression, administrative penalization, the threat of sanctions, and a steady growth in living standards whereby popular aspirations were subdued and funneled toward private material concerns. The Czecho-slovak masses lapsed into political apathy as the process of atomization pervaded all social groups and Party control seeped into virtually every public institution and association. This partial re-Stalinization, involving pronounced repression, cultural dogmatism, and economic rigidity largely survived intact into the 1980s, but has come under increasing scrutiny and criticism in recent years. The long-term Soviet aim in Czechoslovakia and elsewhere in the bloc was to prevent the germination of conditions which would again necessitate a Red Army intervention and a prolonged period of anti-reformist "normalization." However, events in Poland during the early 1980s once more highlighted the brittle nature of the state-society "contract" in Eastern Europe, especially under conditions of economic stagnation or decline.

In order to understand the scope and structure of opposition in Poland it is useful to review the main precursors to the mass-based free labor union Solidarity. In the closing years of Gomułka's rule, intellectual dissent mounted against official censorship and the government's restrictive cultural and educational policies. In March 1968 student protests were held in several major universities, including Warsaw, Lublin, Poznań, and Wrocław. The demonstrators called for limitations on state censorship and democratization in political life. Student turmoil was used as a pretext by the PUWP leadership to unleash a nationwide anti-intellectual campaign couched as an "anti-Zionist" operation. Liberal-minded critics of the regime were expelled from universities and other academic institutions, and the Party itself was purged of non-conformists and rival factions.

In December 1970, a major workers' rebellion erupted in the Baltic Coast shipyards; some demonstrations were also registered in several Upper Silesian mining towns.[55] The protests were sparked by substantial and sudden price increases on meat and other items. Through such hikes the government sought to avoid losing foreign exchange by diverting meat for export following a series of poor grain harvests. The root causes of the demonstrations lay much deeper than mere opposition to price rises; they revolved around persistent political injustice and constant economic deprivation. The protests were violently quelled by security troops and about 300 workers were slain in Gdańsk, Gdynia, and Szczecin. The unrest and ensuing political turmoil within the ruling elite led to Gomułka's ouster as First Secretary. As in other Polish crises, harder-line interest groups within the Communist establishment sought to capitalize on the conflicts but were outmaneuvered by the newly installed Party chief Edward Gierek.

Largely through massive borrowing from the West, Gierek's "stabilization" program managed to raise living standards steadily during the early 1970s. This helped to pacify the population and divert its attention from political issues. Paradoxically, however, society's growing expectations throughout the 1970s increased public frustration when the inefficient, wasteful, and unreformed economic system proved unable to sustain material improvement.[56] Initial economic growth could not be maintained though it stimulated growing consumer demands. Food prices were kept frozen in the early 1970s to perpetuate popular passivity; but any lingering popular support for Gierek quickly evaporated when prices were drastically raised in the latter part of the decade. The initial wave of street protests by workers in Radom and Ursus (near Warsaw) in June 1976 were subdued and scores of workers were imprisoned, beaten by police, or persecuted in other ways. But these protests proved to be simply a foretaste of more serious turmoil in the years ahead.

There were at least two important consequences of the 1976 clashes. First, they led to the creation of several oppositionist groups, including the Workers' Defense Committee (KOR) and the Movement for Defense of Human and Civil Rights (ROPCiO), which campaigned for the release of imprisoned workers and attempted to bridge the gap between the dissident intelligentsia and the alienated working class. Second, the violence of previous clashes with the police convinced a growing number of opposition activists that in any future confrontations occupational factory strikes and peaceful, well-organized mass protests could have more impact by avoiding official provocations and attacks. The potential for conflict in Poland was exacerbated by divisions within the Party during the late 1970s regarding the degree of tolerance for political opposition and reactions to the economic crisis. This contributed to government indecision and inability to deal with the next round of confrontation with the proletariat.

Workers' frustrations were stretched to breaking point by mid-1980; they were fuelled by deteriorating material conditions, numerous petty repressions, and the coming of age of a new generation with high expectations for civil rights and economic opportunities and unencumbered by their parents' haunting memories of Hitlerism and Stalinism.

Once again, sudden price increases ignited mass strikes in numerous Polish cities during the summer of 1980. On this occasion, politically mature workers and dissident intellectual advisers were determined to institutionalize their protests and win specific concessions from the regime. Strike committees successfully pressed the authorities to grant twenty one major demands in the Gdańsk, Szczecin, and Jastrzebie agreements in late August and early September 1980. This workers' victory led directly to the creation of Solidarity (*Solidarność*), the first mass-based independent trade union in the Communist world.[57] Solidarity rapidly gained the membership and support of the overwhelming majority of Polish society. By the middle of 1981, the union claimed nearly ten million members, with a further three million independent farmers registered in Solidarity's rural counterpart.

The Party leadership was clearly unprepared for the scale and resoluteness of popular opposition to Communist policy in 1980–81. It offered various temporary and deceptive compromises to Solidarity while it mustered the means and the muscle to reverse the gathering tide of democratization. The Communist bureaucracy in all arenas of public life now confronted a severe challenge to its political control from a concerted though non-violent mass movement of reform. This grassroots "revolution" was of necessity "self-limiting," as some observers have noted, because workers' leaders generally took a realistic account of limitations to reform in a one-party state and the hovering Soviet menace. Nevertheless, the parameters of popular protest were constantly expanded throughout 1981. They embraced such fundamental issues as: cultural freedoms; public control over economic production and distribution; democratic participation in local government and industrial self-management; and authentic parliamentary elections. Popular strivings for democracy in all gained a momentum of their own, undeterred by official threats, intimidations, and sanctions.

The Warsaw regime rigorously resumed the offensive against Solidarity with the imposition of martial law in December 1981, once the fate of the Party-state had been entrusted to General Wojciech Jaruzelski with Moscow's evident approval.[58] The element of surprise played a crucial part in the success of Jaruzelski's "state of war." Camouflaging the operation as a straightforward army takeover to prevent imminent civil war, armed detachments of motorized riot police (ZOMO) stormed factories, shipyards, and coal mines, liquidated strikes and public demonstrations, and arrested or interned thousands of national, regional, and local Solidarity leaders. The violence of nationwide martial law was relatively restrained, compared to the more localized clashes of 1976 and 1970, as the population was unarmed and unprepared for the showdown. Jaruzelski relied primarily on mass dispersals, beatings, firings, imprisonment, internment, political trials, and verification campaigns to subdue protests, isolate dissident leaders, and eradicate the free union organization. Martial law was accompanied by the imposition of a new layer of administrative, organizational, judicial, and police controls over the populace. The gravely weakened PUWP was reconstructed with the aid of the disciplined Communist military arm. All independent organizations were outlawed and disbanded, with the notable exception of the Roman Catholic Church, which the regime attempted to placate and manipulate to help enforce public submissiveness to government policy. Among the banned groupings were blue and white collar unions, professional associations, farmers' lobbies, cultural associations, and various youth and student groups. Officially sponsored substitutes were promptly established in all occupational and social spheres, including a government supervised labor union, to help assure that mass protests would not be repeated and that any shop-floor grievances could be speedily resolved in the future. Martial law was first suspended and then formally lifted in 1983; but the instruments of Communist political control and police repression remain firmly in place to this day.

Conclusion

The most recent Polish drama, culminating in the official offensive against Solidarity, aptly underscored the severe limitations placed on public autonomy, political democracy, and national self-determination in Eastern Europe's Communist Party-states. It also highlighted the strong undercurrent of conflict between popular aspirations and Party political interests. Our review of post-World War II Soviet bloc history helps to identify some significant fault lines beneath the appearance of Communist Party hegemony. These underlying strains and tensions revolve around several critical issues, such as: deprivations or depredations in living standards; denials of human and civil rights; and persistent struggles for individual and collective liberties, religious rights, cultural self-expression, social self-organization, and the preservation of distinct national identities. Each of these actual and potential fault lines, the accompanying manifestations of dissent and opposition, and the most significant developments in these fissures over the past decade, will be explored in detail in the following chapters.

2

Dissident Strategies I: Roots, Repression, Reformism

Marxist-Leninist systems deny legitimacy to overt expressions of political dissent against Communist Party policy, and outlaw any organized opposition to the Party leadership. Severe limitations are placed on any public manifestations of political pluralism. Rival political parties are not tolerated, though quasi-independent organizations supportive of the ruling Party may be allowed to function. The veneer of unanimity is maintained through coercion and manipulation, whereby individuals are constrained from resisting or reshaping the fundamental constituents of the political and economic structure. The absence of a democratic electoral system for Party and government posts, and the ban on any authentic parliamentary opposition, insures the exclusion of public participation and contestation in state decision-making.[1] In addition to the hierarchical principles of "democratic centralism" present within all Communist-controlled bodies, the Party *apparat* and its various subsidiary organs consistently violate their own laws, periodically purge discredited or unreliable members, and systematically restrict the rights of ordinary citizens.

During the Stalinist period in Eastern Europe, Communist rule resulted in the wholesale liquidation of all forms of political opposition. Since Stalin's death in 1953 various degrees of controlled "de-Stalinization" have been evident, with the elimination of some of the worst officially confessed "errors and distortions." The more notable changes during the post-Stalin era have included: a more pronounced emphasis on "collective leadership" in the ruling Politburo; greater scope for professional administrators or "technocrats" in the implementation of Party decisions; a reining in of the police apparatus, making it more accountable to the Party leadership; and some gradual rationalization in economic policy, with less concentration on developing heavy industry at the expense of consumer needs. Nevertheless, these and other reforms have not greatly affected the core Leninist political principles, particularly as de-Stalinization proved to be highly restrained and selective after the initial post-1953 relaxation.

The dichotomy between the ruling elite and the disenfranchised masses was brought into sharp focus during the process of de-Stalinization. Since the termination of this thawing process, East Europe's Communist regimes have failed to establish any permanent popular mandate or enduring government legitimacy, whether through political democratization or steady material well-being for the bulk of the population.[2] The political stability of the post-Stalin period is built essentially around the curtailment of popular pressure for genuine democratic reform and, according to some observers, a marriage of convenience between the ruling elite and loyal elements of the technocracy.[3] In general, the most stable systems have been characterized by a more pervasive and consistent application of the state's social control mechanisms, and a closer alliance between Party officials, compliant "experts," and other reliable members of the intelligentsia. On the other hand, the mass of the populace, including the industrial working class, the peasantry, and the non-Party intelligentsia, continues to lack any viable independent organizations to defend its interests. In practice, these social groups are atomized, subservient, and dependent on the dominant state-Party apparatus.

The history of East Europe since the dawn of de-Stalinization has been punctuated by a series of social and political convulsions. As discussed in Chapter 1, each regime has endeavored to contain potentially volatile internal developments by subduing popular aspirations for more comprehensive liberalization. Although official reactions to the effects of de-Stalinization were not uniform in each country, they created some major dislocations in the exercise of power. At various important junctures this contributed toward spawning a number of dissident currents and oppositionist movements.[4]

The pace and character of domestic change has varied considerably during the past thirty years, thereby providing diverse opportunities for the germination of political dissent. Specific national and international circumstances have affected both the nature and manifestation of dissent, as well as the extent of official repression. The "northern tier" of Central-Eastern Europe has generally been at the forefront of political and economic reform. Likewise, the more active and widespread displays of dissent and opposition have been concentrated in these more modernized and industrialized states. Several reasons for this can be enumerated, including a more politicized working class, a sizeable independently-minded intelligentsia, national traditions of democratic resistance, rising and often frustrated popular expectations, and the degree to which official restrictions have been eased during pertinent periods.[5]

In the following two chapters we are primarily concerned with the theories and overall strategies of East Europe's political opposition. The concrete application of these strategies in specific national settings will be discussed and assessed in later chapters. The common and diverging attributes of dissent and opposition to the prevailing power structure, aiming to restrict Party-state totalitarianism, will be examined. In particular, the two chapters will focus on developments during the past decade, characterized by the flowering of dissent in several Warsaw Pact states.

Strands of Dissent and Opposition

An all-embracing definition of dissent and opposition will not be offered in this study, but some general parameters of the subject matter will be outlined. In Communist Party states, dissent from official ideology and opposition to government policy has often been forced to assume "extra-legal" forms outside the established political institutions. Although the national constitutions and domestic laws of the Peoples' Democracies and Socialist Republics formally guarantee basic civil liberties, including the right to free speech, assembly, and association, these freedoms have to conform with the often cited "interests of the working people" as interpreted by government officials. But despite their attempts to fully control and constantly direct all aspects of public life, most of the Soviet bloc regimes have experienced periodic breakdowns and crises when political conflicts have re-emerged.[6] Moreover, beneath the tranquil veneer of comprehensive state supervision, dormant dissent is often present and may spill over into overt opposition at opportune moments.

Schapiro has offered a useful starting point for distinctions between "dissent" and "opposition."[7] Dissenters assert their inalienable right to criticize the existing regime, to disagree with its policies, to remind the authorities of their duties, obligations, and laws, and to advocate alternative policies for the government to pursue. Political oppositionists, by contrast, seek to replace the existing government by some alternative administration, or to completely overhaul the prevailing political system. However, the links between "dissent" and "opposition" are more complex and intertwined in practice than in theory. For instance, the term "dissent" in Leninist states does not necessarily signify minority status or muted non-conformism, while the notion of "opposition" does not define any one political strategy or program of change.

It may therefore be more useful to look at the phenomena in terms of a spectrum of orientations, ranging from total rejection of the Communist system to circumscribed criticism of specific government policies. In order to avoid definitional pitfalls and controversies, we will generally employ the terms "dissent" and "opposition" interchangeably simply to indicate some form of individual or collective confrontation with the Party-state. The precise nature of that confrontation will be outlined and elaborated during the course of this study. We will be principally concerned with how dissident-oppositionists during the past decade have conceptualized workable scenarios for change and pressed for transformations of the existing system.

Schapiro proposes a five-fold classification of dissent and opposition in Communist states.[8] This constitutes a useful framework, with the proviso that the categories may overlap and alter over time. First, we have an "all-out rejection" of the system itself and the desire to replace it. The concomitants are the repudiation of all forms of compromise with the regime, and attempts to overthrow it by all available means. Second, there are power struggles or factional conflicts within the Communist establishment, whether at the central, regional, or local levels. This internal strife is usually conducted in conditions of secrecy, where it is difficult to obtain hard facts, and revolves around personal, ideological, or programmatic differences. It is often accompanied by personnel displacements at various levels of the apparatus as new leaders emerge and garner support, or the incumbent leaders reinforce their positions. Third, a variety of pressure and interest groups may vie for influence within the parameters of the existing polity by pressurizing Party leaders to promote some specific policies or group objectives. Such groupings are most often part of the political establishment and may include leading elements of the police, army, Party and government bureaucracies. Key interest groups do not in general seek to oust the Party leadership, though they may divide into more "conservative" or "reformist" factions to promote their own goals. This in turn may undermine the political *status quo*, especially if the struggle for influence is conducted in the public domain, even though the initial objective may not envisage such a challenge.

Fourth, in Schapiro's estimation, there are "pragmatic dissenters" among scientists, technicians, and experts in diverse fields. They are usually unencumbered by doctrinal or political constraints, but primarily campaign for improved economic efficiency, technological progress, and financial support. They commonly fall within the purview of a "loyal opposition" even though they may not necessarily belong to the political establishment. Fifth, "apolitical dissent" may exist which does not advocate an overthrow of the regime or the wholesale replacement of the existing system. It simply claims the right to criticize government policies, and demands the observance of basic human and civil rights. Contemporary dissent and opposition in Eastern Europe fall somewhere within these five categories. The variations and developments in the first and last definition will primarily concern us here, as they encompass numerous forms of non-establishment dissent and extra-systemic opposition.

The vast majority of the population in each Soviet bloc state does not overtly dissent or even consistently disobey or ignore government regulations. Any number of factors operate to discourage and prevent open resistance and politically motivated opposition. Most notable among them are: the fear of repressive sanctions; the feeling of powerlessness and past experiences of failure; self-interest for some, and the avoidance of exposure for others; rational calculations about the risks and prospects for dissent; and pressing socio-economic concerns to satisfy and not endanger personal and familial needs. Open dissent is by definition restricted to a small minority under "normal" circumstances, where officially encouraged passivity and apathy preserve the position of the power elite. The scale and durability of any economic and social crisis may mobilize people on certain occasions when the barrier of fear is breached and the undercurrents of discontent with the regime are successfully tapped. Such conditions rarely persist, however, before the Party regains the initiative and reasserts its control. Nevertheless, numerous sources of discontent persist among aggrieved social groups within East European societies and mushroom into open conflict under pertinent conditions.[9]

The catalyst for much post-Stalin dissent was provided by intellectuals and students in universities and other academic institutions during the mid-1950s. They helped to broaden the bounds of permitted open discussion, particularly in Poland and Hungary, which influenced other social strata and even penetrated the ruling Parties. In many respects the university intelligentsia stood at the forefront of political reform and criticism of official policy, and acted as spokesmen for the "Polish October" and the Hungarian revolution.[10] In countries where the rise of a "revisionist intelligentsia" was thwarted and Party *apparatchiks* maintained a stranglehold over academic life, dissident intellectuals were effectively isolated and the technocracy remained obedient to the governing elite—as evidenced in Romania, Bulgaria, and the GDR. The governments in turn avoided potentially risky reformist experiments and did not make either ideological or political concessions to the humanistic intelligentsia even during the heady days of initial de-Stalinization. Instead, the regimes in question tended to co-opt technocrats as "partners" to rationalize the central planning system.

In Poland, Hungary, and Czechoslovakia, conflicts emerged early on between the "free intellectuals" (including scholars, teachers, and various groups of technocrats) and the Party bureaucracy—the "bureaucratic class."[11] The humanistic, artistic, and creative intelligentsia generally veer towards "anti-authoritarianism" in their political leanings, especially where they have been denied access to positions of influence. The growing political consciousness of East Europe's intelligentsia has therefore resulted in periodic conflicts with the Party's ideological watchdogs.[12] Following the traumatic events of 1956 and 1968, the ruling elites have mounted substantial offensives against "independent reformists" and the "marginal intelligentsia" in order to stymie campaigns for reforms which may endanger Party control.

During the 1960s and 1970s a new type of "intellectual dissident" appeared in Eastern Europe. These were people who felt increasingly disillusioned with the post-Stalin "stabilization" and did not refrain from criticizing the regime even when officially ostracized, sanctioned, or banished. Irrespective of government disapproval, they had no intention of returning to or joining the establishment fold but put forward alternative political, economic, and social policies, and were unwilling to compromise on what they considered to be essential issues. Dissenting intellectuals became increasingly concerned with formulating viable strategies for change while seeking to overcome their isolation and estrangement from other social strata.[13] Since the mid-1970s in particular, a new generation of oppositionist intellectuals has come to the fore and embraced political activism. In broad terms they have set themselves three primary tasks: to forge a cohesive "intellectual opposition" to the Party cadre; to re-evaluate and re-formulate practical strategies for political transformation; and to link up with other aggrieved segments of the population.

Paradoxically, by defining all overt critics of government policy as deviants, the authorities in several states helped to nurture more united groups of dissenters.[14] Official policies even tended to promote bonds between individuals who, apart from their non-conformism, shared little in common by way of backgrounds, interests, ideologies, or programs. Once subject to police harassment and other forms of persecution, their experiences and values tended to converge. Their "subculture of marginality" enhanced their antipathy towards governmental authority and helped to bolster their cohesiveness. Moreover, a pertinent socio-economic factor has been operative during the past three decades. The industrialized Soviet bloc economies have been increasingly unable to absorb the growing stratum of university graduates in appropriate occupations for which they are qualified. This failure has helped to create a breeding ground for political dissenters who share economic grievances against the regime and perceive their deprivations as stemming from the system's limitations.

Since the mid-1950s, East Europe's dissidents have been re-examining the cardinal precepts and principles of Marxism-Leninism and Soviet Communism, while undergoing a process of profound alienation from the Party-state. A growing number have sought viable alternatives while registering their dissatisfaction with the pace of change and the evident ossification of the political system. They have been especially concerned with extending civil liberties such as free expression, and promoting the pluralization of political life. In their efforts to articulate new models and forge closer links with other social groups, an element of "vanguardism" has been evident, in that much of the dissident intelligentsia visualizes itself as the representative of the "overall interests of society" and not simply one social class. During periods of political upheaval, such dissenters have sought to gain public influence by formulating pressing issues in authoritative ways and speaking up on behalf of the silenced majority.[15] Even in periods of relative stability, their programs are often intended to inspire popular confidence and support; indeed, they implicitly concede that without mass backing their chances of success would appear remote.

In Marxist-Leninist phraseology, the working class cannot act as a "class for itself" without a vanguard Communist Party organization, because it lacks collective power aside from exceptional circumstances. Although on occasion workers in Eastern Europe have entered the political fray to campaign for non-economic interests, in general they are motivated by practical everyday concerns rather than abstract ideological or political issues.[16] Some analysts have also pointed out that workers tend to voice protests about material issues because "they are safer for dissatisfied elements in the population to articulate without immediate repression, than political ones."[17] Among the numerous grievances which may stimulate workers' protests it is worthwhile to mention: price increases, their sudden implementation, and the unfavorable economic context in which they are introduced; relative deprivation in comparison with other social sectors; stagnating living standards; rising expectations which cannot be satisfied by the government; the manner in which the authorities deal with specific complaints and protest actions; and persistent frustration with official channels of conflict resolution.[18]

Workers' alienation is actually rooted in unfavorable economic conditions, and their feelings of powerlessness and under-representation in meaningful political institutions.[19] The relative passivity of blue collar workers in the 1940s and 1950s may be explained partly by the maintenance of tight Party supervision, as well as by the economic opportunities available during the period of accelerated industrialization. Workers at this time were on the move, both territorially and socially, with genuine possibilities for educational and occupational advancement. Indeed, a "marriage of convenience" was established between each regime and the working class in which political passivity or loyalty became a prerequisite for survival and personal material improvement.

Since the mid-1950s, however, most governments have displayed a growing inability to provide their side of this post-Stalin "social compact"—entailing full security of employment, considerable economic equality (in terms of equitable pay distribution and low differentials), wage and price stability, consistent work, and acceptable, steadily rising living standards.[20] Workers' aspirations for steady material improvement, good working conditions, opportunities for social mobility, and effective social services, have remained underfulfilled. In many instances, there has even been a marked deterioration in all these spheres. The early phase of upward mobility seemingly cannot be replicated, while the rising aspirations of second generation industrial workers have been thwarted, thus generating a source of potential conflict with the state.[21]

Growing economic expectations have also been accompanied by demands for genuine worker autonomy free from officially controlled organizations, and for greater worker participation in the decision-making process in numerous institutions.[22] In certain circumstances this has developed into demands for a more authentic representation of working class interests through independent labor unions and autonomous workers' councils and self-management bodies. Such demands have fuelled discontent and protest, but it is usually some arbitrary government measure, such as an abrupt price hike, wage decrease, or higher output decree, which provokes work stoppages, strikes, or public demonstrations. According to Woodall, it was young worker-technicians holding foremen posts who were commonly the major organizers of strike committees in Poland's Baltic shipyards both in 1970 and in 1980. Since 1956 this stratum of workers has become especially exasperated by the "lack of promotion prospects, the unresponsiveness of management, and the pressures from the work force."[23] In addition, the alienation of blue-collar workers in large plants in particular, has proved conducive to collective protests against official moves. Indeed, most of the substantive strike movements in Eastern Europe have had their origins in large industrial enterprises.

Any major economic reforms or management restructuring geared toward greater industrial efficiency may in fact increase the disaffection of unskilled and semi-skilled workers in uncompetitive sectors of the economy. The prospects for unemployment, underemployment, more demanding work quotas, stricter work discipline, and larger wage differentials, could intensify working class discontent in the years ahead. Such scenarios have in turn been manipulated by entrenched Party anti-reformers to bolster their case for tighter central control and stringent Communist supervision over wage equality. However, one should not overestimate the extent and depth of popular opposition to economic reforms that may involve both short-term and long-term sacrifices. Workers are evidently less inclined to protest against reforms that are implemented following genuine consultation with shop-floor representatives, especially when they result in noticeable improvements in overall material and political conditions.[24]

There is an unfortunate propensity by some commentators to concentrate on intellectuals as the pre-eminent leaders of any popular opposition to the regime, neglecting the role of workers. Governments that seek to denigrate local protests also frequently portray workers as mere followers manipulated by devious intellectual "troublemakers."[25] Notwithstanding such simplifications, it is still valid to assess the prominent position of the intelligentsia in oppositionist activism throughout much of Eastern Europe. Intellectuals have clearly endeavored to assure continuity during periods of proletarian passivity, and to formulate long-term programs for popular resistance and systemic change. Since the mid-1970s, opposition intellectuals have also attempted to erode the barriers separating them from the working class—barriers often erected by the Party, and compounded by mutual suspicion and isolation between workers and intellectuals. In a number of states, dissidents in both social strata have tried to articulate common values and objectives on a whole range of issues, including freedom from persecution, civil and human rights, improved economic conditions, religious liberties, and positive steps towards national independence.

The resistance of peasants and private farmers to government policy was more pronounced in the early years of Communist rule. This did not usually involve concerted or organized opposition, but stubborn resistance to agricultural collectivization and the forced requisitioning of farm produce. Peasant opposition registered most pronounced success in Poland, where a large private farming sector survived the Stalinist onslaught, and a process of de-collectivization was finally undertaken in the late 1950s. Peasant opposition proved to be least effective in the Balkan states, where less discriminate collectivization swallowed up practically the entire private farming sector. The rural populace in other Soviet bloc nations fell somewhere between the two extremes of predominant privatization and full-scale collectivization. During the past four decades the farming peoples have been steadily and deliberately de-politicized, particularly after the subversion and liquidation of autonomous agrarian political parties and occupational associations during the 1940s and 1950s. Though this substantially lessened overt opposition, it did not signify growing support for the regime. In general, peasants withdrew into private concerns, avoided involvement in officially-sponsored organizations, or only participated in a token fashion, while grudgingly coming to terms with the new social order.[26]

The absence of peasant rebellions in the Soviet bloc can also be explained by the logistical difficulty of organizing sizeable protests in rural areas. Farmers' households tend to be segregated, confront communications problems, and are readily exposed to police harassment and administrative interference. Moreover, many potential peasant leaders left the countryside during the period of rapid industrialization and urbanization, or were co-opted and neutralized by the Party and its peasant-oriented associations. The first post-war peasant generation experienced favorable conditions for upward mobility into the working class and for overall social advancement. Contrary to Communist propaganda, this process was not a consequence of socialism *per se*, but a feature of rapid industrialization and development whatever the actual system of government.[27] The newly emergent "peasant-workers" were largely a transitional group with a low predilection for revolt or organized opposition. Observers have noted that these largely unskilled workers have tended to be less conspicuous in initiating strikes because they are newcomers to proletarian culture and workers' behavioral patterns. They usually lack strong traditions of labor unionism, combativeness, collective bargaining, common action, or "class consciousness." "Peasant-workers" evidently value highly their newly acquired worker status, while forging only tenuous long-term ties with the working class. They generally avoid open confrontation with the government, not wishing to endanger their occupational achievements.

The second generation of "peasant-workers" incline toward a different set of priorities than their parents and increasingly adopt a working-class frame of reference. The relative deprivation experienced by the first generation had its compensations in opportunities for upward mobility, whereas such prospects have gradually decreased since the 1950s. Peasant expectations may also have been raised in recent years because of the expanding gap between town and country with regard to economic conditions, social services, occupational opportunities, and access to consumer goods. But apart from the extensive self-organization of farmers in Solidarity's Poland during 1980–1981, rural discontent has rarely manifested itself in any concerted actions. Nevertheless, some analysts consider that peasants "may increasingly be affected by developments in other sectors of society, and by the discontent of other groups."[28]

Young people in general tend to be more persistent and uncompromising in their demands for change than are their elders. One important generational dichotomy in Eastern Europe is the lessened preoccupation with stability and tranquility exhibited by post-war age-groups. By contrast, the generation which came of age before or during World War II, or during the Stalinist years, is often more cautious and wary of civil strife. The latter's parental influence has tended to restrain young people who are resentful of material stagnation and unfulfilled ambitions. Working-class youths, in particular, will continue to face diminishing prospects for educational, occupational, and economic progress.[29] University and college students have often felt especially alienated from the political system and its values. Their more pronounced idealism has often made them correspondingly critical of the less than ideal realities of "really existing socialism." Universities in Eastern Europe, as in the West, have traditionally served as breeding grounds for new ideas and non-conformism. This potential for dissent has been displayed on different occasions in several states. The *Petofi* circle at Budapest University in the mid-1950s formulated oppositionist programs which gained the support of an ever-widening sector of society. University protests in Poland in 1968 led to clashes with police and provocations staged by Party factions. Several Czechoslovak universities were at the forefront of the Prague Spring reform movement. Even in East Germany, higher educational establishments are in certain cases focal points for political opposition to the SED leadership.[30] An additional phenomenon has been noted in parts of Eastern Europe since Stalin's death: the growing disaffection among the offspring of former Communist officials—the so-called "second generation socialist intelligentsia." The trend has been particularly noticeable in Poland, Czechoslovakia, and Hungary, where many prominent dissidents are in fact the children of former Party functionaries who held high office during the Stalinist era.

East Europe's political dissenters represent a range of ideological and political orientations, though much of their particularism has become submerged during the overarching conflict with the state-Party elite. Nevertheless, personalized political persuasions and objectives often exert an important influence on the strategies pursued by individual dissidents and oppositionist groupings. There is a wide spectrum of political positions among activists operating outside the Communist power structure. Not all oppositionist strands are present in each country under observation, because much depends on national traditions and historical experiences. However, the overall range encompasses neo-Marxist socialists "on the left," non-Marxist socialists, social democrats, liberal democrats, Christian democrats, agrarian populists, and national democrats and nationalists "on the right." There are fringe elements on both extremes of the spectrum, but their general influence and political impact tends to be marginal in all states.[31] Each political tendency is linked with certain long-term goals whatever the short-term priorities and strategies adopted *vis-à-vis* the regime. Though the precise details differ between each country, certain brief generalizations can be offered as to the program associated with each political position.

The nationalist-focused and national democrat opposition principally concentrates on ways of securing full national independence and eliminating the Communist Party dictatorship. In promoting and pursuing such objectives, they often neglect to formulate detailed models for the political structure of a post-Communist state; in many cases other political trends display similar shortcomings. Christian democrats tend to advocate a more pronounced role for Christian Churches and religious-oriented groups within a pluralistic framework. Agrarian populists are primarily concerned with improving rural conditions and enhancing the position of private farmers and other countryside residents. Liberal democrats concentrate on defending and enhancing individual liberties within the framework of a multi-Party parliamentary-type system based on free elections. Social democrats place greater stress on socio-economic equality, a welfare system, and a more pronounced role for the state in pursuing such programs.

A major trend in post-Stalin Eastern Europe has been the emergence of a self-proclaimed "socialist opposition," embracing many of the social democrats together with various shades of Marxist and non-Marxist socialists.[32] This grouping tends to exclude the assortment of "radical Marxists," Trotskyists, Maoists, militant egalitarians, and anti-consumerists who exhibit precious little public appeal and whose numbers are miniscule. The more mainstream "socialist oppositionists" espouse comprehensive nationalization or state control over the major means of production, combined with cooperative ownership of the smaller enterprises in the service, craft, and agricultural sectors. In recent years the position of many socialists has veered towards greater "privatization" in small-scale services and manufacture, thus approximating the West European mixed economy model. The economic proposals of the "nonsocialist" opposition are geared more strongly towards free enterprise, comprehensive marketization, and much restricted state control or government interference in any branch of production aside from the key national industries.

The more devout socialists place paramount emphasis on "workers' self-management" in large plants and "local self-government" in regions, districts, and municipalities; they have also opposed the "unrestricted accumulation of private capital." A loosely defined "socialist political system" has been propounded by some of the leading theorists of the "socialist opposition" which would involve the creation of "socialist political organizations." Even when supporting "political pluralism" they underscore that any newly emerging political organizations must be "working class parties" operating within a "socialist setting."[33] Some of these theorists display a somewhat dogmatic propensity to assume that "socialist democracy" constitutes a system which guarantees citizens "more rights, more freedom, and influence than bourgeois parliamentary democracy."[34]

The "socialist opposition" played an influential role in Czechoslovakia's Prague Spring, and they have made their voices heard on subsequent occasions. Much of the dissenting non-Communist intelligentsia is steeped in socialist principles, though it is highly critical of the Soviet model. Furthermore, much of the socialist political and economic program finds generally favorable resonance among the population while sharing several common features with other political trends. Nevertheless, some degree of polarization is evident between the "socialist democrat" and the "nationalist populist" opposition, not merely with regard to political objectives but even more immediate programs and strategies, as we shall discuss below.

Some of the disparate positions enumerated above trace their ancestry to pre-war or wartime political organizations, while others have based themselves on post-war developments. In the context of this study, it is more helpful to think in terms of specific political strategies to initiate change in the Communist system of government—however far-reaching and whatever the ultimate ideological objectives—rather than attempt to elucidate a Western-type competition between diverse political groupings. Indeed most contemporary dissidents seem able to subdue their individual political beliefs for the sake of the "wider cause." Since the mid-1970s, in particular, the issues of human rights, freedom of speech, civil liberties, and the extension of democratic participation have helped to cross-cut many ideological divisions and offered "a basis for a broad 'national front' into which all democratic forces of Eastern Europe can be integrated."[35] In Hungary, Czechoslovakia, and elsewhere the "new opposition" has indeed included Marxists and former Marxists, libertarians, religious activists, democrats, liberals, apolitical non-conformists, populists, and nationalists of various hues. The prevailing trend has been to avoid outright or singular political activity but to broaden the base of popular opposition within and beyond the intelligentsia. It is the immediate strategies and tactics of political dissenters and their methods for influencing both the government and the populace which primarily concern us here, rather than their protracted political programs.

A spectrum of religious or Church-based criticism and opposition to Communist policy can also be traced in Eastern Europe. It ranges from the prominent and highly visible role of Poland's Roman Catholic church, through the GDR's "constructively critical" though non-confrontational Lutheran Church, the weaker and more subdued position of the Catholic and Protestant Churches in Czechoslovakia and Hungary, to the relatively passive Orthodox Churches in Romania and Bulgaria, which are more effectively integrated into the Party-state framework.[36] Since Stalinist times, especially in countries with large Churches commanding the loyalty of the majority of the population—as in Poland and East Germany—the regimes have reached some tentative *modus vivendi* with the Church hierarchies. Such agreements have benefited the ruling Party by helping to limit popular discontent with the direct or indirect assistance of religious authorities. This was clearly visible in Poland during the initial stages of martial law in December 1981, where Church leaders contributed to cooling the public temperature and preventing more violent mass outbursts. Warsaw thus used the Catholic hierarchy to help subdue public disquiet and limit the scope of protests.[37] In many instances, the Church leadership has proven itself to be equally adept and sophisticated in its dealings with government officials, and has extracted several concessions for the benefit of the Church as an institution and for society as a whole.

Even in reasonably tolerant states such as Poland, however, the Church remains on guard against state repression. Hence there has been a pronounced hesitation to oppose the regime overtly on politically sensitive issues. Such caution has not precluded passive rejection or indifference to Marxist-Leninist doctrine and opposition to the active propagation of atheism. With varying degrees of success, the Christian Churches have remained bearers of an alternative world-view, value system, and social-educational program. Once they take a stand in defending individual and collective freedoms and condemn governmental abuses, East European Churches find themselves more closely linked with the championing of other civil liberties. Church leaders in several states have increasingly demonstrated support for freedom of expression for dissident intellectuals and economic improvements for the working class and peasantry. Undoubtedly, an element of self-interest has also been operative, with the Churches seeking to extend their influence, institutionalize their status, and gain concessions from the government.

In Poland, where the Catholic Church has achieved a fairly secure position by Soviet bloc standards, and commands the loyalty of the bulk of the population, it has provided a protective umbrella for much of the lay political opposition, especially since the mid-1970s. According to the prominent dissident writer Adam Michnik, the Church has "provided a true barrier against totalitarian power . . . defending the nation, its rights and values."[38] Though the Church has consistently warned against any armed resistance to Communism since the Soviet takeover, it has become a moral counterweight to the regime and has even won the backing of non-religious political dissidents for its teachings and activities. The Catholic hierarchy does not put forward a political program but simply promulgates many of the "core values," such as truth, human dignity, and personal liberty.[39] In countries where Churches undertake a more modest teaching role, stringent governmental control over Church funds and activities are usually in evidence.

In recent years the Polish Church has increasingly spoken out against official repression and assisted persecuted individuals and their families. Moreover, under the protective sanctuary of the Church and the resolute posture of many clerics since the imposition of martial law, various independent initiatives "are again being undertaken and new islands of autonomy come into existence among the people."[40] In addition in Poland, a well-organized Catholic lay intelligentsia has crystallized since the late 1950s which maintains close contacts with non-Catholic intellectuals and acts as an indispensible conduit of communication between the Church authorities, the non-religious political opposition, and much of the Catholic working class and private farmers.[41]

Other Soviet bloc countries have also witnessed the emergence of Church-sponsored or religion-oriented dissident groups. Though many of these may proclaim their doctrinal or moral allegiance to the teachings of the Church in question, they tend to maintain an independent political and organizational stance. In the GDR the Lutheran Evangelical Church has in recent years more actively supported the fledgling autonomous peace movement and anti-militaristic East German youth groups.[42] The Czechoslovak Catholic Church has become more outspoken in its protests against the regime's ideological campaigns since the early 1980s, and has endorsed young people's involvement in cultural, social, and ecological affairs outside Party supervision. Hungary has also witnessed a revived interest among youths in religious informal "basic communities," among Catholics, consisting of prayer and meditation groups beyond the purview of the state.[43] Even among the Orthodox congregation in Romania, there seems to be a spreading trend towards independent activism among some of the clergy and among young people.[44]

The attitudes of secular political dissidents towards religion in general and the Christian Churches in particular have radically altered in several countries since the 1960s.[45] Poland provides a striking example in this regard, where a number of post-"Polish October" and post-1968 oppositionists (many of whom initially formed a "socialist opposition") were formerly vehemently anti-clerical. The Catholic Church was viewed as an essentially "reactionary" institution, and indeed all religious groupings were considered anachronistic and regressive. Such attitudes changed in the wake of more pronounced Church support for the dissident movement, at which time it was perceived to be the most effectual counterweight to Party rule. Conversely, whereas Church leaders during the 1950s and 1960s viewed many of the dissenting intellectuals as "leftist atheists," opinions were modified from the mid-1970s onwards, especially as many Catholic political activists became involved in the human rights campaign which supported freedom of belief, worship, and association. Church authorities, local priests, and dissident intellectuals began to concur more closely on several burning issues—including the search for freer channels of information. The Church became an important link between several social classes and occupational groups, and seemed increasingly prepared to defend the rights of each social sector. Whether other Churches in Eastern Europe can successfully help to support any credible opposition movement remains to be explored.

Official Responses

The use of the term "opposition" in Communist states dates back to Lenin, whose intention it was to besmirch critics with charges of disloyalty to the ruling Party, betrayal of the working class, and treason against the proletarian state. Since the Bolshevik takeover, one overriding objective of all Communist regimes is to silence or eliminate critics who challenge the Party's organizational discipline or political monopoly. Communist leaders also strive to prohibit conditions conducive to the birth of public self-organization and independent political activity.

Under "normal" circumstances, the basic tenets of the Communist system cannot be challenged for long without provoking repressive reactions from the Party elite and the various establishment interest groups fearful of any curtailment of their powers. An extensive Party-state apparatus and managerial stratum depends for its survival on stifling dissent and maintaining the *status quo*. These bloated bureaucracies would confront a potential loss of their considerable privileges if a process of authentic democratization were to establish a foothold. A determined resistance is therefore upheld against opening up policy-making to any independent groupings, including those elements of the "technocracy" whose political or ideological loyalties are in doubt, or whose demands for economic rationalization may endanger bureaucratic controls.

The element of fear and the threat of force and other sanctions have remained strong weapons in the governments' arsenals, in addition to the pervasive system of administrative, economic, judicial, and security controls.[46] Fear of repercussions has encouraged general public timidity and an unwillingness to engage in overt oppositionist activity even when dissatisfaction with official policy is widespread. The authorities also instigate and perpetuate a process of social atomization, whereby any organizational links beyond the family circle are controlled by the Party or one of its numerous subordinate bodies. In tandem with these techniques, each regime divides and conquers various sectors of society to prevent any fusion between them outside state control.[47] According to Konrad and Szelenyi, the ruling class seeks to "disrupt the class unity of the intellectuals," and to frustrate any attempts by intellectuals to form alliances with the workers.[48] Party leaders have tried to split the intelligentsia by integrating some sectors into a "loyal technocracy" which shares in elite privileges. The remaining intellectuals, particularly the humanistic and artistic segments, are placed under strict official supervision and separated from other dissaffected classes largely through restricted access to the means of communication.

Since Stalin's demise the use of naked terror against the population has diminished, and a greater emphasis has been placed on other forms of control and manipulation, including administrative sanctions, institutional restraints, propaganda and persuasion, economic levers, religious and cultural safety valves, and what Lewis calls "symbolic manipulation"—involving phoney pluralism, the denial of social conflict, and appeals to national preservation and *raison d'etat*.[49] Some analysts have pointed out that when a society has developed a substantially modern industry in which it is essential to increase productivity and incorporate modern and intricate production techniques, "coercion is no longer enough—and indeed it can run counter to efficiency which becomes the first requirement. Efficiency cannot be obtained by coercion, but only by participation."[50] This in turn has implications for the methods of social control and the limitation of political dissent and opposition.

The intensity of government repression may differ in each country, while the leadership itself may be divided in its reactions to real or potential dissent. Some elements may support the application of greater discipline over the workforce and heightened repression against critical intellectuals, while other functionaries favor the loosening of certain restrictions and more subtle forms of pressure to assure conformity and stability. The latter may propose greater flexibility in dealing with the opposition, even though they may share identical overall objectives with harder-line cadres. The most flexible elements of the government's repressive strategy generally revolve around the timescale for eliminating opponents and the precise methods to be employed at any juncture, taking into account prevailing material conditions, concerns to maintain social stability, and the international ramifications of government actions.

Given that the goal of Party leaders in each Soviet bloc state is to neutralize the "extra-legal" political dissenters and eradicate manifestations of opposition to the Communist system, some important questions follow for political resistance. First, does any regime loosen the reins and tolerate some measure of overt dissent precisely when it feels strong and confident enough, or when it is comparatively weak and incapable of staging a major crackdown? Reasonable arguments have been offered for both scenarios. The answer obviously varies between states, where the context of particular repressive campaigns or periods of tolerance may change. Second, does severe intolerance towards political dissent, without the mass terror of Stalinism, generate further opposition or effectively constrict it? Evidently this largely depends on the effectiveness of the Party's social, political, and economic control mechanisms. Some have argued that repression which is not all-encompassing may breed fresh resentments and even radicalize the opposition by creating a pertinent cause for protest. Conversely, it may simply force the government's opponents to employ different tactics or remain dormant in anticipation of future opportunities for open resistance when oppressive conditions are relaxed or public resentment becomes more widespread.

On the other hand, constant and extreme forms of repression may increase the likelihood of a major popular explosion, or this may become self-perpetuating by fuelling discontent which then requires ever more severe persecution. Contrarily, does a policy of restrained coercion and relative leniency stimulate or mute political dissent? Pertinent cases can be advanced for either proposition; indeed, both overt and latent forms of dissent may be inspired by either excessive repression or increasing tolerance.

The dividing line between what is envisaged as "safe" or "dangerous" varieties of opposition differs in each country. Dahl has indicated a major dilemma faced by "oppositionless" states in this regard:

> If all oppositions are treated as dangerous and subject to repression, opposition that would be loyal if it were tolerated becomes disloyal because it is not tolerated. Since all opposition is likely to be disloyal, then all opposition must be repressed.[51]

As a consequence, Communist regimes attempt to balance repression with degrees of moderation in a way which strengthens or at least does not weaken Party rule. Such a strategy coexists with an undercurrent of official fear that too much leeway may release oppositionist forces which could undermine state control. One should not underestimate the persistence of a Leninist paranoia that views all extra-Party dissent as subversion.[52] Party officials remain on guard against comprehensive reform or the encroachment of political heterogeneity. Nevertheless, in some countries the parameters for criticism and milder forms of dissent have been stretched on occasion either in the official realm or outside it. The more sophisticated Communist elites may even allow for "protective areas" where limited forms of opposition and controllable expressions of non-conformism can operate. Such phenomena are of course subject to contraction or elimination as the government sees fit.

Since Stalin's death Communist leaders have updated their methods for controlling society and disarming menacing forms of opposition. Some observers detect an ebb and flow in the pattern of repression since 1956, in which periods of intensity intermix with moderate spells. A number of similarities can be traced in the forms of repression applied by East European states against domestic dissidents. Sharlet posits a four-fold strategy, consisting of "pacification through consumption, repressive tolerance, differentiated political justice, and suppression by force."[53] Each government has tended to focus on one or more of these methods in its broad anti-opposition drive. One may even propose the existence of several "models of repression" enforced by particular regimes with greater or lesser severity and consistency. These policies span the range of methods outlined by Sharlet, with some notable local variations.

The Romanian, Bulgarian, and East German[54] "models" concentrate on "suppression by force," whereby the authorities seek to eliminate dissenters from the public arena as swiftly as possible—through intimidation, persecution, imprisonment, or expulsion. In addition, the GDR has been more successful at applying "pacification through consumption" by guaranteeing reasonable living standards for the bulk of society and thereby steering it clear of protest actions. The Czechoslovak "model" also combines "suppression by force" with "pacification through consumption"; though it has also employed "repressive tolerance." For example, Prague conducts a prolonged war of attrition against its opponents in the Charter 77 campaign, hoping to harass the activists into submission and eventual oblivion.[55] Officials have tried to confine the human rights movement to a section of the intellectual community and isolate it from the working class, while "differentiated political justice" singles out either the front ranks of Charter 77 or lesser-known dissidents when convenient. More intensive repressive campaigns are usually mounted when the government is less concerned about unfavorable international publicity, or when it feels either emboldened or threatened domestically.

The Hungarian repressive "model" since the completion of the post-1956 "normalization" has stressed "pacification through consumption" and "repressive tolerance." Budapest is less overtly repressive in the economic and cultural domains than neighboring states, though this should not be mistaken for a steady or permanent growth of liberalism or democracy. The administration keeps close tabs on all known dissenters, and the self-styled "second culture" is allowed to function within certain limits. The opposition is customarily handled with some degree of sophistication and delicacy, where administrative sanctions rather than imprisonment or enforced exile are more commonplace if certain bounds are breached.[56] The dividing line between "safe" and "unsafe" dissent is deliberately left vague in order to keep the opposition in a precarious and unstable position. The reasons for Budapest's flexibility, "repressive tolerance," and low visibility are twofold—first, for purposes of foreign consumption to project an image of humanitarianism and liberalism, and second because the authorities may not feel gravely threatened by intellectuals who do not command a challenging mass movement.

Poland presents a somewhat different picture of overt repression, especially since the lifting of martial law, as "repressive tolerance" and "differentiated political justice" have gained increasing prominence. One must remember, however, that behind the veil of martial law and the violent liquidation of strikes and demonstrations, General Jaruzelski's regime constructed an intricate network of new laws and pro-government organizations to subdue, defuse and channel grass-roots disquiet into safer outlets.[57] Dissident workers and intellectuals have been placed on a short leash and subjected to numerous persecutions short of prison since the 1986 "amnesty decree" for political prisoners.

Specific forms of repression applied at different junctures against the opposition can be subdivided into two main categories—police persecution and administrative sanctions. Police harassment includes: sporadic or around-the-clock surveillance, bugging of apartments and telephones, direct or indirect threats, blackmail attempts, house searches, monitoring mail and visitors, confiscation of private property (such as typewriters, documents, books, and valuables), short or long-term detentions, interrogations, beatings and other kinds of physical mistreatment and violent attacks by "persons unknown," whose links with the security services are often barely concealed.

Administrative or legalistic sanctions include various forms of bureaucratic obstruction, job demotion, deprivation, or dismissal; discontinuation of welfare and health care benefits; disruption of mail and telephone services; withdrawal or withholding of passports, driving licences, or other necessary documents; expulsion from a labor union or other social or economic association; exclusion from participation in official cultural or scientific activities; eviction from homes; separation from families and friends; internal or external exile; psychiatric repression; political or "criminal" trials; and imprisonment for various periods. Some states employ the entire gamut of repressive techniques on appropriate occasions, while others are more selective and only revert to more direct methods of persecution on rare occasions. The regimes in question have two further weapons at their disposal—propaganda pressures and economic levers. The former includes media campaigns slandering the opposition in general, character assassinations to discredit specific individuals, rumor-mongering, and comprehensive disinformation offensives both at home and abroad. Among the economic levers employed to prevent, limit, or deflect workers' discontent, the authorities may arbitrarily improve working conditions, wages, and other material benefits in certain enterprises; suddenly make available stocks of food and other valuable consumer items; or even change the management in individual factories to forestall protests by a disgruntled workforce. Economic levers can also be negative and involve the denial of certain rights and privileges, or the blocking of access to much needed goods and services. Such policies can of course also be applied against intellectual and other dissenters.

Notwithstanding the numerous forms of pressure at the governments' disposal, dissident individuals and oppositionist movements have persisted in several states. A number of factors operate in this regard, including the perceived and actual weakness of official organs, and their inability to liquidate all resistance; an unwillingness by the regime to take the opposition too seriously as a challenge to the system; and the deliberate retention of an unthreatening safety valve to help release and dilute popular pressure. In some instances, Party officials may even allow some latitude for criticism within or outside the ruling establishment, which they intend to maneuver in a desired direction and help promote some policy alterations or personnel changes. Moreover, East European dissidents have persistently attempted to circumvent their governments' various repressive strategies. The successes and failures they have registered while devising their own strategies for major political, economic, social, and cultural change will now be examined in some depth.

Revisionism and Reformism

Following Lenin's dictum and the Resolution on Party Unity at the Tenth Bolshevik Congress in 1921, "factionalism" or political opposition within Communist Parties was deemed impermissible. Henceforth, dissent on fundamental policy issues and the most important doctrinal and organizational principles of Marxism-Leninism was implicitly denied and explicitly outlawed by the Party leadership. Despite such prohibitions, in the absence of legalized opposition parties, intra-systemic opposition in Communist regimes is generally confined to factionalized inner-Party groupings. However, under normal circumstances the existence of any such coherent or corporate Party factions is largely obscured.

Despite administrative and disciplinary safeguards, various sectional groupings periodically coalesce around particular policies or around individuals who uphold and promote specific objectives. These may occasionally concretize into more durable interest or pressure groups within the Party apparatus or other Communist bureaucracies. Though potential interest groups outside central or regional Party tutelage, which could compete with the power elite, are proscribed and eliminated, sectional interests intent on extending their influence within the system's parameters continue to function. In many cases, ranking cadres or groups may seek support among lower levels of the Party and among an assortment of occupational strata. They endeavor to pressurize the leadership to adjust its programs in line with their particularistic interests or with some overall program of reform. Various interest groups may form temporary and informal alliances to further their goals, and may even establish provisional links with individuals or groups outside the Party-state establishment. Under ordinary conditions, however, most occupational groups and social organizations are not in a position to influence official policy in any meaningful or lasting way.[58]

The breadth or regularity of sectional strife, or the extent and significance of power struggles within the Party, cannot be readily assessed because of their customarily highly secretive nature. One can only glean certain indicators of their existence from reported conflicts over programs, and delays in decision-making and policy implementation. But certain generalizations can be advanced, particularly as they relate to overt manifestations of conflict and opposition. Inner-Party struggles involving powerful interest groups are not necessarily "revisionist" or "reformist" in nature, or even simply a question of pressure groups promoting specific interests. They may entail an essential loyalty to the Leninist political system during maneuvering for positions of influence by potential or rival leaderships. Serious power struggles between Party groups or individuals who have garnered sufficient support to challenge the ruling clique may originate either within the Party's ideological "left," "right," or "center," or they need not be linked with any precise ideological or political tendency.

A notable "rightist" inspired bid for power within the Party was attempted by the "Partisan" group in Poland in the late 1960s. This faction tried to capitalize on the student disturbances during 1968 to dislodge the incumbent Party leadership, but were repulsed by First Secretary Władysław Gomułka. Though the "Partisans" employed nationalistic symbols and sought to appeal to patriotic sentiments, their purported "nationalism" camouflaged their inherent neo-Stalinism, subservience to Moscow, racialist chauvinism, anti-semitism, and predominant reliance on the security service apparatus.[59] A "leftist" oriented inner-Party grouping seeking to gain power and transform the ruling SED, signalled its existence in East Germany in the late 1970s.[60] A "manifesto" was issued in Berlin in October 1977 by the Central Coordinating Group of the "League of Democratic Communists of Germany" (BDKD). Purportedly consisting of several middle and high-ranking officials dissatisfied with Party policy, it sought to stimulate a

Prague Spring-type reform movement for reconstructing a more ideal form of "democratic communism."[61] The League's program called for "party pluralism," popular elections to an independent parliament, elimination of the "bureaucratic features" of democratic centralism within the SED, and German reunification within a strictly communistic framework. The group gave little subsequent indication of its existence, as no one either claimed membership in the League or responsibility for its manifesto.

Popular aspirations for democracy, civil liberties, and national independence, and public discontent with government policy, have often been exploited or manipulated politically by segments of the Party or security apparatus, especially during struggles for power and influence. In Poland, strikes, demonstrations, and riots have been exploited periodically by ambitious individuals and sectors of the *apparat* to bring about leadership changes. Some analysts have even argued that it is primarily conflict within the ruling elite which provokes political crises in Eastern Europe. Though this may be an exaggeration, it seems clear that various Party elements are prepared to benefit from manifestations of popular discontent to further their own interests. The Party leadership itself is clearly not immune from such political ploys. Groups within the Party may even deliberately cultivate self-serving contacts with some extra-Party opposition elements to enhance their struggle for power.[62] Such contacts are discarded when they cease to be advantageous. Numerous issues may be exploited during intra-systemic conflicts for political preponderance. For instance, the more skilled administrators may challenge their opponents by questioning their competence and capability.[63] Various other personal, professional, or political attributes may be equally manipulated to promote or resolve differences within the establishment.

According to the Soviet Political Dictionary "revisionism" is:

A trend in the working class movement that, for the benefit of the bourgeoisie, wants to debase, to emasculate, to destroy Marxism by means of a revision—by way of re-examination, distortion, and negation of its basic tenets.[64]

Lenin avowedly "proved" that any attempts to weaken the "leading role" of the Communist Party objectively assist "anti-socialist" forces, and pose the threat of a capitalist restoration. "Revisionism" has therefore traditionally been portrayed as a gross betrayal of Marxism-Leninism, "scientific socialism," and the working class movement. Party ideologues insist that revisionism prepares the soil for counter-revolution by undermining "revolutionary vigilance," creating ideological confusion, and softening-up Communism. It also purportedly forms an external threat to the socialist camp, because "counter-revolution" and "revisionism" are supposedly the two major weapons employed by the international bourgeoisie and imperialism to combat all "revolutionary action."

Revisionism in Eastern Europe sprang to life during the post-Stalin thaw and before the hatches were again battened down by the Party elites on guard against creeping counter-revolution. Nevertheless, revisionism has re-appeared in various guises since 1956. The post-war Communist revisionists in the Soviet bloc had less in common with a theoretical revision of the standard Marxist-Leninist analysis of capitalism and socialism, than with a critique of actual developments in Communist states. For the purposes of this study, by "traditional revisionism" we understand the flowering of Communist dissent between 1953 and the extinction of the Prague Spring in 1968–1969. It consisted of attempts by Marxist intellectuals to rejuvenate and update Marxism-Leninism in theory and in practice. The supposedly "original values"—such as humanism, egalitarianism, and genuine internationalism—were to be restored, together with their practical political expressions in enlarged social freedoms, an end to police terror, and comprehensive cultural liberalism.[65]

Lenin distinguished between "right revisionism" and "left revisionism"; he also contrasted "revisionism" with differing forms of "reformism."[66] "Right revisionism" was associated with a "social democratic distortion" of Marxism and constituted a dangerous international phenomenon threatening to divide and dilute the Communist movement.[67] "Left revisionism" was linked with various forms of "revolutionary syndicalism," anarchism, and "left-wing communism." By definition, "revisionism" in all its guises presented an inherent challenge to Leninist "democratic centralism" and the Party's monopolistic "leading role." In Lenin's estimation, "reformism," similarly to "opportunism", could be either good or bad, depending on its content, context, and consequences. Communist theorists have generally followed their mentor's premises and practical guidelines for coping with the phenomenon, but have made additional adjustments to meet current Party requirements. Lenin believed that Marxists should support reformist tendencies in capitalist countries seeking to improve working class conditions and enhance the power of the revolutionary movement. However, Communists must resolutely oppose those "reformists" in both capitalist and socialist states whose goal is to "restrict the aims and activities of the working class to the winning of reforms."[68] Such "liberal reformism" has been lambasted as a "bourgeois deception of the workers." In Communist states "reformism" is always suspect, as it may weaken "Marxist-Leninist discipline" and disorganize the Party. Since Stalin's time in Eastern Europe certain kinds of reforms, whether they are defined as such or not, have been recognized as useful if not indispensable—whether to assist economic productivity and modernization, or to improve the country's international position. This pragmatic application of "reformism" is always partial, circumspect and provisional, lest it overstep certain bounds and endanger the Party's supremacy.

In the wake of Stalin's death, each Soviet bloc Party chief has grappled with unacceptable manifestations of revisionism and reformism. The offensive has assumed both ideological and practical proportions. In the majority of these countries, revisionists were ousted from the Party and their influence effectively neutralized by the end of the 1950s. The Czechoslovak "revisionist" and "counter-revisionist" struggle, however, erupted during the 1960s and was eventually extinguished with the help of Soviet tanks in 1968. Cross-bloc, post-Stalin revisionism has shared a number of common features. Dissident Polish historian Adam Michnik succinctly summed up these characteristics:

> Revisionism was an intellectual movement that accompanied the corrosion of the Party apparat's iron ideology. In its attempt—in principle—to be a movement aimed at repairing the Leading System, revisionism tried to moderate and restrict the system's totalitarian character, violating—at least unconsciously—the very essence of communist rule.[69]

Kusin has traced nine major elements of the reformist-type programs put forward by Communist revisionists in the 1950s and 1960s.[70] Their significance in each state has differed somewhat, and they have often been applied in a self-serving manner by the governments in question. These ingredients focused on: relations with the Soviet Communist Party; inner-Party relations; reform of the political system; workers' self-management; economic changes; the role of law and the rehabilitation of political victims; cultural and scientific freedom; the "humanization" of Marxism; and "peaceful co-existence" with the West. When these issues merged into a coherent program for far-reaching reform the Party apparatus reacted strongly to preserve its political control, and the revisionist-reformist movement was eventually extinguished.

Following the Soviet-led invasion of Czechoslovakia and the subsequent "normalization," it was officially claimed that the authentic Marxist-Leninist nucleus of the CPCS Party had "defeated revisionism"—a political deviation which had sided with "bourgeois ideology," and whose propositions served as a theoretical justification for "opportunism" intended to split the "working class movement."[71] The attempt at Party self-improvement in Czechoslovakia, through internal reform and economic, cultural, and political liberalization, and the campaign against "dogmatism" and "conservatism" during the Prague Spring, was later denounced as a serious deviation from Marxism-Leninism. According to the victorious ideologues, revisionist-reformists sought to abolish "socialist relations of production" under the guise of economic reform.[72] The "democratic socialist" system proposed by Prague reformers was henceforth equated with a "bourgeois system" which would restore capitalism in Czechoslovakia, and threaten the cohesion of the entire socialist bloc.

Since 1956, Soviet leaders have endeavored to forestall any repetition of the Hungarian, Czechoslovak, or Polish crises by stymieing the growth of rival groupings within the ruling Communist Parties. The fear of uncontrollable reformism is one major reason why factionalism is discouraged and combated, particularly factionalism with revisionist underpinnings.[73] During the early phase of de-Stalinization, factional strife was commonplace as various Party groups vied for influence and control, while the Stalinist leaders were replaced in the midst of sweeping personnel reshuffles. The post-thaw leadership in turn tried to eradicate factional conflicts, including any potentially destructive revisionist tendencies. Though both revisionism and factionalism have resurfaced at several periods in some of the states under observation, they have been stringently regulated and confined to moderate bounds. However, in the absence of any institutionalized forms of opposition to the current Communist Party line, and with the presence of often disgruntled technocrats, intellectuals, and other interest groups within the administration, some conflict is likely to resurface periodically and even spill over into the public domain.

For the purposes of this study, "neo-revisionism" and "neo-reformism" refer to post-1968 attempts at substantive economic and political change emanating from within the Communist political structure. These terms may also encompass efforts to reform the political system either by Party members or by "outsiders," without recourse to any extra-systemic or "extra-legal" channels. This "modern" form of revisionism-reformism often entails some reinterpretation of Marxism in general, and a reconstruction of Leninism in its Soviet variant in particular. The avowed political positions of such reformers may range from an "independent Marxism" through various shades of "socialism" and "social democracy." One common characteristic is a pronounced criticism of Leninism as a specifically "Russian" phenomenon inapplicable outside the Soviet revolutionary era and largely irrelevant, or even regressive, for the "highly developed" industrialized East European countries.[74] Leninist-Stalinist totalitarianism is dismissed as a "bureaucratic-statist distortion" of Marxian socialism. Some neo-revisionists have posited the need for a return either to pre-Bolshevik Marxism, or for the development of authentic "neo-communist" social formations and political structures. Self-styled "real socialism" in the Soviet bloc is therefore disparaged for being at variance both with Marxist theory and with practical needs and potentials.

The assortment of neo-revisionist positions are strenuously attacked by Communist governments concerned with internal influences undermining Party doctrines, programs, and institutions. Revisionist intellectuals have advanced a "new model" of socialism, involving a "democratized" single-party system and heightened public involvement in decision-making, alongside overall state planning. Party stalwarts argue that the intended or unintended consequences of such proposals would be to deprive "scientific socialism" of its "revolutionary character."[75] Doctrinaire ideologists maintain that revisionists are waging an undeclared war against Marxism-Leninism under the guise of an attack against Stalinism. Some Party theorists have even posited various "levels of revisionism" corresponding to the degree to which the culprits have departed from official Marxist-Leninist prescriptions. Such attacks contain a few kernels of truth, in that many Marxist revisionists have increasingly turned towards Eurocommunism, "democratic socialism" or Western-type social democracy since the 1960s. This of course is largely the product of their disillusionment with prospects for reforming Warsaw Pact Communist Parties. Many revisionists have in effect discarded several key Leninist principles—such as "class struggle" and the "dictatorship of the proletariat"—and gradually embraced some indeterminate "third way" of organizing society, neither fully capitalist nor communist.[76] Internal dissent by critical Communist intellectuals may indeed start as a simple disagreement with certain Party policies, and subsequently evolve into more fundamental misgivings over political conditions and developments.

The impact of neo-revisionism on Party policy since the 1968 Czechoslovak catastrophe, especially in the political realm, has not proved to be of enduring significance in any East bloc state. Party leaders have remained on guard against "social democratic" or "left communist" encroachments, and have attempted to swiftly subdue any emergent political reformism. Michnik points out that in demanding "liberal political reforms" the revisionists have been faced with an important choice— either to recognize the Party *apparat's* view of social order and thereby "identify with the authorities against society's aspirations," or to continue calling for political reform and "part ways with the Party to become an opposition group."[77]

A segment of the revisionist tendency, whose basic loyalty to the Communist system has taken precedence over propositions for far-reaching political change, has increasingly turned toward some variant of gradual domestic reform. This has principally focused on economic issues, where they envisage change to be not only possible but essential. Such economic reformers have usually been careful to avoid explicit political connotations in their "restructuring" proposals. They generally do not dispute the system of central planning and Party control, but seek more salient roles for technocrats and the largely apolitical scientific and technological intelligentsia. Reformist technocrats are far from being political democrats, but are primarily rationalists, utilitarians, and problem-solvers within the system's parameters. Their emphasis on greater efficiency and rationalization has nevertheless generated some cleavages among official economists over the precise content of any reform package, and produced conflicts with the traditionalist bureaucratic establishment.

Some reformists have programmatically proceeded further along the road of marketization and economic decentralization, particularly in Hungary, and have implicitly criticized the rigid command model. However, their political influence as a viable opposition movement has tended to be restricted as a result. Many of these "experts" are periodically co-opted by the ruling apparatus as economic advisers, while some of their reformist proposals have been applied under strict government supervision. Even where reformist propositions are considered valuable, their implementation often proceeds prudently and in a piecemeal fashion lest it disrupt the Party's political machinery. Nevertheless, economic refomers may continue to present a long-term challenge to time-honored Communist Party control mechanisms and management policies.

For the non-Party "democratic socialists" in Eastern Europe, "reform" is understood as a vehicle for establishing or extending "socialist democracy" by political, economic, or other means. This contrasts with the premises of intra-systemic "Communist reformers," whose objective is to enable the current structure to operate more efficiently and productively; for the latter, pluralism and devolution in decision-making are not pursued for their own sake. Notwithstanding the reluctance of Party officials to advocate far-reaching political changes, some members of the "socialist opposition" have cultivated contacts with self-styled "moderates" and "reformers" within or close to the apparatus, usually with limited ultimate success.[78] The categories of "reformer" and "conservative" within the ruling Communist Parties are rarely watertight or even mutually exclusive. Polish, Czechoslovak, and Hungarian Party leaders and lower-level functionaries have on occasion donned reformist robes when convenient in internal power struggles, or as a useful tactical device to gain public support. Such reformist inclinations were later discarded, diluted, or adapted to suit government requirements when prevailing conditions no longer warranted their use.[79]

It is helpful at this point to discuss some pertinent examples of neo-revisionism and intra-Party and extra-Party reformism in the Soviet bloc.

The Czechoslovak and Polish cases will be sketched briefly, while the Hungarian and East German examples will be considered in more detail. The Czechoslovak revisionists played an important role during the years preceding the Prague Spring. Some remnants were still active after the post-invasion purges in the opposition movement that pre-dated Charter 77. During the period of "normalization" they formed a "socialist opposition" among the more active ranks of the "Party of the expelled"—a designation for the approximately half a million members removed from the Communist Party in 1969–70. These former "Prague Springists" continued to question the viability of the Party dictatorship and its undemocratic pyramidical structure.[80] Their actual influence on government policy since 1968 has not proved significant. However, some eventually provided a crucial stimulus for the creation of the human rights movement centered around Charter 77. The "ex-communist" or "reform communist" ingredient has been present in the Charter since the group's inception. Though they have not formed a coherent political group, and have lacked a binding program, their persistent influence is noticeable in Charter 77 campaigns—particularly in the movement's repeated calls for dialogue with the regime, in its singular avoidance of conflict, and in the underlying belief of some Charter 77 signatories that the Communist Party is still capable of reforming itself and the political and economic systems. These modern-day revisionists have helped to put brakes on Charter 77 from evolving into a distinct political movement, or into an overt oppositionist force.

Revisionism and reformism in Poland, as in other states, began as a movement of criticism and disillusionment within the Party concerning the pace and scope of de-Stalinization. Following the reversals and eventual failures of the "Polish October" many reformist activists left the Party. After the violent suppression of students' protests in 1968 and workers demonstrations in 1970 and 1976, they increasingly sought new strategies to initiate political change outside the purview of the state. They became progressively more pessimistic about the likelihood of reforming the Party itself; hence their links with revisionism, and in many instances with Marxism itself, were effectively severed.[81] The remaining Polish Communist reformers were preoccupied with economic issues and less attentive to any major political transformations. According to Michnik, by 1980 and the dawn of Solidarity the remaining political reformers within the Party proved to be a caricature of their Polish October and Prague Spring "ideological mentors," having no real links with the "tissue of intellectual life." For these "reformers" the question of "how should the Party be made more democratic" was central, whereas for those working outside the system "the focal issue was how to tear the largest possible area of public life out of the *diktat* of the Party *nomenklatura*."[82]

The most significant recent display of inner-Party reformism in Poland was visible during 1981, when the "horizontalist" movement of middle and lower ranking Communist activists attempted to forge more effective political linkages by-passing the traditional hierarchical structures of Party control.[83] The movement was resolutely suppressed and outlawed by the Communist leadership even before the imposition of martial law. In post-revolutionary Hungary, with the gradual implementation of Kádár's unwritten "social compact," political opposition within and outside the Party was stifled. What remained for the most part was a strong current of economic reformism co-opted and manipulated by the ruling elite, and a small critical intelligentsia tolerated by Budapest and advancing essentially moderate policies for liberalization. During the 1970s and 1980s, the government left the oppositionist intelligentsia largely at liberty, simply harassing it in petty ways to ensure that it would not exceed permitted bounds. The influence of the more outspoken dissidents has been deliberately restricted and isolated from the working masses, in order to preclude the crystallization of any sizeable social movement.

The Hungarian dissidents themselves have been extremely cautious about encouraging or establishing any mass movements. There are several interrelated reasons for this: the trauma of the 1956 Revolution, the discouraging examples of Czechoslovakia in 1968 and Poland in 1981, the fear of more severe repression, and the difficulty of garnering public support. Many dissidents also maintain that a popular and strident campaign for political and economic changes could also undermine the current gradual and often precarious attempts at reform within the Party. Critical intellectuals have therefore avoided open ideological and political clashes with the regime. In their estimation, Budapest should not feel threatened by an independent intelligentsia, and neither should Moscow be alarmed that Hungary could once again become a focal point of social tension and conflict.

One of the leading Hungarian pro-reformist dissidents, Gyorgy Konrad believes that Party leaders seek to achieve an "enlightened, paternalistic authoritarianism, accompanied by a measured willingness to undertake gradual liberal reforms."[84] In this respect, Magyar dissidents should support even piecemeal measures which aim at a "democratic reform of state socialism," and realize the long-term "conjunction of interests" between the government and the opposition in improving the workings of the system. Konrad succinctly summarizes the position of Hungarian neo-reformists:

Since we cannot be either contractual allies, or a sharply defined opposition, we must be reformists, critical players for democracy against those who play to defend the Party-state's monopoly of power. We must be their opponents on behalf of democracy, and at the same time their collaborators on behalf of undisturbed national survival.[85]

Hungarian dissidents form a "subculture within the larger intelligentsia," and are primarily a cultural opposition and not a fully fledged political grouping. Moreover, they generally advance reformist programs and not wholesale political changes. They have not cultivated contacts with the working class in attempts to forge any mass movement, but have sought to influence other intellectuals, especially those in a position to wield some power, and thus encourage liberalization "from the top" downwards. At present, the majority of reformist dissidents think that the Party dictatorship can be curbed and loosened, primarily through economic reforms, gradually accompanied by the necessary political adjustments.[86] Such gradual economic shifts, involving a partial decentralization of industrial management, increasing "privatization," and a corresponding democratization in decision-making, will evidently encourage the "embourgeoisement" of Hungarian society, and of the Communist Party itself. An expanding middle class intelligentsia could in turn purportedly swallow up the "dictatorial bureaucracy." According to Konrad, the power elite displays some tendency to develop into a "rational bureaucratic elite of professionals" willing to delegate decisions to lower levels of the power hierarchy, and to permit the eventual separation of the various political and economic spheres of authority.[87]

The prevailing idea among the pro-reformist Hungarian dissidents is to encourage gradual change, political stability, and the emergence of a strong middle class that would soften the Party from within. In this scenario, although the framework of Communism remains intact, "the spirit and style in which power is exercised" can evidently become more flexible and democratic.[88] Proponents of these views are clearly banking on the good will, rationality, and enlightened self-interest of Communist officials. They seem equally assured that the system can consistently evolve toward some "democratic socialist" model without stimulating more far-reaching political and nationalist demands among the Hungarian population, or without provoking a major backlash from Party dogmatists or from Moscow.

Dissident reformers perceive definite limits to the process of reform within Communist systems; indeed they explicitly preclude the emergence of "new decision-making centers" operating outside Party control or supervision. In Konrad's estimation, because the Kremlin will not countenance the dissolution of Communist rule in Budapest or the "Finlandization" of Hungary, society has to cast its lot with a "milder tyranny." Nevertheless, the role of dissidents is apparently to test the flexibility of the system without questioning the legitimacy of the regime or employing "illegitimate methods."[89] The long-range success of this neo-reformist strategy in the Hungarian context remains in doubt, particularly in the light of deteriorating economic conditions, growing public discontent, and the persistent conflicts between reformers and anti-reformers of various shades within the Party leadership.

A small group of political dissenters in the GDR have veered towards neo-revisionism, and propounded more substantive political and socio-economic changes than the Hungarian reformist dissidents.[90] But given the highly repressive conditions in East Germany and the effective pacification of the working class since the 1953 revolt, political dissidents have been sealed off from the masses. They have failed to develop links with either discontented industrial workers or with any significant reformist trend within the ruling SED.

A fundamental neo-Marxist revisionism is evident in the works of Robert Havemann[91] and Rudolf Bahro. It involves an updating of Leninist theory and praxis, and prescriptions for the "renewal" of the Party on account of the "ideological bankruptcy" of the Soviet system.[92] Bahro does not simply want to modify "actual socialism" by introducing liberal economic features, but aims at a thorough remodeling of the Party. For Bahro, the "crisis of proto-socialist societies" in the Soviet bloc is deeply rooted in the "socio-economic contradictions" inherent in the "relations of production." The abolition of private property has evidently not resulted in a socialist transformation whereby the "means of production" are genuinely the "property of the people"; in fact, "the whole society stands property-less against the state machine."[93] A patently wide chasm exists between Marx's classical vision and the realities of the new society, as envisioned by Bahro. This state of affairs calls for a "new revolution," though not a violent clash, which would transform "actual socialism" into actual "communism."[94]

Bahro and other like-minded Marxist revisionists in the self-proclaimed "communist opposition" posit the need for a "cultural revolution" which must involve "all progressive elements" in the country, whatever class or section of society they may be "objectively" ascribed to. The "communist movement can no longer take up the standpoint of exclusive and particular class interests," because the proposed "new party" needs to have a mass following as the "general representative of a new order."[95] Bahro's stated objective is the elimination of the privileged power of the "bureaucratic structure" which exercises tutelage over society, so that the relationship between state and society is drastically re-arranged. In an evident idealization of the Prague Spring, Bahro conjectures the existence of "progressive communist" latent forces in East German society. The "born-again" Party would need to direct its energies not against state socialism as such, but against the "dictatorship of the politbureaucracy." For Bahro, simple economic restructuring without extensive political reforms are insufficient to build a "new organization of non-capitalist industrial society."[96]

Bahro evinces a somewhat illusory notion that the state, under pressure from "progressively minded socialists," will "gradually become less dominant."[97] By dissolving the "politbureaucracy" society will apparently "liberate itself," through a wide-ranging "emancipatory movement" involving the "creative elements of all strata and spheres of society." The "new model" of society proposed by the East German theorist is highly elusive—it is neither capitalist nor communist, and is to consist of an unclear mixture of central economic planning and "controlled democracy," together with self-management in "all social institutions," and the creation of a novel form of communal life based on "autonomous group activities."[98] Neo-revisionists such as Bahro appear more concerned with reviving some idealized form of communism, than with constructing a society based on individual liberties, political pluralism, and participatory democracy. They are explicitly opposed to "party pluralism," which is considered anachronistic from a Marxist standpoint because "the plurality of political parties rests on a class structure," which has avowedly been eliminated throughout Eastern Europe. With clearly Leninist undertones, Bahro argues the necessity for a "vanguard organization" and an "intellectual leadership" over society, and specifically opposes the reconstruction of any liberal or social democratic parties.

Marxist neo-revisionist ideas about "post-bureaucratic societies" in the Soviet bloc seem idyllic and utopian, and they leave numerous pertinent questions unanswered—in particular, the actual opinions and aspirations of the non-ruling social strata.[99] Bahro believes that the number of committed "communist oppositionists" is steadily growing in East Germany, but the evidence does not appear to confirm such suppositions.[100] He neglects to mention that by all accounts much of the population in the GDR and other East European states consider "communism" *per se* to be discredited. They are unlikely to heed calls for any new "communist revolution" or to support the emergence of a "new communist party" promising a "communist transformation."

In the GDR, the fragmented and persecuted dissidents have an additional problem in stirring the masses, and indeed in speaking a common language with them. Vocal East German dissident intellectuals have remained more committed to Marxism than their Polish, Czechoslovak, or Hungarian equivalents, even while rejecting the official Party version.[101] Their consequent alienation from the working class has plainly proved to be a major factor inhibiting the formation of any sizeable oppositionist movements.[102] A similar problem has been encountered by Romanian dissidents operating on an equally small oppositionist scale.[103]

The self-proclaimed "communist opposition," especially since the collapse of the Prague Spring, has been little in evidence throughout Eastern Europe. Political dissidents have increasingly adopted and pursued new strategies outside the revisionist-reformist framework, seeing little need or prospect for transforming the ruling Parties from within, or in devising any workable "new model of communism." Nevertheless, a gradualist, reformist-leaning platform may offer some reasonable scope for the future, without necessarily entailing an evolution towards a democratic, multi-party system, but rather a more "tolerable dictatorship" of "authoritarian paternalism." Though the prospects for any Communist Party rejuvenation along Bahroist lines appear to be remote, we are witnessing some revival of inner-Party reformism in the Soviet bloc during the Gorbachev era, but it will probably be devoid of any ideological revisionist fervor. One should not be unduly optimistic at this stage about the outcome, or exclude the possibility of an eventual anti-reformist backlash. The ruling Communist Parties have learnt some painful lessons from previous attempts at comprehensive political and economic reform, and will remain careful not to unleash mass demands which could seriously undermine Party-state absolutism and Soviet bloc cohesiveness.

3

Dissident Strategies II: Social Activism

Revolutionism and Evolutionism

The overwhelming majority of the population in each East European state, whatever the extent of its disillusionment, alienation, frustration, and opposition to Communist government policies, purposively avoids involvement in revolutionary or violent activities. With the notable exception of the 1956 Hungarian Revolution, national insurrectionary or political revolutionary campaigns have proved to be extremely isolated and easily containable incidents following the Communist seizure and consolidation of power in the 1940s.[1]

A number of factors and counter-pressures discourage and effectively preclude the emergence of violent revolutionary movements. These include: the omnipresence of the police and security apparatus; the network of stifling political and social controls; the fear of repression and other reprisals; psycho-social barriers involving pronounced apprehension about personal isolation and the ultimate futility of revolt; awareness of previous failed attempts to overthrow Communist Party rule; the unlikelihood of outside assistance; and the improbability of either gaining sufficient arms or determined mass support to neutralize or effectively challenge the security forces. The ever-present threat of Soviet intervention plays an equally important role in discouraging violent rebellion throughout the bloc.

As a result of these factors, violent outbursts by workers and other demonstrators have usually been sporadic, small-scale, and short-lived. In addition, they have rarely been linked to any systematic revolutionary program of political and social transformation, or to a campaign of national liberation. In general, such outbursts have only evinced temporary, slender, and easily reversible concessions from the government in question. Furthermore, violent acts have tended to provoke the regime and served as pretexts for liquidating a whole spectrum of internal opposition irrespective of its attitude to violent revolution. Riots and other destructive protests have also been staged or manipulated by Communist regimes, or by vested interests within or on the margins of the power structure, to promote their own objectives in the process of eliminating active oppositionist leaders, organizers, and participants. People are generally aware that after a successful official "pacification" of a major demonstration, strike, or rebellion, the opportunities for any concerted challenge to the government tend to recede substantially. At such a time public fear is inclined to increase, while the arrest and punishment of oppositionist activists discourages the staging of further organized protests, whether violent or peaceful.

Since the late 1950s, Eastern Europe has witnessed the demise of quixotic, revolutionary idealism among both the Marxist and non-Marxist political dissidents. First, this has involved a lessened emphasis on some vanguard of "professional revolutionaries" planning, undertaking, and leading any major political transformation. Second, it has led to a repudiation of violent tactics, and precluded any strategic planning for a violent showdown with the regime. In many respects, this has reflected a growing sense of realism, given the highly unfavorable internal and external conditions for a popular uprising. Few political oppositionists in the Soviet bloc make calls for or place any hopes in dramatic, violent, or wholesale revolution to overthrow the government and eliminate Soviet domination.[2]

The Polish opposition movement in the late 1970s, even before the rise of Solidarity, categorically repudiated insurrectionist and violent revolutionary methods, declaring that they would not allow themselves to be "driven into conspiracy . . . (we) will not be provoked, and will never resort to acts of terror which could be exploited to liquidate any authentic, spontaneously formed outlets of social initiative."[3] The prominent Polish dissidents Jacek Kuroń and Karol Modzelewski implicitly supported the concept of "revolution" during the politically stagnant 1960s, and evidently did not discount the possibility of a violent overthrow of the "bureaucratic system" through some "genuine" form of "proletarian revolution."[4] However, they lost enthusiasm for revolutionary activities and sweeping political changes after the 1968 student protests and government repression. They subsequently discarded much of their youthful Marxist zeal and utopian pro-communist inclinations, and developed novel prescriptions for more gradual social change.

A similar pattern has been visible in other East European states since the 1960s. Echoing the ideas of a substantial segment of the post-Stalin opposition embracing various political persuasions, the Hungarian dissident theorist Konrad considers that:

Nothing would be a bigger mistake for the East European democratic opposition, nothing would hurt our real interests more, than falling captive to the style of thinking, rhetoric, and mythic tendencies of the Jacobin-Leninist tradition. I could only regard as a demagogue anyone who deemed himself a revolutionary today on our political soil.[5]

According to Tokes, repeated failures to bring about drastic changes through armed uprisings and revolutions have left "all would-be insurgents with no alternative to accepting gradual reforms as the only realistic strategy of political change in the shadow of the USSR."[6] The only questions to be resolved would revolve around three key issues: how gradually the process of change should develop; what the precise content of any political, social, and economic reforms should be; and what would be the most effective non-revolutionary strategy for achieving the desired objectives.

Clandestine, conspiratorial, and "underground" political opposition has been little in evidence—with the notable exception of Poland—since the Communist regimes broke the backbone of the immediate postwar resistance movements. Some clandestine anti-government activities were pursued after the crushing of the Hungarian uprising, and following the post-Stalin crises in other states, but in general these were small and ineffectual campaigns. Moreover, the majority of political dissidents have increasingly come out in favor of overt, publicly visible oppositionist work, particularly since the late 1960s. By basing their programs on openness, clarity, peaceful change, and gradualism, most dissidents have purposively avoided official charges of criminal deviance, subversive conspiracy, and of fomenting violence. Simultaneously, they have tried to fortify public trust, confidence, and participation in oppositionist work, campaigned to dismantle the pervasive barrier of popular fear, and sought to generate positive publicity for their cause both within and outside the Soviet bloc.

Notwithstanding these developments, in certain instances the impossibility of expressing ideas freely or working openly for reform has driven dissenters into various forms of clandestine or semi-clandestine activities.[7] Secretive work may be pursued for differing reasons, whether to avoid exposure, capture, and persecution; to maintain intact certain elements of the dissident movement and shield them from police persecution; to gather, produce, and circulate unofficial information; or to preserve reliable and regular contacts with supporters and organizations providing financial and material aid from the West. All this does not of course signify the existence of a revolutionary conspiracy or the advocacy of violent methods of resistance, despite repeated government charges to the contrary.

Several notable intellectual figures have been engaged, to a greater
or lesser degree, in clandestine and anonymous oppositionist ventures.
The fear of exposure, demotion, dismissal, blacklisting, imprisonment,
and other forms of repression, have encouraged certain critics of the
regime to seek "extra-legal" channels to disseminate their views. For
instance, the clandestine Polish League for Independence (PPN) was
formed in the mid-1970s as an intellectual think tank to stimulate free
debate among the Polish intelligentsia on sensitive political, social, and
economic issues.[8] Its members maintained complete anonymity because
of fears about official harassment, but seemed to have achieved little
more than issuing documents and provoking discussions without establishing any cohesive organizational structure or political program. Similar
initiatives have been periodically undertaken in Poland and other East
bloc states with variable levels of durability and effectiveness.

The most substantial and lasting clandestine movement of resistance
was painstakingly constructed in Poland soon after the declaration of
martial law in December 1981. This was as much a strategy of necessity
as choice under grossly repressive political conditions, involving the
destruction of the "overground" and legally functioning Solidarity movement and other non-governmental organizations. Dissidents such as
Michnik and Kuroń, who were previously opposed to underground
operations, fully supported the newly established "conspiratorial" labor
union structures because "Jaruzelski has made the choice for us." All
branches of the underground movement explicitly opted for peaceful
methods of pressure on the regime, dismissed the idea of revolution
and armed insurrection, and implicitly avoided any replication of the
war-time anti-Nazi resistance movement—with its underground state,
an alternative national government, and clandestine political parties.[9]
Indeed, the Solidarity underground has tended to steer clear of political
activity as such, amid a wide-ranging debate within the opposition
movement about the efficacy and moral dimensions of secrecy, deception,
and underground activities in general.

The principal aims of the Polish underground during martial law were
to preserve the spirit and substance of Solidarity under extremely adverse
conditions, to prepare for any future resumption of legal or overt
operations, and to counter and undermine the process of Communist
"normalization." Activists avoided the construction of a centralized,
hierarchical organization with an apparatus of professional conspirators,
and instead opted for a loose decentralized network of factory, local,
regional and national cells which coordinated some but not all of their
activities.[10] An internal "molecular doctrine" was developed in the
underground, whereby each activist was aware only of the identity of
a handful of trustworthy collaborators. This minimized the chances for

police liquidation of an entire local structure, even if a number of individuals or complete local cells were discovered by the security services and dissolved. The existence of small secretive units lessened the chances of capture, whereas a mass underground organization may have proved more vulnerable to penetration, exposure, and elimination.

The development of a comprehensive infrastructure of underground networks in Jaruzelski's Poland was accompanied by the establishment of clandestine safe houses, hiding places, escape routes, meeting points, printing and distribution networks, and a system of couriers linking cells, factories, and regions. The latter also transmitted material support and independent information between Poland and the outside world. The maintenance of organizational secrecy was paramount, and it necessitated the activation of latent sympathy among wide sections of Polish society. In addition to publishing underground texts, collecting trade union dues, organizing protest actions and various other visible forms of resistance, the underground has undertaken numerous attempts to disrupt oppressive government policies. It has conducted campaigns to discredit the most sadistic and corrupt officials, militiamen, and prison wardens; arranged symbolic public protests; forged some official documents and personal identity papers; spread rumours detrimental to the regime; and mounted occasional mild acts of sabotage against state property.[11] Some actions have been deemed constructive and others counter-productive by activists during the course of the struggle. In fact, the limited "dirty tricks" campaign subsided once the worst excesses of martial law had passed. Concurrently, street demonstrations and workers' strikes were discouraged after their repeated failure to influence government policy; they merely provoked violent police "pacification" drives.

Oppositionist strategists have argued that the Polish underground must not simply vent anger toward the regime, but should construct a patient and consistent campaign avoiding militancy and acts of desperation. Furthermore, the underground was to be part of a wider movement of "national resistance," flexible and adaptable, and co-existing parallel with other forms of opposition depending on prevailing circumstances— whether these are "overground," overt, semi-legal, or semi-clandestine.[12] The Polish opposition clearly intends to keep its options open by upholding various forms of pressure on and resistance against the government. The clandestine element in their operations has remained one essential ingredient since the official attack on Solidarity was launched.

Some observers believe that clandestine, conspiratorial operations tend intrinsically to breed militancy and radicalism. Among the factors that allegedly encourage this process of radicalization one can mention: the feeling of isolation and frustration experienced by activists concerning the pace and direction of actual change; their overall detachment from and idealization of the popular mood, leading to an increasing divorce from reality; a self-destructive competition for public attention; an overzealousness to provide visible proof of the authenticity of the opposition movement; intolerance and mounting vindictiveness resulting from incessant government repression; and the search for some dramatic manifestation of the significance of the clandestine campaign.

In the case of the major part of the Solidarity underground, extensive radicalization seems to have been avoided. This has been partly due to the presence and influence of a moderate leadership and a sizeable core of activists closely associated with the "evolutionist" dissident intellectuals. Though clandestine organizers have tended to be more outspoken than above-ground oppositionists, because of their anonymity and relative safety from official reprisals, Polish independent union activists astutely calculated that any drastic militancy would play into the government's hands and help buttress official propaganda campaigns against "Solidarity extremists." Radicalism, it was argued, could also alienate activists from the mass of workers and contribute to the former's demise by dissipating popular support. In general, the pre-martial law, Solidarity-type gradualist approach to political and socio-economic change has been continued in the post-martial law underground movement.

Non-Solidarity clandestine groupings and networks have also emerged in Jaruzelski's Poland, including several avowedly political movements with their own publications and programs.[13] Some indications of clandestine activity have also been registered in other states, though on a smaller scale and with less clear-cut public support or coherent internal organization; these groups have also operated under seemingly even more inauspicious political conditions. For instance, a clandestine body styling itself as the Revolutionary Action Group (SRA) was formed in Prague in late 1981, expressing support for Solidarity's struggle in Poland and calling upon Czechoslovak workers to stage sympathy protests on behalf of their neighbors.[14] The group scored little success in stirring the population out of passivity or in expanding its membership and effectiveness; the SRA evidently dwindled away soon after its inception. The success or failure of any clandestine endeavor hinges on numerous interrelated factors, including the degree of public support; the structure, size, and durability of the movement; the group's program, platform, tactics, and activities; the nature and effectiveness of non-clandestine opposition in the country; government methods of disruption, and the efficacy of police penetration of the movement.[15] Clandestine and clearly "illegal" groupings generally face an uphill struggle throughout Eastern Europe in trying to dispel widespread feelings of public impotence, pessimism, and apathy, and in preserving their organizational viability.

As de Weydenthal points out, dissident movements in the Soviet bloc since the late 1970s have "essentially focused on the political conditions of their individual countries; so their specific programs and methods of operation have been quite different."[16] Notwithstanding such differences, however, a trend has emerged during the past decade as political oppositionists outside the ruling Parties have adopted similar if not identical strategies to promote extensive political change—these strategies generally fall under the rubric of "new evolutionism."[17] By contrast, the "old evolutionists" were primarily inner-Party revisionists and reformers of various stripes who sought to alter the political and economic system from within during the 1950s and 1960s.[18]

The aim of the "neo-evolutionist" strategy, unlike that of the revolutionists, is not to win any outright victory over the government or, in contrast to the reformist-revisionists, to initiate change within the ruling Communist Parties. The central objective is to try and maneuver the government either into granting lasting concessions to the populace, or into tolerating various social initiatives that gradually extend the horizons of individual freedom and public autonomy. As a result, certain lasting compromises may be sought between state and society as dissidents attempt to make Party leaders realize that their "common interests" are best served by means of a social evolution that does not endanger the State's geostrategic and political survivability, but helps to release and constructively channel public pressures for change. However, the evolutionist platform does not ultimately depend on any actual negotiations between representatives of the Party-state and society. In fact, the overall program for the population focuses on seeking and obtaining freedom of action in various public and private spheres with or without explicit government permission. Any such gains can subsequently be presented to the authorities as a *fait accompli*, while campaigns for wider liberties continue.

The neo-evolutionists do not necessarily base their strategies on the good will or reasonableness of the ruling elite; indeed their propositions are pitched more toward society than the state. A little leeway in one area, they maintain, stimulates and accelerates demands and possibilities in other spheres, thus contributing to a gradual transformation of the social system. This "strategy of liberation" is supposed to be loose and flexible, feeling its way along the path of least resistance and growing "in the direction of the possible."[19] New evolutionism is fundamentally opportunistic, and attempts to create or widen any cracks in the state edifice and its network of social controls. It is also tinged with a high degree of realism which is based on past dissident experiences and evident in the supposition that any freedoms gained by society can be swiftly rescinded when government pressures increase or social pressures relax. Though they do not entirely reject the use of violence, especially for purposes of self-defense and as a last resort, neo-evolutionists pointedly oppose revolutionary tactics because of the overwhelming power of the security forces, their counter-productiveness in provoking extensive repression, and the supposed moral-political congruence between means and ends.

The strategy of "instant change," encompassing a comprehensive reformist or revolutionary political package from the outset, is thereby counterposed by the policy of the "long march"—a gradual, step-by-step process intended to restrain the masses from undertaking radical oppositionist measures. New evolutionist thinkers, embracing various political persuasions, posit both shorter and longer term objectives—the former may be very modest and specific, the latter are usually far-reaching and general. The maximalist platform, which may include full national independence and major political transformations towards a multi-party parliamentary system and a representative democracy, may appear comparatively remote. By contrast, the process of "social self-determination" is a more immediate proposition, with its emphasis on freedom of choice, civil liberties, respect for human rights, and the recreation of a "civil society" in each Communist state.[20]

The notion of a "self-limiting revolution" is applicable in this context; its influence was clearly felt during the "legal" Solidarity era in Poland. Throughout its overground existence, the free labor union leadership was prepared to negotiate compromises with the authorities on any number of issues pertaining to economic or social policy, and thereby delay or indefinitely postpone any longer-term popular political aspirations. This gradualist position became more problematic when Solidarity leaders found themselves caught in the cross-fire between provocative government delaying tactics and growing grass-roots militancy and public impatience. Nevertheless, the majority of union officials and advisers, even after the imposition of martial law, essentially continued to believe in the possibility and necessity of some measure of accommodation with the regime, calculating that there was no viable alternative.

The neo-evolutionists evidently consider that time is on their side, and perceive a long-term trend in Communist states towards a technologically advanced consumer society dependent on greater economic efficiency and political rationality. One concomitant of this process of modernization would apparently involve a slackening of tension and conflict between state and society, and a loosening of government controls in several areas of public life even without necessitating the introduction of a novel post-Communist political model. The evolutionist strategy of gradualism and self-limitation has been most widely developed in Poland since the late 1970s, following the failure of student and worker protests to alter government policy and the general disillusionment with Communist reformism. As Pravda notes, there was:

> A growing realization, especially among younger intellectual dissidents, that traditional attempts to convert reformist-minded politicians to the cause of democratization must be replaced by a strategy for the implementation of human rights in the broadest sense, embracing economic as well as political liberties, in alliance with the working class.[21]

East Europe's new evolutionists have displayed some affinity with individuals who opted for "organic work" in 19th century partitioned Poland, following the failure of several uprisings against Russian and Prussian overlordship, as well as with the program of "small-scale work" in the Czech lands under Austro-Hungarian suzerainty. In contradistinction to the revolutionaries and insurrectionists, the "organic workers" or "positivists" favored a slow but diligent course to preserve national and cultural identity and instill national self-confidence against the onslaught of Russification, Germanization, and Austrianization. Heroic, symbolic, and ultimately wasteful human sacrifices against overwhelming odds were disdained.[22] A similar process of adaptation developed throughout Eastern Europe in the shadow of Soviet domination. Indeed, between the failures of post-Stalin revisionism and the emergence of the more forthright neo-evolutionist strategy, a "neo-realist" political philosophy was visible among many activists who rejected the official Party-state system but avoided outright political opposition.

Similarly to the 19th century organic positivists, the 20th century neo-evolutionists stressed a strengthening of the "social organism"; involvement in autonomous communal affairs; conducting work "at the foundations"; stimulating links between intellectuals, workers, and peasants independent of the state; comprehensive educational and cultural work; and the recreation of an "integrated national community."[23] Much as "organic work" was intended to be a practical vehicle and constructive preparation for future national self-determination, neo-evolutionism has been visualized as a pragmatic and creative apprenticeship for participatory pluralistic democracy.

There is a certain degree of overlap between the positions of some of the new evolutionists and the neo-revisionist reformers discussed in the previous chapter. However, all forms of revisionism are intrinsically system-oriented and concentrate on internal Communist Party "renewal," whether such pressures for reform operate within or from outside the official political structures. Nevertheless, neo-evolutionism and reformism are not mutually exclusive strategies, and they may be pursued in tandem. By promoting social activism and enlarging the scope of "civil society," dissidents may seek to encourage some reformation within the Party itself or in the institutions it controls, even though this may not be the major aim of the exercise. In Pelikan's estimation, the essentially revisionist "socialist opposition" has "never ruled out the need and the possibility of acting within the Party and within legal institutions, in short whenever an opportunity should arise."[24] In fact, the revisionist theorists argue that "far-reaching political transformations are only possible when they are advocated by forces within the ruling Communist Party—even though the initiative may emanate from the population."[25] During the past decade, many former Marxist revisionists have opted to concentrate their efforts outside the official political system through a mixture of choice and necessity, even while retaining most of their socialist ideals and objectives.

Several attempts at "entryism" or "legalism" have been made by dissident activists during the past few years, particularly in Hungary and Poland. Some oppositionists have proposed a technically "legalistic" approach towards reform, by deliberately entering government controlled organizations and institutions in order to change them entirely from within, to alter some of their policies for the benefit of society, or simply to undermine the Communist monopoly over political and social life. In the wake of martial law, some Polish activists have supported Solidarity infiltration into the official labor unions, self-management bodies, and local administrative "peoples' councils." Similarly, a number of Hungarian dissidents have openly stood for elections in local government bodies to test the limits of democratization. The results so far have been disappointing, and have underscored that the infiltration, manipulation, and domination of democratic institutions by dictatorial Leninist group-ings has historically proved more effective than the penetration of Communist institutions by democratic forces. East European regimes maintain strict supervision over any subordinate bodies to preclude their takeover or exploitation by political opponents, and are prepared to undercut the position of any organization that may have been successfully infiltrated. Some dissident groups may nevertheless continue to propound entryism either as one element of a broader reformist or evolutionist strategy, or as an essentially opportunistic method for disrupting certain governmental operations.

Neo-evolutionist theories were developed in the late 1970s after successive waves of disenchantment with government policy. They were based on the premise that self-generating internal reforms of the Party-state offered only limited prospects for genuine democratization.[26] Evo-lutionists in the late 1970s and the 1980s have not specifically set out to forge links with groupings and individuals in the ruling Parties, even though they hoped to encourage independent thought and diversification within the political establishment, including its ruling echelons.[27] Whereas revisionist-reformers espoused changes implemented "from above," the new evolutionists clearly placed greater faith in effective action "from below," through the emergence of autonomous groups and programs that could energize the "internal evolution" of society toward democracy rather than the state.

During the past decade a number of proponents of neo-evolutionism have themselves evolved away from a traditional socialist political platform. Current evolutionism, particularly evident in Poland and Czechoslovakia, embraces more diverse political orientations than its revisionist-reformist antecedents. Indeed, part of its strength rests on its pluralistic tolerance in which ideological and political differences between activists concerning the eventual format of a "post-totalitarian" Eastern Europe do not preclude close cooperation on numerous more practical issues and concrete ventures.

New evolutionism can be usefully subdivided into two broad strands or tendencies: the "social evolutionist" and the "political evolutionist." Contemporary Poland offers the most pertinent case study of this distinction.[28] Among the "political evolutionists," the Confederation for an Independent Poland (KPN), Fighting Solidarity (SW), and other like-minded pro-independence groupings, have enunciated far-reaching but concrete programs for political transformation, entailing neither a violent revolution nor revisionist reformism.[29] Revolutionary activity in itself is not categorically discounted, but terrorism and other forms of violence are eschewed as being counter-productive. The stress here is on comprehensive independent political education; the gaining of mass support for the movement; the establishment of overt or clandestine political groups, parties, and alliances espousing diverse political programs; and the creation of an "alternative political system" operating initially in largely conspiratorial conditions but leading to an eventual, largely peaceful replacement of the Leninist system with a democratic multiparty structure. The specific political programs of Poland's independent political groupings, which seem to have mushroomed since the onset of martial law, will be discussed in the next chapter.

The second distinctive trend of "social evolutionism" was most clearly applied by the Committee for Social Self-Defense–Workers Defense Committee (KSS-KOR) during the late 1970s.[30] KSS-KOR founders propounded the creation of a multitude of self-directed social organizations that deliberately avoided political activism but captured ground from the state by leaving the Party with a constantly shrinking area over which it could exercise effective supervision. In order not to provoke comprehensive police persecution, both the Communist Party and the most essential elements of the monoparty system were to remain intact while society patiently carved out independent niches for itself. The "social evolutionists" in Poland proved to be more consequential than their "political" counterparts by the turn of the decade, and evidently developed a more rewarding policy for social change. However, some cross-fertilization of ideas and programs between the two strategies has occurred since their inception; for example, more overt political activity has been undertaken by former KSS-KOR theorists after the lifting of martial law. The regime has sensed the dangers inherent in both forms of "new evolutionism" and seeks to undermine their public influence and liquidate their most obvious manifestations.[31]

Though both forms of neo-evolutionism suffered a severe setback during Polish "normalization," there seemed to be precious little alternative under extremely oppressive conditions. The "state of war," with its attack on all autonomous social organizations and initiatives, appeared to disprove the supposition that genuine and lasting democratic changes were possible, whether emanating from the Polish United Workers Party or from peaceful and sustained public pressures on the regime. Though a substantial volume of debate and dispute over programs and tactics has already taken place in post-martial law Poland, no clearcut "post-evolutionist" position, or a singular dissident strategy that supersedes the premises of evolutionism, has emerged thus far. In addition, much of the oppositionist movement appears to be fragmented, frustrated, and indecisive about specifying any single long-term platform *vis-à-vis* the regime. In general, persistent calls for compromises with the government and the restoration of organizational pluralism, coexist with the concept of a "long march" in pursuit of the "alternative society" irrespective of the regime's stance. Much of the neo-evolutionist program and its gradualist tendencies continue to be visible among the Polish opposition, particularly in the espousal of restraint, compromise, and the avoidance of open confrontation after the failure of strikes and demonstrations in 1982 and 1983.

The "new evolutionist" strategy has also been pursued in Czechoslovakia, though at a generally slower and more hesitant pace than in Poland. The Charter 77 human rights campaign was established neither as a mass protest movement nor as an oppositionist political grouping to challenge the Prague regime's monopoly of power. Rather it is a "citizens' initiative" aiming to restore all fundamental civil, cultural, economic, and social rights to the populace.[32] Its "social evolutionist" tendency has been most evident in the shunning of outright political activity and in the absence of an organizational structure, formal statutes, a specified membership, or an all-encompassing program of political reform. Since its inception in January 1977 the Charter has encouraged independent initiatives by Czechoslovak citizens in a multitude of non-political spheres. For instance, it has sponsored the Committee in Defense of the Unjustly Prosecuted (VONS); a host of independent publishing, educational, and cultural activities; and the nascent state-free peace movement and ecological protection campaigns.[33]

The reformist bent in Charter 77 appears to be more pronounced than that in the statements and ventures of the Polish opposition, possibly because of the presence within the movement of "ex-communist" officials who continue to uphold the prospect of an inner-Party rejuvenation along the lines of the Prague Spring. One of the Chartists' main activities has been the drafting of substantive documents critical of particular aspects of government policy, evidently in the hope of stimulating debate with and within the power apparatus. Various pressing social, economic, and ecological problems are discussed in Charter 77 texts, and pertinent propositions for amelioration are put forward. Indeed, while the Chartists stress their significance as an "embryonic, independent, checking capacity from below," a principal objective is to influence and bolster reformist tendencies inside the ruling Party and among the half a million former Communists purged after 1968. Polish evolutionists, by contrast, seem to place less hope in reformist trends inside the Party-state, and attach greater value to creating and expanding independent social groups while narrowing the parameters of state control.

A markedly smaller degree of development toward any "new evolutionist" strategy has been evident in Hungary until recently and in the German Democratic Republic. This can be partly accounted for by the subdued nature of post-1956 political dissent in the former, and the pre-emptive governmental counter-measures in the latter, as well as by the unfavorable public climate discouraging the emergence of broad, autonomous social initiatives. Nevertheless, several single-issue campaigns have been undertaken by dissident activists and other disgruntled citizens in recent years, largely revolving around specific human rights grievances. A wider evolutionist approach embracing numerous areas of public concern may indeed blossom in the years ahead. Even more discouraging circumstances prevail in Romania and Bulgaria, where social and political dissent is kept tightly sealed and has displayed little sign of bursting on to the public arena, aside from occasional, short-lived workers protests over specific economic grievances. However, one should not discount any future growth of some aspect of neo-evolutionism as a viable method for countering state control and wresting various spheres of social activity from the Party's monopolistic control.

Unorganized Dissent and Non-Violence

The overall aim of independent criticism and public non-conformism in Eastern Europe is not to provoke rebellion or violent revolution to overthrow Communist regimes, but rather to indicate the deficiencies and failures of official policy, encourage programmatic reforms, and facilitate a consequential social momentum.[34] However, the atomized and often personalized nature of individual criticism tends to preclude sustained pressure on the government to alter its policies. On the other hand, its amorphous and often moderate character may help to protect individuals against repression.

The drawbacks of individual criticism and non-conformism are fairly obvious: they may involve prolonged social isolation, a lack of public coordination, and a limited resonance in either the population or the administration. Even where criticism may be prevalent within a certain profession or workplace, it may be quelled either by official concessions or reprisals following a realistic government assessment of the public mood. In fact, such low-key dissent and verbal criticism may persist for some time without seeking or finding any tangible outlets of expression or visible protest acts. Notwithstanding the obvious limitations of latent dissent, muted criticism, and fragmented non-conformism in the Soviet bloc, individual and even private discontent and deviance can acquire political connotations and thereby enter the public domain. In some instances, essentially laconic criticism, particularly when it purportedly influences neighbors, colleagues, and workmates, and encourages acts of civil disobedience, may be officially perceived as a display of political opposition and therefore resolutely combated. Some East European regimes have demonstrated a greater tolerance for individualistic criticism and non-conformism than others, although this is liable to alter depending on a number of factors explored in Chapter 2.

In Poland and Hungary in particular, it is possible to publicly berate specific economic and social policies and unsatisfactory government performance, and even to criticize lower ranking officials in the mass media. However, the inclusion of critical opinions in the official media should not be mistaken for an official acceptance of open political opposition. Nevertheless, on some occasions permitted criticism may be one manifestation of a conflict of interests within the ruling Parties over certain policies or methods of implementation. The tolerance and even instigation of internal criticism is often a sophisticated ingredient of the regime's propaganda package, whereby official mechanisms of communication encompass and thus help to neutralize potentially threatening condemnations of the political system. Sharlet, in his discussion of the tolerated varieties of dissent in Hungary, mentions the "circumscribed public agenda" for debate and criticism, and a "sanitized social space that fosters the illusion of critical involvement at little real cost to the regime."[35] Hence it is permissible to disapprove publicly and debate an "array of depoliticized economic issues." This "official embrace" of certain domestic critics may additionally help to confuse, divide, and defuse any potential for coordinated political opposition.

In the case of Poland, a prime government objective in allowing some expressions of criticism from unofficial sources is to discredit a number of moderate dissidents in the eyes of the public through their association with the state media, while enhancing the regime's externalized liberalizing image.[36] Nevertheless, certain central issues remain strictly off-limits to public criticism, most notably the country's political structure, the legitimacy of the Party and government leadership, and the regime's defense policies and foreign "alliances." Individuals may be allowed to disagree with various features of the system's operations, but the avowed aim must be to repair its malfeasance and improve its functions and not to postulate its replacement by a non-Communist alternative.

The domain of culture has traditionally constituted an important sphere for expressing critical, divergent, and non-conformist opinions in Eastern Europe, even if only in a roundabout and allusive manner.[37] Whether through literature, art, film, music, theater, or other means of communication, individual dissenters have tried to elude or bypass the censor's grip and develop autonomous pockets of free expression. Some dissidents have also exerted pressure through their particular cultural formats for a far-reaching relaxation and liberalization in official cultural policy and, by a process of osmosis, in other state-controlled spheres. Cultural activities, especially where they involve overt and concerted manifestations of popular aspirations and an independent national identity, form a valuable rallying point for broader political demands.

Cultural instruments can also serve to amplify critical and oppositionist viewpoints and platforms among the population. This vehicle has been widely and competently used in some states to ridicule, admonish, or explicitly challenge government policies. The official record in suppressing and controlling independent cultural activities or nullifying the political message generated through cultural channels has also varied with regard to method, intensity, and effectiveness. Conversely, non-conformist cultural expression may also benefit the political system, both as a window dressing for avowed cultural autonomy, and for diverting potentially damaging political dissent into spheres which are perceived to be safer for the regime.

The miscellany of non-conformism is not confined to the critical intelligentsia or to cultural life, but tends to be more widely dispersed. This is evident in numerous work enterprises and offices, even though it need not assume any organized form or result in work stoppages or other protests. In addition to fairly commonplace public cynicism and grumbling, workers have developed numerous ways of displaying their dissatisfaction over economic and non-material issues. Absenteeism from work is a popular method of indirect and spontaneous protest; it is also a form of informal bargaining with state employers for improved pay and working conditions in the absence of an effectual collective mechanism for defending workers' interests.

East European state-controlled industries are characterized by high rates of employee absenteeism, "sick leave," and an extensive job turnover, in addition to the all-pervasive apathy, low rates of effort and productivity, shoddy workmanship, the output of inferior quality goods and sloppy services, the careless handling of machinery, misuse and theft of plant property, a deliberate indifference to work discipline, the violation of factory regulations, and a host of other displays of "deviant" working class behavior. Much of this widespread non-conformism is not reported by management, and is generally ignored and tolerated by the authorities as an indispensable safety valve in an alienated populace. The acceptance of these passive forms of worker discontent undoubtedly contributes to releasing tensions and maintaining some level of stability within state enterprises, but they are obviously not conducive to economic efficiency. These individualized acts of dissent and non-conformism also divert disaffection away from concerted acts of protest and more menacing forms of popular pressure against the Communist authorities.

Individual acts of dissent do not preclude occasional or regular forms of collective action, whether this is organized or spontaneous. There are both advantages and disadvantages associated with unorganized protests by workers, students, farmers, or other aggrieved groups. Such demonstrations may take the authorities by surprise; they could quickly spread if disquiet is widespread and the regime is unable to undertake swift preventative measures, or has incorrectly assessed the public mood; and they could win some instant concessions from management or the central authorities intent on placating the protestors. However, government agencies are well aware of the damaging consequences of sudden protests escalating out of control, spilling over and affecting wider segments of the population; as a rule, they take careful precautionary measures against such an eventuality.[38] On the other hand, spontaneous protests may simply amount to self-defeating acts of despair, born of anger, and entailing poor preparation for any sustained struggle. Such manifestations are often readily exposed to police provocations and repressions, and lack a binding, self-sustaining program of action or a long-term set of achievable objectives.

The inefficacy of unorganized, spontaneous, collective protests in previous crises contributes to demoralizing workers, and may either result in a wholesale avoidance of future protests whatever the actual grievances, individualistic acts of despair or destruction, or more careful pre-planning for an organized protest given the right conditions. A sequence of lessons about the strategy of protest seems to have been learned by both Polish workers and the Warsaw government since the early 1970s. Walk-out strikes followed by street demonstrations were swiftly and violently crushed by the security forces on the Baltic Coast region in December 1970, and in Radom and Ursus in 1976. As a result, during the next round of confrontation in the summer of 1980 workers staged occupational strikes and avoided open street clashes with militia units. Once the regime had mustered its forces and decided to resume the offensive with the imposition of martial law in December 1981, occupational strikes were forcibly terminated by armed detachments of ZOMO riot police; strike organizers and participants, in addition to the free labor union leaders, were arrested and interned.

The element of surprise played an important role during General Jaruzelski's anti-worker operation, as the population had assumed on past experience that factory terrain was reasonably sacrosanct and the government would therefore refrain from violent attacks. The subsequent propositions by some oppositionists about "absentee strikes," rotational work stoppages, and other coordinated protests to circumvent police intervention bore little fruit during Polish "normalization." Where conditions become difficult for staging organized, pre-planned protests, and there is an absence of sufficient cohesion, as well as limited opportunities for free assembly and mass organization, workers may revert back to spontaneous, spasmodic stoppages and latent forms of non-conformism to display their displeasure.

When they do take place, unorganized and individualized forms of dissent among any number of social groups may be more characteristic of extremely repressive states, and occur where there is little post-war tradition of concerted collective action. The GDR is a case in point. Since 1953 dissent in East Germany has been commonly restricted and fragmented; there have been individual protests by intellectuals or occasional localized strikes of short duration. Such displays of protest have rarely coalesced into any durable opposition groupings, or evolved toward unified and systematic "class activism."[39] Political dissent has revolved around individual critics of the government; these are often political theorists, artists, and other intellectuals who may exert some influence over sections of the intelligentsia but whose public exposure is extremely restricted and whose political programs carry little popular weight.[40]

Small independent literary and artistic groups critical of the GDR regime "at weekends" also operate in the country, but are loose and flexible and do not appear to have sought any substantially wider audience. The East German regime deals firmly with political dissenters, either through imprisonment or severe harassment or by forcing them to emigrate and then revoking their citizenship.[41] Voluntary emigration may also be considered a form of dissent and a passive form of protest through an abandonment of the system, whether or not the individual concerned subsequently campaigns in the West on behalf of his or her countrymen.[42] Since 1963, the GDR regime has allowed selected political prisoners to leave the country upon payment of what is in effect a ransom submitted by the West German government or paid by private agencies.[43] In general, official disruption and intensive social controls serve to keep dissent in East Germany largely disorganized and politically ineffectual.

Romania provides another example where stringent government measures stifle the emergence of coherent dissident strategies. Aside from the occasional work stoppages, strikes, and demonstrations over falling living standards, as in the Jiu Valley in 1977 and in Brasov in November 1987, political opposition in Romania has been confined to a handful of creative intellectuals or disgruntled Party officials and army officers.[44] Overt and organized dissent has little popular appeal or opportunity to crystallize among the masses. The development of more substantive forms of opposition appears to be some way off, though one needs to be careful not to posit some inevitable evolutionary progression toward the varieties of dissent characteristic of Poland or Czechoslovakia. Nevertheless, some experts have put forward the thesis that Romanian dissent has had a late start compared to other East European states, largely because of the initial optimism surrounding the relative liberalism during the first few years of Ceausescu's reign in the early 1970s—this tended to discourage the emergence of any united oppositionist forces.[45] In the period since this "false liberalization," repression and atomization have increased, as has material hardship; political and social conditions have become increasingly unsuitable for mass dissident action.[46]

Unorganized forms of dissent may also be more likely in states where the uncodified "social compact" between government and citizens is fairly consistently upheld by both sides. In Hungary, for instance, the post-Revolutionary population relinquished any demands for political freedoms in exchange for certain economic guarantees—such as tolerable living standards, security of employment, and a level of material opportunity outside the state sector.[47] As a result, dissent was fairly narrow in scope, less organized and harmonized than in Poland, and displayed little evidence of propounding extensive programs for social or political transformation. Opposition tended to be confined to urban intellectuals who concentrated on creative work rather than organizing sizeable pressure groups and pursuing contacts with the working class.[48]

The political criticisms of Hungary's self-styled "semi-legal opposition" seem to be directed primarily at other intellectuals rather than toward the country's working class or peasantry, in order to stimulate thought and discussion on philosophical, ideological, political, and ethical issues. Magyar dissidents have never felt strong enough to challenge the regime in any concerted way, especially in the uncertain and complex political and economic climate fostered by Kádár since the late 1960s.[49] However, Liehm has postulated that increasing economic difficulties in states such as Hungary will make the "social contract" increasingly more difficult to uphold without sweeping socio-economic reforms.[50] The consequences of any breakdown of the compact for dissent, political opposition, public protest, and other forms of independent social activism could well prove substantial.

The basic rationale and purpose of non-violent collective protests is to apply pressure on the authorities and their agencies in a systematic and prolonged manner in order to alter government policies. People in Communist Party-states are likely to opt for non-violent forms of struggle because of a multitude of social, political, ideological, strategic, and tactical factors. It is widely assumed that given current geopolitical conditions a localized armed revolt will not dislodge Soviet interests and the national Leninist regimes. Society is literally and figuratively disarmed and has little prospect of arming itself in the face of greatly superior firepower. Moreover, violence as such is generally viewed as futile and counter-productive: armed resistance can be swiftly isolated and its practitioners eliminated without evincing any notable policy changes.

Zielonka points out that a complex relationship exists between the strategy and objectives of non-violent resistance.[51] Success in organizing a non-violent action does not necessarily signify the ability to achieve the desired goal; indeed, some protests may have an opposite effect on official policy to the one intended. The achievements of any non-violent strategy hinge on several related issues—the size of the movement, its cohesiveness, discipline, and morale; the attainability of immediate or more distant objectives; the program and ideological-political underpinnings of the campaign; as well as the strengths, weaknesses, and tactics of the government under pressure.

Official concessions are highly unlikely unless the regime in question is confronted with an active form of non-violence that threatens to disrupt vital civilian or military communications networks, production schedules, or similar critical state concerns. The resolve of the government needs careful scrutiny throughout any non-violent protest action. So does its willingness to resort either to coercive and disciplinary measures at any juncture, or to negotiate tactical compromises in order to terminate the protest before it spreads further afield. In Soviet bloc states, the Party's security apparatus has severe sanctions at its disposal to eradicate peaceful protests and punish the leaders, organizers, and participants. In such cases, non-violent demonstrations stand little chance of victory unless they are sufficiently large and resilient, and the regime is unwilling or unable immediately to resort to armed repression—either because of indecision, weakness, internal differences of opinion, logistical inferiority *vis-à-vis* the protestors, or fear of even more damaging consequences.

In Zielonka's opinion, "the Polish case represents the most effective application of nonviolent action in the history of communism."[52] Concerning the rise and rapid growth of the Solidarity movement during 1980–1981, this is undoubtedly correct, but one needs to examine the longer-term successes and failures of any non-violent campaign before making a final judgment. In stark martial law realities, despite its mass nature, its popular appeal, and its revocation of all violent means of protest or pressure on the regime, Solidarity was clearly unable to meet or maintain even its most limited initial objectives. These included legalized free labor unionism, organizational pluralism, an end to official media censorship, and the participation of freely elected workers' representatives in any formulations of economic reform. Despite its myriad early successes and the government's evident retreat on many minor and some major issues, Solidarity clearly miscalculated the regime's long-term objectives, its duplicity, mendacity, and eventual willingness to forcefully crush non-violent protests and restore its power monopoly.

Many dissidents in Poland and elsewhere have developed an ethical aversion to coercive methods in general, associating these closely with the Leninist method of rule. This aversion has become a linchpin of most oppositionist strategies; other ingredients have included public activism, long-term gradual social change, the protection of human and civil rights, and a stress on ethical means serving ethical ends such as human dignity and equal justice. In sum, non-violence has become part and parcel of a wider strategy of democratization intended to reduce the Party's "structural violence" in all aspects of public life. Nevertheless, Solidarity's continuing emphasis on non-violence should not be confused with pacifism. Many pacifists contend that no cause is worth fighting or dying for, whereas Polish oppositionists admit the possibility of armed defense against unbearable despotism if all other methods fail and sheer physical survival is clearly endangered. In a similar vein, Hungarian dissident Konrad, who espouses only peaceful change in Communist systems, also affirms the right of every community to actively defend itself against its "occupiers."[53] The eminent Czech dissident Vaclav Václav believes that the opposition can only accept violence as a "necessary evil" in extreme situations when "direct violence can only be met by violence" and where "remaining passive would in effect mean supporting violence."[54]

An additional factor of some relevance in this assessment is the question of the "self-limiting" aspects of non-violent dissident activism in Eastern Europe. Unfortunately, the concept has given rise to some misunderstanding over the aims of the varied oppositionist movements and the contexts in which they operate. The term "self-limiting revolution" has been applied most frequently to Solidarity's Poland, to signify the purportedly self-imposed restrictions on public demands and likely government concessions, and an apparent cut-off point beyond which no sane activist would willingly venture. Granted that Solidarity, even in its heyday, eschewed violence and tended to avoid provoking a coercive state reaction, it must be remembered that the strategy of government-union negotiations contained an inbuilt dynamic.

Self-limitation was not an end in itself, but before martial law it proved to be a viable method for drawing concessions and winning "social space" from the government. For many independent union leaders and advisers, not to mention the more militant rank-and-file, self-limitation was not a conscious ploy but an essential means of approach involving trial and error, and trial and success. The strategy employed placed no finite limits on political goals and achievements, though logically and practically the most far-reaching demands were postponed until some future date. The scope, development, and utility of "self-limitation" were largely dependent on government reactions, where the central, regional, and local authorities were consistently pressed to cede territory to independent social control. Indeed, even the vocal proponents of "self-limitation" and gradualism expanded their political horizons and assented to increasing grass roots pressures. During the latter part of 1981, before Jaruzelski's crackdown, the spectrum of social, economic, and political demands was consistently enlarged.

"Non-violence" in Eastern Europe may cover an expansive range of individual and collective protests, methods of non-cooperation with the authorities, and acts of civil disobedience. Strikes and work brakes of various kinds are probably the most common form of collective protest by blue collar workers. They are generally easier to arrange in large plants where rapid communication within a sizeable workforce is fairly straightforward, and a collective withdrawal of labor can be quickly organized. Though comprehensive political demands are uncommon during strikes, these may develop during the course of a protest against essentially "economistic" issues that stimulate proposals for greater worker participation in decision-making.[55]

Strikes may be threatened or actual, spontaneous or planned, partial slow-downs or complete stoppages, "work-to-rules," or "no-work-to-any-rules," absentee strikes or occupational strikes. "Sit-in" strikes help to hold participants together, provide an opportunity for discussion and planning, selecting leaders, formulating demands, maintaining morale and discipline, and avoiding direct confrontation with the police. Short strikes may be a symbolic token act of protest rather than a means for slowing down or stopping production.[56] In the absence of genuine collective bargaining arrangements or free labor unions to protect workers' interests, employees may pressurize management to grant specific demands by threatening stoppages or directly petitioning employers. This has been the case in numerous large Polish factories since 1982, where pay demands to compensate for almost annual price hikes have been granted by the authorities to prevent any major strike or outburst of protest.

"Solidarity strikes," widespread in Poland during the summer of 1980, proved to be a powerful weapon against an unprepared regime. They involved numerous large factories and smaller workplaces in practically all industrial branches, towns, and regions. In some instances, solidarity strikes can theoretically escalate into a "general strike," whether local or nationwide, intended to disrupt economic life and bring the country to a standstill while evincing concessions from the authorities. Such far-ranging paralyzing actions have been extremely rare; even during the short national Solidarity stoppages in 1981, essential production and services were purposively maintained to avoid unnecessary material losses and to minimize public inconvenience.

Peaceful street marches and public demonstrations may also be staged to express discontent and influence the authorities. These may traverse specific routes before dispersal, or lead to assemblies at particular destinations for variable periods of time in order to garner public support and gain publicity.[57] "Hunger strikes" may be conducted by political prisoners or dissidents and sympathizers at liberty; these can be individual or collective, partial or complete, rotational or continuous, short-lived or prolonged.[58] This form of protest has usually been employed to help inform the public about some government abuse of human rights, to campaign for the release of political detainees, or to put pressure on the regime to alter some unpopular policy.

Boycotts of official organizations and unofficial embargoes on certain goods and services may also be attempted. Two pertinent examples here are the mass boycott of government sponsored labor unions in Poland following the outlawing of Solidarity, and the widespread boycott of official elections to local Peoples' Councils and the national parliament (*Sejm*) in 1984 and 1985 respectively.[59] These were forms of collective protest designed as a public act of defiance against government "illegality," its ban on authentic free trade unions, and the facade of democracy the regime was constructing in the wake of martial law. Boycotts indicate an overt refusal to recognize the legitimacy of the regime and its various subordinate institutions and associations.

Milder forms of boycott have included a slow compliance with government directives; avoidance or only token participation in numerous social, political, cultural, and occupational associations and official events; and refusals to perform certain unpopular acts, such as close collaboration with the authorities. An alternative form of civil disobedience either disguises actual non-compliance by apparent obedience to official laws and regulations, or more overtly disregards some formal directives. Officials and participants in government-supervised activities may be blacklisted as "collaborators" with the regime, and various non-violent sanctions applied against them—such as ostracism, taunting, the public exposure of misdeeds, humorous pranks, and comprehensive public shaming. Pressures may be equally exerted on the uncommitted to participate more energetically in the anti-regime struggle.[60]

In a veritable encyclopedia of non-violent action, Sharp enumerates the myriad additional forms of possible anti-government protest which preclude any deliberate acts of violence.[61] Though many of these methods should not be naively transposed from conditions prevailing in open Western societies to closed, strictly controlled Communist states, some of the procedures listed have been attempted by East Europeans at different junctures. They include: public meetings and rallies; public speeches and deputations; letters of protest, declarations and petitions; the painting, printing, or verbal expression of slogans; the display of banners and posters; leafleting and the showing of flags and other symbolic paraphernalia; prayer, public worship, and pilgrimages; delivering symbolic objects to officials; displays of portraits and other visual images; oral or mechanical sounds, and public gestures of disrespect or resistance; public singing of national, religious, or political protest songs; non-official or private radio and television broadcasts; the production and distribution of illicit texts, videotapes, and audio cassettes; political jokes and public rumor; honoring the dead at significant spots, particularly symbolically important political figures, or paying homage at burial places and demonstrative funerals; and public silence and walk-outs from official state functions.

Though the effects of such miscellaneous public protests in positively influencing government actions may be slight, and indeed the more overt demonstrations may provoke police repression, in the long term they could help preserve and reinforce public morale and sustain social resistance. Small acts of peaceful protest may be a prelude to other forms of collective opposition, and could be part of a wider strategy to secure specific objectives. In East Europe's Communist states, it seems that only a concerted campaign of mass non-violence can bring some positive results, particularly if it is focused at opportune moments, such as during periods of intense internal crisis or pronounced weakness within the ruling Party. On the other hand, experience has indicated that even changes wrought by oppositionist forces on such occasions may be of short duration once the authorities regain the initiative and launch an anti-dissident offensive with the full force of their political armory.

Social Movements

The premises of social resistance and "social self-defense" are in many respects encapsulated in Konrad's description of the "antipolitician":

> The apolitical person is only the dupe of the professional politician, whose real adversary is the antipolitician. The antipolitician wants to keep the scope of government policy . . . under the control of civil society.[62]

The strategy of social self-defense has become an essential element of the gradualist "neo-evolutionist" program developed by dissidents in Poland and Czechoslovakia since the mid-1970s. The defense of specific persecuted individuals in Poland by groups of intellectual dissenters evolved into a method for defending certain key values, goals, and autonomously arising groupings, while resisting the Party's monopolistic tendencies. The Workers' Defense Committee (KOR) was organized by disaffected intellectuals to provide moral, financial, and legal assistance to workers victimized for their anti-government protests in June 1976, and to protect them from official repression. After 1977, KOR evolved into the Social Self-Defense Committee (KSS-KOR) to encompass a broader range of social and economic issues and grass roots public activism. These local initiatives were intended to stimulate informal self-help associations, aiding the emergence of independent spheres of public life.[63]

Practical considerations played an important role in Poland, as both revolution and reformism were effectively blocked and direct forms of political opposition seemed impractical. Violence and clandestine conspiracy were rejected in preference for establishing "new patterns of social behavior" modeled on national, social, and cultural preservation in the face of totalitarian compulsion. Student, worker, peasant, and intellectual self-defense committees were intended to "defend all social initiatives aimed at implementing human and civil rights."[64] The creation of independent publications, such as KOR's *Robotnik*, served to publicize popular grievances and aided the formation of elementary links between the working class and dissident intellectuals (as well as forging informal ties within these social categories) through the gathering and dissemination of unofficial information. A similar process has been discernible in Czechoslovakia since the rise of Charter 77.

One important aim of the self-defense program is to stir the "silent majority" out of "inactive passivity," and guide it through "active passivity" toward "social activism." Bypassing the Party and other state-supervised organs, dissidents attempt to counter and redirect commonplace public apathy, and involve citizens in constructive independent pursuits. Even direct confrontation with the regime, it is argued, could help to educate, politicize, and mobilize the workforce; while the cumulative effect of resistance and self-defense would contribute toward reinforcing public confidence in pressing for further demands.[65]

Evolutionist dissidents have contended that informal networks of mutual support, multilateral assistance, and the exchange of independent ideas, would prove difficult for the government to suppress, especially in the absence of large structured organizations. Such a process could vigorously counter the Communist process of social atomization and manipulation.[66] A spirit of "solidarism" or "social solidarity" has been evoked to pierce the barrier of widespread popular fear. The notion of flexible, fluid, non-structured, informal groupings was intended to promote varying degrees of coordination and protection within and between public groups. Such affiliations would evidently be less susceptible to repression while covering numerous initiatives in which citizens could voluntarily participate, depending on their individual inclinations and social circumstances.

Activists maintain that social self-defense can set limits to state control and help initiate a process of gradual destatization and more active "social offense." Another objective was to expose the shortcomings of the Communist system, and the incompetence, corruption, and inefficiency of Party and government officials, while proposing alternative policies and kindling popular pressures for improvement. An essential element of self-defense has been the issue of human and civil rights. This entails a largely "legalistic" approach to relations between state and society, whereby the authorities are pressed to abide by their own laws and the numerous international agreements they have signed. The systematic monitoring of official human rights abuses developed after the signing of the 1975 Helsinki Final Act agreements, which contained specific humanitarian provisions in "Basket Three." The accords established an international obligation for the signatory states, including each Soviet bloc government, to abide by the updated human rights charter.[67] Among the numerous issues falling under the rubric of "human rights," Tokes mentions: "adequate political representation, meaningful participation in public affairs, equal protection under the law, equal access to education, welfare, and cultural benefits, and fair sharing of the material comforts and psychic benefits of rapidly developing or already highly developed economies . . . "[68]

Czechoslovakia's Charter 77 has placed the most pronounced emphasis on the Helsinki process as a major rationale for its existence and campaigns. The movement has concentrated on the whole gamut of human rights and civil liberties:

> By drawing attention to various individual cases where human and civil rights are violated, by preparing documents and suggesting solutions, by submitting other proposals of a more general character aimed at reinforcing such rights and their guarantees, and by acting as a mediator in various conflict situations which may lead to injustice . . . [69]

This pattern has been partially replicated in other Soviet bloc states. The Movement for Defense of Human and Civil Rights (ROPCiO) was established in Poland in March 1977 to monitor, report, and lodge protests against official violations. Many of its functions were subsequently performed by committees established under Solidarity's auspices following the legalization of the free labor union. After Solidarity was outlawed, dissidents in several towns created a number of informal committees to examine and publicize police abuses, while the clandestine Polish Helsinki Commission compiled, recorded, and published information on government human and civil rights violations.[70] Romanian dissidents have tended to focus on more specific human rights provisions contained in international covenants, particularly on the right to travel and all its concomitants—to establish interpersonal contacts, to communicate and otherwise exchange ideas—which have been severely restricted by the Ceausescu regime.

Through the creation of "social self-defense mechanisms," East Europe's political dissidents have attempted to construct a "new model" of society in which respect for individual liberties is deemed to be paramount.[71] The flexible new evolutionist strategy for social change has thereby sought to channel practically any grassroots demands which are often stimulated by numerous individual grievances against the regime. The defense of particular persons, groups, rights, and values has become a rallying point in several states for sustained forms of social resistance. Strategists calculated that such initiatives could provide momentum for the dissident movement by arousing mass support and applying constant pressure on the authorities. Whether consciously or unconsciously, political oppositionists thereby sought finally to break out of the post war pattern of "outburst—repression—concession—and stabilization."[72]

Through an increasing involvement of citizens within groups independent of Party-state control, political dissidents have attempted to shift "the focus of social activity away from the institutions of the communist system and towards more open public domain."[73] The emphasis on self-organization was designed to remove from official jurisdiction entire areas of public life which in ideal democratic conditions do not belong under state tutelage. A gradual "detotalitarianization" of society was propounded as a successive "step" in solidifying and extending the parameters of social self-defense. In the words of Hungarian dissidents Bence and Kis:

> The evolution of independent social movements is not merely a tactical means for radical reformism. Organizational autonomy of society is a goal in itself. The better organized a society, the smaller the overweening power of the political leadership, the nearer the point in time when a transformation of the power system may be attempted.[74]

The search for "pluralism" in its widest meaning was to entail a broadening of public participation in social, cultural, economic, political, and national affairs. The objective was to initiate and extend a process which Ionescu and Madariaga call "institutionalization"—the expansion of a number of independent bodies and institutions, accepted by law and forming "a system of order based on legality."[75] In the East European context, it was a question of gaining the passive tolerance of the regime and not necessarily its active approval or the legal enshrinement of each autonomous public body. An additional goal was to encourage the regime to extend the public's input into the formulation of socio-economic policies and a range of other issues, or at least allow divergent voices to stimulate a broader debate within and outside government circles.

The latter strategy has clearly been applied by Czechoslovakia's Charter 77. Several Charter activists claim that their overall effect on the Prague authorities has been positive. Whether the regime overtly attacks the human rights movement or ostensibly ignores its existence, Charter 77 documents are apparently carefully scrutinized by officials who, in some instances, evidently take some account of the problems analyzed therein. Several topics highlighted in a Charter text have been subsequently discussed by officials and either the dissident thesis is countered or partial solutions to the problems raised are advanced. Prague evidently considers it is occasionally important or expedient to address certain complaints and criticisms, even if only in a roundabout way without naming the original source of criticism. Charter spokesmen maintain that some sections of the administration are fully cognizant of this "embryonic, independent, checking capacity from below," whose influence could purportedly expand in the future.

Demands for organizational pluralism in Poland since the early 1980s have principally focused on trade unionism, especially after the initial successes of Solidarity. These calls have had a visible resonance among workers seeking organizations to protect more effectively their economic and social rights. Since the imposition of martial law "trade union pluralism" has provided a rallying cry for the opposition, which has been pressing for the restoration of some semblance of independent activity. Even though dissidents have avoided directly challenging the "leading role" of the Communist Party through demands for "political pluralism," any appeals for organizational plurality tend to be interpreted by officials as an implicitly political claim which could open the floodgates to more wide-ranging pressures and concessions. Against such an un-promising background, opposition activists have sought to devise policies best suited to local conditions for creating informal autonomous groups, often as a *fait accompli* in the struggle for "social space."

Independent movements in Eastern Europe often arise either as a result of specific public grievances, or as a consequence of protest actions that may be initially individualistic or uncoordinated. In many respects, these are roundabout or indirect methods of political opposition, whereas direct political dissent through the creation of politically oriented groups could more easily incite outright repression and supply the regime with credible pretexts for intervention. Numerous single-issue groups have been created at various junctures, and either persisted or were quickly suppressed and dissolved.[76] In addition to the organizations and groupings already mentioned, each state has witnessed the emergence of several other autonomous initiatives of variable size, duration, program, and objective. For instance, in 1979 Hungarian dissidents established the Foundation for the Assistance to the Poor (SZETA) to provide material help for the impoverished sectors of society outside any official channels.[77] SZETA also proved to be a valuable propaganda device against the self-proclaimed reformist government, by exposing the growing material inequalities and persistent injustices within Magyar society.

In pre-Solidarity Poland, among the numerous independent occupational, self-defense, or single-issue groups one can mention the Students Solidarity Committees (SKS), the Believers Self-Defense Committee (KSLW), and the Flying University (LU). Similarly, in post-martial law Poland, the Freedom and Peace (WiP) group was founded by military oath protestors, and Clandestine Factory Committees (TKZ) were created by Solidarity activists in a host of work enterprises. East Germany and Czechoslovakia can claim small and informal autonomous peace groups, and ecological protection campaigns spurred by severe environmental deterioration. Social movements of all descriptions have been much more restricted in Romania and Bulgaria for the reasons we have discussed previously.

Propositions for the establishment of independent labor unions have been raised in several countries, even before the idea came to fruition in Poland during the summer of 1980. The campaign for workers' organizations free of state control struck at the heart of the ruling ideology, and undermined the legitimacy of the governing Parties which claim to fully represent proletarian interests. Even before the birth of Solidarity, several small free trade union committees were founded in Katowice (February 1978), Gdańsk (April 1978), and Szczecin (October 1979), but proved not to be very influential among workers or consequential *vis-à-vis* management.

Attempts to create autonomous workers' associations were also made in Romania, though with little lasting success. The clandestine Free Labor Union of Working People in Romania (SLOMR) was formed in February 1979, initially by twenty individuals; during the following month it was joined by 1,487 members of another independent, secret labor body.[78] By April 1979, before it was disbanded by the authorities, SLOMR claimed approximately 1,600 members. In addition to protesting over economic issues such as low wages, excessive work norms, low living standards, and forced retirements, SLOMR demanded the abolition of special material privileges for the ruling elite, an end to official censorship, and the right to freedom of travel. It spoke up for the social and economic rights of workers, peasants, and soldiers, and embraced other issues germane to wide sectors of the population. In this way it ventured beyond the more immediate "economistic" demands lodged by the Jiu Valley miners in 1977.

Poland's Solidarity was a pertinent experiment in applying the program of an expanding "civil society," beginning with free trade unionism and later extending into other areas. In many respects, the rapid growth of Solidarity and its multi-faceted challenge to totalitarian rule proved to be a somewhat premature attempt to realize the "civil society" envisioned by dissidents. Though the union increasingly sought to develop a political system based on authentic public participation, and it provided an umbrella for numerous autonomous civic initiatives, it did not possess a clearcut vision of ultimate goals or a well defined concept of co-existence with the government. It seems that the larger the social movement, the bigger the dilemma it faces—whether to become an alternative to the regime, or to renounce such aims and simply concentrate on limiting the scope and substance of Communist control.[79] The problem was never actually resolved, while martial law decapitated all independent organizations and refocused their attention on sheer survival. Much of

Solidarity's problem centered on the lack of precedents or models for such an enormous and cumbersome democratic movement in a Communist state. Moreover, the government exploited Solidarity's inexperience, openness, and internal wrangles to wear down and ultimately liquidate the movement.

Centrifugal and centripetal forces were constantly present within Solidarity, pulling and pushing the movement simultaneously toward centralization and decentralization. In addition, the union contained numerous divergent occupational groups and social strata, each with specific complaints against the government and campaigning primarily for their own particular interests. Moreover, splits emerged between "gradualists" and "fundamentalists"—the latter wanted the movement to push much further in its confrontation with the regime and adopt more explicitly political demands.[80] Given these internal antagonisms, plus the lack of an established medium for conducting negotiations and reaching binding agreements with the government, as well as the regime's deliberate provocations and manipulations, a united, consistent strategy proved difficult to sustain by the union's leadership. The rise and rapid growth of Solidarity took much of the political opposition by surprise, though some intellectual dissenters later made claims to the contrary. Curry correctly notes that intellectuals, whatever their strategies, were largely reacting to events rather than leading or directing them in the wake of the 1980 strikes. They were co-opted as advisers by workers' leaders and were unable to impose themselves on what remained an essentially dispersed mass working class movement.[81]

At least two important lessons may be gleaned from the Solidarity experience for the movement for "social independence." First, in a favorable setting, large public campaigns can assume a life of their own, as they are fuelled by enormous latent public discontent with the Communist system. Second, a rapidly expanding social movement may need to restrict its immediate objectives while guardedly constructing a viable program of "peaceful coexistence" with the authorities. Dissidents have to contend with Eastern Europe's inferior geostrategic placement in which current domestic conditions are inauspicious for wholesale democratization and the rapid termination of single-party rule.

The long-term program of a number of Soviet bloc oppositionists envisages the creation of an independent social structure once public resistance to the regime becomes sufficiently widespread. By broadening the scope of self-determination in various spheres of public life, "parallel structures" could theoretically emerge alongside official institutions and organizations. These would eventually share in decision-making by negotiating with the government on issues of crucial concern, and ultimately limit the Party and state to executive or administrative functions implementing the decisions of a "self-governing society."[82] In effect, this would involve an intensification of the new evolutionist strategy, particularly its "social evolutionist" components, whereby a strictly non-violent mass movement would establish an "alternative" or "second society" through mass participation in autonomous groups and the avoidance of official bodies. In this scenario, political activism would be avoided, and instead of overthrowing, reforming, or democratizing the Leninist government, society would steadily extricate itself from state tutelage, determine its own interests, and govern its own affairs—thereby molding a virtual "state within a state."[83] Fundamental social transformations would thereby precede and motivate any substantive political changes in each country. Oppositionist forces and dissenting social groups would not therefore have to wait patiently for the Party to initiate reform, or for circumstances to become more conducive for mass action, but could themselves generate more favorable conditions.

The idea of "parallel structures" within an increasingly assertive "alternative society" free of Party supervision has been proposed and elaborated by several authors. Notable among them has been the Warsaw Solidarity activist Wiktor Kulerski who, soon after the declaration of martial law called for the creation of an "underground society"—"a loosely structured, decentralized movement composed of independent groups and committees."[84] Though Kulerski's propositions were considered to be especially worth exploring under "state of war" conditions, his program for the "alternative society" seemed to embrace many of the distant objectives of various evolutionist thinkers throughout the bloc. According to Kulerski, this independent movement:

> Should strive for a situation in which the government controls empty shops but not the market, employment but not the means of livelihood, the state press but not the flow of information, printing houses but not the publishing movement, telephones and postal services but not communications, schools but not education.[85]

Independent activities, groups, and networks were to be established in all possible arenas, where many of the Polish seeds had already been sown in the late 1970s and during the legal Solidarity period. An important element of this process would be to stimulate shop floor activism among blue and white collar employees, including demands for greater factory and office self-management, and local self-government in city districts and rural areas. Dissidents maintain that practical experience in genuine democratic participation and decision-making at the grass roots would lay the foundations for more comprehensive "destatization" and help educate the masses in participatory and representative democracy. The free labor union campaign could continue to be a pertinent method for stirring workers out of sullen passivity and involve them in concrete endeavors with visible results, rather than in ephemeral and distant causes. Associations such as free trade unions could evidently strengthen non-Party links between enterprises, occupations, branches, and regions, and provide an indispensable supplement to any democratized self-management organs.

Intellectuals are also encouraged by advocates of the "alternative society" to push for their own autonomy and engender the growth of independent social, cultural, and educational institutions. Konrad postulates the idea of eventual "economic autonomy" for the East European intelligentsia.[86] Instead of being dependent on the state for all essential goods and services, free-thinking intellectuals in all professions should supposedly attempt to set up "alternative enterprises" through which to sell and distribute their products to the population. Simultaneously, this pursuit of "ideological pluralism" would encourage the emergence of "political pluralism" among various social classes.

The "alternative society" platform envisages a network of autonomous activities gradually enveloping all spheres of life formerly under state supervision. Some of these proposals have been put into practice on a greater or lesser scale in several countries. Independent publishing of various dimensions is a case in point—whether home produced and individually typed *samizdat*, or the more extensive "illegal publishing houses" printing several thousand copies of unofficial documents, newspapers, journals, and even full-length books. *Samizdat* production is vast in Poland and Czechoslovakia, somewhat smaller-scale in Hungary and the GDR[87], and extremely embryonic in Romania and Bulgaria. The primary goal here is to break or bypass the official monopoly over information and to establish workable distribution networks to avoid police interception.[88]

Independent education, research, and study encompass another potentially fertile area in which social initiatives could bloom. Among the numerous attempts to initiate such movements, it is worth mentioning the Polish Society for Academic Courses in the late 1970s and its later underground offsprings, and the Hungarian "flying kindergartens" and "flying libraries." The programs offered have included study seminars for students and workers covering subjects deemed too sensitive or "ideologically suspect" by the authorities, as well as the distribution of books banned by the education ministries dealing with historical, religious, philosophical, and political themes.

A host of discussion clubs have also surfaced in Poland and Czechoslovakia. Even during martial law and after it was formally rescinded, the Polish "alternative society" claimed numerous clandestine, semi-secretive, semi-legal, unofficial, loosely structured educational and cultural associations, many of which have been sheltered by the Catholic Church. Similarly, Charter 77 has promoted literature and scholarship with a view to developing autonomous educational programs. It includes a curriculum of learning for young people excluded from higher education because of official political discrimination against their parents. The independent "Patočka University" consisted of lectures presented in private apartments by academics who were barred from teaching in the state system.

Culture and the arts provide another rich field of unofficial endeavor. Polish, Hungarian, and Czechoslovak dissidents have been avidly encouraging the extension of a "second culture" during the past decade. Among the many initiatives one need mention private musical concerts, theatrical performances, poetry readings, and art exhibitions. In postmartial law Poland, funding and coordinating bodies have been established to promote independent culture, education, and the arts by raising and dispensing money to artists and works outlawed or neglected by the regime.

An assortment of other spheres have been explored for a possible evolution toward public autonomy. Economic self-help initiatives, mutual assistance networks, private crafts and services, and unofficial trading arrangements beyond government reach have all been attempted with mixed results. They are either effectively combatted by the police or partially tolerated to minimize the failures of the official economy without greatly challenging overall state control over the economy. Furthermore, as Matejko indicates, not all informal social bonds and networks, or the transactions concluded in this "second economy" should be considered "positive" from the dissident point of view.[89]

Throughout Eastern Europe there exist workplace, neighborhood, and friendship linkages geared less toward "social activism" in the sense normally understood by the political opposition, but more toward venality, careerism, and outright theft. In many respects, this systematic corruption and pervasive self-interest serve the government by breeding cynicism, selfishness, and apoliticization while hastening the process of social atomization. Such conditions conflict with the "solidarism" so often proclaimed by dissident theorists as an essential instrument for creating the "alternative civil society" under Communist rule. Despite their obvious shortcomings, informal self-help networks with less "negative" traits also function under state socialism. Conversely, not all aspects of the "second economy," including its "black" and "grey" markets necessarily preclude "social activism" and the forging of Party-free social bonds. Indeed, the "second economy" may foster both individual entrepreneurship and public cooperation while extending the frontiers of public independence.[90]

The evolutionist strategy of the "alternative society" has been likened to a "long march" undertaken outside any governmental institutions instead of "through them," as was proposed by reformists in the 1950s and 1960s.[91] Dissident strategists thereby attempt to stimulate and constructively guide the potentially powerful social forces suppressed but never fully eradicated in totalitarian states. The wholesale recreation of civil society is to be based on the rights of individuals and groups, protected by the "rule of law" against Party privilege and government repression, and moving in the direction of full "social independence." This "long march" or gradualist program was most vividly articulated in Poland by Solidarity's underground leaders during the "state of war." It is not necessarily inapplicable to other countries, given a favorable admixture of public frustration, mounting social protest, and government retreat. However, just as reformists have been charged with displaying a naive attitude to the possibility of reforming Communist Parties from within, the evolutionist proponents of the "alternative society" may be accused of propounding somewhat optimistic social objectives. One should neither overestimate the extent of public stamina nor underestimate the multi-faceted Party-state offensive against autonomous public life.

Dissident Foreign Policy

Similarities and differences between East European dissidents over domestic political strategies are also reflected in their international priorities and programs. The overwhelming majority of oppositionist writers reject the consequences of the Yalta-Potsdam postwar division of Europe into two externally dominated "spheres of interest." They also appear to favor the "Europeanization" of Central-East Europe, and a drawing together of the "two halves" of the continent—culturally, socially, economically, politically, and eventually militarily—to counter "superpower interests" and establish a "fully independent Europe." However, divergences arise between dissidents on questions such as how far and how fast East European independence can proceed, what concessions are to be made to Soviet interests, how East Europe figures in the Soviet-American conflict, and the timescale and exact calendar for implementing "Europeanization."

An overall division is discernible among dissidents on international questions. On the one hand, we find the revisionist-reformers and social "neo-evolutionists" with socialist, social democratic, or liberal political persuasions. On the other hand are the political "neo-evolutionists" with populist, Christian Democratic, or avowedly nationalist orientations.

These two categories exclude the more radical but less significant revolutionist positions of both left and right extremes.

The gradualist social evolutionists espouse a slower and more "realistic" process of regaining national autonomy and sovereignty. They underscore that self-determination for the countries of the Soviet bloc will need to be "self-limiting," by exploring the bounds of the possible and settling for less than full independence given the remoteness of a complete Soviet imperial collapse. Instead, they visualize a prolonged period of semi-autonomy revolving around national divergences on domestic economic, cultural, and social policies; but they also define clearcut parameters as to foreign and defense programs as well as continuing Warsaw Pact membership. The limits of autonomy would need to be extended circumspectly and with a careful eye on Moscow, but they should apparently aim toward the "Finlandization" of Eastern Europe and strict national neutrality in line with "geopolitical realities."[92]

By contrast, the nationalist and populist-oriented political evolutionists voice a more forthright and wholesale repudiation of any remaining Soviet "sphere of influence" in East-Central Europe. They oppose any interference by Moscow in the internal affairs and external relations of these states, and propound more strident progress towards full national independence in the shortest possible time. Their mid- to long-term objective is a mutually arranged "free confederation" of East European states between the Baltic, Adriatic, and Black Seas, and equal treaties of non-interference and non-aggression with Moscow. In addition, several dissidents point out that treaties would need to be signed with a genuinely independent Ukraine, Belorussia, and the three Baltic States once the Soviet empire has been dismantled. The content of such international agreements has also been a source of some dispute among the opposition, particularly in Poland. These discussions revolve around the issue of territorial boundaries, the nature of German reunification, the status of national minorities in each country, and the actual process of de-Sovietization throughout the Communist world.

A more immediate issue which has increasingly preoccupied Soviet bloc dissidents concerns the "national" versus "bloc-wide" road to liberation and the significance of "Europeanization." The "national road" has clearly shown its limitations during various local outbursts against Communist rule which were successfully contained, isolated, and extinguished. As a consequence, numerous theorists have argued that a more consistent, "internationalist" movement is essential to initiate changes in each state and to present a "united front" of dissent *vis-à-vis* the local rulers and the Kremlin. In practice thus far, this has amounted to little more than sporadic exchanges of documents, joint letters of protest, statements of intent, a degree of mutual support between certain oppositionists, and occasional clandestine meetings. Consistent contacts between dissidents in different states have proved difficult to maintain, even between individuals in neighboring countries. Each regime has made strenuous efforts to seal off its dissident movements from the outside world and avoid exposing its populations to politically dangerous ideas. The hermetic isolation of Poland during the legal Solidarity period by the GDR, Czechoslovak, and Soviet authorities proved to be merely an extreme example of this process.

Nevertheless, despite severe official harassment, symbolic meetings between Czechoslovak and Polish dissidents, first staged in the summer of 1978, were resumed in August 1987.[93] During the intervening years a "Polish-Czechoslovak Solidarity" working group has maintained some contact between Charter 77 signatories and the Polish opposition. Various illicit texts have also been smuggled across the Polish-Soviet border to "Solidarity sympathizers" in Russia, Bielorussia, and the Ukraine.[94] In an unprecedented display of inter-dissident solidarity on 1 February 1988, simultaneous demonstrations against severe repression in Romania were held in Prague, Budapest, Warsaw, and Moscow at the request of Charter 77. They included hunger strikes, vigils outside Romanian embassies which were quickly dispersed by the police, and other symbolic protests, in addition to messages of support for "social resistance" in Romania.[95]

Such displays of support are likely to be repeated if a sufficient degree of international planning, coordination, publicity, and participation can be arranged despite government dissuasion. A joint communique, which was something of a landmark in East European dissident solidarity, was issued on the 30th anniversary of the Hungarian Revolution. It was dated 23 October 1986, released simultaneously in Budapest, East Berlin, Prague, and Warsaw, and contained the signatures of 120 prominent opposition activists from Hungary, the GDR, Czechoslovakia, and Poland. Several Romanian dissidents later appended their names to the document.[96] Subsequent joint statements have also been issued in support of East German dissidents jailed or expelled to the West in January and February 1988, and in recognition of the right of conscientious objection to military service, in March 1988.

Although attempts to promulgate bloc-wide exchanges of ideas, joint policies, and common activities have thus far registered only limited success, their longer term impact should not be dismissed. The experiences of the Prague Spring, Poland's Solidarity, and other national endeavors to initiate change, have undoubtedly influenced the programs, strategies, and tactics of opposition movements elsewhere in the bloc. In some cases they have provided a stimulus to local opposition. For instance, the operations of Czechoslovak and Polish activists have provided a frame of reference for less sizeable or effective groups in other states. Schopflin points out that the Hungarian opposition "emerged into the open" in January 1977 with the publication of a letter in support of Charter 77.[97] By focusing on basic human and civil rights, activists across the bloc hope to promote common causes with which dissident groups in each country can readily associate and campaign for in their domestic contexts.[98]

Campaigns launched against abuses of citizens' rights and violations of the rule of law, in addition to numerous economic, political, and social grievances may find an increasing resonance among broader sectors of the population. Mutually reinforcing single-issue movements concerned with ecological deterioration, military conscription, nuclear disarmament, and other popular causes, could fortify East European social activism in the years ahead. Oppositionist strategists are evidently seeking ways to channel public disaffection and frustration into collective and effective forms of bloc-wide pressure and political leverage.

Problems of communication between independent groups are likely to persist, though contacts between intellectuals are obviously easier to maintain than those between largely unorganized working class protestors. Dissident intellectuals in several states have purposively sought links with the West in order to gain publicity and rally support for their cause. The West also serves as a valuable transmission point between country-based opposition movements. Konrad and others have stressed the importance of an "international solidarity of intellectuals," as a "mutual defense alliance" against state repression.[99] This should apparently involve a network of communications, the cross-fertilization of programs, the circulation of political and non-political texts, and more practical joint activities. Intellectuals with well developed international contacts will continue to form an important conduit of information between and within Communist states, and with the outside world, while seeking to extend their influence and establish lasting cooperation among oppositionist forces.

A difference in approach toward the West can be noted among dissidents holding divergent political views. Traditionally, the more devout socialists have adopted a fairly pronounced anti-NATO stance—partly to court the support of Western left-leaning intellectuals and political groups, partly to ascertain their socialist credentials, and partly to parry government attacks.[100] East European Marxist revisionists from the mid-1950s onwards have cultivated contacts with like-minded Western Communists and courted nascent Eurocommunism with a view to promoting a visionary "socialist Europe," characterized by a "non-aligned" foreign policy and the toleration of "separate" or "national roads to socialism," entailing "humane socialism" and a reformation of the ruling Communist Parties.[101]

Non-Communist socialists and social democrats have also displayed some propensity toward favoring links with left-oriented organizations in the West, but generally pursue a wider range of potential democratic support.[102] Avowed non-socialists, liberal democrats, conservatives, and nationalists of various hues may have a broad spectrum of potential backers in the West, but in turn are constrained by overall ignorance about their programs and an underlying Western "realism" which places more emphasis on internal Party reforms and gradual "accommodations" between state and society rather than a Western-type political transformation. Western leaders and political bodies therefore hesitate to support dissidents whose programs focus on political pluralism and full national independence, in case such overt backing chills their relations with Moscow.

Mindful of constraining their opportunities for obtaining Western support, many dissidents since the mid-1970s—including those with evident socialist ideologies—have tried to extend their campaigning platform in the West. This has been especially noticeable in the light of mounting disillusionment with various left-wing parties and organizations who, despite their rhetoric, tend to avoid providing tangible support for the East European opposition.[103] The broadening of the range of contacts by the new evolutionist strategists has been fostered by the increased mobility of Soviet bloc intellectuals during the past two decades. The expulsion or voluntary emigration of a sizeable segment of the Czechoslovak and Polish non-conformist intelligentsia, after the events of 1968 and during the Solidarity era, has also reinforced communications with the West. The various waves of visitors and emigrants provide an indispensable channel of contact between independent groups in the East and public opinion in the West. Relative freedom of movement in the West also assists East bloc "international intellectual solidarity" on democratic soil.

Both the exiled and home-based dissidents have gradually acquired greater skills in gaining, maintaining, and directing support in the West. In some cases, they have managed to obtain fairly reliable sources of financial support, political backing, and outlets of communication. Through the accurate monitoring and reporting of internal conditions, and by carefully assessing the priorities of the Western media, governmental institutions, and other pertinent organizations, some oppositionists have become adept at circulating unofficial information and campaigning for various forms of support. The focus on numerous attractive and "newsworthy" single issues has evidently helped their overall cause.

In the case of Poland after the rise of Solidarity, free labor unionism became a prominent issue. International labor union federations, national trade union councils, and individual trade unions in the West, theoretically became natural allies in the Polish struggle. However, the ingrained resistance by some traditionalist pro-Soviet labor union executives in aiding essentially anti-Bolshevik workers' movements in the East, proved difficult to overcome in many Western countries.[104] With regard to Czechoslovakia, the Western spotlight has been focused on the human rights issues encapsulated in numerous international agreements and their infringements by Prague. Czechoslovak dissidents have also cultivated contacts with Western peace movements in recent years, partly to gain support for autonomous peace and disarmament crusades in the Soviet bloc, and partly to underscore the anti-democratic nature of East Europe's regimes. The issue of world peace has been closely linked by Charter 77 activists with government respect for human rights. The similarities in patterns of repression and resistance throughout the bloc have also been highlighted by political dissenters with some access to Western public opinion.

Campaigns on behalf of political prisoners and other persecuted individuals have also been mounted in the West, with varying degrees of success. Help has been sought from governments, international organizations, and numerous professional and human rights associations. Dissidents have tended to discover that aside from prolonged "crisis periods," such as the rise and fall of Solidarity, international protest campaigns are difficult to sustain. Communist authorities are well aware that Western concern and "interference" in their "internal affairs" can rapidly wane when the international spotlight turns to another part of the globe; hence they often adjust their policies accordingly.

The role of emigres in supporting political opposition in Eastern Europe and campaigning on behalf of dissidents also needs to be considered. Emigre politics are clearly not uniform, programmatically homogeneous, or always internally consistent. Each of the major exiled populations conducts its own diverse political and cultural life in its adopted country. This is compounded by the emigres' wide dispersion among several Western countries, their usually small size and restricted influence, frequent generational differences of approach, and the existence of successive waves of emigrants holding dissimilar aspirations and pursuing divergent policies. Inter-emigre contacts are also a potential minefield. Mutual suspicions and historically rooted animosities are not always easy to overcome, even when attention is concentrated on common causes and interests *vis-à-vis* the Soviets and the West. Nevertheless, some emigres continue to play important roles as political lobby groups in several Western states, as points of contact with indigenous dissidents, and as sources of material assistance for oppositionist movements.[105] For example, many *samizdat* documents reach the West through the respective emigre communities, while messages of support from the West often traverse the same route.

The West provides a valuable point of reference for East Europeans, particularly through the popularly perceived contrasts in living standards, political freedoms, and other civil liberties. This tends to generate disenchantment, disquiet, and criticism of Communist Party failures and the unfulfilled promises of "really existing socialism." It may also equally fuel higher expectations for future change and help mobilize the public in this direction. East European contacts with the outside world have expanded enormously during the past decade, as a result of individual visits to the West and through the influx of foreign tourists, students, and emigres. In the case of the GDR, approximately eight million West Germans annually visit family and friends in the East. Their East German compatriots measure their own welfare against standards prevalent in the FRG about which information is readily available. The influence of Western radio broadcasts, such as those of Deutsche Welle, Radio Free Europe, the Voice of America, and the BBC, as well as television and other means of communication, on the populations of the Soviet bloc must also not be underestimated.

The postures and pressures adopted by Western administrations and non-governmental agencies will continue to impinge on East European developments, though the relationship is not straightforward.[106] The encouragement of economic reform, political and cultural liberalization, and respect for human rights through various incentives and pressures has evidently scored some successes. However, one would need to scrutinize the context and durability of any purported Communist Party concessions before extolling the efficacy of Western levers and responses. In many respects, temporary improvements on the human rights front are used as tactical maneuvers by Soviet bloc regimes to disarm Western criticism while reverting to more subtle, hidden, or sophisticated methods of social control and repression. Nevertheless, during the era of detente in the 1970s, Communist regimes displayed some sensitivity to Western criticisms and generally avoided major acts of repression to stymie international censure and to curry economic favors. A similar process of calculated tolerance has been visible since Gorbachev's accession to power in 1985. However, when major internal developments threaten to undermine the Party's pre-eminent position, the authorities rarely hesitate to revert to more comprehensive crackdowns.

While the East European regimes fail to honor all the commitments contained in "Basket Three" of the Helsinki Final Act, these and other human rights stipulations help to legitimize the activities of domestic dissidents. They also provide legalistic credibility to Western pressures for internal reform. The West engages in a policy of "differentiation" *vis-à-vis* these regimes, by offering more favorable economic and political treatment to governments which either display greater respect for human rights or conduct a more independent foreign policy. In considering such outside influences over the internal developments of Eastern Europe, it is worthwhile to repeat Kusin's observation in the light of several decades of evidence that "reform certainly breeds detente. Conversely, however, the relationship is not causal."[107]

Conclusion

Political dissidents and discontented social groups in Eastern Europe confront largely inflexible political systems. Communist governments are hesitant to incorporate new methods and ideas, are preoccupied with potential threats to single party rule, and are unwilling to devolve power to any significant extent. Even where some economic or cultural diversity and experimentation is tolerated, the system's political structures have been shielded from encroachment by decentralizing and democratizing tendencies. The past thirty years have demonstrated the pitfalls and difficulties involved in trying to alter East Europe's internal *status quo*— whether through popular rebellions, reformist pressures, or peaceful mass movements. The limits of political and socio-economic change are largely fixed by the domestic Party-state establishment and the military-strategic interests of the Soviet leadership.

Periodic revolts against the Communist system have been regularly followed by massive repression, the imposition of further preventative measures by the government in question, and attempts by political dissidents to apply new strategies to alter the system. The opposition movement in several states has endeavored to break out of this self-perpetuating cycle of revolt and repression, by devising appropriate methods for constructively stimulating and channeling public energies into effective pressures for social and political change.

As we have discussed, many dissident strategies are reactive and flexible, taking full account of government capabilities and intentions, the public mood, and the current international political climate. An important ingredient for the success of any form of opposition is an accurate assessment of popular stamina and official reaction. The appeals of dissidents therefore vary between states and alter over time. It seems that only in the event of a comprehensive collapse of Communist authority and a severe contraction of Party-state power, coupled with intolerable mass grievances and frustrations, is the bulk of the population willing to engage actively in concerted opposition. Under "normal" circumstances, however, economic conditions are evidently adequate, or more precisely the mechanisms of social control and the organs of repression are sufficiently effective, to discourage overt mass opposition.

Most Soviet bloc regimes have attempted to balance repression with concession, in order to prevent the emergence of menacing public opposition. An important element here is the pursuit of some viable though uncodified "social compact" between rulers and ruled, whereby the state provides economic stability and social security in exchange for the public's political compliance. The authorities endeavor to drain and dilute popular interest in oppositionist activity while isolating overt dissenters from the working masses. The Party may even be willing to tolerate the existence of a "dissident community," as long as the movement for independent social action does not appear to take root among the populace or menace the regime's political monopoly. During crisis periods the government aims to exhaust the public and increase their fear of reprisals, while fostering pessimism, confusion, apathy, and the avoidance of open confrontation.

Despite their numerous internal problems, the Soviet bloc systems are not doomed to disintegrate rapidly. Moreover, one cannot assume any inevitable process of liberalization, democratization, and structural political and economic reform, with or without the existence of various forms of dissent. The question of whether Communism will break before it bends has preoccupied many opposition theorists; they seem to have concluded that a gradual and prolonged bending process must at least be tried and tested.

An additional long-term problem concerns the transformation of Soviet overlordship into some form of genuine internationalism of equal national partners. Many have argued that only the progress of democratic reform or a systemic breakdown in the USSR itself will lead to any lasting changes in Eastern Europe and in the latter's relations with Moscow. The interplay of internal and external factors may place definite constraints on political dissent, but it may also provide opportunities that we will discuss in the concluding chapter. In the final analysis, however, it is difficult to escape the conclusions drawn by numerous East European oppositionists that the most significant domestic freedoms can only be won by indigenous social forces in confrontation with the vested interests of the Communist Party power elite. In this context Konrad's observation seems particularly apt:

> Our defeats are milestones on the road to East European liberation. Defeat is part of the game: we will not be cast down by it for long, we will get up and go on, and if we don't, then our children will.[108]

4

Political and
Human Rights Movements

In this chapter we are primarily concerned with the broad phenomenon of public non-conformism, citizens' self-defense, human rights lobbying, and nascent movements pressing for greater political liberties or transformations of the political system. Single-issue campaigns focusing on particular social, religious, cultural, and economic freedoms are assessed in subsequent chapters. Ramet points out that dissatisfaction and disaffection are more widespread in the Soviet bloc than known cases of politically inspired dissent may indicate.[1] It is often manifest not in overt, public acts of protest but in a withdrawal into private life, perfunctory work performance, the avoidance of official institutions, absenteeism, pilfering, and various forms of "social deviance." Active dissent, by contrast, involves some conviction that the structure or function of government can be changed, and that pressure should be applied accordingly. Even displays of seemingly non-political dissatisfaction, such as workers' strikes sparked by poor pay or worsening economic conditions, sometimes have underlying political roots. All attempts to alter official policy outside the formally prescribed channels constitute a form of independent social activism with definite political consequences.

We will focus on significant campaigns launched during the past decade to expand the scope of human rights and political liberties, particularly those which pertain to freedom of expression, association, and organization. The demands of some of these groups may not be overtly political, in that they do not attempt to rearrange the structures of power; however, the very existence of autonomous human rights associations has clear political import in a Leninist state. Independent citizens' pressure groups are designed to influence official policy on a broad range of issues, and they constitute an embryonic expression of organizational pluralism. The more explicitly political groupings differ in their programs, ideologies, and strategies *vis-à-vis* the regime. Human rights and political movements span a range of organizational formats, and their size, composition, significance, longevity, and achievements vary considerably both within and between East European states.

Solidarity's Poland

In assessing the condition of the Solidarity opposition in post-martial law Poland, an historical synopsis of this independent mass movement would be helpful. The formal agreements between the Warsaw regime and workers' strike leaders in August 1980 led to the founding and eventual registration of the Independent Self-Governing Trade Union "Solidarność."[2] Though technically a labor organization designed to represent and defend workers' interests, during the sixteen months of its legal existence the movement evolved into a multi-faceted campaign to democratize all social institutions and establish new associations free of Party supervision. Solidarity was governed at the central level by a National Coordinating Commission (KKP), later the National Commission (KK), which elected a small National Presidium to provide day-to-day leadership of the union. The KK consisted of representatives from 33 regional committees, and coordinated Solidarity policies vis-a-vis the government under elected chairman Lech Wałęsa. The union maintained a highly democratic decentralized structure based largely on independent and sometimes contradictory initiatives at the regional, municipal, and factory levels. Solidarity also spurred the formation of numerous autonomous occupational associations among all social sectors, including farmers, students, technicians, writers, and artists. The liberal climate in 1980–81 also stimulated the formation of numerous single-issue campaigns and political clubs, as well as a plethora of uncensored publications, events, and public gatherings.

By the close of 1981 Solidarity publicly endorsed a wholesale transformation of the country's political structures, social institutions, and economic mechanisms. It supported democratic elections to local Peoples' Councils and to parliament, and pressed for power-sharing in economic decisions with a greater role for workers' self-management and enterprise autonomy. The union was drawn into ever-widening demands for public control over state institutions, but proved unprepared to operate in the political vacuum resulting from official paralysis as Poland's economic crisis escalated.[3] Solidarity was distracted and manipulated during protracted negotiations with government representatives as General Jaruzelski prepared his counter-offensive.

Solidarity was suspended following the imposition of martial law in December 1981 and was formally banned in October 1982. The authorities were intent on restoring full Party control over public life and eradicating autonomous social activism. Though mass repression fractured Solidarity's organizational backbone and eliminated an effective pressure group, a loose nationwide underground union structure was painstakingly created to resist official persecution.[4] In addition, several Solidarity leaders and advisers, in or out of prisons and internment centers, continued to demand the full implementation of the August 1980 agreements. Clandestine union networks developed in several regions, with variable membership and programs. In general, underground Solidarity steered clear of outright political activity and focused instead on defending workers' interests, providing truthful information, and simply keeping itself intact. By mid-1985 the majority of union regions had re-established some organizational structure, consisting of plant, inter-enterprise, and regional committees; underground publications; and communications networks. It is difficult to estimate accurately the total number involved in the Solidarity underground. Though only several dozen activists have actually stayed in hiding, several thousand people lent their support, and tens of thousands more provided backing for specific Solidarity causes. Membership in the underground network has remained highly fluid, and dependent on the extent of police penetration, government repression, local commitment, and organizational effectiveness.

A prolonged debate has raged in oppositionist circles concerning the preferred structure of the Solidarity movement: whether it should be mass-based or vanguardist, covert or overt, centralized or decentralized. Immediate and longer term programs, and the positions to be adopted toward the regime over numerous pressing issues have also been debated. In general, Solidarity has adhered to the notion that a "long march" is the most appropriate strategy to resuscitate the union while supporting other autonomous political, social, and economic initiatives. This standpoint has been reinforced by repeated failures of strikes and demonstrations to influence government policy and reinstate trade union pluralism. Solidarity leaders appear acutely aware of the limitations involved in rebuilding a mass movement under current conditions, as well as their restricted capability to influence and coordinate the bulk of the workforce. The strikes of April, May, and August 1988 may have underscored the deep-seated resentment of government policy on the shop floor, but they also highlighted the constraints Solidarity faces in organizing, controlling, and channeling workers' protests.

To understand the scope and impact of "post-December" Solidarity one must survey the union's structures and activities at the central, regional, and local levels.[5] At the national tier, the Interim Coordinating Commission (TKK) was established in Warsaw in April 1982 to set overall guidelines for the underground union, to coordinate inter-regional activities, and to provide a domestic and international symbol of Solidarity's legitimacy and continuity. The TKK's membership has fluctuated due to police capture of leading activists representing the major union regions. With the arrest of its chairman Zbigniew Bujak in May 1986, the TKK lost significant prestige and authority, and indeed throughout its lifespan has found it difficult to direct or respond promptly to grassroots activism under acutely demoralizing conditions. Since the 1986 "amnesty" for the majority of Polish political prisoners, the national Solidarity leadership has been rearranged to test governmental "liberalization" and push for the legal reactivation of the union. The Provisional Solidarity Council was established "above ground" in September 1986, consisting of seven prominent union leaders presided over by Wałęsa. But the TKK and much of the underground network was retained in case of renewed persecution, and continue activities that could not be practically conducted overground. However, the existence of two Solidarity leadership bodies created more problems than it solved, and led to a damaging division of authority as well as confusion over responsibilities and decision-making. As a result, a new governing organ, the National Executive Commission, was formed in October 1987. It was headed by Wałęsa and replaced the TKK and the Provisional Council, both of which were formally dissolved. Nevertheless, there was no immediate improvement in the effectiveness of the national union in terms of organizing popular protest or in pressurizing the regime to grant meaningful concessions.

About twenty regional Solidarity structures recognize the authority of the new national leadership. Regional networks are especially well developed in Gdańsk, Lower Silesia (Wrocław), Mazowsze (Warsaw), and Małopolska (Cracow), but more amorphous in the remaining areas. Regional committees endeavor to coordinate union activities between work enterprises and with the Solidarity center. The most important and well-organized committees have maintained representatives in the TKK. They also channel funds from within and outside the region to subsidize various local union operations, such as publishing and providing aid to sacked or imprisoned activists. One of the most developed regional organizations, in Warsaw, has a "bureau" to monitor the location of Solidarity leaders and distribution networks, and to disperse funds to various sub-bodies and non-union groups. Additional cells exist to uphold inter-regional contacts, arrange "special communications," and oversee financial affairs. Since the 1986 amnesty for political prisoners, several regional commissions have emerged from hiding or have been newly created to function openly; however, the majority have remained underground.[6]

At the enterprise or office level, hundreds of Clandestine Factory Committees (TKZs) function in Poland, though their size and impact vary considerably between plants. They are most entrenched in the larger factories or among tightly knit working-class communities that manage to resist police penetration. The TKZs have been subject to substantial pressure arising from shrinking funds, official repression, and the withdrawal of members due to fear, apathy, cynicism, or despondency. They cannot openly defend the workforce and are often ignored by the management as an employee pressure group. Few such committees have surfaced as overground entities because many activists remain concerned about government persecution. Since the fall of 1986, Solidarity organizers have campaigned to register plant-based union chapters. They have also tried to stimulate the formation of new independent factory committees involved with specific grievances concerning working conditions, health care, and self-management.[7] The idea was to present union pluralism as a *fait accompli* even without formal registration; however, clandestine cells and networks would not necessarily be disbanded. Achievements to date have not been dramatic even where free union representatives have attempted to deal directly with plant managers. The authorities remained unwilling to restore Solidarity whether at the national, regional, or factory level; both overt and covert union activity have been branded as an illegal "threat to public order." Solidarity's Provisional Council was outlawed in October 1987, though union leaders claimed that they were operating in accordance with international labor conventions and therefore did not require formal government approval.

In general, free union cells concentrate on producing and distributing the unofficial press, maintaining clandestine factory libraries, collecting union dues, and assisting repressed employees, while attempting to influence management decisions over specific shop-floor grievances. Local factory committees have registered some success in campaigning for higher wages, as witnessed in the wave of demands voiced in early May 1988.[8] Solidarity activists and supporters helped to organize stoppages and issued strike alerts in protest over falling living standards, and in some cases managed to gain support from several thousand workers. Possibly, by their very existence, the TKZs have spurred the official labor unions into competition; the latter have campaigned more actively on behalf of workers' interests in order to gain public credibility. The regime has refrained from all-out repression, hoping that all Solidarity structures will disintegrate through a mixture of political ostracism, economic attrition, public disillusionment, and rifts within the opposition.

Rural Solidarity has found it even more difficult than its urban counterpart to resume pre-martial law activities. Various attempts have been made to establish local, regional, and national farmers' councils, including the National Farmers Resistance Committee "Solidarity" (OKOR"S") and the Independent Peasant Activists "Roch."[9] OKOR"S" and other clandestine groups have spoken out for more substantial political work among independent farmers, especially those of the younger generation, leading to the formation of an independent agrarian party.[10] However, free trade union activism has remained limited and scattered in rural Poland. The difficulties are compounded by the geographic dispersal of farmers, their long working hours, a weaker tradition of organizational work and collective protest, and the frequent susceptibility of villages to police encirclement and intervention. Nevertheless, other independent agrarian-based initiatives have proliferated, even without a normally functioning Rural Solidarity structure. These include parish groups or "pastoral communities" in over 10,000 locations that arrange informal discussions, cultural events, self-education courses, and religious retreats with parish priests. They also obtain legal counsel for farmers and assist the families of persecuted activists.

Numerous human rights groups and social self-defense movements were formed in Poland before and during the Solidarity era. The Workers' Defense Committee (KOR) was established in September 1976 by dissident intellectuals following government reprisals against nearly 2,000 workers who had publicly protested three months earlier in Radom and Ursus against steep price rises.[11] KOR provided financial, medical, and legal aid to persecuted workers and thereby laid much of the groundwork for more fruitful contacts between intellectuals and workers during the next round of conflict with the state. About forty individuals were particularly active in KOR, including the historians Jacek Kuroń, Adam Michnik, and Antoni Macierewicz, the economist Edward Lipinski, and the writer Jan Józef Lipski. Several dozen more intellectuals and students provided tangible assistance by gathering, publishing, and disseminating KOR material, and directly aiding repressed workers. Following Gierek's "amnesty" for the victims of June 1976, KOR was renamed in September 1977 the Committee for Social Self-Defense (KSS-KOR). It attracted support from a wide cross-section of Polish society and encouraged or inaugurated numerous independent ventures in education, culture, human rights advocacy, and free labor unionism. KSS-KOR dissolved itself in September 1981, out of a conviction that it had become superfluous with the surge in social activism after the birth of Solidarity. Its former members served in various union bodies as advisers, spokesmen, or officials. They also participated in shaping much of the underground movement after the declaration of martial law.

The Movement for the Defense of Human and Civil Rights (ROPCiO) was created in March 1977 to monitor Poland's compliance with international agreements such as the Helsinki Accords.[12] It also provided aid to victims of state prosecution and campaigned for changes in Polish law to protect civil rights. ROPCiO's founders and chief activists, including

Andrzej Czuma and Leszek Moczulski, intended to broaden the opposition movement after the creation of KOR. ROPCiO established "information centers" in several major cities, and drew various nationalist activists into the dissident campaign who might otherwise have remained on the sidelines. Like KSS-KOR, ROPCiO disbanded in late 1980 during the growth of Solidarity in late 1980. However, its original members continued to be active in oppositionist work.

The Polish Helsinki Commission was established by Zbigniew Romaszewski and several other KSS-KOR members in 1979 to document and publicize human rights abuses. After submitting several reports to CSCE follow-up meetings, it was dissolved under official pressure in 1982. A new Helsinki Committee in Poland (KHP) was set up in early 1983 to collect and publish material on human rights violations during and after martial law.[13] It declared its independence from all political and Solidarity groupings while maintaining its members' anonymity. The KHP produced several bulky reports on civil liberties that were submitted to the UN Commission on Human Rights, the International Labor Organization, and other international forums. In July 1988, the Helsinki Committee revealed the identity of twelve of its chief organizers. In addition to monitoring official repression, they pledged to undertake "citizens' legislative initiatives" and openly use existing laws to protect "individual and collective rights."

After the murder of Father Jerzy Popiełuszko by four police officers, several citizens' committees were set up in late 1984 and early 1985 to monitor and report on police violence.[14] Prominent dissidents helped to found these groups as open public initiatives that reacted swiftly to official lawlessness. This was the first systematic attempt following the imposition of martial law to organize overtly. The authorities promptly outlawed the committees and harassed their members; as a result they gradually lost steam. A few subsequent human rights intiatives have been undertaken; for example, the Polish League for Human Rights was created in Szczecin in October 1986, with representatives in nine cities. The group styled itself as a recreation of the prewar Polish League for Human Rights, which was affiliated with the International Federation of Human Rights. All such groupings have remained avowedly apolitical and primarily concerned with defending rights guaranteed in international conventions, the Polish constitution, and in domestic laws.

A series of small, decentralized neighborhood Committees for Social Defense (KOS) were formed after December 1981 as a means of channelling local resistance against the Jaruzelski regime.[15] Several hundred KOS cells are believed to operate in over a dozen cities, though it is difficult to gauge their size and impact. They have little formal structure and are dependent on the degree of local commitment and activism.

Many have arisen and disbanded over the years, and they often overlap with the Solidarity network or provide support to union cells. KOS activities have included organizing aid for political prisoners and their families, helping activists in hiding, and printing and distributing underground texts—over thirty KOS-inspired publications have been produced, mostly in Warsaw and Cracow. The KOS program centers on the "long march" social evolutionist strategy, focused on building an "independent society" from the grassroots upward, and energizing citizens' involvement in all manner of non-state pursuits. They have avoided political activities on the assumption that the politicization of the opposition is divisive, premature, and currently counter-productive.

Since the trauma of martial law, the number of independent political groupings has increased dramatically in Poland. They exhibit an ideological and programmatic diversity that remained largely submerged during the legal Solidarity period. Some of the loosely organized political initiatives predate Solidarity, others coalesced after the rise of the union, and the majority were spawned during or after the "state of war." Many groups trace their political roots to prewar or wartime political parties, while others have more contemporary programs and strategies. The political opposition has largely developed and operated independently of Solidarity, though the actual membership frequently overlaps. Most of the groups support Solidarity, but they are sometimes at odds with specific union programs or leaders. Indeed, the fact that they emphasize politically oriented work tends to overreach the more circumscribed union objectives. However, this also contributes to their generally small size, public isolation, and limited effectiveness. Much of the political opposition is highly critical of the moderate and concessionary tone of Solidarity spokesmen; it considers union policies inadequate for the sort of wholesale changes deemed necessary to curtail or terminate Communist control in Poland.[16] Some political activists view Solidarity's previous avoidance of political initiatives to be partly responsible for the lack of public preparedness for Jaruzelski's crackdown. By contrast, other political dissidents tend to be more conciliatory than the union leadership toward the regime. They base their operations around periodicals and discussion clubs, and seek to extract maximum room for maneuver from the government—whether this involves partial cooperation, official registration, or the infiltration of official and semi-official institutions.[17]

Though a majority of the population has stayed aloof from any political groupings, either as a result of fear, apathy, or cynicism, a substantial minority numbering in the thousands has remained active irrespective of government intimidation. About thirty independent political groups, including self-styled parties, are known to exist in Poland, though only a dozen or so can claim some established structure, membership, regular publications, and a concrete program.[18] This survey will encompass the most significant groups and outline their history, strategy, and activities. Some are fully clandestine or semi-conspiratorial, others are largely overt. Ideologies and policies often overlap; we shall trace some common strands and indicate points of distinction. Each of the groups discussed falls into one of two categories: political "absolutists," "fundamentalists," or "radicals" who argue that only a complete overhaul of the system and the removal from power of the Communist Party will suffice to institute democracy and national independence; and political "gradualists," "pragmatists," or "realists" espousing piecemeal reforms and a slow evolution eroding the Party monopoly. Within this dichotomy, the groups span a spectrum of orientations on a left-right axis, with regard to the long-term direction of desired change, though it is often problematic to place them exclusively on any one wing.

The Confederation for an Independent Poland (KPN) was established in September 1979 as a self-proclaimed political party seeking to bring about a sovereign parliamentary democracy terminating one-party rule.[19] During the legal Solidarity era the KPN claimed a membership of some 60,000 and opened offices in several cities. The group's strategy called for a "creeping revolution" through the creation of several political associations and the eventual convocation of an alternative parliament that would proclaim new national elections. While not advocating violent revolution, KPN sought an intensification of political activism among workers and intellectuals outside regime control. It rejected any compromises or cooperation with Warsaw as diversionary and self-destructive. KPN leaders were harassed by the police and imprisoned. Under martial law the organization was paralysed and its four key leaders sentenced for "attempting to overthrow the government by force." After their release in August 1984, the KPN has resumed its work under the auspices of a Political Council that called for free elections. But despite occasional meetings, statements, and publications, until recently KPN has displayed little sign of recapturing a sizeable following. This may be due as much to internal organizational splits as to incessant official persecution.

Fighting Solidarity (SW) was founded in Wrocław in June 1983 by activists who broke away from Solidarity's regional committee in Lower Silesia. SW asserts that it has several hundred active members and supporters, a central leadership with considerable local autonomy, and a youth wing—the Council of the Fighting Solidarity Youth Movement. Initially led by the former Solidarity official, Kornel Morawiecki, SW claims about two dozen publications, including an underground bulletin with the same name.[20] It runs a news agency, self-education programs, and a clandestine radio station, and has mounted numerous protest actions in Wrocław, Poznań, Gdańsk, Lublin, Katowice, and other cities.

Dissatisfied with Solidarity and Church moderation, SW opposes any accommodation with Warsaw. It stresses social self-organization based on "solidarism"—consisting of industrial syndicalism, strong local self-government, a cooperative focused mixed economy, and a multi-party parliamentary democracy. Its program is more far-reaching than that of the Solidarity committees, though it cooperates with the union in its ongoing struggle for economic pluralism.

The Liberal Democratic Party "Independence" (LDP"N") emerged in November 1984 after publishing the underground political monthly *Niepodległość* for over two years.[21] Centered in Warsaw with branches in Cracow and Katowice, the LDP"N" claims several dozen anonymous members organized around a Political Council. The group has been highly critical of Solidarity's concessions to the regime and it dismisses any prospects of "democratizing Communism." It proposes the creation of an elaborate "underground political league" as the basis for a future interim government and the eventual overthrow of Communist dictatorship. In the short term, LDP"N" emphasizes political education and activism among all sectors of society but remains suspicious of the alleged elitism of the pre-Solidarity intellectual opposition. The group espouses laissez-faire capitalism, and like other dissident organizations underscores the importance of international cooperation in Eastern Europe to hasten the disintegration of the Muscovite empire. Since early 1985, LDP"N" has collaborated with other underground groups but tends to dismiss the entire Solidarity network as a largely spent force.

Freedom-Justice-Independence (WSN) declared its existence in August 1982 and called for the creation of an underground state based on local self-government.[22] Its social democratic Political Declaration, released in May 1983, favors a mixed economy with a sovereign democratically elected state. WSN expresses little faith in Communist reformism or in legalistic ventures by the opposition. It is based in Warsaw with little evidence of support outside the capital. The Congress of National Solidarity (KSN), which issued its founding declaration in 1983, purportedly has cells in Warsaw, Cracow, Łódź, Gdańsk, and Poznań. Its leadership comes largely from the veteran opposition activist Wojciech Ziembinski. KSN has not declared itself a political party but claims continuity from the earlier Clubs in Service of Independence (KSN) founded in September 1981 and the Committee for National Self-Determination (KPSN) formed by Ziembinski in February 1979. The KSN is intended to function as a broad discussion platform for independence-minded Poles, and is less concerned with the political or economic shape of a future Poland.[23] It rejects all forms of collaboration with Warsaw and has proposed a complete boycott of all Party-sponsored institutions and initiatives.

The Polish Socialist Labor Party (PSPP) was founded in September 1981 by Edmund Bałuka, the Szczecin strike committee leader in December 1970.[24] With several dozen members who are mainly shipyard workers, it is fully clandestine, publishes unofficial texts, and arranges political discussion clubs. It has sought neither government registration nor pursued legal endeavors, and remains staunchly opposed to Communist Party rule. The Warsaw-based "Robotnik" Political Group also declares itself "democratic socialist," dismisses any possibility of binding agreements with the regime, and criticizes apolitical social activism as being unnecessarily restrictive.[25] "Robotnik" holds that democracy and independence can be won only by a tightly knit political opposition, but it believes that the time for such a scenario has not yet arrived. It therefore concentrates on educating and recruiting cadres during the prolonged "preparatory stage."

Among other small independent groupings veering toward an "absolutist" position, it is worth mentioning Liberation ("Wyzwolenie"), a Warsaw-based organization with a publication of the same name and engaged in fully covert operations.[26] It is strongly "anti-collaborationist," viewing any dialogue with the authorities as an illusory exercise because the system is ultimately "irreformable." Also notable are the Fatherland ("Ojczyzna") group, which draws upon the heritage of the prewar pro-Church National Workers Party; the Polish Independence Party (PPN)[27], composed of former KPN activists; the anarchist Alternative Society Movement (RSA); the Independent Workers Movement (NRR); the Workers Opposition Compact (POR); and the Workers Thought Club (KMR).[28] Some attempts have been made to coordinate activities among groups with compatible ideologies and programs. The Compact of Independence Parties and Organizations (PPION) was formed as a loose federation of such associations to produce joint statements and provide mutual aid.[29] But little progress has evidently been made in forging a united front. Most inter-organizational activities revolve around publishing, issuing joint programs; organizing discussions, education programs, and demonstrations; and engaging in "symbolic politics" by way of patriotic commemorations and displays. The political campaigns also act as pressure groups, with varying degrees of influence, within the diversified oppositionist movement.

Dissident "pragmatists" have also formed politically oriented groups of various tendencies. They emphasize the potential flexibility of the existing system and the ability of unofficial associations to influence government policy—at least on certain pressing concerns such as the need for economic liberalization. In some cases, they shelter under the Church umbrella while testing the limits of independent political activity.

They try to avoid being drawn either into adopting "radical positions" or exposing themselves to manipulation by the regime.

The Polish Socialist Party (PPS) was established by 42 dissidents in November 1987 as a revival of the splintered and co-opted PPS of the 1940s. Its chairman is the one-time KOR activist Lipski, while several other former Solidarity leaders and advisers joined the Party's presidium and Central Committee.[30] As an openly active group, the PPS has sought to test the sincerity of Warsaw's "democratization" and "restore the true meaning of the word socialism." The PPS has endeavored to cooperate with all democratic bodies while expanding its branches and membership. It has sought government tolerance while arguing that there is no law in Poland that requires the official registration of any political party. PPS leaders have tested the limits of Warsaw's proclaimed "socialist pluralism," and underscored their intention to abide by the constitution and comply with any procedures that would guarantee their party's security. The regime responded negatively by branding the group "illegal" and hounding its leaders and members. The PPS's long-term objectives are "socialist democracy and national independence." Its short-term focus is on trade union pluralism, respect for human rights, and increasing public control over government decisions. Interestingly enough, the PPS was created by activists who previously rejected political activism in favor of social evolutionism. They may have altered their strategy because of the growth of political competition among the opposition, apprehensions over being outpaced by events, cognizance of the limitations of a KOR-type approach, and appreciation of the opportunities emerging during the post-martial law "thaw."

The Political Group "Wola" (GP"W") was founded in February 1984, and is centered around one of the leading Warsaw underground weeklies, *Wola*.[31] GP"W" is closely identified with Solidarity but believes that a political approach is essential alongside union work, and supports the politicization of some segments of the opposition. However, it has also voiced the opinion that the dissident movement could be weakened by excessive political diversification under current conditions. GP"W" is less concerned with long-range programs than short-term actions for building an "alternative society." It espouses the infiltration of official institutions and the transformation of semi-official bodies into independent pressure groups. The stress is on gradual, patient change rather than a complete repudiation of working within the system. GP"W" is evidently left-leaning with a strong penchant for "workers' control" and "democratic socialism."

The "Głos" Group is a continuation of the pre-Solidarity *Głos* journal established in September 1977 and associated with one stream within KOR. Its leading light is Antoni Macierewicz who has criticized KOR's "leftism" in the past. The group went underground during martial law, but after initially speaking out against any hopes of reforming the system, "Głos" has increasingly steered toward compromise It presented a controversial proposal in 1983 calling for cooperation between the Church, army, and Solidarity against Communist Party interests. Should such an accord prove unattainable, "Głos" espoused a "long march" approach while staunchly defending Cardinal Glemp's conciliatory policies toward the regime. Clearly Christian Democratic in orientation, the group maintains close links with Solidarity ideals and activists.[32]

Res Publika appeared in 1978 as a "liberal conservative" publication, faded away during martial law, but re-emerged in 1984 after negotiations were undertaken with the authorities to legalize the journal. Since *Res Publika* was formally registered in 1986, the editorial team has insisted on its independence from the Church, Solidarity, and government. It follows a "legalistic" approach as an "open opposition" venture testing the bounds of censorship and government permissiveness. Its chief editor Marcin Król is particularly concerned with expanding cultural, educational, and intellectual freedoms by taking advantage of any official openings and concessions. The group's willingness to operate with Warsaw's blessing created some friction in the opposition, and it was initially denounced as "collaborationist"; but since 1987, its political strategy has won greater acceptance in dissident circles. The regime perceives *Res Publika* as a trial balloon in its efforts to split and neutralize intellectual dissent by tolerating some critics while prohibiting others.

Polish Politics (PP) emerged from the Young Poland Movement (RMP)—an independence-oriented group founded in July 1979, which claimed members in Gdańsk, Szczecin, and Warsaw, until it was dissolved during martial law. PP upholds a national democratic (*endecja*) political line, but rejects some of the more extremist tenets of this prewar ideology.[33] Its views are put forward in a quarterly publication bearing the group's name, which first appeared in the fall of 1982. In December 1987, PP disclosed the identity of its spokesmen, including its leader Aleksander Hall, and declared support for a gradualist approach to political change and for lasting compromise with the regime. The group stresses a unitary "national identity," Christian values, a strong national leadership, and a close alliance with Russia, while disputing full state control over the economy. It opposes the notion of an "underground society," but favors an open campaign to limit Party interference and "soften the system," and a "national agreement" between political groups based on dialogue and moderation.

The "13 December" (*13 Grudnia*) group is located in Cracow, where it operates the autonomous "Liberum Veto" publishing house. It considers itself practical and "realist," but its long-term objectives are full blown

free-market capitalism and parliamentary democracy.³⁴ Its leading or-
ganizer and theoretician is Mirosław Dzielski, who eschews the creation
of a political party and avoids associating either with Solidarity, the
political opposition, the government, or the Church. According to "13
December," instead of arguing aimlessly about political alternatives, the
opposition should seek to "open the floodgates" of individual economic
enterprise and increase personal liberty by altering the economic system.
It strongly supports the black market economy and all efforts to form
free enterprise associations. It views uncontrolled market activity as an
essentially positive phenomenon. Its apolitical approach can be classified
as "economic evolutionism"—a gradualist and accommodationist strategy
that avoids major confrontations with the regime while backing a slow
erosion of state economic control, whether through Party reforms or
unofficial economic activities. "December 13" stresses individual freedom
as the basis for reform. It denounces a whole spectrum of political
opposition as "social democrat," placing unacceptable limitations on
personal freedom, and forecasts increasing government tolerance for new
economic initiatives given the perilous state of the economy.

The Catholic Church in Poland has also sponsored political discussion
clubs, meetings, and independent pro-Catholic publications. The Arch-
diocese Council of the Ministries of the Working People in Warsaw has
included a number of prominent Catholic intellectuals, such as Piotr
Naimski and Wiesław Chrzanowski, involved in devising a Church-
oriented workers' organization as an alternative both to Solidarity and
Party institutions.³⁵ Moves have been made to lay the basis for a Christian
Democrat Party, or a likeminded pro-Catholic movement under Church
auspices and tolerated by the regime. The Club for Political Thought
"Dziekania" (KMP"D") has been organized by the veteran Catholic
activist Stanislaw Stomma, who seemingly benefits from Cardinal Glemp's
patronage.³⁶ At least four unofficial political groupings have participated
in the Club's meetings since 1986—"Res Publika," Polish Politics, "13
December," and "Głos." The Club espouses gradualism and has ambitions
to shape the opinions and activities of intellectuals, students, and workers.
Warsaw may indeed allow a more structured political group to crystallize
in its efforts to dissipate and fracture the opposition into "safe" and
"extremist" currents, while maintaining cordial relations with the Church.

Several other efforts have been made to test the government's pluralist
declarations. But applications for the registration of political clubs and
debating societies have borne little fruit. Warsaw may in future purposively
tolerate "constructive" oppositionist groups in order to enhance the
impression of democratization, divide dissent, and entice "moderate"
Catholic intellectuals into some sort of "anti-crisis pact" regularly discussed in the official media. Nonetheless, according to government

spokesmen "socialist pluralism" principally signifies "pluralism within the framework of the socialist system . . . corresponding to legal, political, and constitutional rules."[37] This gives the authorities enormous scope for prohibiting those organizations that ostensibly challenge or undermine Party supremacy. Prominent opposition figures willing to reach some *modus vivendi* with Warsaw face the danger of manipulation without necessarily obtaining tangible or lasting benefits. Their relationship with the Party-state remains fundamentally asymmetrical, in terms of political power, social control, and public influence.

Charter's Czechoslovakia

During the past decade political dissent and public opposition in Czechoslovakia has revolved around the Charter 77 human rights campaign. Charter 77 was essentially the product of debate among disenfranchised intellectuals and reform Communists purged from the CPCS after 1969. The initial signatories, including writers, academics, journalists, former politicians, Party functionaries, technicians, students, and a smattering of blue-collar workers, represented a fairly broad spectrum of Czechoslovak society. The instigators of the Charter sought the widest possible movement of citizens in defense of fundamental civil liberties.[38] According to its founding declaration, dated 1 January 1977, "Charter 77 is a free, informal, and open community of people of different convictions, different faiths, and different professions, united by the will to strive, individually and collectively, for the respect of civic and human rights."[39] The Chartists stressed that they were not establishing a political organization, because Charter 77 had no rules, statutes, permanent bodies, or formal membership. Furthermore, the Charter did not avowedly propose a program of political reform, "but within its own sphere of activity it wishes to conduct a constructive dialogue with the political and state authorities."[40]

Charter 77 urged the involvement of citizens in guarding a spectrum of civil rights.[41] The Chartists demanded that Prague obey its own laws and respect the international obligations it had freely undertaken, including the Helsinki Final Act. The appearance of Charter 77 was psychologically important, because it breached the barrier of fear cultivated by the regime since 1968. The avoidance of political overtones and its commitment to act openly and strictly within the law broadened the Charter's appeal. Though the founders harbored few illusions that the authorities would respond positively to their propositions, they reasoned that Charter 77 could at least create a climate in which far-ranging political changes could eventually materialize.

The question of whether the Chartists should function openly or clandestinely was resolved early on. It was decided that secretive and anonymous activities would be counterproductive, because they would provide Prague with a clear-cut excuse for strangling the movement at birth and dismissing it as an "anti-state conspiracy." On the other hand, by operating openly and disclosing the names of its signatories from the outset, Charter 77 depicted itself as a fully legal human rights campaign without subversive intentions. Moreover, by declaring itself in favor of "constructive dialogue" with the government, the Chartists could further deflect the inevitable official offensive. Several vexing questions have preoccupied the signatories—including whether to opt for a restricted or mass membership. Anyone was at liberty to sign the Charter, but because the movement lacked any formal structure there was little need to recruit masses of activists. Moreover, the Chartists evidently did not rate their success according to the number of signatories, but rather by their effectiveness in influencing the regime and stimulating autonomous citizens' initiatives. The majority of Chartists reasoned that the best compromise between restricted and mass membership was to encourage various cultural and educational pursuits parallel to those controlled by the state.

Charter 77 combines several political and nonpolitical groups and individuals. The Charter does not constitute a formal union or federation of these groups, does not publicly represent any of them, nor has it evolved into a mouthpiece for their views. It has simply provided a platform and an opportunity for action by people who could subordinate their personal opinions and ideological orientations to the larger human rights cause. When the Charter was launched, one of the largest groups to sign was made up of "ex-Communists" or reform Communists, including Dubček's Minister of Foreign Affairs Jiri Hajek. Initially, they formed about half the signatories, but over the years their percentage of the total has declined to a small minority. Little open support for Charter 77 has been forthcoming from the majority of former Party members expelled after the Soviet invasion. Many have become thoroughly disillusioned by the results of "normalization," or were simply not prepared to risk involvement in another reform movement. The influence of reform Communists within Charter 77 has been most noticeable in the signatories' repeated calls for dialogue with the regime, and in the underlying belief that the Party was still capable of instigating reform.

A second sizeable group within Charter 77 consists of a mixture of "democratic socialists" and "independent liberals," including such notable figures as the sociologist Rudolf Battek. A number of them periodically criticize the ex-Communists for unnecessary moderation and have urged more direct political activism. Some of them have even suggested the creation of an avowedly political organization. Although many of the "independents" envisaged little prospect for systemic reform, they conceded that given the political impasse only the application of consistent pressure on the authorities could bring dividends. A campaign for respect for human rights seemed to offer the most realistic chance of success, and could ultimately evolve into a more substantive oppositionist force if circumstances become more favorable. The independent liberals appear to have been the most ardent supporters of independent initiatives in culture and education, and fully supported the pursuit of international contacts with Eastern dissidents and Western sympathizers.[42]

The third significant element within Charter 77 consists of religious activists, including the much persecuted Catholic priest Father Vaclav Maly. The role and influence of religious activists in the Charter has increased steadily during the last decade. The movement provided a forum that helped Protestant, Catholics, and other denominations unite around the campaign for freedom of belief, worship, and assembly. The religious groups have not adopted any specific political orientation, but instead have espoused a practical humanism that enables them to act in concert with nonreligious Chartists. A growing number of practicing Christians have joined the campaign or provided support; some have also been involved in the unofficial "underground Church." In addition to the more well-defined groups and tendencies, Charter 77 has attracted an assortment of unaffiliated intellectuals such as the acclaimed playwright Vaclav Václav, young people from the "cultural underground," and ordinary citizens without strong political views. The wide spectrum of orientations within the Charter apparently has not included any explicitly nationalist or overtly anti-Communist elements. Splinter groups or factions have not materialized and a general unity of purpose has been maintained since 1977.

Despite its longevity, Charter 77 has been unable to kindle widespread and active support among the majority of the population. The crushing of the Prague Spring reforms and two decades of paralyzing "normalization" have left most Czechoslovaks in a resigned mood. Although a majority is latently hostile to the regime, there is little immediate prospect for citizens to exert real influence on government policies. Events in Poland since 1981 have reinforced this standpoint. Like subjects in most other Communist states, Czechoslovs remain skeptical about the advisability of independent action and prefer to divert their attention to private or consumer concerns. The number of Charter 77 signatories stood at under 2,000 in 1988, but calculating the precise number of active supporters or passive sympathizers is more problematic. Irrespective of how many thousands are actually involved in human rights activities, popular support has proved sufficient to enable the movement's active minority to persevere despite constant government harassment. The backbone of Charter 77 activities has consisted of compiling, producing and disseminating various unofficial texts. These include communiques and statements signed by the three annually selected spokespersons, letters, petitions, political or literary essays (*feuilletons*), and current situation reports.[43] These documents explain Charter initiatives and outline concrete proposals for economic and political reform. They are intended for domestic and international audiences by highlighting conditions in Czechoslovakia and canvassing support for the human rights campaign. Besides defending civil liberties and sponsoring independent publishing, educational, and cultural pursuits, Charter 77 has sought to restore "humanism" in social relations. It stresses ethics, morality, honesty, and individual responsibility. Chartists maintain that people need not become members of any specific organization or even sign the Charter, they should simply aim to recreate "elementary human values" in a hostile political setting that favors bribery, dishonesty, corruption, greed, and selfishness.

Charter 77 has stimulated and nurtured the formation of other unofficial groups that have set themselves more specific goals. The most well known and active of these is the Committee for the Defense of the Unjustly Prosecuted (VONS)—established in April 1978.[44] VONS was inspired by individuals who perceived the need for effective assistance to the victims of repression. Its prime objective is to chronicle the case histories of people facing judicial prosecution, imprisonment, or other forms of repression for their independent activities. VONS keeps detailed records of specific cases of persecution, which it makes available to citizens and foreign organizations, including Amnesty International. The Committee provides a lifeline, which the regime has tried to sever, between prisoners, their families, and the outside world. Since May 1978, VONS has regularly issued its own communiques, documents, and extensive lists of prisoners of conscience. Over 750 reports on specific human rights violations have been compiled to date. In December 1978, VONS became a member of the Paris-based International Federation of Human Rights—an associate member of the United Nations. VONS subsequently adopted the subtitle: the Czechoslovak League for Human Rights. Its membership has remained fairly small, numbering about thirty people. But there are several prominent opposition activists in its ranks, such as Ladislav Lis, Vaclav Václav, Rudolf Battek, Otta Bednarova, Stanislav Deraty, and Petr Uhl.

A small, clandestine organization calling itself the Revolutionary Action Group (SRA) was formed in Prague in late 1981. It declared strong support for Poland's Solidarity and called on Czechs and Slovaks to stage protest actions on behalf of Polish workers.[45] Although the SRA scored little success in stirring the masses, the government's repressive response indicated that it viewed the group's efforts with some seriousness. Several workers were apprehended, charged and sentenced for "subversive activities"—consisting of duplicating and distributing material published by Czechoslovak emigres and by Solidarity which "slandered the leading role of the Communist Party" and the "socialist character of the Republic." One of the defendants, Vaclav Sokoup, was accused of trying to "contribute to the importation of the Polish crisis situation into Czechoslovakia." Another prisoner, Jan Wunsch, was assailed for founding an independent organization—the Independent Group for Press and Information—and attempting to "subvert" young workers and high school students. One can deduce from SRA statements that, from a "revolutionary socialist" perspective, it is more explicitly and militantly opposed to the Communist regime than much of the dissident community. In April 1982 the group asserted that it benefited from "the full support of the Czech opposition" and had "significant support among working people, particularly in the industrial areas of central Bohemia."[46] Such claims cannot be verified. The SRA has no formal ties with Charter 77 or VONS, and its influence in the country has proved marginal.

A group of independent political activists, the Democratic Initiative, surfaced in Czechoslovakia in the summer of 1987.[47] It despatched several statements to the Prague government containing four main proposals: economic reform must be accompanied by substantive political change guaranteeing the rights of individuals; the *nomenklatura* system of political appointments should be abandoned; the free flow of information and free access to the media must be assured for all citizens; and a climate of political and religious tolerance should be created. The Democratic Initiative has also requested an amnesty for all political prisoners, freedom to establish independent social organizations and cultural associations, and the cessation of Party control over the country's Churches. The group's appeal to the government in support of sweeping democratization was signed by 184 people. Some of the signatories are linked with Charter 77, others are not; indeed, not all participants have previously been involved in any known dissident activity. The fate of the Initiative under Prague's less than benign "liberalization" remains uncertain.

In recent years Charter 77 itself has increasingly spoken out in favor of political pluralism and announced that it is ready to support and defend almost any independent political endeavor. However, the movement also cautioned that it would continue to avoid formulating any political program or establishing an oppositionist grouping under its auspices.[48] Charter 77 has also attempted to become more visible and gain wider influence by organizing outdoor rallies, symposia, and demonstrations on pertinent occasions. For example, Chartists tried to arrange a rally in Prague on Human Rights Day in December 1987. Despite police harassment and the detention of Charter signatories, several thousand people assembled in the Old Town Square. The Chartists have also appealed for greater grass roots activism in all manner of independent pursuits.[49] Their objective is to expand public activities beyond the narrow confines of the traditional dissident circles. The cautious reforms enacted by the Prague regime are clearly insufficient to satisfy dissident demands and growing popular aspirations.

Dissidents' Hungary

Until the early 1980s criticism of government policy and the workings of the political system in Hungary was confined to a small circle of the intelligentsia. The 1960s had witnessed the emergence of a pro-reformist stream influenced by the writings of the Marxist philosopher Gyorgy Lukacs and the "Budapest School" of Marxist criticism.[50] Its proponents approved of liberal economic reforms and proposed greater political pluralism. The Soviet invasion of Czechoslovakia and reformist reversals in Hungary in the early 1970s came as a blow to these revisionists, many of whom became increasingly disillusioned with official Marxism. By the late 1970s, a number of younger critical intellectuals had largely left reform-Marxism behind and turned to human rights issues to initiate far-reaching transformations in the political system. Nevertheless, they remained reformist oriented rather than "neo-evolutionist," styling themselves as the "democratic opposition."

Budapest upholds a thin and changeable dividing line between permissible criticism and proscribed dissent. This demarcation shifts according to current political requirements and is frequently tested by the opposition in its attempts to extend the reformist debate. Hence Hungary's dissenting intelligentsia is often referred to as the "semi-legal" opposition. Budapest usually avoids open confrontation with the "dissident community," calculating that it can isolate and confine them into obscurity. Occasional crackdowns have been staged when officials perceived a threat of dissident resurgence or the danger that their ideas might gain wider public support. Hungary's economic decline and stringent austerity measures may indeed attract more alienated intellectuals and frustrated workers toward oppositionist activity. A forceful anti-dissident drive could radicalize even wider sectors of the intelligentsia or broaden the popular appeal of oppositionist views.

Links between Magyar dissidents and workers are scant; there are few opportunities to establish such contacts, little sustained effort to cultivate them, and difficulties in maintaining them under the government's watchful eyes. The critical intelligentsia concentrates instead on producing and disseminating uncensored documents and publications, thus acting as an influence group and a rival source of information, analysis, and prognosis for other intellectuals. Fewer than 300 activists are probably involved in the "democratic opposition," though the number of sympathizers far exceeds this figure. The most notable representatives include the architect László Rajk (son of the former Foreign Minister), writers George Konrad and Janos Kenedi, sociologist Miklos Haraszti, philosopher Janos Kis, and the independent publisher Gabor Demszky. Since the early 1980s Hungarian dissenters have increasingly embraced a form of social evolutionism, in calling for an independent press, citizens' defense committees, free labor organizations, and other grassroots public initiatives outside the official system. Even though no durable or sizeable human rights monitoring committees have been formed, several small *ad hoc* groups have sprung up in recent years.[51] The "March 15th Human Rights Group" was formed in Budapest in early 1987, to publicize police action against demonstrators during celebrations of the national anniversary of the abortive 1848 revolution. The independent "Democratic Youth of Hungary" has issued periodic statements since 1986 on specific human rights violations, as has the more "established" dissident press.[52] These initiatives also signal an attempt to forge closer links between dissident intellectuals and young people at the forefront of various antigovernment protests or nationalist manifestations.

Political demonstrations have been staged in Hungary, either on important national anniversaries or in support of dissident calls for democracy and free speech. Protest letters or statements of support have been sent to the government, to other Communist regimes, to oppositionist groups in neighboring states, to Western governments and organizations, and to international forums. Several large meetings have been arranged by dissenters to discuss reform and expand the reach of the opposition. Informal discussion clubs, such as the "Democratic Club" for young people, have proliferated of late, and some have applied for official registration. Efforts have also been made to influence public opinion through "legalistic" or "entryist" channels. For instance, several members of the "democratic opposition" fielded candidates in the May 1985 parliamentary elections, as the new electoral law formally permitted some candidates to be nominated "from the floor." Though the aspirants were excluded from the final election lists, they managed to raise various sensitive issues during public discussions which arguably reached a wider audience than normally has access to the *samizdat* press. Thousands of ordinary citizens thereby obtained some inkling of dissident views on domestic and international issues.

In official estimations, the urbanite, intellectual "radical bourgeois" opposition is divided between a "moderate" and a "confrontationist" wing. Their differences revolve around methods of operation rather than ultimate political objectives. This contrast may mirror our distinction between reformers and evolutionists, or between social and political evolutionists, as well as signifying divergencies in the programs espoused by particular individuals or groupings. The Party has noted an increasing radicalization of the urban opposition since the mid-1980s. Indeed, some dissidents have called for greater unification and a more concrete and concerted program of action to pressure the regime and influence the public, even if this means stepping outside the "semi-legal" parameters. Several *samizdat* journals have put forward liberal democratic programs for a free parliament, political pluralism, and fully independent law courts, as well as proposals for a more cohesive oppositionist organization along Polish or Czechoslovak lines.[53] To prevent the emergence of a stronger dissident lobby, which could undercut their policy of cautious, supervised reform, the authorities have pursued a policy of cooptation and neutralization. Proposals for a "pro-government opposition" have been made by some officials, in which non-Party people would be allowed to criticize publicly certain state programs. These advances have been treated with suspicion by dissidents because Budapest has adopted such tactics previously to emasculate political opposition. Harassment of the "democratic opposition" has continued by way of house searches, confiscations, blacklists, and the levying of heavy fines.

In recent years, several dissident journals have started to campaign for political pluralism in Hungary. In 1986 the outspoken publication *Demokrata* issued a draft program calling for major political reform and institutionalized pluralism.[54] Its demands included: limitations on the Party's "leading role"; tolerance for other "democratic political currents and organizations," as well as social and professional associations; an enhanced role for parliament; a full separation of Party and state; greater local self-government; an independent judiciary; a mixed economy operating according to market principles; and complete individual freedom in the fields of learning, culture, religion, and scientific research, with the abolition of obligatory Marxism-Leninism as a state-sponsored ideology. However, the *Demokrata* group has not proclaimed itself an independent political party and appears to have no immediate plans to do so. In 1987 the leading unofficial journal *Beszelo* also published a detailed project for reform in all important public domains, after prolonged consultation with different strands in the "democratic opposition."[55] Entitled "The Social Contract: Prerequisites for Resolving the Political Crisis," the study is a mixture of proposals for internal Party reform, restrictions on state power, and organizational pluralism. According to the editors and authors, *Beszelo* does not represent any specific, organized oppositionist grouping, but simply endeavors to coordinate dissident work and stimulate public self-organization. It also seeks to influence reformist elements within the establishment to embark on major political changes. The "Social Contract" is designed as a contribution to an urgently needed "national debate" on pressing political and economic issues.

Several *samizdat* publishers regularly issue joint statements about official policy. For example, after the government reshuffle in June 1987, *Beszelo, Demokrata, Hirmondo,* and *Egtajak Kozott* stated that "popular reception to the personnel changes indicates a vote of no confidence for the new leadership." In March 1988 several hundred people signed an appeal calling on the regime to enter into meaningful discussions with independent groups of citizens to overcome the country's deepening crisis. They also backed the creation of a multi-party democracy. More militant political tendencies have also shown some signs of life. For instance, the second issue of *Demokrata* printed a twelve point program by a "radical group of the democratic opposition" that calls for an "end of the Communist Party's monopoly of power."

In the late 1980s there appears to be a more pronounced focus on political and organizational work among Hungary's dissidents. The Federation of Young Democrats was founded in March 1988 as an independent "social organization" for young people aiming to end the monopoly of the Communist Youth League.[56] It was established by 37 students and oppositionist activists whose objective is to create "a social alliance, grouping together politically active, radically reform-minded youth groups and individuals." The Federation did not apply for official registration to avoid state manipulation, but expressed willingness to work openly in accordance with the constitution. The police have issued warnings and threats against the group's members, but it has nonetheless managed to hold meetings and appoint spokesmen; by mid-1988 it claimed some 1,000 members. The Federation has received numerous letters of support from prominent dissident intellectuals.

An umbrella organization for all independent campaigns, called the Network of Free Initiatives, was inaugurated in May 1988 in Budapest.[57] Its purpose is to "express views different from the official version," especially about "political issues of national importance," and to "coordinate the work of independent democratic movements." The Network seeks to provide a framework "independent of state power" that could evolve into an "autonomous political force." The group elected a fifty member council whose members include Kis, Haraszti, the writer Peter Esterhazy, and the historian Gyorgy Litvan. It also selected several spokespersons along the lines of Charter 77, to represent the Network vis-a-vis the government and other interested parties. The organizers have urged the population to "renounce fatalism" and participate in

Network ventures. The group held its first national conference in June 1988 with the participation of all major oppositionist movements, despite official attempts to prevent the meeting. Budapest seems uncertain as to how best to deal with such initiatives; while avoiding comprehensive repression it has been unable to neutralize them. During the current period of economic reform and the regime's self-proclaimed "liberalization," a major crackdown against the opposition could prove damaging by alienating influential intellectuals and further impairing economic performance. In the long term, however, repression may be essential if the Party's political monopoly is to be preserved, and if measures to provide a "legal framework" to depoliticize non-state associations prove inadequate to restrain growing dissent.

A long-standing division exists in the Hungarian opposition between urban based, social democratic or liberal intellectuals, and the pro-agrarian, traditionalist or nationalist populists. A segment of the "populist opposition" draws upon the political traditions of the Smallholders Party, the strongest postwar political organization before the Communist seizure of power. Since the late 1950s the populists, mainly of the older generation, have largely accommodated themselves to the prevailing system of government without necessarily sharing the HSWP's ideology or objectives. They acquiesced to a regime which claimed to be seeking "national unity," echoing Kádár's dictum that "whoever is not against us is for us." Populist activists appeared more fearful of a decimation of the population through bloodshed or emigration than of an authoritarian government engaged in national reconstruction. Exploiting such passivity or muted support, Budapest gave some populists prominent positions in a number of Party-controlled institutions.[58]

In 1985 several former peasant-populist activists expressed their disillusionment with Kádár's policies and embarked on bolder oppositionist work. Discussion clubs and unofficial meetings have been organized under the aegis of the Writer's Association in which populist viewpoints carry some weight. One of its most prominent representatives is Istvan Csurka, a writer and playwright whose works have been banned for several years but who has recently reemerged from relative obscurity. The leading pro-populist literary monthly *Tiszataj* is published openly with government permission, though occasional crackdowns have been engineered when particularly critical articles have appeared. *Tiszataj* and other populist publications and discussion forums intend to extend their base of support by influencing students, teachers, and rural intellectuals.

The Budapest regime styles the more outspoken populists as a "radical nationalist" trend. In fact, some prominent populists have become increasingly critical of the Party's record on patriotism, nationalism, morality, ethics, and the Magyar minority question in Romania and elsewhere;

their chief spokesman is Sandor Csoori. The minority issue has preoccupied populists in recent years and has become an important rallying point for all government critics. Hungarian nationalists within and outside populist circles have been perturbed by the government's inadequate response to Romanian discrimination against the large Magyar population in Transylvania. The Grosz regime has evidently taken note of such criticism and endeavored to use the minority controversy to its advantage by protesting against Bucharest's policies and deflecting attention from growing domestic unrest.

Populists boast a loose association of writers disseminating their ideas primarily through rural cultural centers and literary journals. They benefit from strong influence in the Writers Association and in several universities where tolerance of Party interference is reportedly decreasing. Though they have not yet undertaken organized political work, government reports estimate that the "potential base" of the "radical nationalists" is far larger than that of the urban liberal intellectuals because of the broad popularity of their views.[59] Many populists have become perturbed and galvanized by mounting economic problems and various social ailments including alcoholism, drug abuse, family breakups, and a high suicide rate. Less concerned with Party reforms or even extra-Party political activity, they concentrate on restoring what are perceived to be traditional Christian and Hungarian values, such as the work ethic, morality, humanism, and honesty. They assert that these values must be resuscitated either by the regime or by organizations beyond its purview. Budapest fears that pro-populist intellectuals, workers, and students may increasingly dismiss the Communist system as an alien and alienating force, rather than viewing it as an indigenous compromise under unfavorable geopolitical conditions.

Populist activists have staged occasional mass meetings and conferences—in Monor in June 1985 and at an important session in Lakitelek in September 1987—to discuss major national problems. The Lakitelek meeting was presided over by Gyula Fekete, a prominent populist writer, and Imre Pozsgay, secretary of the official Peoples' Patriotic Front who became a Politburo member in May 1988.[60] Populism evokes apprehension in Party circles, so the regime has attempted to channel such influences away from overt opposition and into the HSWP. The Lakitelek conference was highlighted by the creation of the Hungarian Democratic Forum, which is to be open to all "democratic and national forces,"[61] that support a "radical reform of the socialist system." Its reformist focus is evident in appeals for various improvements in the functioning of parliament; but its program also transcends the confines of the one-party system by proposing a "democratic elective franchise law" and a new national constitution. The Forum has reportedly garnered wide public support, while the authorities, wary of its appeal, have withheld official recognition or legalization. The Grosz regime may decide to handle the Forum through a delicate mixture of concession, negotiation, and division, as any outright repression could further damage the tentative reform process. Populist and other independent initiatives are evidently to be closely monitored and controlled by the regime where possible, and isolated where necessary.

In April 1988, four prominent reformers within the HSWP who had attended the Lakitelek meeting were expelled from the Party for expressing views critical of the official line. They were Mihaly Bihari, a political scientist and author of a salient study on political reform barred from official publication; Zoltan Kiraly, an editor and reporter; the writer Zoltan Biro; and the economist László Lengyel. All four affirmed that successful economic reform depends on substantive political change limiting Party control. The leadership of the Democratic Forum expressed dismay at the expulsions, declaring that they made any genuine consensus between Party and society all the more improbable. There have also been signs of greater cooperation between populists and the "democratic opposition" since 1982, with periodic consultations and some coordination of protest actions, such as collecting signatures for petitions. In the past Budapest has exploited rifts between the two political strands to guarantee the fragility of any proposed oppositionist alliance. In the future the regime could find it more difficult to prevent such independent dissident initiatives from coalescing, as their campaigns for reform may increasingly converge.

Rudimentary Political Resistance

The seeds of political opposition and human rights activism have been sown in the remaining three Soviet bloc states, but these are still amorphous and small scale. In the GDR political dissent has been submerged and restricted by government repression, stifling social controls, and deliberately fostered apoliticization.[62] During the mid-1970s prominent government critics, including disheartened former Party officials, surfaced in East German intellectual circles. Many adopted a revisionist Marxist or Eurocommunist position, including Robert Havemann, Stefan Heym, Rudolf Bahro, and Wolf Biermann.[63] Until his death in 1982, Havemann was a symbol and a focus of East German intellectual opposition. In recent years dissent in the GDR has become less fixed on individual intellectual non-conformists; it is now more decentralized and issue-oriented. It consists of informal networks of small local groups meeting in private homes and churches to plan strategy. Occasional anti-state protests have also occurred, involving leaflet distribution and public gatherings in opposition to particular government policies. Individual acts of non-conformism are often apolitical, but collide with Party-state interests when they are manifest in the public domain by artists, musicians, religious believers, or members of the youth counter culture. Such groupings rarely display ties with the industrial workforce or the technical intelligentsia operating within the ambit of the SUP. Occasional worker protests have been staged, usually over specific economic grievances though sometimes encompassing wider political demands. For instance, anonymous East Berlin workers in 1981 distributed printed flyers containing an "Appeal to All Working People" and calling for nineteen concrete political and social reforms and an amnesty for political prisoners.[64] Other workers' protests and work stoppages have had narrower objectives, such as pay rises, increased food supplies, and decreased work norms.

Human rights activism in the GDR has concentrated largely on freedom to emigrate to the West. Several hundred people have been arrested for attempting to leave the country illegally. East Berlin periodically eases pressures for emigration and attempts to deflate the civil rights movement by granting "amnesties" for prisoners of conscience and issuing exit visas to persistent "troublemakers." The GDR's human rights campaign also has links to the movement for disarmament. Its main organ appears to be the Peace and Human Rights Initiative, which specifically tied together the issues of peace, human rights, and political freedoms, and set out to monitor official violations of civil liberties.[65] The group, initially known as "Menschenrechte DDR," purportedly has contacts in three cities with about 100 active sympathizers who write and circulate letters and collect signatures. The group was formed in early 1985 according to the Charter 77 model, with three spokespersons in East Berlin issuing moderate pro-human rights statements, providing information to Western visitors, and inviting the regime to engage in dialogue and implement reforms. The Initiative has suffered police persecution, and several of the founders have left the country under duress.

Other loose local groups have been established in the GDR to press for human rights, and for fewer restrictions on foreign travel and East-West communication in general. Public demonstrations have been staged in East Berlin and other cities in support of freer emigration policies. For example, about 1,000 people protested in the capital in September 1987, and 2,000 people gathered in February 1988 in St. Bartholomew's Church demanding the right to emigrate; similar meetings have reportedly taken place in over thirty towns.[66] In some cases individuals barred from emigrating have formed self-help groups in the face of government intimidation to publicize their grievances and issue petitions. Not all of the protestors are political dissidents; many simply seek family reunification or better economic prospects in the West. In some instances, conflicts have arisen between dissidents campaigning to alter the political system but intent on remaining in the GDR, and individuals principally concerned with securing their own emigration. The authorities have exploited such antagonisms to sow confusion and prevent the spread of a unified opposition. This is often accomplished by allowing some individuals to emigrate or by pressuring into exile those who would prefer to stay.

A handful of independent political groups have appeared and disappeared in the GDR, leaving little imprint on official policy. The majority have been small, loosely structured, and cemented by friendship and shared life styles or professional interests. An anonymous left-wing group announced its existence in early 1981, styling itself as an underground political party. It demanded political reform, free trade unions, and a return to "genuine Communism," and claimed cells in East Berlin, Magdeburg, Leipzig, and Rostock.[67] Ten members of the group were arrested on charges of agitation hostile to the state, and little subsequent activism was reported. In addition to creating an unfavorable climate for the germination of organized opposition, the regime undertakes periodic clampdowns. For example, in January 1988 dozens of dissidents were exiled, imprisoned, or otherwise deterred from further resistance to official policy.[68] Periods of relative tolerance are designed to lull Western public opinion and to avoid creating visible martyrs that might radicalize the opposition movement.

Public dissent in Romania can be traced back to the late 1970s, especially to the writer Paul Goma who called for the implementation of human rights provisions guaranteed by the country's constitution and numerous international accords. The Ceausescu regime has dealt swiftly and severely with dissenters by isolating them, forcing them to emigrate, applying administrative and police reprisals, or imprisoning them.[69] Most prisoners of conscience are held for individual acts of protest rather than organized opposition. Their courageous non-conformism has had little resonance in Romanian society, at least in terms of visible public support. Outspoken statements by Romanian intellectuals periodically reach the West, signalling that dissident currents have not been entirely extinguished by Bucharest. Prominent among the dissenters are: Dorin Tudoran, a writer critical of the intelligentsia for its passivity, pessimism, and subservience, who has called for greater intellectual activism; Mihai Botez, a mathematician and former government economic adviser disparaging of Ceausescu's megalomania and disastrous economic policies who has emerged as the most prominent dissident spokesman; and Silviu Brucan, a social science professor and former ambassador to the U.S. and U.N., who has appealed for political reform to avoid a profound domestic crisis.[70] Brucan is a Marxist revisionist who questions the Leninist principles of "democratic centralism" and "anti-factionalism." He has called for "democratization" of the ruling Party, rather than a genuine multi-party parliamentary system.

Other known oppositionist pioneers in Romania have included: Radu Filipescu, an electronics engineer who produced and disseminated leaflets in Bucharest in May 1983 calling upon citizens to "show courage" and stage peaceful demonstrations against the regime[71]; Nicolae Stanescu, an engineer, and Ion Fistioc, an architect, both of whom held middle-level positions in economic ministries and issued documents in 1987 attacking Ceausescu's "dogmatism" and "personality cult." Stanescu and Fistioc have demanded a larger role for professionals and technocrats in economic planning and management; they espouse a reformist rather than a political evolutionist or pluralist platform. Such outspokenness may indicate increasing discontent with the incompetence of the regime among Romania's professionals and intellectuals. Despite sporadic industrial unrest during the past decade, no organized mass movement or durable pressure group has emerged in Romania. Spontaneous workers' demonstrations over falling living standards and wage cuts were held in Brasov in November 1987; 10,000 workers from two major factories conducted a march through the streets and ransacked the local Party headquarters before being forcibly dispersed by the police.[72] Other protests were held the same month in the Danube port of Braile and the Moldavian city of Sibiu; some sympathy protests by disgruntled students were also reported. Such explosions have been effectively isolated and quelled by the government; its leaders and organizers are imprisoned or confined in "re-education" institutions.

Some critics have focused on Bucharest's poor human rights record and demanded speedy improvements. Efforts have been made to establish monitoring groups, but the authorities swiftly suppress such endeavors. The independent Hungarian Press of Transylvania has for several years remained the sole functioning human rights group in the country, primarily concerned with abuses against the large Magyar minority. In 1986 the Romanian Association for the Defense of Human Rights was formed by National Peasant activists, with members in Bucharest, Sibiu, and Reghin.[73] The group's founding charter contained a thorough critique of Romania's civil rights record. This presaged a severe crackdown: its organizers, including Florian Russu and Christian Batusina, were jailed and harassed without any formal legal proceedings so as not to draw publicity to the incident. Other human rights activists have been accused of "parasitism" or "anarchical conduct," summarily tried, and given "corrective labor" as punishment.

The rudiments of autonomous political activity have also been evident in recent years. Romania's "historical parties" subdued by the Communists after World War II—the Liberal Party and the National Peasants Party—continue to signal their existence though in a substantially weakened form.[74] Both have issued documents since early 1985 advocating specific political and economic policy changes. Ion Bratianu, who died in September 1987, belonged to a family which for over a century produced prominent leaders of the Liberal Party. He addressed several letters to the regime with concrete reform proposals, and spoke out in favor of individual liberties, free debate about reform, and greater governmental accountability. Well-known members of the outlawed National Peasants Party have continued meeting privately and striven to develop some form of organization. Much of their political activity is symbolic, such as issuing statements to Romanian exiles in the West. The funerals of several aged Peasant Party members in Bucharest and Transylvania were occasions for sizeable gatherings promptly dispersed by the police.

Efforts have also been made to attract new recruits to the National Peasants. Several workers in Bucharest were interrogated in 1982 and 1983 for allegedly supporting the group, and a National Peasant Youth Group was established in 1986 claiming young workers as members. Ion Puiu, a former Peasant youth leader, authored a party policy document in 1985 and petitioned to run as an independent candidate for elections to the National Assembly in March 1985. The Peasant platform is pro-pluralist and reformist within the "existing constitutional framework," it demands legal guarantees for civil liberties, the depoliticization of the legal and educational systems, the abolition of Communist Party privileges, and a mixed economy.[75] Both of the independent Romanian parties remain small, with little or no effect on government policy. However, they do signify the continuity of non-Communist political currents despite Ceausescu's tyranny and they could presage some political resurgence in the event of future domestic instability or internal reform.

The Romanian Democratic Action, a small anonymous and explicitly political group appeared in November 1985 with the publication of a policy document reminiscent of the independent Liberal Party platform. The program was smuggled out of the country late in 1986. Signed by 13 political dissidents using pseudonyms, it called for parliamentary democracy and the restoration of a mixed economy.[76] Though the group has not issued a concrete plan of action to achieve its political objectives, it has distributed leaflets in several towns calling for public demonstrations against the regime. It appears to have no extensive links with any major strata of Romanian society, and seems less concerned with internal Party reforms than with extra-systemic democratic pluralism along pre-war lines. The group's activists meet infrequently and maintain a loose organizational network to avoid police detection. Reports suggest that its participants are mostly white-collar employees and older intellectuals whose political involvement predates RCP rule.

Political dissent in Bulgaria has been asphyxiated under Zhivkov; its rare appearance is quickly combatted and silenced. Difficulties in obtaining direct information from non-official sources hinder a full appraisal of the scope of political opposition. But despite government denials of the existence of dissent, occasional statements and attacks by Party officials indicate that some oppositionist undercurrents persist in the country. Public warnings and threats are used to underscore that open dissent will not be tolerated.[77] Criticisms of the Zhivkov leadership have occasionally surfaced in rough *samizdat* form or even in some approved publications before being suppressed with their authors punished. Individual or collective acts of protest may in fact be more frequent than is commonly supposed, but without ready outlets there is little or no public record and the "culprits" have been "neutralized." Some dissidents have been forced into exile or voluntarily emigrated, others have been given little opportunity to express their dissatisfaction.[78] According to Bulgarian exile sources, several hundred political opponents of the regime languish in prison, convicted of spying, sabotage, conspiracy, hooliganism, obstruction of the police, fighting with the militia, or trying to leave Bulgaria "illegally."[79]

Human rights activism has been sporadic and individualistic. Unofficial documents periodically reach the West from civil rights advocates protesting official abuses and urging guarantees of a broad range of liberties. "Declaration 78" was signed by a group calling itself "ABD" and demanding freedom of the press and religion, authentic elections, the establishment of autonomous labor unions, free emigration, and the revocation of repressive laws against would-be emigrants.[80] Throughout the 1980s a few courageous Bulgarians petitioned the authorities to respect their human rights pledges. For instance, Yanko Yankov was sentenced to two years in prison in 1984 for visiting Western embassies to discuss human rights issues and for allegedly being a member of a monitoring group; in 1983 Volodya Nakov was diagnosed a "psychopath" and thrown out of work for seeking information on international human rights and peace accords.[81] In January 1987, six activists sent an appeal to the CSCE conference in Vienna complaining about Sofia's poor human rights record and proposing that an international commission monitor the observance of the Helsinki accords in Bulgaria.[82] All six were arrested and interrogated; one of the protestors, Ilya Stoyanov Minev (who has served 27 years in prisons and labor camps) has been adopted by Amnesty International as a "prisoner of conscience" on two occasions. Several others are recognizable for their civil rights activism in the past, including Tzeko Krustev Tzekov, Bozhidar Evstatiev Statev, and Eduard Genov Genov.

Human rights protests signal some attempts at dissident coordination, through appeals for international recognition and protection. The regime regards public criticism of its policies as inadmissible, and activists have been given little opportunity to meet, gather information, issue documents, campaign for changes, or create any coherent movement. But despite government obstruction, in January 1988 a group of Bulgarian dissidents formed the Independent Association for the Defense of Human Rights, to seek international support for civil liberties.[83] The Association has issued several documents and exposed various cases of official persecution in the country. Though it is premature to speak of an active, organized political opposition in Bulgaria, some collective public protests have taken place during the 1980s—including the distribution of flyers, small street demonstrations, and sit-in strikes.[84] In late 1985, *samizdat* material was circulated in the capital, supposedly produced by unidentified workers in a local locomotive factory and signed "Dimitrov."[85] The lengthy document contained pointed criticisms of the government, and demanded substantial pay increases. It appealed to the population to stage protests against the "machinery of exploitation and oppression." The text was distributed in several districts outside the capital, and called upon readers to reproduce and further distribute the appeal. Some anti-Zhivkov opposition has also appeared over the years within the political establishment or on its peripheries, but has been firmly dealt with by the regime. It is difficult to determine, however, whether this is a disguised internal power struggle, a reformist current within the BCP, or simply cases of individual opposition to particular features of Communist rule that are manifested during periodic lapses in official supervision.

Conclusion

During the past decade, human rights movements and politically oriented oppositionist groups in Eastern Europe have varied greatly in terms of size, longevity, program, strategy, and impact. Their size and durability has often been closely related to the intensity, pervasiveness, and effectiveness of Party control and police repression. Also significant is the leeway allowed by Communist regimes for a non-state private and public domain, whether through temporary tactical convenience or long-term political necessity. The extent of organized dissent and opposition is also influenced by national post-war traditions of collective resistance to the Party-state.

In Poland, despite the crushing of Solidarity as a mass organization and cohesive social movement, human rights, social self-defense, and autonomous political groupings proliferate in both overt and covert conditions; also intact is the dispersed network of the free labor union. The Warsaw regime has attempted to eradicate, divide, co-opt, and neutralize those movements which benefit from substantial public support or challenge the Party's key privileges and powers. But in their quest for economic reform the authorities tread a precarious dividing line between outright repression and guarded liberalization. In Czechoslovakia human rights activism centered around Charter 77 has remained relatively constant since the late 1970s. But the civil liberties campaign has helped to spawn various citizens' movements harboring specific economic and political grievances, and has laid some groundwork for organized opposition in a highly repressive domestic climate. In Hungary, dissident currents among the "democratic opposition" intellectuals and the traditionalist "populists" are assuming more politicized forms. The Budapest regime is exploring ways to incorporate acceptable or "constructive" displays of popular criticism in its reform program without surrendering the Party's pre-eminent role. In the GDR, Romania, and Bulgaria political dissent has been seriously hampered by official persecution. It has tended to concentrate where feasible on specific government human rights abuses and proposals for their rectification, as well as the general extension of freedoms in the cultural, social, religious, and economic realms. Political opposition in these three states has remained basic and small-scale; it shows little immediate sign of expansion, particularly in the shadow of the regimes' limited reformist agendas.

5

Religious Activities

On paper, there is considerable religious freedom in Eastern Europe. Freedom to congregate for worship and to observe religious ritual is enshrined in most of the state constitutions of the region. Though there is a constitutional separation of Church and State, and dominance is conferred upon atheistic propaganda, religious belief *per se* is not outlawed. In practice, however, laity and clergy are strictly circumscribed by secular law. Seen through the prism of official Communist ideology, religion is essentially an atavistic pursuit doomed to irrelevance in an "advanced socialist" state. Religious leaders and religious institutions are, with varying degrees of success, subjugated to the Communist Party's "leading role" in society and politics.

Aggressive attempts to eradicate religion in Eastern Europe reached a peak of zeal in the Stalinist era. Historic churches and cathedrals were desecrated and turned into museums, warehouses, and ruins. Religious leaders who refused to sign loyalty oaths to the Communist authorities were imprisoned *en masse* and, in some cases, summarily executed. Religious seminaries, schools, publishing houses and charities were severely threatened by budgetary cutbacks and outright closure. From the training of clergy to the religious indoctrination of young people, religion was placed under threat of extinction by order of Communist orthodoxy.

The historic bridge between the theory and practice of Marxist-Leninist atheism was erected in Eastern Europe by Stalin.[1] The Soviet leader's aggressive war on religion in the USSR was faithfully transposed to the East bloc by staunchly pro-Moscow regimes and Party chiefs. The Stalinist period was characterized primarily by the use of brute force and the application of mass terror to carry out the dictates of state policy. In the arena of religion, total eradication was declared by atheist officials; the ensuing battle was a one-sided attack, frequently violent, inexorable, and underhand. Nevertheless, the state did not emerge as unchallenged victor. Responses to the Stalinist offensive against religion varied from country to country. Attempts to coerce and co-opt religious leaders were not wholly ineffective, but sometimes resulted in pro-regime and anti-regime dichotomies within religious hierarchies and communities. Officially sanctioned religious organizations, such as PAX in Poland or, later, *Pacem in Terris* in Czechoslovakia, emerged with strong government sponsorship; members of these organizations endeavored to win the hearts and minds of believers without arousing the ire of their Communist overlords. While serving as mouthpieces for official policies and positions, they frequently alienated segments of their flock instead of winning new adherents.

The battle to preserve the morals and morale of traditional religious groups did, in several notable cases, inspire spirited resistance. Cardinals Wyszynski and Mindszenty in Poland and Hungary, respectively, did, for example, come to stand for unflinching and uncompromising religious conviction. Both men sought to protect the moral authority and autonomy of their Churches against State encroachment; both scored a number of historic victories amid occasional defeats. At the grassroots, there have also been in recent years spontaneous outpourings of religious fervor in Poland, Czechoslovakia, East Germany, Romania, and Hungary. Dissident intellectuals and workers have fought religious persecution as well through such agencies as Solidarity in Poland and Charter 77 in Czechoslovakia.

This chapter will focus above all on popular resistance to official atheization drives in the past decade. We will explore the independent social initiatives of religious activists as well as the organizational initiatives of intact religious hierarchies. We will not trace the entire evolution of Church-state conflict in Eastern Europe from its inception in the postwar era, but rather highlight the main currents of religious activism, particularly as they have developed in the recent past. Rather than provide a country by country summary of religious upheaval, we have opted for a comparative study that groups together countries under the rubrics of distinct religious creeds. Hence, we will consider the origins and aspects of opposition to state policy in the religious communities of Roman Catholicism, Protestantism, the Orthodox Church and smaller faiths and sects.

Roman Catholicism

Although the institutional infrastructure of the Roman Catholic Church has suffered serious postwar deterioration in some countries, such as Czechoslovakia, even here there has been an unmistakable stirring in recent years of grassroots revival. The picture is considerably rosier in Poland and even Hungary, where the Church has shown marked vitality in the past decade. One factor behind this phenomenon is the 1978 selection of a Slavic Pope who has been an outstanding world leader and a source of special solace and inspiration throughout the region. Another equally significant development has been the emergence of a younger generation throughout Eastern Europe that has demonstrated its disillusionment with Marxism-Leninism and turned to the Church— not only, it must be emphasized, the Roman Catholic Church—as a moral authority above and relatively autonomous from Communist Party or government authorities.

In assessing the importance of Roman Catholicism as a focal point for dissent and popular opposition, it is important to note that the Church has played institutional, symbolic, supportive, and protective roles in buttressing activities and viewpoints opposed to official secular policies at many historical junctures. Perhaps the most striking example of Roman Catholicism fulfilling all of these functions in conjunction can be seen in contemporary Poland, not only during the legal Solidarity era, but also in successive periods of crisis and convulsion before and since. One of the greatest achievements of postwar Catholicism in Eastern Europe has been the emergence of religious leaders of towering moral stature. Personalities such as Archbishop Stefan Wyszynski of Poland or Archbishop Joszef Mindszenty of Hungary were inspiring in their postwar resistance to Communist repression.[2] Their many acts of protest galvanized anti-Communist sentiment within their respective countries, dramatized the plight of their Churches in the West, and safeguarded for a time the relative independence and moral authority of their national Churches. More recently, Cardinal Karol Wojtyła of Cracow, now Pope John Paul II, has been an outspoken and influential defender of human rights in his native land and Eastern Europe generally.

In Poland, as in no other East European country, expressions of religion and nationalism merge. Some 33 million Poles are adherents of the Roman Catholic Church[3], constituting well over 90 percent of the total population. At times of social upheaval, when the populace and the Party have met in direct confrontation—as in the worker protests of 1970, 1976, and 1980—the Catholic Church has played a key role as mediator for and moderator of popular discontent. Indeed, through many centuries of foreign occupation and partition, the Polish Church has served as "the guardian of the nation's language, history, and culture."[4] In this role, it continues to function to this day. Prominent among its various educational endeavors is its administration of the Catholic University of Lublin (KUL)—the only independent university in the East bloc. Catechism classes and Sunday schools run by the Church offer young Poles an alternative vision of history, and a value system that is distinct from Leninist dogma.

The emblems of religious faith were very much in evidence when striking workers at the Lenin Shipyards made history in Gdańsk in August 1980. Impetus for the Solidarity free trade union movement was, many analysts have noted, to be found in the popular euphoria and national optimism created by Pope John Paul II's first trip to his homeland in June 1979.[5] Among the earliest demands of the striking workers on the Baltic Coast was the request that a Catholic mass be nationally broadcast on state-controlled Polish radio every Sunday. Solidarity leader Lech Wałęsa was himself a living symbol of creative social resistance and, concomitantly, deeply held religious belief. Throughout the upheaval he attended mass daily, carried a rosary, and wore the image of the Black Madonna of Czestochowa on his jacket lapel.[6] Though the union was nondenominational in character, most of its leaders were devout Catholics, and many, including Wałęsa, claimed to draw crucial political inspiration from their religious faith, conferring frequently with sympathetic clergymen. Additionally, lay Catholics played an important role as advisors to the union at all organizational levels.

Until 1980, when Solidarity was formed, the Polish Catholic Church was the only organized, or institutional, force in the country which cut across all social groups and confronted the government when the latter abused the civil and human rights of individuals or autonomous groups.[7] Yet the Church, despite defending dissident groups, prudently maintained a formal distance from them.[8] This distance was, however, not always expansive enough for the Communist apparatus, which employed a variety of tactics designed to undermine the widespread popular appeal of the clergy and limit its potential political influence.[9]

There is a long history in postwar Poland of official attempts to split the unity of the Church and "buy" influence among priests who have not been outspoken in opposition to government policies or actions. Such attempts to co-opt segments of the clergy began in the late 1940s, when the authorities launched their misleadingly named "patriotic priests" movement, designed to create a body of regime-loyal clergymen.[10] The initiative enjoyed limited success and survives today in a stunted form under the aegis of the PAX Association. Founded in 1946 by a former Fascist, Bolesław Piasecki, PAX was intended to provide a rallying point for pro-Communist Catholics. The organization has never been recognized by the Catholic hierarchy, and priests are actually forbidden to join it.[11] In the mid-1970s, it claimed approximately 4,000 members, but is now believed to be very much smaller. Its chief activities are in publishing, where its work attracts a fairly wide readership. Since Piasecki's death in 1979, the hierarchy has been slightly more open to the organization, although still disapproving of it. PAX is represented in the Polish Parliament, or Sejm.

A Catholic association established in 1956 with the approval of the hierarchy was "Znak" (The Sign). The group launched a highly respected monthly magazine that bore its name. The publication was suppressed during the Stalinist era, but when the Gomułka regime came to power in 1956, the group was allowed to take over from PAX the weekly newspaper *Tygodnik Powszechny*. Perhaps more important, "Znak" at the same time was permitted to establish Catholic Intellectual Clubs, or KlKs, in Warsaw, Cracow, Wrocław, Toruń, and Poznań. These clubs have since been an extremely important source of alternate thinking about Communist policies and actions, often providing a strong current of oppositionist philosophy and commentary. Until 1976, the "Znak" movement also had five deputies in the Sejm "who constituted the nearest thing to an opposition party in the whole of Eastern Europe."[12]

The first KIKs were established in 1956 as local branches of an emergent national lay Catholic intelligentsia movement.[13] Two years later, however, the movement was stifled by an intolerant regime and only a few clubs were permitted to operate in selected major cities. The situation changed in 1980 and 1981 when, prompted by a spontaneous mass movement toward public self-organization, many new clubs surfaced throughout Poland and were registered by local authorities. All these clubs were suspended following the declaration of martial law in December 1981. Though some of them were never officially registered, more than 40 continue to operate. Financially self-sufficient but closely cooperating with the Church, the clubs sponsor lectures and organize social gatherings and cultural events for lay Catholics.[14] They thereby serve an important role as shelters and supporters of independent cultural activities in the form of educational seminars, art exhibitions, poetry readings, and lectures.

In recent years, Warsaw has repeatedly made efforts to attract to its ranks well-known Catholic intellectuals, most of whom are active in the clubs and critical of the Jaruzelski regime. Few KIK members have responded positively to these official overtures, regarding them as a tactic to split and weaken groups that had been disparaging official policies rather than as a means of real involvement in the political process. Meanwhile, though enjoying a reputation for prudence and moderation, KIK leaders continue to maintain close contacts with opponents of the government, notably in the Solidarity movement with its strong links to grassroots lay Catholic intellectuals and workers.

The Church in Poland found itself in a very difficult position after the government attack on Solidarity in December 1981. The Catholic leadership did not want to be drawn into the political vacuum left in the wake of martial law, but a large segment of the population clearly expected the Church to more resolutely defend human rights, and to campaign strongly for the reinstatement of Solidarity. As a result, the Polish Primate, Cardinal Józef Glemp, has been performing a delicate balancing act between public aspirations for democracy and civil liberties, and incessant government pressure against the Church's political involvement. Criticisms of his performance from both sides largely stem from this unrewarding predicament. But despite Glemp's concern lest the Church be drawn into a major political confrontation with the regime, he has spoken out strongly against official repression and backed the pronouncements of his bishops. The Church has aided thousands of persecuted individuals and their families and provided sanctuary to an assortment of independent social activities.

Post-martial law Poland has also witnessed the political radicalization of a significant number of clergymen who maintain supportive relations with imprisoned or persecuted members of the banned Solidarity movement. The response of the Communist authorities has been vigorously hostile, resulting in a war of attrition that has been characterized by vicious official propaganda, veiled warnings to priests against political activity and, in some cases, direct physical assault. The best known case of violent retribution concerns the abduction and murder of the outspoken Warsaw cleric Jerzy Popiełuszko in October 1984.[15] The crime against the 37 year-old priest was committed by four secret police officers later convicted by the Polish Supreme Court. It is widely believed that the murderers were acting with the prior knowledge and possibly a direct mandate from the upper echelons of the Polish Politburo. Popiełuszko had previously been harassed by security police and received numerous official warnings to cease making political pronouncements from the pulpit.

At the beginning of September 1984, government spokesman Jerzy Urban singled out three extremely popular priests with strong Solidarity links and gave them an ominous warning.[16] During one of his weekly press conferences for foreign correspondents, Urban said:

> Some priests, among them [Jerzy] Popiełuszko in Warsaw, [Henryk] Jankowski in Gdańsk, and [Kazimierz] Jancarz in Nowa Huta, continue to transform religious masses into political rallies and attempt to stir up people's emotions. They do this contrary to the recommendations of the Episcopate and in defiance of our patient warnings that such activities will not be tolerated. Everyone in Poland should be convinced by now that we do not throw our words to the wind.[17]

After this and similar statements from official sources, priests continued to preach morally uplifting sermons from the pulpit, supporting the aims and ideals of Solidarity. But many took unprecedented precautions, such as the installation of bodyguards selected from their local communities. Some also began to implore their congregations to disperse immediately following Church services. They did so to avoid government charges of provoking attacks by ZOMO riot police on unarmed demonstrators at spontaneously arranged marches following Sunday masses in the major cities.

Opposition to government policies on religious issues assumed wider proportions in Poland in 1984 during the so-called "war of the crosses."[18] The nationwide conflict arose when the Warsaw government took active steps to remove religious symbols and icons from the premises of all public buildings, such as schools and university halls. Large scale protests resulted, with pupils and students organizing demonstrations of nonviolent or passive resistance. Officials, at first unmoved by the protests, were later compelled to discontinue their campaign. As a result, an estimated 50 percent of crosses and icons were left untouched by the regime; but the potential for renewed conflict between the secular authorities and young believers persists to this day.

Poland has witnessed both a growth in religious observance since the late 1970s and an expansion of the Catholic Church as an institution. For example, recruitment into the clergy has risen steadily during the past decade. According to Church statistics released in January 1984, there were 20,198 clerics in 1979, and 21,643 by 1983; the figure has increased since. In addition, the number of churches has grown significantly during the same period—over 100 new ones were reportedly built between 1982 and 1985. The Communist regime has tolerated this phenomenon in order to release social pressure, deflect domestic and international criticism of its religious policies, and appease the Church hierarchy at a time of grave social and economic crisis. Further "concessions" to the Catholic Church are also in the process of negotiation, including the legalization of the institution, and the establishment of formal diplomatic ties between Warsaw and the Vatican. In some respects, this has helped to obscure the fact that the overriding and long-term goal of the Party is to restrict the Church to an officially defined "religious role" devoid of all meaningful political involvement in public affairs.

Of the three principal Christian churches in Hungary, the Roman Catholic is by far the largest. Until 1945 it was—aside from the years immediately following the post-Reformation period—the dominant power in a feudal Hungarian society, owning vast tracts of land and claiming the allegiance of the nobility and major landowners.[19] Historically, the Catholic hierarchy has enjoyed considerable influence in the corridors of power. Thus, during the interwar years, when Admiral Miklos Horthy served as Regent, it was unquestioned that his deputy should be the Primate of Hungary.[20] The Catholic Church in Hungary has historically drawn adherents from the whole of the country, which is divided into eleven dioceses. However, its main strength is rooted in the area to the west of the Danube. There are presently about six million baptized Catholics, representing 65% of the country's total population of 10.5 million. In 1980 there were 3,600 Catholic priests, of whom 2,800 were actively ministering, serving an estimated 2,000 Latin-Rite parishes and about 150 Uniate parishes.[21] Priests are trained in five diocesan seminaries, one of which is Uniate, and there is also a Catholic theological academy located in Budapest. This same academy offers three-year correspondence courses in theology for lay people, with week-end consultations. In 1980, 250 seminarians were being trained and an additional 62 were completing their compulsory military service. In that same year, there were 26 monks and 55 nuns (representing the legal Benedictine, Franciscan, and Piarist orders, and the Sisters of Our Lady), and in addition approximately 700 elderly members of banned orders were residing in special State-run retirement homes.

Due to the Communist nationalization of Hungary's Church schools in 1948, there are merely eight Catholic schools in operation in the entire country. These are secondary schools giving a comprehensive Catholic education to some 2,000 students. They are staffed by members of religious orders who are paid by the State. Although this is a miniscule sample of religious instruction, it is highly significant, for it is almost unheard of in Eastern Europe for the Church to operate any schools. This phenomenon demonstrates the comparative religious freedom in Hungary, where relatively tolerant government policies make it possible to worship and study with fewer of the impediments found elsewhere throughout the region. Since the mid-1970s, the Hungarian Catholic Church has successfully pursued a policy of "small steps" in its dealings with the secular authorities. This has afforded the Church sufficient latitude to oversee the building of new churches, expand contacts with Western congregations, offer limited religious instruction, maintain its publishing facilities, and readily fill vacant apostolic posts. In return, the Catholic Church hierarchy has by and large refrained from overt criticism of State policies and actions. It has reined in a few extant dissident priests and shied away from making bold demands of the secular authorities. Nonetheless, it has not entirely skirted controversy within its ranks.

The emergence in Hungary of small independent religious study and prayer groups dedicated to a deepening of spiritual life has created intractable problems across the board: within the Church hierarchy, between religious activists and the Communist State, and in relations between dissenting clerics and the Vatican. These loosely organized cells, widely known as "basis" or "basic" communities are estimated to number several thousand throughout the country and have been in existence for nearly two decades.[22] Consisting mainly of young people, they are largely inspired by the teachings of the Piarist father Gyorgy Bulanyi, who was suspended by the Church hierarchy in June 1982.[23]

Perhaps most controversial of the basis communities' activities has been their advocacy of pacifist ideals and their active promotion since 1979 of conscientious objection to compulsory military service, which has greatly alarmed Communist authorities. At the State's urging, the national hierarchy has publicly opposed such views and disciplined several priests supporting them. The basis communities have also disputed the Church hierarchy over doctrinal matters; moreover, they have accused the Church of being too compliant and of having compromised too much with the Communist regime.[24] The Vatican's position toward the basis communities has been somewhat ambiguous. While endorsing the Hungarian bishops' decision to suspend Father Bulanyi, the Pope did not issue a final condemnation of him, perhaps because of other similarly delicate cases still pending in the Vatican. Some basis community members sought to interpret the Pope's "authentic" decision in their own way, a clear indication that the basis communities, far from submitting, were resolute in their determination to fight back.

Hungarian government officials have vehemently condemned those within the Catholic Church—presumably basis community leaders and members in particular—who encourage "inexperienced young people to refuse military service," something that violates State law and allegedly cannot be tolerated by the regime. The growing nervousness of the authorities and their vigilance toward any sign of "anti-socialist" activity was demonstrated a few days before Christmas 1983 when police seized several hundred unauthorized religious books in a car belonging to two Catholic activists. Both belonged to a basis community group that traditionally distributes religious books as Christmas gifts to its members. They were fined and did not receive a court hearing. According to dissident sources in Budapest, this was the first time that a 1983 amendment to the press law concerning publications printed without official authorization had been implemented.[25] One of the two men involved, Jozsef Merza, had been imprisoned and later confined to a psychiatric hospital in the late 1970s for refusing to join the armed forces on the grounds of conscientious objection.

The Hungarian hierarchy has expressed displeasure with the unwillingness of some basis communities to return to the fold. The late Primate of Hungary, László Cardinal Lekai[26], in an unusually outspoken statement, reviled the communities for accepting neither the authority of the Church hierarchy nor that of its bishops and claimed they "went their own way in opposition to the teachings of the Church."[27] The

Cardinal characterized the groups as "wild offshoots" originating from neither the roots nor the stem of the Church. The hierarchy was endeavoring, he said, to prune them "carefully and with love" so that they did not harm the discipline and unity of Hungarian Catholics.

Members of the basis communities have offered spirited resistance to pressures from above. In late 1983 eight Catholic priests sent a letter of appeal to Cardinal Lekai in which they urged him not to take administrative action against the basis groups but rather to seek unity through "paternal encouragement, in accordance with the Pope's intentions." The eight signatories also complained that priests affiliated with the basis groups were being requested to sign promises of obedience to the Church hierarchy. Admittedly, they themselves had recently been removed from their parishes as a punishment for arranging private religious retreats for basis groups. The priests said Lekai was not empowered to conduct such a "persecution campaign" and appealed (unsuccessfully) to the Vatican to revoke their forced transfers.[28] Shortly before, Father Angel Ruiz, head of the teaching Piarist Order, came to the defense of the suspended Piarist Father Bulanyi, adding that he did not support the policy of the Hungarian Catholic Church in this case and would resist the pressure to have Bulanyi removed from Hungary to Rome.[29]

Budapest's State Secretary for Church Affairs, Imre Miklos, suggested in February 1988 that the government was prepared to discuss a further expansion of the Church's social role.[30] Taking advantage of increasingly relaxed relations with the regime, religious leaders began to demand more legal opportunities for reaching the populace through the media, religious instruction, and pastoral and charity work. Among the matters to be discussed, Miklos included a possible increase in the number of schools operated by the Church, the extension of the Church's network of charitable services, and the possible relegalization of some of the monastic orders outlawed in 1950. Even the subject of alternative non-military service for conscientious objectors was reportedly under review. There are two subjects that appeared too controversial for compromise in the late 1980's. Regular religious broadcasts on television were to be prohibited, allegedly due to "organizational problems" and "limited time." An official reappraisal of the late Cardinal Mindszenty was also ruled out—Miklos called him "a bad politician" whose activities had "ill served" Church-state relations.

Czechoslovakia can claim one of the worst records among Leninist states with regard to the observance of religious freedoms.[31] The Prague government strictly controls the Roman Catholic Church, as well as various Protestant Churches. The Church hierarchies yield to official directives concerning all their activities. In total, 18 Churches and religious communities are legally permitted to function, the largest being the Roman Catholic Church.[32] The secular authorities have attempted for nearly four decades, however, to erode their social base and influence. In this they have enjoyed considerable success, particularly in Bohemia and Moravia.

The State Office for Church Affairs oversees and approves the appointment of Czechoslovak clerics and can withdraw their licenses to practice without warning or explanation. It controls the Churches' administration and finances, manages Church property, regulates religious instruction in schools, supervises religious publishing, and strictly limits contacts with Church groups in the West. Individuals employed in education, health, and numerous other professions are subject to sanctions at work or outright dismissal if they openly attend church services or participate in other religious ceremonies. Children who have received (or applied to receive) religious instruction are frequently barred from opportunities for advanced education and desirable career prospects.

The government-controlled Association of Catholic Clergy, *Pacem in Terris*, which closely monitors the activities of officially approved priests and involves them in Prague's peace campaign propaganda, was formally proscribed by a Vatican decree in March 1982. The Czechoslovak Primate, Frantisek Cardinal Tomášek, has on occasion been vilified by the regime for boldly condemning *Pacem in Terris* and for allegedly seeking to "destroy socialism" in the country. Because of the government's antireligious policies, there is a general shortage of clerics[33] and religious literature, and educational facilities for religious instruction are clearly inadequate to meet popular demand.

Due to relentless official pressure on all independent organizations, Charter 77—the autonomous human rights campaign in Czechoslovakia—has received little or no formal support from any of the nation's Churches. Nevertheless, a significant number of clerics and lay workers sympathize with the dissident human rights movement, and some of them actively provide help. During the past decade, the Charter has also gained the support of ordinary religious believers, both Catholic and Protestant, whose influence on the civil liberties front has grown apace. Religious observance in Czechoslovakia has been revived in recent years, especially among the young. The Communist regime itself estimates that there are nearly five million "active" religious believers—out of a population exceeding 15 million—and several million more who do not hold "atheistic attitudes." Officials often complain about the number of young people attending church services, particularly in Slovakia. The government has waged a vitriolic antireligious campaign in both word and deed, against which Charter 77 has protested many times. It is estimated that at least 100 Catholic priests and other clerics were serving prison terms in 1981, and the figures increased during 1983 when police actions against believers multiplied. The repression frequently takes place in the provinces and therefore receives little publicity in the West.[34] Priests who conduct religious services, provide Bible instruction, or disseminate religious literature without the authorization of relevant state bodies, are charged with "obstructing state supervision of Churches and religious societies" under Article 178 of the country's penal code.

Recent years have witnessed the blooming of what has been designated the "underground" or "catacomb church" in Czechoslovakia. This description is, however, misleading because no alternative or parallel Church structures have been formed; on the contrary, the idea is to supplement official Church activities by ignoring state directives and operating independently. The chief followers of unofficial religious activity are young people who participate in clandestine religious classes conducted by several hundred priests who have been denied official permits. There is also an interest in monasticism among the young, even though monasteries and convents are officially banned and monastic activity is outlawed. Catholic *samizdat* in Czechoslovakia is probably the most prolific of all religious *samizdat* in the Soviet bloc and reportedly enjoys a wider circulation than Charter 77 materials. Publications include books, translations, philosophical tracts, reports on the persecution of believers, and the monthly Czech religious periodical *Informače o Cirkvi* (Information about the Church).[35]

The election of a Slavic Pope has energized religious believers in Czechoslovakia, and not only the Catholic population.[36] In opposition to government policy, Catholics sent a petition to Pope John Paul II, inviting him to visit the country; possibly as many as 30,000 people were said to have appended their names to this document by early 1985. Such a pilgrimage is not likely in the foreseeable future because of Prague's hardline stance. However, more recently, almost 600,000 people nationwide signed a 31-point petition calling for an end to state interference in religious affairs.[37] The petition, supported publicly by Cardinal František Tomášek, was drawn up in December 1987 by a group of Moravian Catholics. In contrast to previous appeals sponsored by the Church, the document was openly circulated, read by priests from their pulpits, and displayed in duplicate form at church exits.

Many believers in Czechoslovakia find the current government policy toward the Churches grossly oppressive and religious freedoms practically absent. There was a prodigious police operation against priests and believers during September and October 1981. During another severe crackdown in March 1983 against the Franciscan and Dominican orders and various other clerics and laymen, some 250 people were taken into custody and interrogated. During house searches conducted in more than a dozen cities, religious literature, money and typewriters were confiscated.[38] This action sparked off protests, including a letter of complaint to Cardinal Tomášek signed by nearly 4,000 Catholics and Protestants. It was the first occasion since 1968 that opposition to official policies manifested itself on such a large scale. All the detained monks and priests were gradually released during the following months. Amnesty International, the human rights monitoring group, regularly reports on cases of religious persecution in Czechoslovakia. According to its data, in July 1984, ten young Catholics were convicted of "incitement" by the district court in Olomouc and received suspended sentences, ranging from six to 18 months.[39] Religious activists are often detained and charged under Article 178 of the penal code for "offenses" that include teaching religion to children, using their apartments to provide religious instruction, and preparing young people for Holy Communion without official permission.

The religious revival in Czechoslovakia has continued unabated despite a host of legal restrictions on religious life, the incessant detention of priests and laymen, and the harassment of practicing believers. An estimated 150,000 people took part in the celebrations in Velehrad, southern Moravia, on July 7, 1985, to mark the 1,100th anniversary of the death of Saint Methodius; about two-thirds of the attendants were young people. The regime appeared to be surprised by the large turnout and disturbed by how the event evidently strengthened the position of the Catholic Church.[40]

Observant Catholics began to experience greater persecution during the months after the Velehrad commemorations, as tensions between the State and Church visibly mounted. Forty Catholic activists were arrested in the Gottwaldov region of Moravia in November 1985 and their copying equipment and religious literature were confiscated. Since January 1986, the official atheistic campaign has been revitalized in the media.[41] Meanwhile, the number of newly ordained clergymen who have been denied a license to perform their religious duties was said to have reached 400 by May 1986, provoking protest letters to the then Czechoslovak President Gustáv Husák from aggrieved clerics. Furthermore, reliable estimates indicate that about 100 priests and activists of various denominations have been incarcerated in prisons or psychiatric clinics for several years for engaging in unofficial religious work.[42]

Charter 77's relations with the Church hierarchies are likely to remain restricted in the future, largely because of the state's strict supervision of religious affairs. One of the Chartists' main postulates is the complete independence of all Churches and religious communities from the State, including easy access to religious education for all citizens. Similar demands from a growing number of ordinary people, such as Moravian

Catholics, could signify potential problems for the regime in the years ahead.

In the late 1980s, Primate Tomášek evinced a marked new assertiveness in confrontation with the regime that resulted in a worsening strain in Church-state relations.[43] The Primate defiantly signed his name to the 31-point petition for religious freedom drawn up in December 1987. In separate letters addressed in April 1988 to Prime Minister Lubomir Strougal and to all Catholics in the country, he spoke out passionately in defense of believers' rights and for the Church's autonomy from the state.[44] Referring to the "repressive and unjust character" of the regime's religious policy, the Cardinal appealed for dialogue with Prague, while deploring *Pacem in Terris*. In May 1988, the Czechoslovak government stiffly rejected the Primate's letter to Strougal. Deputy Prime Minister Matej Lucan said it was at variance with "ethical principles" and constituted a "confrontation platform." The official rebuff did not appear likely to dampen the Primate's enthusiasm for his cause. Whether as a response to popular pressures from his flock or to Vatican inducement, Cardinal Tomášek's role as advocate and activist has set the agenda for Church-state relations in the foreseeable future.

There are slightly more than 1.3 million Roman Catholics in Romania, comprising about 6% of the total population.[45] Approximately 85% of them are of Hungarian or German origin and live in Transylvania. However, there are five diocesan administrations covering the country as a whole. Only one of these—Alba Iulia—possesses a bishop; the others have diocesan administrators, or priests who indefinitely enjoy the pastoral responsibility of a bishop and may administer confirmation, but not ordination. Sixty percent of Romania's Roman Catholic priests are over 65 years old. The Vatican does not publish statistics relating to the country, but the number of parishes is believed to be approximately 650. Theological seminaries exist at Alba Iulia and Iasi. Since the Roman Catholic Church has not submitted a statute for approval by the state, it is tolerated but not officially recognized. Nonetheless, a Roman Catholic priest has sat in the Grand National Assembly.

From the onset of the Communist rule in Romania, relations between the government and the Roman Catholic Church were strained.[46] The Hungarian and German origins of this Transylvanian based Church were crudely seen as a threat to Romanian national unity. The Church's vital links with the Vatican were viewed as a sign that the supreme loyalty of the Catholic community lay outside Romania's borders. In 1948 the old concordat with the Holy See was denounced. Some members of the Roman Catholic Church in Romania have voiced unhappiness about their lack of religious freedom.[47] In December 1978, a small group of priests and laymen appealed by letter to Pope John Paul II to intervene with the Romanian government on their behalf. They emphasized that their parishes were often undermanned or served by very old priests, and that they were inadequately provided with literature and other materials. Among the group's requests was permission to print their own literature; to establish religious communities and lay associations; to restore banned Catholic educational establishments; and to participate in pilgrimages to Rome, Lourdes, and other shrines. Earlier in 1978 a priest, Father Peter Mares, appealed to President Ceausescu to permit more Catholic churches to be built and to allow Catholic public festivals.[48] He also requested that vacancies in the Catholic hierarchy be filled and the Uniate Church be re-established. Mares was subsequently expelled from the country. Another priest, elderly Father Michael Godo, was fined and sentenced to six years in prison in 1980 for collecting funds to build a new church.

The East German Roman Catholic Church has followed a tradition of avoiding political issues, which accounts for the comparatively quiet role it has played in GDR society.[49] Closely cultivated ties with the Vatican have helped to protect the Church's position. Catholic leaders have circumspectly maintained a guarded distance between Church and state. For example, the head of the Berlin Bishops' Conference, Joachim Cardinal Meisner, has reportedly never met with East German head of state Honecker. The approximately 1,050,000 Roman Catholics, constituting 6.2% of the population, remain, in the words of the Apostolic Administrator of Erfurt, Bishop Joachim Wanke, a "small flock (in a) secularized, materialistic environment."

East German Catholics live in 920 parishes and are served by nine bishops, 1,500 priests (diocesan and religious), and 26 permanent deacons.[50] There are 3,244 nuns and 56 lay monks in 20 religious orders. Within the GDR there are only two recognized dioceses—Berlin and Meissen— as the Vatican has not formally acknowledged the postwar frontier between East and West Germany, and the ecclesiastical areas which border West Germany have been designated apostolic administrations. The bishops work closely together through the Berlin Conference of Ordinaries. Catholic priests receive their training primarily in the large seminary at Erfurt, and there are minor seminaries in other parts of the country. Some 270 students were being trained in 1980. Training centers for catechists have been set up throughout the country; at Magdeburg there is a training center for female pastoral assistants.

Until recently, the small size and political squeamishness of the Catholic Church in East Germany led to an isolation that was not entirely approved of by the Vatican, nor even by every Catholic in the country.[51] The 1.05 million Catholics are dispersed rather thinly, with greater concentrations in the regions around Erfurt and Dresden. Cardinal Alfred

Bengsch, who was Bishop of Berlin from 1961 until his death in 1979, was pastorally and theologically conservative. He continued the policy of his predecessor, Cardinal Dopfner, which was to maintain the unity of the Catholic community and not to become involved in political matters. The political acquiescence of the Catholic hierarchy has been considerable, with its public statements on social matters limited to the expression of disapproval about abortion and military instruction in schools. But the priests have preserved a united front and not a single one has joined the "Berlin Conference of European Catholics," a state-sponsored organization that invites Catholics across Europe to Soviet-style meetings which invariably support Warsaw Pact foreign policy positions. Reportedly, the leadership of this body is composed entirely of laymen and is atypical of rank-and-file church members.

Although the Catholic Church has carried out some administrative reorganization[52] to enable it to operate more efficiently in the GDR, it has not revised any of its diocesan boundaries. The diocese of Meissen, which was recreated in 1921 and relates directly to the Holy See, is the only Catholic diocese whose boundaries lie wholly within East Germany. The GDR government continues to be nettled by this, but the financial benefits to the Catholic Church of the present arrangement are substantial. Their parishes and buildings are beautifully maintained by the Catholic Church in West Germany, and bishops' residences are commodious.

In June 1972, the Catholic bishops of the GDR issued a pastoral letter on the subject of the *Jugendweihe*, taking an unusually firm stand.[53] The *Jugendweihe* is an official state dedication ceremony for boys and girls, in which they formally declare their readiness to accept civic responsibilities. Leading up to the ceremony there is training in Communist doctrine and practice, often including unabashed atheism. An estimated quarter of a million young people undergo the ceremony each year. In their pastoral letter, the bishops confirmed earlier statements in which they had adjudged the *Jugendweihe* to be essentially a non-Christian and atheistic substitute for confirmation. They called on all Catholics to boycott the ceremony, adding that any Catholic who voluntarily participated in it while aware of its atheistic overtones committed a sin against faith. The bishops alleged that pressure to take part in the *Jugendweihe* had mounted in recent years, and their letter ended with a reminder of the GDR constitution's guarantee of freedom of conscience and faith. According to these constitutional guarantees, a citizen who refuses on conscientious grounds to participate in the *Jugendweihe* should experience no disadvantage.

In July 1987, the first Catholic convention in the GDR took place over three days in Dresden, amid signs that the hierarchy was assuming a more assertive role in East German society. In January 1983,[54] the

Catholics emerged tentatively from their "ethical vacuum" by issuing a pastoral letter condemning the arms race and speaking out against the East German Communist Party's policy on conscientious objection and military indoctrination. In May 1985 in St. Hedwig's Cathedral in East Berlin, the Church held a three-day youth congress that dealt with the problems confronted by young Catholics in education, employment, and society as a whole. In addition, Catholics have stepped up their ecumenical contacts with the East German Evangelical Church, which had been made difficult in the past by divergent views on social and political activism; the latter was and remains considerably more strident.

The Bulgarian Catholic Church has an estimated 60,000 to 70,000 members, including approximately 10,000 Uniates—followers of the eastern Byzantine rite.[55] Small and advanced in age, the Catholic communities are sprinkled throughout Bulgaria in several isolated pockets. To the south, the main centers are Plovdiv, the nearby town of Rakovski and its surrounding villages, and the town of Malko Tarnovo near the Turkish border. In the north, the Catholic Church see is in Ruse and its following is concentrated in numerous small towns and villages in the vicinity of Svishtov on the Danube. These include Belene, where Bulgaria's second nuclear power complex is under construction.

Sofia's relations with the Vatican have been strained in recent years. However, in late June and early July 1987, Archbishop Francesco Colasuonno, the Vatican's envoy to Eastern Europe, spent one week in Bulgaria as a guest of the government. He was the first papal emissary to visit Bulgaria since the trial in Rome of three Bulgarian citizens accused of complicity in the attempted assassination of Pope John Paul II in 1981. Though the precise nature of Colasuonno's official talks was kept secret, he almost certainly appealed for further government concessions to improve catechism instruction and rejuvenate the aging Bulgarian Catholic priesthood. Although the Vatican and Bulgaria have yet to establish full diplomatic relations, there have been important high-level contacts between the two states in recent years. A major thaw in relations came in 1975[56], when, in the midst of an official visit to Italy, Party leader Zhivkov had an audience with Pope Paul VI. At this meeting, Zhivkov consented to the appointment of bishops to the two Latin-rite dioceses that had, officially, been without bishops since 1962. Not long after the Papal audience, thirty Catholics—including eight priests and seven nuns—were permitted to go on a Holy Year pilgrimage to Rome, and became the first Bulgarians to leave the country on a religious pilgrimage for over thirty years.

The Sofia government has refused on a number of occasions to reconsider its proscriptions on religious instruction.[57] The publication of Catholic literature is also severely restricted, with the Church allowed to publish nothing more than an annual calendar. Catholics are also disturbed by an aggressive emphasis on atheistic education in schools, the armed forces, and mass organizations. Vatican officials have frequently protested government claims that the private practice of a religion and the public propagation of atheism can be equated as civil rights. Probably the most pressing problems confronting the Roman Catholic Church in Bulgaria are the advanced age of priests and the shortage of suitable candidates for ordination. In 1980, only three priests were under the age of fifty.[58] During the first twenty-five years of Communist rule, the government permitted the ordination of only seven priests—all former students of the closed seminary in Plovdiv.[59] According to the West German Catholic journal *Informationen und Berichte*, in 1983 there were only 42 priests in Bulgaria (22 of the Latin Rite) to minister to more than fifty parishes. Their average age is believed presently to be between 65 and 70. Sofia granted permission in 1981 for one Roman Catholic (and one Uniate) to study each year in Rome. However, this concession alone will not remedy the chronic shortage of priests in the country.

Protestant Denominations

Among the panoply of religious and national oppositionist patterns in Eastern Europe, the case of the German Democratic Republic stands alone. It is the only country in the region that claims an absolute Protestant majority, and its leading Church—the Evangelical-Lutheran Church—has at times assumed a strong, unchallenged role in opposition to key regime policies. The Church has lent unswerving support to the unofficial peace movement in the GDR; aspects of this phenomenon will also be dealt with in Chapter 7. Here we shall look at the unique organizational structure of the Evangelical-Lutheran Church, discuss its priveleged relations with the regime, and anatomize the religious community that is the mainstay of its support. Finally, we shall assess the recent pressures for bold political reform that have come from Church representatives.

The popular strength of the Evangelical Church in the GDR has undergone profound changes since the postwar Communist takeover. In 1946, out of a total population of 17 million in the Soviet zone of occupation in Germany, some 15 million were adherents of the Evangelical Church and 1.75 million were Catholics.[60] By contrast, in March 1983, the Evangelical Church claimed 7.7 million believers, while the Catholic Church numbered 1.2 million members.[61] More recently, however, there are signs of a popular resurgence of interest in the Evangelical Church, as believers and non-believers alike crowd into Sunday services to hear the outspoken, explicitly political sermons of popular ministers. Following the postwar division of the German nation, the Protestant Church in East Germany retained a unified institutional structure with that of West Germany until 1969.[62] This provided the Evangelical Church with substantial added resources and hampered government harassment and containment. After the ruling SED instituted a Stalinist program in 1952, the religious establishment met with an atheistic frontal assault, but was never entirely neutralized and retained a powerfully influential base among believers and clerics.

In June 1969 the Federation of Evangelical Churches in the GDR was officially formed, thus severing the structural contacts between the Protestant churches of the two Germanys. Thereafter the Evangelical Church of the GDR continued to voice prudent opposition to regime policies on a number of salient issues, notably the emigration of East Germans to the West, the collectivization of agriculture, and universal conscription into the armed forces. In September 1964, it was successful in winning an important concession: the introduction of a "construction soldier" service for conscientious objectors drafted into the military. Nevertheless, veterans of the construction units are liable to experience severe discrimination; they frequently find that they are barred from higher education and suitable employment. As yet, despite Church pressures and proposals, there is no strictly non-military option open to conscientious objectors in the GDR. Those who refuse to enter the military as construction unit soldiers, or *Bausoldaten*, are summarily tried and imprisoned.

The philosophical and political stance adopted in the 1970s by the Evangelical Church has been effective in safeguarding its moral integrity and autonomy into the 1980s. Albrecht Schonherr, formerly Bishop of Berlin-Brandenburg and Chairman of the Federation of Evangelical Churches, gained respect and renown for his concept of "a Church within socialism," which was committed neither to opposition to the state nor to subservience to the regime.[63] Other Church leaders have followed Schonherr's lead, paying particular attention to grassroots pressure for dialogue on the subjects of peace education, environmental pollution, nuclear energy, and the growing "militarization" of East German society.

Since March 1978, when Church and State leaders met amid great fanfare at the highest levels, a delicate but decisive framework has been worked out for greater religious freedom in the GDR. Following the meeting, the state perfunctorily reaffirmed its commitment to guaranteed equality for all citizens, regardless of ideology.[64] In addition, concrete concessions were made by the regime: the Church was accorded increased radio time and granted access, for the first time, to television; more prison chaplancies were approved; and a building program to erect new churches throughout the country was inaugurated. There is no State interference in episcopal appointments, and synods have yet to elect a bishop from the minority of clergymen who voice uncritical support for the ruling SED.[65]

East German Churches are financed primarily by their members, who contribute payments in the form of a voluntary tax on personal income, donations and collections. The Evangelical Church remains the sole non-State landowner in the country, owning approximately 500,000 acres of agricultural land and operating some 50 farming enterprises. The regime, in addition, annually provides the Churches with funds for clergy salaries and general overheads. From the government also come monies each year for the maintenance and restoration of Church buildings that are viewed as historically or architecturally distinguished. The theological faculties of the state universities also receive official subsidies. The regime, for its part, offers no resistance to other generous subsidies to the Church from the West; they supply the national economy with a steady stream of sorely needed hard currency and defray costs that would otherwise need to be met by East Berlin.[66]

Pressures for political reform from East German Protestants have increased friction between the Church and state in recent years. Emboldened by Gorbachev's perceived democratization campaign in the Soviet Union, groups of believers have called upon the SED to initiate a free and open dialogue, leading to "social and political renewal."[67] The demands were circulated in June 1988 in a document at a national Church congress. They envisaged a broad-based liberalization of socialism, extending to reforms in electoral procedures, but stressed that the Church should not wait for "democratization from above," and must begin to exert pressure from below. Radical factions in the Church, active for several years, have met with resistance from Party leaders, who have been slow to implement Gorbachevian-type reforms. Even mainstream clerics have become outspoken proponents of change. Thus, in the spring of 1988, the Vice-Chairman of the Federation of Evangelical Churches, Manfred Stolpe, publicly stated that "a qualitative leap forward (by the SED) is in order;" he added that "without *perestroika*, things will not work anymore."[68] In June 1988, Lutheran-Evangelical Church leaders approved Twenty Theses on Societal Renewal, demanding that the Communist Party renounce its monopoly on truth and its fundamental claim to superiority over other institutions. The theses also called for electoral laws that would allow for a choice in the selection of political candidates, an accountable court system, and a revision of the GDR's criminal law.[69]

Though Protestants are a religious minority in Hungary, they are a sizeable and significant one. They have a historic tradition which rivals that of the majority Roman Catholic Church in regard to the wellsprings of religio-nationalist sentiment in some regions of the country.[70] To be a "true" Magyar patriot carries different religious connotations, depending largely on which group of believers one questions, for neither Catholics nor Protestants can claim to possess fully the Hungarian "national church."[71] Western Hungary is predominantly Catholic, while in eastern Hungary the picturesque town of Debrecen has come to be known as "the Calvinist Rome." Lutherans, who are broadly spread over the northern part of the country, are in general of Slovak or German descent.

The two largest Protestant Churches in Hungary are the Reformed Church and the Evangelical Lutheran Church, with two million and 400,000 baptized adherents, respectively.[72] Members of the Reformed Church comprise an estimated 20% of the population and are distributed among 1,250 self-supporting independent parishes. They are concentrated primarily in urban areas and in the large rural region east of the Tisza River. Each parish is governed by a parish minister and around 250 assistant ministers. There is a 100-member General Synod which takes contributions from the parishes for a central Church fund. Interestingly, the Reformed Church of Hungary has bishops—one of the few churches of the Reformed tradition that actually does. Clergymen are trained in the theological academies of Budapest and Debrecen; at Sarospatak and Papa there are also theological institutes. The Church runs seven homes for the aged, one children's home and six homes for handicapped children. It also operates two grammar schools.

The Hungarian Lutheran Church[73] has a considerably smaller foothold in the country, constituting less than 4% of the total population. Some 80,000 Lutherans reside in the capital. The remainder—numbering 320,000—are widely dispersed and usually constitute local minorities throughout the country. There are approximately 300 main parishes clustered into 16 seniorates and served by some 400 pastors. In addition, there exist approximately 1,900 scattered groups known as sub-parishes or "daughter" congregations. Lutherans have a theological academy in Budapest which offers five-year programs to several dozen students at a time. The same institution also gives post-graduate courses for pastors, and in January 1980 it started a new theological "extension" course for lay men and women. The Church operates 18 charitable agencies, which include homes for the elderly, orphans, and those with incurable diseases. Since 1945, the Lutherans—who lost many church buildings during World War II—have sponsored extensive reconstruction of churches and parsonages.

As is the case with the Roman Catholic Church, the Protestant Churches in Hungary have by and large pursued a policy of accommodation rather than confrontation with the Communist regime. The President of the

Reformed Church, Bishop Tibor Bartha, and the President of the Lutheran Church, Bishop Zoltan Kaldy, are both active members of the political establishment. Bishop Bartha has sat on the Presidential Council and, with Bishop Kaldy, has been a longstanding member of the Foreign Relations Committee of Parliament. Bishop Kaldy has often made public pronouncements lending unconditional support for socialism and the foreign ("peace") policies of the Kádár government.[74] Both clerics have been decorated ceremoniously for their unambivalent service to the state, without any overt signs of disapproval from their flocks.

In Czechoslovakia, as in Hungary, Protestantism is a minority religious orientation. And again, there is a schism between Catholics and Protestants, with each denomination making less than definitive claims to being the country's "national church." Protestantism in Czechoslovakia has its strongholds in the Czech lands of Bohemia and Moravia, where most of the population lives. Its historic course has been troubled, encompassing periods of triumph and defeat at the hands of rival religions in the sway of foreign powers.[75] According to the latest available statistics, 1.3 million Czechoslovak Protestants pay membership fees.[76] Lutheranism is the predominant Protestant faith in the country.[77] Its largest body is the Slovak Evangelical Church of the Augsburg Confession with 370,000 members and a total of 510,000 when one includes so-called "affiliated" members.[78] The second largest Protestant grouping is the Evangelical Church of Czech Brethren with 81,000 members and 295,000 affiliates. The Silesian Evangelical Church of the Augsburg Confession has 36,000 members and 50,000 affiliates; it is a Polish-speaking Lutheran denomination based in Tesin, Karvina and Ostrava. The Reformed Church in Slovakia, which has 120,000 members and a total affiliation of 165,000, was created in 1918 after Slovakia was sliced off from the Hungarian part of the Hapsburg empire.

The Protestant Churches of Czechoslovakia have not had tempestuous relations with the Prague regime, as has the Catholic Church, but they are subjected to the same strict official antireligious policies. Protestant believers have not considered it necessary to develop their own *samizdat* activities to protest against atheistic propaganda and persecution, as have Czechoslovak Catholics. There are no major problems in occupying vacant bishoprics or seniorates in the Protestant churches or in publishing Bibles or hymnals. Nevertheless, the Protestant Churches do encounter various difficulties.[79] A 1983 report by the Reformed Church of Slovakia characterized the general situation for its adherents as "desolate," adding that "in many parishes only 5% of the population attend worship."[80] In addition, there is evidence to suggest that relations between the Protestant Churches and the state are not altogether copacetic. In 1977 the Evangelical Church of the Czech Brethren, a smaller grouping with several thousand members, issued a document informing the deputies of the Czechoslovak Federal Assembly about the oppression of its members. The document enumerated the principal areas of oppression, such as the restriction of Church activities, the withdrawal of professional licenses from priests, and official measures against religious publishing and ecumenical work. It went on to decry a precipitous decline in the numbers enrolled for religious instruction in Bohemia and Moravia.[81]

In Romania and Poland, there are extremely strong national Churches—the Orthodox and Roman Catholic, respectively—representing the vast majority of the religious population. In both countries, Protestantism is a minority faith greatly overshadowed by the relative splendor and security of the larger denominations. Nevertheless, Protestants have shown remarkable vitality and dynamism in recent years. Accumulated evidence from Romania suggests that Protestants are winning converts at an impressive rate. In Poland since martial law, the Jaruzelski regime has on occasion attempted to confer a special, largely symbolic status on Protestants in the name of "religious pluralism," to weaken Catholic authority and influence. In both countries, there has been a growing tendency in official circles to recognize the potential significance of the Protestant minority, whether as a threat to official atheist campaigns or, as in Poland, as an expedient political tool manipulated to counterbalance the weight of the Catholic majority.

The recent experience of Romanian Protestants provides an illustration of a government sponsored propaganda offensive that sorely backfired. Despite attempts by Bucharest's Department of Cults to contain the spread of neo-Protestantism, minor sects have burgeoned. They appear to be fuelled in their growth by widespread alienation from the mainstream Orthodox Church, which has been almost entirely co-opted by the Communist authorities. Disaffected adherents of the Orthodox Church have joined forces with Protestant groups in large numbers; notably they have entered the Baptist and Pentecostal faiths. As a result, there are an estimated 450,000 new Protestants in Romania. Almost half of them are Baptists—more than in all other East European countries combined.[82] The Baptists of Romania have demonstrated a spirited resistance to official moves designed to extinguish their vitality. As Socor has observed:

> Owing to the sense of mission they have brought to the service of their faith and the determination they have displayed in resisting regime pressures, the Baptists' visibility and their impact on the Romanian religious scene has been far greater than their number might suggest. They have been especially active in proselytizing, in disseminating throughout the country Bibles received from abroad, and have engaged in a constant war with

the authorities for permission to acquire or build prayer houses and churches.[83]

The Romanian authorities have become painfully aware of expansive neo-Protestantism. At a seminar for Romanian academics involved in atheistic propagandizing, one participant, Georgeta Florea, drew a direct connection between the regime-sponsored "reversal of religious belief" and the propagation of smaller sects. Increasingly, she noted,

> This reversal of religious belief has created a paradoxical situation. It has only meant loss of confidence in the traditional religions and preservation of the illusion that there must be a better faith. In one way or another, this has brought (disaffected believers) under the influence of the neo-Protestant sects, which are becoming increasingly militant.[84]

It may well be an overstatement to suggest, as Florea does, that neo-Protestants in Romania are becoming "increasingly militant." Nevertheless, it is accurate to say that they have evinced an energetic activism. In 1978, Baptists and Seventh Day Adventists created an independent organization to monitor religious repression, and to press for stricter government adherence to laws and statutes guaranteeing religious freedom. Calling themselves the Christian Committee for the Defense of Believers' Rights (ALRC), members of the organization became affiliated with the Swiss-based Christian Solidarity International, and succeeded in publicizing numerous cases of religious persecution throughout the country.[85] Other steps taken by neo-Protestants in the realm of independent activity include religious publishing, proselytizing and petitioning for houses of worship.

The response of the Bucharest regime to this surge in neo-Protestantism has gone far beyond official expressions of concern. By early 1986, there were approximately 200,000 baptized Baptists, 200,000 Pentecostals, and 45,000 Plymouth Brethren in Romania. According to Joseph Ton, these three denominations have been growing collectively at a rate of 15,000 to 20,000 new converts a year.[86] In an effort to stem the tide, the Romanian secret police and the Department of Cults have worked in tandem to wipe out religious fundamentalism and dissent. The antireligious campaign, which gained momentum in the mid-1980s, has been targeted in particular at activist members of Protestant sects, although some outspoken Orthodox clerics have also been silenced.[87]

In recent years, the Ceausescu regime has brought dozens of clergymen to trial, almost all of them Protestants.[88] Clerics have been sentenced to long prison terms, usually on patently trumped-up charges; some have been strategically released due to international pressure before serving their entire terms. Others have been defrocked and stripped of their pastoral licenses. Many have been harassed by official agents, and there are reports of physical attacks on influential ministers. In addition, since late 1983, the authorities have closed or demolished Baptist and Pentecostal churches in Bucharest and provincial towns. The demolitions and closures, which have also affected Orthodox congregations, are said by the regime to be necessary for the construction of new apartment buildings and ambitious housing complexes. In September 1984, the government decreed the demolition of the Second Baptist Church of Oradea; claiming 2,000 members, this church is thought to have housed the largest Baptist congregation in Europe.[89]

Though Poland is often thought to have a monolithic, all-encompassing faith in Roman Catholicism, not all Poles are Catholics. The country has a small but significant Protestant community, though it accounts for less than 5% of the total population. Largest among Poland's Protestant groups is that of the Lutherans, who claim approximately 80,000 members and 100 pastors in six dioceses.[90] Adherence to the Lutheran Church has weakened gradually in recent years due to the permitted emigration of hundreds of adherents to West Germany. Following far behind the Lutheran Church in terms of membership, but retaining its place as second largest, the Polish Baptist Church now has about 2,500 baptized members and some 7,000 adherents. There are 50 Baptist churches and more than 70 other centers of Baptist worship served by 60 ordained pastors and lay preachers. A new headquarters for the Baptists opened in Warsaw in the early 1970s. Less than 40,000 Poles are affiliated with other Protestant Churches, notably the Reformed Church, the United Evangelical Church, the Methodist Church, and the Seventh Day Adventist Church.

Because the Warsaw regime does not view the Protestant Churches as a threat, most of them have a legal status and Church-State relations are relatively relaxed.[91] As noted earlier, however, the authorities have attempted to use the Lutheran and other Protestant Churches as a symbolic counterweight to the Roman Catholic Church, thereby deliberately downplaying the enormous social and political influence of the latter. This has been accomplished by repeated emphasis in official statements on the religious "pluralism" of the country, heavily implying that the Catholic Church does not have the moral authority to speak for every Pole.

The Orthodox Church

By far the dominant religious faith in Romania is Orthodox Christian, with some 17 million adherents in the country. The historic tradition and current demographic reality of the Orthodox Church in Romania is such that it is truly a national church, embracing the loyalty of the majority of citizens, including, it has been asserted, a sizeable number of Communist Party members.[92] But it would be erroneous to assume that there is an essential conflict or contradiction between simultaneous adherence to the Church and the Party-state, for the former has been almost entirely co-opted by the latter. With a few notable exceptions, Church officials refrain from overt criticism of government policies or actions; those who challenge the *status quo* are defrocked or moved to remote parishes. Indeed, in crucial respects, the Church is called upon to support and echo regime dictates, and hierarchs are not reluctant to join in the general public apotheosis of President Ceausescu, in line with the officially orchestrated personality cult.

The activities of the Orthodox Church in Romania are strictly regulated by the State's Department of Cults, which approves all ecclesiastical appointments. There are two Orthodox theological institutes of university rank in Bucharest and Sibiu. These cater in an average year to some 1,500 full-time students, recruited entirely from six seminaries. In addition, there are approximately 120 Orthodox monastic foundations housing around 2,200 religious devotees—1,500 nuns and 700 monks. In recent years, Romania, in keeping with a trend sweeping much of Eastern Europe, has experienced something of a popular religious revival. Though this has been especially pronounced among Baptists and other neo-Protestant denominations, the Orthodox Church still attracts sizeable congregations, and a significant number of the worshippers are young people. Religious festivals and Sunday masses bring crowds of believers into churches and cathedrals, and the usual religious fervor of the masses is often compared to the level of pious devotion in Catholic Poland.

The extent of dissent and opposition within the Orthodox Church should not be overstated, though there have been noteworthy cases in recent years of courageous stands taken by maverick priests. Perhaps the best known of these is Gheorghe Calciu. Arguably the most articulate critic of the Ceausescu regime, he served over 20 years in political detention before emigrating to the United States in the mid-1980s.[93] Between lengthy periods in prison, Calciu took an uncompromising moral stand on the issue of religious freedom in the face of increasing official "atheization" campaigns. His inspiring sermons were directed above all to the youth of Romania, and struck a responsive chord there. His texts were duplicated, circulated clandestinely, and avidly read countrywide.

In 1978, Calciu became a founding member of the interdenominational Christian Committee for the Defense of Religious Liberty and Freedom of Conscience. The group issued a comprehensive 25-point program of demands for greater religious freedom, which it sent both to the Romanian authorities and to religious and human rights organizations in the West. Calciu wrote a separate appeal for support to Pope John Paul II and to the prestigious French Committee of Intellectuals for a Europe of Liberties (CIEL), which later appointed him a member. He was similarly active in a broader sphere of social concerns. In 1979, Calciu provided spiritual guidance to a group of Romanian workers and intellectuals who attempted to set up a Free Labor Union of Working People in Romania (SLOMR).

Other priests have mounted opposition to the co-opted policies of the Orthodox Church hierarchy and to the state; they have been dealt with equally severely. An example is provided by the experience of Father Radu Pamfil, who was active in rural Timis county. Pamfil's conflicts with Church and state began in April 1981. He was called before an ecclesiastical court in 1985 and charged with carrying out "occult practices." In a matter of months, he was transferred from his parish.[94] A concerted expression of dissent occurred in the early 1980's, when five Romanian Orthodox priests banded together to make their dissatisfaction known in a formal plea to the Romanian patriarch. In their resultant "Testimony of Faith," the clerics called for

> The implementation of the right to give children a religious education and the organization of a young Christian movement; individual ecumenical freedom without any constraints; the right to have access to the information media, radio and television; the release of Father Calciu from prison; the reintroduction of the "Lord's Army" movement (a banned Orthodox renewal movement); and the recognition of the Uniate Church as the sister and supporter of Orthodox spiritual life.[95]

The penalties imposed on the authors of this document were draconian. Two of the priests who composed the statement were physically assaulted by members of the local militia. A third was arrested, threatened with torture, made to sign a confession, and stripped of his license to do priestly work. A fourth cleric also lost his job.

Resistance to the subservient posture of the Romanian Orthodox hierarchy *vis-à-vis* the Communist authorities exhibits a mass character in the dogged persistence of one clandestine organization, the "Lord's Army." Founded in 1923 by Iosif Trifa, a Romanian Orthodox priest from Transylvania, the banned movement still claims upwards of 400,000 underground members.[96] Essentially a moral renewal movement, aimed at countering the influence of evangelical Christians, the Lord's Army evolved into a lay-initiative mission movement within Orthodoxy. At the height of its popularity in the mid-thirties and forties, millions of

Romanian Orthodox, including priests, participated in its proselytizing activities, publishing, and open-air mass meetings. In 1935, the movement rejected efforts by the hierarchy to curb the lay role in its leadership. Father Trifa was defrocked and the movement continued to develop independently of the Church leadership, though its members remained part of the Romanian Orthodox Church.

After seizing power in 1947, the Communists outlawed the "Lord's Army" and imprisoned its leaders. One of the most prominent, Traian Dorz, a poet and hymn writer, spent 17 years in prison; he was placed under house arrest in 1965. The movement, which operates clandestinely and under constant harassment, still holds a powerful appeal for Romanian Orthodox youth. In recent years, the plight of the "Lord's Army" has been publicized in the West by the Romanian ALRC (Christian Committee for the Defense of Believers' Rights). In a document dated August 23, 1978, ALRC tried to clarify the movement's history and aspirations. In a chronicle of persecution, the authors observed that

> The name "Lord's Army" was enough to give rein to the most ridiculous and fantastic hypotheses. Anyone who belonged to the Army was suspected of belonging to an Army organized for regular armed combat. Arrests (in the late 1940s) followed one after the other; people were rounded up by region. A total of 500 "soldiers" were arrested. Many were not released until 1964.[97]

The ALRC document was poignantly entitled, "A Limb of the Orthodox Church Which Continues to Bleed: The Lord's Army."

The postwar history of the Orthodox Church in Bulgaria is a chronicle of almost unrelenting co-optation and domination by the state.[98] Organized opposition to the anti-religious policies of the Communist regime is practically unknown; even maverick actions or statements by individual clerics and laymen are relatively rare. Punitive actions against dissenting clerics who opposed hierarchical compromises were severe, usually culminating in long prison sentences in the immediate postwar years. At the time of the Communist takeover in Bulgaria, the Orthodox Church had a leader of exceptional moral integrity, Metropolitan Stefan of Sofia.[99] At first he welcomed a regime that promised much-needed social reforms, but when he realized its totalitarian and aggressively atheistic nature, he complained strongly about the abolition of religious education and freedom of conscience, and about official encroachments on Church life. He also suggested a plebiscite on the question of political rights of all citizens. He was exiled to a monastery in 1948 and died there in 1957. His popularity at home and his international reputation saved him from the harsher fate of lesser known religious figures.

Today there are some three million members of the Bulgarian Orthodox Church. Many are not active worshippers, and according to periodic accounts from Western travelers, most Orthodox Churches are not especially well attended on a regular basis. Yet the Church, as a national institution, commands an undeniable place of high esteem in the history of the nation. It is widely credited—even in official statements by Bulgarian government spokesmen—as having played a key role in the country's centuries-old struggle for freedom from Turkish domination. It was invaluable in helping to preserve the distinctive history, language and culture of the Bulgarian people under the yoke of foreign rule. In recognition of this, the Church has assumed a secure place in contemporary Bulgarian society. But the moral price it has paid for this security is rather high. Essentially, the Bulgarian Orthodox Church functions as a sub-department or bureau of the Ministry of Foreign Affairs, and it has been of considerable utility to the regime in supporting its foreign policy initiatives.[100] Primarily the Church is called upon to decry NATO arms build-ups and applaud Warsaw Pact escalations. It is intensely active in international peace seminars and conferences, sponsored by Moscow or other East bloc countries. Church representatives also travel to Third World states with government officials, where they praise the foreign policy achievements of Bulgaria and her allies. Needless to say, Church hierarchs are expressly forbidden to make any public or private criticisms of Communist programs, either at home or abroad.

Assorted Minority Religions

The Uniate, or Greek-Rite, Catholic Church is an illegal religious group in parts of Eastern Europe, denied formal recognition by the Communist state. At the end of World War II, the Uniates numbered 1.57 million in Romania, and 320,000 in eastern Slovakia, with much smaller communities in Bulgaria, Poland, and Hungary.[101] The larger Uniate Churches in Romania and Slovakia were forcibly incorporated into the Orthodox fold, following the Soviet model of absorption in the Ukraine. The smaller Churches, which were not seen to pose a political or nationalist threat, fared somewhat better. Hungary's Greek-rite Catholic Church was permitted to function and Miklos Dudas, the Hungarian Uniate Bishop of Hajdudorog, was even allowed to attend the Vatican II Council in Rome.[102] Bulgaria's 15,000 Eastern-Rite Catholics (numbers estimated in 1975), most of whom are Ruthenians, enjoy toleration by the Sofia regime, while the 150,000 Uniates in eastern Poland have suffered various subtle forms of official discrimination.[103]

Romania was the first East European state to ban the Uniates, after making an abrupt about-face on the issue. In September 1948, a government decree recognized the Greek-rite Catholic Church and granted it the right to organize two eparchies. Then, less than three months later, another decree banned the denomination. Clergymen were imprisoned, as were resistant laity. New Uniate leaders were selected from a collection of Communist sympathizers, who proceeded to announce the incorporation of the faith into the Romanian Orthodox Church. There was, however, widespread popular opposition to the move. Two-thirds of Uniate priests and three-quarters of the Uniate believers resisted implementation of this decision.[104] The regime responded with severity; by the end of November 1948, even before the Uniate Church was formally outlawed, approximately 600 Uniate clergymen were imprisoned, including Bishop Ion Suciu, vicar of the Blaj Metropolitan See, and Bishop Valeriu Traian Frentziu of Oradea.[105] Romanian Uniates and their sympathizers have, in subsequent years, appealed for relegalization of the denomination, hoping that the occasionally deviant policy-making of the Ceausescu regime would countenance the reversal of a decision made in the Stalinist era under more pronounced Soviet influence. An early petition was submitted to Ceausescu by Reverend V. Vorobchievici.[106] No less than 32 more petitions were received by August 1977. These measures have evidently failed to influence the decisions of the Romanian Department of Cults or the Romanian Communist Party.

Initially, Czechoslovakia's Uniate Church was also banned by the Communist authorities. Its union with Rome was abrogated by order of the State on April 28, 1950, and its adherents were pronounced Orthodox.[107] At the time, there were more than 300,000 Uniates in Slovakia's Presov diocese, outnumbering by far the 35,000 Orthodox believers in three dioceses. But the Uniate Church was relegalized in Czechoslovakia less than twenty years later. Under the reformist Dubček administration in 1968, a committee of some 135 Uniate clerics won an annulment of the 1950 legislation and full rehabilitation of their denomination. Since 1970, the Prague authorities have targeted Uniate areas for successive militant atheization drives, exerting severe pressure on believers. Yet they have not banned the Uniates once again. This may be due to the regime's perception that it risks a flare-up of widespread popular disaffection if it dares to go too far in suppressing the religionationalist character of the Uniate faith.

There are numerous small Protestant sects scattered throughout Eastern Europe which number a few thousand members each. Most of these are not officially recognized by their respective governments, so a precise calculation of their numerical strength is not possible at this time.[108] The institutional framework within which these sects operate is often informally organized, with preachers trained and ordained secretly and worship conducted in the homes of the faithful. Often, published religious material is in short supply, so *samizdat* literature is circulated within the community, enabling limited private religious instruction of children. Financial support is typically denied by the State, so that contributions from believers are crucial for the provision of religious materials, which are usually kept to a minimum. Frequently, in the case of fundamentalist Protestant denominations, there is some contact with sister Churches in the West that furnish material and financial assistance. In some instances, these foreign contacts are used by Communist regimes to persecute believers, who are accused of cooperating with an international network of antisocialist "enemies of the State."

Denied legal status by the Leninist authorities and starved of funds, it is clear that these sects labor under a heavy burden. Nevertheless, they are typically active in evangelical work, and—as in the case of the Baptists of Romania—they have sometimes increased their numbers by recruiting adherents who are disillusioned by the moral compromises of larger, co-opted religions. Moreover, there is evidence to suggest that several Protestant sects have opposed official policies through their stalwart support for conscientious objection and their denial of national health service treatment.

Official reprisals against pacifists are under review in many East bloc states, as will be discussed in Chapter 7. In the GDR, an estimated 200 conscientious objectors are imprisoned each year; about half are Jehovah's Witnesses.[109] In Hungary, some pacifist Christians—notably Nazarenes and Seventh Day Adventists—have been permitted to do unarmed military service since 1977. However, according to Amnesty International, by 1986 as many as 150 conscientious objectors were serving time in Hungary's Baracska Prison, most of them Jehovah's Witnesses who refused to perform any kind of military service.[110] In September 1985, a military court in Budapest tried eleven conscientious objectors and sentenced ten Jehovah's Witnesses (and one Roman Catholic) to prison terms ranging from two years and six months to two years and ten months.[111] In Poland, according to reports by Western correspondents, several dozen Jehovah's Witnesses were in jail in 1987, pending trial on charges of refusing military service.[112] It is worth noting that in Poland, as in other East European countries, the Jehovah's Witnesses are denied formal legal status by the state.

Among the smaller Protestant groups in the region, one of the more sizeable is that of the Pentecostals in Bulgaria. By unofficial estimates, this sect is comprised of some 10,000 members and 120 churches, and it is experiencing a recent revival, with membership growing at a rapid rate.[113] Some Pentecostals have run afoul of officialdom by refusing state medical assistance. In one notorious case, Boyanka and Ivan Vanevski,

Pentecostals from Veliko Turnovo, were tried as murderers for allegedly letting their six year-old daughter die of diphtheria rather than summon medical help.[114] Folk remedies and rituals are often used by small sects in predominantly rural areas in preference to relying on medicines and hospital care provided by the regime. This phenomenon is a longstanding reality throughout Eastern Europe, though it appears to be gradually diminishing as urbanization and advanced formal education spread to outlying rural areas.

There are small Muslim communities throughout Eastern Europe, with a substantial concentration in Bulgaria. Around 2,000 Muslims live in Czechoslovakia and East Germany, 15,000 in Poland, and 35,000 in Romania.[115] In Bulgaria, where Muslims comprise no less than 15% of the population, there are an estimated 700,000 to 900,000 ethnic Turks—and much smaller groups of Pomaks, Tatars, and Gypsies—whose professed faith is generally Islam. These Muslims have been targeted as an ethnic and religious threat by the Sofia regime, and since late 1984, they have suffered severe persecution. Virtually overnight, hundreds of thousands of Muslim Turks ceased to exist—officially—in Bulgaria.[116] Due to a government-inspired "Bulgarization" offensive, which reached a peak of intensity in early 1985, the ethnic minority was forced—sometimes at gunpoint—to exchange Turkish and Islamic names for Bulgarian and Christian ones. This was part of a systematic persecution that severely curtailed religious and civil freedoms. Birth certificates, passports, marriage licenses and job applications were changed from Turkish into Bulgarian. Mosques were closed, and copies of the Koran confiscated. Amnesty International has estimated the number killed for resisting the drive at 300 to 1,500.[117] One aim of the campaign has been the abolition of the Islamic ritual practice of circumcision. Soon after the name-changing was initiated, examinations of all sons of Turks were carried out. Circumcision was formally banned and follow-up checks ensued to ensure that the new law was being observed. Failure to comply could result in a fine or imprisonment for the boy's father, for the person who performed the circumcision, and for anyone who assisted in arranging the ritual.

"Bulgarization" has been fuelled partly by official fears that the ethnic Turkish birthrate has far surpassed the low birthrates of ethnic Bulgarians. Sofia, by implementing its discriminatory policies, hopes to avoid any separatist or fundamentalist upsurge on the part of its Islamic minority. By unilaterally declaring the country a one-nationality state, the regime aims to defuse any potential division of ethnic loyalties. But the resentment at the grassroots is considerable; though the "Bulgarization" drive has been accomplished with a massive show of brute force, a backlash has been reported, with whole villages offering passive resistance.

Once several million strong, before the Holocaust, East European Jewry has dwindled in the postwar era to a vestige of its former extent. There are small Jewish communities scattered throughout the region, with few exceeding 6,000 or 7,000 members. A majority of Jews are aged; the younger generation has limited or no institutional facilities for learning Hebrew or otherwise receiving a traditional Jewish education.[118] It is difficult to estimate the precise numerical dimensions of contemporary East European Jewry, due to problems of definition: those who identify themselves as Jews are frequently of the older, moribund generation; many more are of Jewish descent, although they are generally not observant.

The largest Jewish community in Eastern Europe can be found in Budapest, where a majority of Hungary's 80,000 Jews reside.[119] Out of a prewar Jewish population of 725,000, only 125,000 survived the Nazi genocide. In the immediate postwar period, there was a further reduction due to emigration and a declining birthrate. Around 20,000 Jews fled the country after the 1956 Revolution, though emigration to Israel is now greatly reduced. In 1978, there were almost a hundred synagogues, sixty congregations, and 26 rabbis affiliated with the Central Board of Hungarian Jewish Communities. The largest synagogue, which is located in Budapest, has room for about 3,000 worshippers, and the regular Friday evening services are well attended. Hungary also permits the operation of the only rabbinical seminary in all of Eastern Europe. Situated in Budapest, it had in 1980 thirteen Hungarian students, three Russian, and one Czech, though not all of them planned to become rabbis.[120]

In late 1987, a Jewish *samizdat* publication appeared in Budapest. Entitled *Magyar Zsido* (Hungarian Jew), it may well be the only exclusively Jewish underground periodical in Eastern Europe.[121] The first edition's lead article described the sympathies of the editors thus: "Our loyalty is twofold: We are Hungarians and Jews." The orientation of the publication appeared to be cultural and political rather than religious. A number of articles were reprinted from other journals, including Western emigre papers. For example, a report about the background to the disappearance of Raoul Wallenberg, the Swedish diplomat who saved thousands of Hungarian Jews from Nazi slaughter, was reprinted from editions of the Munich-based journal *Nemzetor*. Though the future of *Magyar Zsido* is not assured, its appearance testifies to a welcome pocket of vitality in the Hungarian Jewish community.

Anti-Semitism has been an unfortunate but trenchant feature of the Jewish experience in Eastern Europe, before and since the advent of Communism. The age-old stereotype of the Jew as an outsider, even a "fifth column," has been enhanced in official circles by the sympathies and loyalties of Jews toward Israel. In several East bloc countries, such as Poland[122] and Romania, Jews have periodically been the target of officially sanctioned anti-Semitic campaigns. Even though there are few actual scapegoats left, Communist governments have attempted to manipulate and rekindle old popular prejudices by orchestrating a politically distracting "anti-Semitism without Jews." For example, in March 1968 the Polish Communist Party launched a nationwide "anti-Zionist" campaign to hound critical and non-conformist intellectuals from the universities and other prestigious institutions; many Jews were thereby pressured into permanent exile. More recently, before and after the imposition of martial law some sectors of the political establishment blamed Jews for a gamut of dire social and economic problems in the country.

Conclusion

The persistence and revival of religion in Eastern Europe, despite periods of intensified antireligious measures, is a tribute to the independent initiatives of clerics and lay activists, who have sought to preserve and extend freedom of conscience in both word and deed. Some Churches have played an important institutional role in securing and broadening religious rights, serving often as a mediator for popular demands and a moderator of public discontent. But Church-state relations in the Soviet bloc differ from country to country.

In Poland, the Roman Catholic Church is a powerful counterweight to the Communist Party and wields significant influence in Church-State negotiations. In Romania and Bulgaria, on the other hand, the Orthodox Church rarely deviates from a course of strict conformity and obedience to government directives. Between these two poles are the Churches of the GDR, Hungary, and Czechoslovakia. In the GDR, the Evangelical-Lutheran Church has pursued a philosophy of a "Church within socialism," which has not precluded occasional confrontation with the Communist regime on political issues. In Hungary, the Catholic Church hierarchy has followed a "small steps" policy that has won notable government concessions at the price of foregoing any open criticism of Budapest. The Czechoslovak Catholic Church has endured severe persecution and slow deterioration under Communism, but in recent years it has asserted more vigorously its demands for greater religious freedom and social independence.

The struggle to protect religious rights in aggressively atheistic states has been fought in public and in the privacy of the home. It has involved the sacrifices of some of the best minds and moral fiber of the religious communities, as the most outspoken have been repeatedly incarcerated, forced to emigrate, or otherwise silenced. Despite the threat of swift and severe official retribution, religious activists, to varying degrees between states, continue to engage in unofficial publishing, clandestine group meetings, religious instruction, secret ordinations, and proselytism. Often, they are sustained by contacts in the West, who publicize their persecution, their gains, and their grievances. Chiefly, they are sustained in their cause by their deep reserves of faith.

It would be unwise at this juncture to prophesize any victor in these struggles between the atheists in power and the dispossessed who continue to believe. But if the past forty years are to serve as a basis for understanding, it would be fair to say that opposition to militant atheism is substantial, deeply ingrained, and enduring. Far from showing signs of abatement in recent years, religion has demonstrated a new vitality and popularity, particularly among the younger generation. This phenomenon augurs perhaps an intensification of opposition to regime policies in the future, which may trigger even more antireligious propaganda, increased harassment of believers, and harsher penalties for religious dissenters.

6

Economic Initiatives

Party-state economic planning, instituted throughout Eastern Europe during the Stalinist period, was not simply a device to accelerate industrialization, but had clear ideological, political, and social implications. The pivotal objective was to extend, centralize, and consolidate Communist controls over the growing industrial proletariat and each strata of the urban and rural population, through the Party's grasp over all important economic levers. The command economy was also designed to aid the expansion of a highly costly state bureaucracy, police and security apparatus, and the armed forces. This was accompanied by the liquidation of the capitalist sector, which was dismissed as "reactionary" and "retrograde." Since the mid-1950s a restricted private sector has been tolerated in the East bloc, though its scope and development has varied substantially between states. Party planners thereby hoped to bolster the flagging "socialized" economy by meeting consumer demands and diverting public attention from meaningful political reform. The enfeebled private sector and the unregistered informal exchange networks were designed to complement the state-controlled economy; they were not to compete with or erode the latter. Economic reforms and liberalization were counterbalanced by the long term interests of the ruling bureaucracies which sought to stymie the emergence of a large and powerful entrepreneurial class or autonomous working class pressure groups such as free labor unions and independent self-management councils. The economic muscle of either stratum could theoretically stimulate political opposition and encourage social emancipation from Party tutelage.

A fundamental conflict has persisted in the Soviet bloc between economic liberalization and the centralized distribution of power and decision-making. The Communist elites have therefore been concerned lest economic decentralization—including some measure of privatization in agriculture, small production, and local commerce—weaken their mechanisms of comprehensive social control.[1] As Brezinski has noted, the entire private "second economy" may serve as a lubricant for the economic planning system and as a social mollifier "which stabilizes the social order in the short term." However, "in the long run, it is to be expected that its effect will erode and corrode the system" if it is allowed to expand.[2]

Privatization and Free Enterprise

Under Stalinism, capital was generated and accumulated with little regard for efficiency, diversification, balanced modernization, fiscal discipline, or consumer consumption. In addition, the military and security apparati absorbed the best materials and expertise, which deprived the civilian sectors of the economy. Since the 1950s adjustments have been made to the Stalinist development model, with lessened emphasis on heavy industry at consumer expense. But each state continues to experience problems in converting from "extensive" to "intensive" growth, reconciling central planning with market forces, and motivating workers to raise output. Major difficulties are involved in revitalizing and reforming a command economy without undermining Communist controls over the economic process.[3]

The failures and shortcomings of East European economic reform should not be viewed as aberrations, but rather as a consequence of state policies that do not address the root problems of central planning but primarily focus on rearranging the existing model. The intrinsic maladies are manifested in, among other things, "faulty information and planning without facts, distorted evaluations and destruction of corrective mechanisms, the incompetence and inhibitions of decision-makers, and an absurd complexity of procedures and rigidity of targets."[4] The majority of Communist reformers do not oppose the principles of central planning or "socialization." They aim to trim the bureaucracy and replace incompetent administrators with more efficient personnel. A measure of decentralization may accompany such streamlining and reshuffling, by devolving some decision-making powers to the enterprise management level. But the government is empowered to retain control over the national economic plan. In McFarlane's estimation, all economic reforms enacted since the 1950s have "represented some re-division of economic power, sometimes within the elite (from Party secretaries to managers), as well as some from the elite to the non-Party masses (e.g. concessions to peasants concerning free market sales from private plots.)"[5] However, privatization and free enterprise have not been allowed to flourish, even in the midst of the most far-reaching reforms.

The parameters of economic reform are evident during attempts to boost productivity and develop a more efficient non-state sector. The reforms adopted by each state have differed considerably, with numerous retreats, accelerations, and retrenchments en route. The ruling Parties have been ambivalent over the scope, pace, and duration of such adjustments, and feared any loss of control over major economic processes. Various direct and indirect official constraints on marketization and decentralization have been in evidence. Each regime has resolved to uphold the centrally planned economy, even while utilizing market elements to boost national production. This is a far cry from introducing a market economy controlled in a few key nationalized sectors by a central plan. The Party edifice remains distrustful of market forces, while the reformist conflicts within the elite revolve around the extent of bureaucratic trimming and the degree of tolerance for private enterprise.

Even in Hungary, where many compulsory plan targets for industry were abolished after 1968, and much of the economy decentralized, state interference has persisted and many proposed reforms have been blocked.[6] Bureaucratic recalcitrance, aimed at controlling the private sector and preventing inefficient state enterprises from declaring bankruptcy, has been evident. In January 1988 Budapest levied a 25% general enterprise tax on all private and cooperative businesses to boost state income and keep company profits and autonomy in check.[7] Even the most reform-minded governments send ambiguous signals to private entrepreneurs; some leeway and encouragement has been combined with administrative obstacles and disincentives. The authorities endeavor to maneuver private businesses into filling supply gaps without allowing them free rein to expand. State tolerance of some private enterprise is related to its absorption of excess purchasing power and labor capacity. This eases pressures on the authorities to create job opportunities, particularly if unemployment were to grow with the closure of unprofitable state industries.[8] Nevertheless, the economic *nomenklatura* fears that private industry could attract the best workers, highlight the incompetence of state plants, and spread income differentials that could prove politically destabilizing. The ruling Parties may seek to exploit economic inequalities to prevent any unified opposition. However, the emergence of a visible new privileged class alongside an increasingly impoverished working class could exacerbate public protests against a system avowedly based on egalitarianism.

East Europe's private sector consists of an officially sanctioned private agriculture, manufacturing, and domestic commerce, and a parallel or unofficial economic system, encompassing "black" and "grey" markets and informal, personalized distribution networks. The non-state economy provides more than one-third of all goods on the domestic market in some countries and over half of essential labor and services.[9] Private initiatives are often hidden and difficult to tabulate, though they help supply crucial goods and services on the domestic market. Oppositionist groups throughout the Soviet bloc support de-nationalization and privatization as a means of stimulating the floundering economy, restricting Party control, and extending political liberties. Poland's Solidarity has voiced support for "varying forms of ownership" in its blueprints for economic reform. Extensive marketization would purportedly lead toward a "multi-sector economy," consisting of state ownership of public utilities and large self-managed key enterprises, and a multitude of small and medium-sized private and cooperative businesses. Such an arrangement would allegedly help remove barriers to individual initiative.[10] A segment of the post-martial law opposition in Poland, whose members consider themselves "economic evolutionists," strongly supports any measures that would galvanize free enterprise. Such a development, they argue, would progressively erode Party control even without a head-on political challenge to the regime, and it could prove difficult to reverse in the long haul.

Hungary's "democratic opposition" has also spoken out in favor of greater pronounced privatization, in which independent small enterprises would perform a "fundamental" instead of a "peripheral" or "supplementary" role in the economy. Budapest dissidents propose that a legal framework be created to protect private enterprises from Party encroachment and stimulate free market competition.[11] Far-reaching proposals for economic decentralization and privatization were also put forward in November 1986 by several leading economic experts under the auspices of Hungary's official Peoples' Patriotic Front. They were subsequently rejected by Party leaders as being too radical. A condensed version of the economic report has been circulated in *samizdat* to evade official censorship.[12]

To forestall the emergence of a strong private sector, even the most reformist East European regimes have undertaken periodic retreats from liberalization, while their bureaucracies have engaged in persistent obstruction of free enterprise. The ministerial and managerial apparatus is uneasy about losing its privileges in a system constructed around political loyalty rather than merit and achievement. Even while introducing market elements, the Hungarian Party retains its "guiding hand" by setting "macro" parameters and general industrial targets. Middle and lower levels of the bureaucracy continue to view with disfavor the growth of private businesses, and tightly control the issuing of necessary business permits and material supplies. Without institutionalized guarantees for private ownership, there is little long-term security or legal protection for the few businesses allowed to operate. There are constant irritants to free enterprise, such as prolonged registration procedures and other administrative hindrances, with threats of license withdrawal, heavy fines, and eviction for tax evasion, as well as various "control commissions" combatting "speculation."[13]

Ingrained features of the Leninist political system, including four decades of public dependence on the state and periodic campaigns against "resurgent capitalism," have stifled the development of entrepreneurial skills and self-motivation. The state has also fostered a negative stereotype of private businessmen as unprincipled "wheelers and dealers" or "parasites." Such an image enjoys some popularity, particularly where people perceive widening disparities in income and make little distinction between money earned through hard work and resourcefulness or through bribery and corruption. Wide differentials in acquired wealth increase resentment among those meagerly paid state employees who benefit only minimally from the private sector. Growing inequalities may fuel workers' pressures for higher wages and have adverse effects on productivity. Anti-entrepreneur sentiments in society have been manipulated by Party dogmatists to stall further economic liberalization. Their propaganda barrages have focused on fears of unemployment, more demanding work norms, higher consumer prices, and falling living standards. They are aware that factory workers suspect the personal cost of reform may far exceed any imminent material benefits. In Poland, Hungary and Czechoslovakia opposition activists have tried to counter the anti-reformist argument and erroneous popular assumptions, by stressing that private initiative and an expanding market system will stimulate economic recovery, and possibly political pluralism, which will eventually benefit the entire society.

It is useful at this juncture to survey the extent, character, and implications of private enterprise in Eastern Europe. In agriculture, the immediate post-war land reform programs, in which plots were distributed from expropriated large landowners to private smallholders, were designed to destroy the pre-Communist rural order and to neutralize the peasantry during the consolidation of Party rule. With the onset of Stalinization, private farmers were either coerced or cajoled to join collective or state farms. The collectivization drive was slowed down after Stalin's death, and reversed in Poland, largely because of passive peasant opposition and the sharp decline in agricultural output.[14] The pursuit of "agricultural socialization" was resumed in all states except Poland once the political situation had stabilized throughout the bloc by about 1957. In Bulgaria collectivization was practically completed by 1958, in Czechoslovakia and the GDR by 1960, in Hungary by 1961, and in Romania by 1962. Party functionaries and their political appointees managed state and collective farm property with minimal interference from peasants and agricultural workers.

Since the early 1960s, improved agricultural productivity has been pursued in the region, not primarily through widescale reprivatization but by technical improvements and various organizational changes in planning and management. In Wadekin's estimation:

> The rigid Stalinist system of "command agriculture" had to be made more flexible by relinquishing strictly centralized planning, procuring of produce, and price setting—some reform of the system was necessary, although at the same time, the leaders were eager to uphold central control and to prevent the re-emergence of "petty bourgeois capitalism" on the farms.[15]

Some allowance was made for restricted forms of private cultivation and small household allotments for collectivized peasants. But private farming continued to be hindered by administrative pressures; inadequate access to machinery, feed, and fertilizer; and low state purchase prices for crops. Peasants, in turn, endeavored to evade state supervision by using unofficial trading channels for foodstuffs to boost their living standards.

Bulgaria, Czechoslovakia, the GDR, and Romania permitted a circumscribed individual farming sector. It was based on small, subsidiary family plots for collective farm members and some private land use in marginal and hilly areas. Despite the restricted size of private plots belonging to collective farmers, their output has generally provided about one-third of total agricultural output in these states. Regardless of numerous official obstacles, individualized farming has remained the most cost-efficient sector for practically all varieties of produce.[16] In recognition of the vital role played by family farming, restrictions have been loosened somewhat on private production in several "collectivized" states since the early 1980s. In an effort to maintain domestic food supplies while expanding agricultural exports, state intervention in managing collectivized farming has decreased, and more incentives have been presented to private rural producers.[17] Nonetheless, secure legal guarantees for the peasantry, including the permanence of private land ownership, have not been forthcoming from the state.

Under the NEM, Hungary devised a system of semi-independent cooperative farming and treated the private sector somewhat more equitable. It has involved decentralized decision-making over farm targets, production schedules, the purchasing of machinery, building materials, fodder and fertilizer, and the choice of crops and livestock to be raised. Within these "self-financing" cooperatives, bureaucratic intrusions have been curtailed even though farm managers remain Party-approved appointees. Some leeway has also been given to private "homesteads" and household plots, but with clear limitations on their size. Though non-state farming of all descriptions accounts for over one-third of Hungarian agricultural output,[18] private farmers have been denied proper opportunities for investment, expansion, and self-organization as an independent lobbying group.

In Poland, unlike other East bloc countries, a large private farming sector has persisted. Some 2.8 million private farms occupy 75% of arable land and produce the bulk of foodstuffs for domestic consumption and export.[19] Tolerance for individualized farming was part of Gomułka's compromise with the Catholic Church and the rural population during the "Polish October." However, state planners deliberately neglected the modernization of private farming in the hope of squeezing out the aging peasant population and gradually expanding the socialized sector. A disproportionate share of government resources have been invested in persistently inefficient state farms, while private cultivators have been denied much needed credits, capital, machinery, spare parts, pesticides, insecticides, fuel, and fertilizer. In many cases, peasants have had to resort to the "illegal" economy to procure essential supplies. In addition, low state purchasing prices for agricultural produce have operated as a disincentive to family-centered farm production. In recent years Polish peasants have been given some legal guarantees regarding the permanence of private land ownership and inheritance; they have also received official promises of equal access to credits and agricultural machinery. Despite such assurances and the raising of procurement prices, farmers remain deeply skeptical about the regime's ultimate intentions. They are more concerned to obtain necessary equipment and capital rather than to amass paper safeguards that can easily be rescinded or ignored by officials. Warsaw's negative attitude toward peasant activism after the destruction of Rural Solidarity is discernible in its unwillingness to approve a Church-sponsored agricultural fund for private farmers. After five years of prevarication, a much truncated foundation was legalized in December 1987, after the Church had formally abandoned its efforts to register the original project.[20] The regime clearly has misgivings about unconditionally encouraging private farming with sizeable funds that could be used to circumvent the official system of allocation.[21] Warsaw also fears the resuscitation of Rural Solidarity and other pressure groups under Church protection. The decision to tolerate a circumscribed agricultural foundation is primarily motivated by Warsaw's severe economic travails and its eagerness to obtain any available Western aid.

The ultimate agrarian objective of each Party-state appears to be the creation of state-owned agro-industrial concerns and a proletarianized, wage earning rural population. In this schema, private farming and semi-autonomous cooperative farming may be permitted for prolonged spells to relieve economic pressure, but their spread and influence is closely monitored lest they undermine state plans. All East European countries endeavor to inhibit rural producers from forming independent occupational or political organizations. Indeed, aside from Poland in recent years, there has been little sustained autonomous organizational work among private farmers. By and large the rural population has been atomized and denied the political openings to lobby effectively for their interests.

Communist states have allowed small entrepreneurial initiatives to operate in manufacturing and servicing. However, business growth and efficiency is hampered by government regulations, including stipulations against business expansion, legal restrictions on property rights, high levels of taxation, low ceilings on hiring, constraints on capital investment, and frequent changes in official policy that exacerbate business insecurity. As a result, instead of re-investing to bolster the economy, entrepreneurs generally seek fast profits to minimize losses through state interference. These earnings are invariably spent in various forms of non-productive consumption. Though the degree of official tolerance varies between states, legalized free private enterprise involves a range of activities, such as the private leasing of state stores, the operation of small-scale "cottage industries," and the work of self-employed craftsmen or repairmen. Numerous other potential outlets for larger scale operations have been barred to individuals. Often private manufacturers and service providers maintain two jobs—in a state plant or office during the daytime, and in their private ventures during evenings or at weekends. In this way they try to assure themselves of steady though inadequate state salaries and health and vacation benefits, but at the same time their income is supplemented by private earnings. State employment can also provide an illegal supply of valuable tools and machinery, as well as personal contacts for private business pursuits.

During the past decade legal private enterprise has helped to assuage chronic official shortages of goods and services. In Poland about 700,000 people were engaged in non-agricultural private employment in 1982, though growth of this population has been intermittent and subject to unpredictable reversals. About 300,000 of the total participate in extremely small artisan concerns that only employ one or two individuals. The majority experience frequent shortages of essential materials. According to the deputy chairman of Poland's Central Association of Artisans, the regime maintains "organizational and psychological barriers" against artisans, and places various obstacles in the way of private initiative which continues to be officially disparaged as "capitalism."[22] The registration of small private businesses in Hungary has increased steadily since 1982, when Budapest eased some of its stultifying legal restrictions. Over 150,000 craftsmen, repairmen, and traders currently run independent ventures.[23] Many of them are only part-time entrepreneurs because of the high incidence of bureaucratic meddling which acts as an important disincentive for small businesses. Private businesses require official authorization that is contingent on the attitude of local authorities and their interpretations of the law. Even legally operating firms often have to resort to bribery to acquire essential supplies. Because of government restrictions on the number of employees, the most common form of private business is small family-centered operations. Due to widespread business insecurity most entrepreneurs tend to skim the most lucrative markets to earn fast personal profits.

The various local and national associations for independent craftsmen and other entrepreneurs do not properly represent business interests. For example, Hungary's small Craftsmen's National Association and Tradesmen's National Association do not defend the rights of members but are state-sponsored bodies designed to oversee the private sector. In February 1988, an independent National Association of Entrepreneurs was established by nearly 900 businessmen in order to campaign more effectively for craftsmen and traders, particularly in interpreting Budapest's new tax regulations.[24] Similar initiatives have been undertaken in Poland to support free enterprise. At least one such grouping has been officially registered and allowed to function: the Industrial Association in Cracow; it issues information on how to establish private businesses. Organized attempts to coordinate and assist entrepreneurs on a nationwide basis have been less successful. Warsaw's Economic Society, representing about 400 private businessmen since early 1987, has been denied registration, probably because of its candid support for Solidarity's economic program.[25] To counter such autonomous initiatives, in December 1987 the regime set up its own Society for Supporting Economic Initiatives in Warsaw, but its effectiveness remains in serious doubt.

East Berlin has grown more tolerant of its handful of entrepreneurs who display loyalty to the regime and do not erect any independent pressure groups. Currently, about 400,000 people are involved in the legal private sector, which includes about 25,600 retailers, restauranteurs, and landlords accounting for 8.5% of the retail trade and 16% of the catering trade.[26] The government avowedly intends to further expand the private retail trade. Nevertheless, conflicts persist between successful businessmen and Party functionaries, based on ideological divergencies, economic competition, and differing political priorities. Cautious state support in the past has been insufficient to invigorate private enterprise, and many craftsmen have retired since the mid-1970s. In early 1988 the GDR regime passed legislation to encourage small businesses and help buttress the faltering national economy.

Free enterprise in Czechoslovakia has continued to be severely restricted. Only 22,000 miniscule and often part-time businesses operate
there. In recent years the government has begun renting out premises
to individuals for retail, catering, and service outlets providing meals,
beverages, and parking and cloakroom facilities on a contractual basis.
However, supplies for these businesses have to be purchased from the
state or from official organizations at set rates, while the maximum
prices charged by entrepreneurs are officially regulated. This policy
clearly constrains free-market competition.[27]

Bureaucratic obstruction has been reported even for this limited private
initiative, as local *apparatchiks* are often unwilling to issue business
permits for fear of creating "modern millionaires." Bulgaria has announced
that some small businesses will be publicly auctioned and leased out
to individuals to provide important services. They will include catering
establishments, bakeries, repair outlets, and small motels, but no hired
labor will be permitted.[28] Individuals will be allowed to produce certain
scarce goods and provide some essential services in their "recreation
time," if they manage to arrange the necessary permits from local
authorities.

Private storekeeping has also developed in the more reformist states.
For instance, there were 30,000 private retailers in Hungary in 1986,
double the total of five years before. The majority operate outside the
food sector because of the limited opportunities for profit available in
the latter.[29] Also in the "reformed" Hungarian economy, larger quasi-
independent enterprises employing up to thirty people have been officially
approved.[30] These "semi-private" ventures are based on informal contracts
between state-run cooperatives and private entrepreneurs. They often
operate as co-op subsidiaries, in which the businessman runs the venture
independently but contributes a sizeable portion of private net income
to the state enterprise, which in turn guarantees administrative protection
and provides the premises.[31] Agricultural cooperatives and some industrial
plants are allowed to undertake a wide range of "sideline" ventures in
manufacturing and services, and the workers involved can substantially
supplement their incomes.

In 1982 Budapest introduced the Economic Work Collectives in industry,
which surpassed in number 35,000 by early 1987 and engaged nearly
half a million employees. The EWC's are not fully autonomous concerns,
as they are subject to management interference, but they do afford
workers a chance to increase their take-home pay. Since early 1988 the
regime has increased taxation on the Collectives because their rapid rise
has purportedly hurt the nationalized sector. In their state-run jobs
workers minimize their output and conserve their energies for EWC
operations, which consequently achieve higher levels of productivity

than official industry. Heavy taxation and bureaucratic restraints tend to thwart initiative but they also help to rein in economic energies that undermine the socialist sector and the powers of its Party overseers.

Some East bloc states have made strenuous efforts to attract foreign investments in specific industries, in which the investor would manage the venture and could make a sizeable profit. "Polonia" firms owned primarily by emigres or expatriates were introduced in Poland in the mid-1970s. By this move, Warsaw endeavored to attract Western capital and business expertise by granting favorable conditions such as low taxes and permission to employ more workers than can domestic entrepreneurs. About 700 "Polonia" firms were functioning by 1985, notable for their efficiency, dynamism, flexibility, growing productivity, and high wages that attract qualified staff from state industry. Their success has irked the managers of socialist enterprises who are easily outcompeted. As a result of opposition from the Communist establishment, restrictions have been placed on "Polonia" expansion by voivodship authorities.[32] Taxes have been raised, red tape lengthened, and the transfer of profits abroad has been curtailed. Not surprisingly, some companies have closed down their operations and the future for growth looks less than promising. Joint ventures with Western companies have been encouraged in several states to attract much needed foreign capital. Hungary has about 50 such enterprises that often benefit from preferential treatment such as tax exemptions. Poland passed a law in 1986 to encourage joint ventures, and a number of such firms have been depicted in the media as "models" for state enterprises.[33] Even governments which have traditionally prohibited foreign investment, such as Czechoslovakia and Bulgaria, have relaxed the regulations somewhat in recent years. In the long term, however, the small number of joint ventures are unlikely to make any durable imprint on the centrally controlled economy or the growth of independent economic intiatives. The Party apparat treats the private sector, including foreign capital, as a "transitory phenomenon" or a necessary temporary compromise that ultimately conflicts with the interests of socialism by spreading unsavory "capitalist attitudes" among the populace.[34]

Parallel Economies and Informal Networks

The boundary between legal or tolerated and illegal or unregistered economic activities is often indistinct and fluid in Eastern Europe. The "second," "parallel," or "underground" economy consists of a vast network of unreported transactions, whether in competition with or complementary to the official economy and the registered private sector.[35] Because the latter two supply systems have been unable to meet consumer demand, many people have turned at least partially to the "black" or "grey" markets. The "black economy" has tended to thrive under repressive conditions that outlaw a free domestic market. Some observers estimate that the non-legal economy is larger in states where the overt private sector has been more effectively suppressed. Other analysts posit that the "second economy" is more extensive in countries with a larger private sector and greater government leniency.[36]

Communist regimes generally recognize the value of the "parallel economy." It contributes to consumer satisfaction by supplementing inadequate state supplies, and helps forestall the necessity of implementing far-reaching market-oriented reforms. Moreover, by tolerating unlicensed economic pursuits, or failing to eradicate them, the authorities are "buying themselves a measure of stability, in that the ambitions of potential trouble-makers are channelled into individualistic consumerism."[37] In some instances, the ruling Parties try to absorb or decriminalize parts of the informal sector for purposes of taxation and overall supervision. Communist governments are aware of the dangers of unrestrained private initiative. It may undermine their mechanisms of public control, or increase social tensions because of wide disparities in peoples' access to alternative sources of cash and goods.

Though the informal economy serves as a safety net for the state by partially alleviating widespread material deprivations, it also extends the horizons of social activism and may have political undertones. Korbonski asserts that where the Party system is popularly perceived as illegitimate, parallel economic networks are endowed with a degree of public legitimacy. In fact "illegal economic activities have been viewed by many as representing a form of resistance against the Communist system," carrying little stigma but viewed as a permissible method to evade state control.[38] Periodic government clampdowns on "speculation," "corruption," and the parallel economy leave little visible mark because these activities are often sophisticated, wide-ranging, and deeply rooted. The Party endeavors to keep the underground economy within certain bounds or to exploit its apoliticizing effects on society. On the other hand, it remains concerned that some independent exchange networks may coalesce into or assist the political opposition. The second economy has flourished throughout the Bloc in the past two decades as a result of rising consumer aspirations that the state cannot meet. Black and grey markets for foodstuffs, goods, and cash, which balloon or contract according to variations in consumer demand, have expanded because of the insufficient number of legal businesses and the retailing deficiencies of state socialism.[39] In most cases, the parallel economy simply acquires and distributes scarce items to match demand and purchasing power, rather than manufacturing new products for the domestic market. There is a close dependence of the unofficial economy on the official economy, as the former often syphons off goods and labor from the latter. In some instances the illicit production of furniture, clothing, and other consumer items also takes place, but its volume is difficult to calculate. By all estimates this contributes little to national output; for example in the GDR it reportedly accounts for less than one percent of national income.[40]

Black market transactions involve household goods, medical supplies, cosmetics, and toiletries in chronically short supply through official outlets. These are often "liberated" from state plants, warehouses, or stores. Cars, spare parts, various mechanical equipment, and building materials can also be acquired unofficially from full or part-time black marketeers or state employees. Aslund compares the legal and unregistered entrepreneurs in Eastern Europe to "war speculators" seeking quick returns rather than long-term investments.[41] A wide network of "cowboy" entrepreneurs and traders avoid taxation and operate without any authorization; they incur few overheads or financial risks. State employees who have slim opportunities to trade illicitly or appropriate state property for personal gain, often "steal time" by reducing effort and output in their official jobs and conserving energy for their private concerns. Others also perform unregistered work during their normal working hours.

Trade in foodstuffs is also widespread, whether such goods are sold for cash or bartered. The degree of government tolerance for private food markets varies and helps to determine the "greyness" or "blackness" of unofficial commerce. Many farmers conceal their actual output from the authorities, and evade purchasing agencies in order to sell directly to urban consumers. In Poland a relatively wealthy stratum of entrepreneurs has arisen, specializing in private domestic production of vegetables, fruits, and flowers that are in high demand. Similar patterns are replicated in the other states. Some black marketeers concentrate exclusively on illegal cash transactions. The "dollar millionaires" may be in a minority but large amounts of foreign currency are handled outside official purview by wide sections of the population. The use of "hard currency" is an alternative and more effective means of acquiring scarce goods, while wide discrepancies between official and unofficial exchange rates provide sizeable profits for individuals illegally trading in Western cash. The black market for foreign currency is further stimulated by the official "Pewex" stores in Poland, and similar outlets in other states, where customers can legally purchase otherwise unobtainable luxuries, such as cosmetics, foreign liquors, and electronic equipment.[42] Other highly valued Western items also function as a medium of exchange or bribery in Communist countries. In Romania,

"Kent" cigarettes serve as an unofficial local currency that can be used almost anywhere to obtain scarce goods and services.

"Moonlighting" is commonplace throughout the region, with many individuals receiving payment for unreported jobs for friends, neighbors, colleagues, or acquaintances. "Moonlighting" occupations range from house construction, trucking, and home repairs, to private tuition, and medical and dental care.[43] The government, unable to eradicate the practice, either turns a blind eye or legalizes some second jobs because they help relieve universal scarcities. Budapest has imposed income tax on monitored "semi-legal," secondary jobs to divert funds to the state, but this may have the effect of either restricting the informal economy or compelling individuals not to declare their gross earnings. "Moonlighting" may bring both advantages and disadvantages to the state. It may contribute to overall economic growth, but the government loses substantially in terms of uncollected taxes, supplies pilfered from the state, and diminished productivity in official jobs. Problems in controlling "moonlighting" are compounded by the involvement of managers and other officials who perform or benefit from various secondary services. In most cases, "moonlighters" are in extremely heavy demand, and obtain high payments in a "sellers market." Moreover, their competence and workmanship is usually far superior to that of state employees.

In some instances, illegal private enterprise reportedly flourishes within state industry, by utilizing official premises as well as any available tools and resources on site. In Romania groups of enterprising workers, sometimes with the connivance of plant managers and local Party functionaries, have benefited from factory property—including buildings, equipment, raw materials, and energy supplies—to manufacture various items, even during working hours, that are subsequently sold privately for profit.[44] Such collective "abuses of public property" are evidently widespread and remain undetected for many years, while those involved earn substantial sums "on the side." These practices contribute to the inefficiency and poor productivity of the state economy, even though they help to meet public demands for scarce products. They also indicate the depth of worker alienation from the goals of state industry and the inviolability of nationalized property.

East Europe's "second economy" also has an international dimension, manifested in illicit "merchant tourism."[45] Private commerce, involving cash transactions and barter, is conducted by tourists during trips to or through other East Bloc countries. Products that are virtually unavailable in the country visited are smuggled in, and local goods are purchased for re-sale or consumption at home. Unofficial currency exchanges are also conducted during such trips. For thousands of travellers vacations become a highly profitable commercial venture, and may be repeated several times a year, especially when a merchant establishes a reliable network of local buyers and sellers. Poles and Yugoslavs appear to be the most outstanding "tourist traders" throughout the region, due perhaps to the comparatively liberal travel policies of their respective governments. But other nationalities are not immune to this pioneering business spirit. Communist governments have in recent years become alarmed by the scale of this independent economy, and have enforced stricter frontier checks, tighter visa controls, and more stringent foreign exchange regulations.

There is an inherent ambiguity in the relationship between Party-state planners and the voluminous underground economy. While illicit commerce helps to compensate for shortfalls in official supplies, it simultaneously deprives the state of sparse resources and distributes goods and services in ways that the authorities have not sanctioned or controlled. Such transactions undermine the legitimacy of the socialized economy and its functionaries, and breeds in state plants cynicism, apathy, a negative work ethic, and shoddier workmanship. Moreover, in the long term the national economy suffers more than the regime, because profits gained in illegitimate economic activities are not reinvested for purposes of expansion, research and development, and modernization. They are primarily expended on consumer goods and serve to perpetuate the widescale bribery network. This in turn results in further economic imbalances, damaging inflationary pressures, and unfulfilled consumer demands. Long-term economic instability may indeed be the price for short-term material gains.

Extensive self-help and mutual aid networks operate in Eastern Europe outside state control.[46] While such informal exchanges give some vent to entrepreneurship and public ingenuity, they are focused not on raising productivity but on circumventing a cumbersome government bureaucracy. Personal and familial crisis-management are characteristic of self-help networks in Communist countries. Webs of kinship, friendship, neighborhood, and other personal contacts provide access to various goods and services for many people. The system commonly operates on the basis of trust, reciprocity, and self-interest, though it may also be characterized by conflict and exploitation rather than mutuality and solidarity. This hidden network also has a political dimension, in that through it people avoid unnecessary contacts with official agencies and help insulate themselves against shortages and bureaucratic interference. Though the self-help system operates according to utilitarian rather than political principles, it nevertheless maintains and enlarges the non-state public sphere.

Kenedi provides a fascinating account of the underground system of distribution and mutual favors in Hungary, in which millions of individuals are involved to some extent.[47] People seeking goods or services generally unobtainable from the state or legal private sectors exploit an intricate mesh of personal contacts. This long-term "credit system," arranged through friends, acquaintances, relatives, neighbors, work colleagues, and other individuals in useful occupations or positions, involves a host of favors and exchanges, and creates a sequence of durable interpersonal obligations. Wedel describes the complex private distribution networks in Poland, which average citizens manipulate to their advantage.[48] Circles of family, kinspeople, acquaintances, and neighbors help to arrange everything from acquiring household items to circumventing governmental red tape. Wedel estimates that about twenty to thirty percent of Poles' incomes are spent on informally obtained goods and services, though the degree of illegality, and the extent or effectiveness of personal connections varies considerably; factors such as class, status, and sheer opportunity weigh heavily in the balance. These systems of "social insurance" embrace diverse forms of reciprocity, whether direct or indirect, immediate or delayed; they also revolve around enduring loyalties and mutual obligations that tend to perpetuate the self-help relationship.

Token gift-giving, routine bribery, and tipping are commonplace in the Soviet Bloc. They extend into virtually every public sphere and involve officials and staff in numerous institutions and agencies. Often it is individuals with the best contacts and influence-peddling techniques who obtain necessary materials enabling them to engage in legal or unregistered business ventures. Private sector producers rely heavily on permits and supplies regulated by state officials, which breeds bribery and corruption as businessmen try to keep their threatened enterprises intact. Many state employees earn extra income by charging clients for information, services, or goods that they are supposed to provide during normal working hours. Self-help cliques and bribing networks exist within practically all state bureaucracies, whereby officials not only build their own power bases but avail themselves of numerous scarce goods and services.[49] Bribery, corruption, nepotism, and patronage are practically institutionalized, and bureaucratic cliques may sabotage proposed economic reforms that could weaken their hold over such processes and privileges. Party leaders often tolerate such practices as a "necessary evil" that helps to assure political loyalty and stability. Administrative corruption includes the bribing of officials, illicit use of state supplies and premises, embezzlement, employment of unpaid labor, and the syphoning of state funds to pay for private villas, cars, foreign trips, and luxuries. Indeed, many bureaucrats do not seek a more efficient economy as this could jeopardize the material benefits accruing from their informal contacts.[50] Elaborate "pay-off" networks also exist, not simply to line the pockets of officials but to keep the wheels of industry moving and achieve plan targets. Through them managers and plant directors obtain essential materials, machines, and components that cannot be easily acquired through normal channels.

At the opposite end of the self-help–mutual aid spectrum are the various charitable initiatives undertaken by non-state agencies. The extensive humanitarian assistance program conducted by the Catholic Church in Poland provides food, clothing, medicines, and other vital items to needy families, orphans and old age homes, hospitals, victims of police persecution and their dependents.[51] Many of these supplies originate in the West from various governmental and private donors, and they are shipped directly to the Church to by-pass the inadequate state distribution system. Though Warsaw has not overtly restricted this invaluable humanitarian work, particularly during times of severe social distress, it has persistently barred the Church from dispersing large funds free of state control or re-establishing a charitable institution affiliated to the worldwide "Caritas" network.[52] In the absence of such an institution, the Church supervises a Charitable Commission attached to the Polish Episcopate with a network of diocesan and parish branches staffed by volunteers who distribute urgently needed aid. Solidarity also runs a charitable health care program, largely subsidized by the West. Its Social Foundation for Workers' Solidarity dispenses medical supplies to needy workers and their families.[53] Fund organizers hope to establish prophylactic and diagnostic centers independent of the rapidly deteriorating state health service. An autonomous, secular charitable initiative has also been undertaken in Hungary. The Foundation for Assistance to the Poor (SZETA) was created in December 1979 by a number of young Budapest intellectuals.[54] For several years SZETA raised money, distributed clothing and other items, and offered legal assistance to the homeless, Gypsies, and other underprivileged groups. In 1981 SZETA claimed about 500 members, but subsequently it appeared to decline in scope. The Foundation has come into conflict with the government, which resents its exposure of official failure to alleviate poverty.

Informal economic activities in some states also help channel funds to opposition groups. This may involve donations from home or abroad, the clandestine use of state property and supplies, the illicit purchase of materials prohibited to average citizens, or self-generated business financing by dissidents. The economic dimensions of political resistance appear to be well developed in contemporary Poland, where the "samizdat market" in particular has been thriving. Though in many instances underground publications are distributed freely, the sale of other books, periodicals, newssheets, audio and video cassettes, posters, badges, and assorted insignia raises money for the opposition movement. Direct financial contributions are regularly or sporadically paid by thousands of Solidarity supporters to help sustain the opposition network; substantial funding is also obtained from sympathizers abroad. The money collected is used to purchase printing equipment and materials, and to provide stable salaries to underground printers, distributors, editors, and writers. Furthermore, numerous individuals contribute valued goods or services to the opposition, or help collect and distribute funds for secret publishing operations. To insure *samizdat* publications against financial shortfalls and police seizure of equipment, manpower, and publications, an underground Foundation for Independent Publishing was set up in Warsaw in the wake of martial law.[55]

Labor Unionism and Self-Management

In most East European states, the official labor unions continue to function as standard Leninist "transmission belts" enforcing official policy through the union hierarchy, while monitoring the mood on the shop floor and filtering information upward to the government.[56] Trade unions supervise the workforce, while union officials are screened, selected, and scrutinized by the Party. In post-martial law Poland, however, the new government-sponsored labor unions have assumed a more refined role with the aim of averting further workers' protests.[57] Since 1982, unions have been carefully reconstructed from factory to central level to entice former Solidarity members and to prevent the emergence of independent worker organizations. Poland's "new unions" have posed both as independent "partners" for the regime, concerned with revitalizing the economy, and as capable defenders of workers' material interests. Nonetheless, though union officials have publicly opposed regular price increases and other unpopular government measures, their impact on Warsaw's policies has been limited. Their officially publicized opposition may indeed be a device to gain credibility among the workforce, and to dispel the appearance of impotence or automatic compliance with the will of the authorities. Solidarity leaders have accused the official unions of ineffectiveness in protecting living standards and improving working conditions, and they have been treated with suspicion by workers.[58] Official union members in several factories have participated in strikes called by workers over price rises on numerous occasions. This demonstrates the depth of dissatisfaction with the formal "negotiations" between state and union representatives. Despite early promises of trade union pluralism, Warsaw has disallowed the creation of rival unions even at the plant level, fearful as it is of Solidarity influence. The current situation is in stark contrast to the pre-martial law phase when in addition to the vast Solidarity structure over eighty "autonomous unions" and about two dozen "branch unions" were also in existence.

Some initiatives have been undertaken in other states to establish independent labor unions. Such attempts have occurred either during periods of domestic turmoil or in the midst of workers' protests against economic deprivation, when the official unions were perceived to be worthless. During the 1956 Hungarian uprising, independently elected workers' councils were established in all major factories, mines, and state farms after the Trade Union Central Council had freed itself from Party tutelage. They gained some control over management and backed various protests and strike actions after the Russian invasion. Following the Revolution, free associations were resolutely suppressed and employees again placed under Party-union supervision. During the past decade some disgruntled workers in Hungary have called for withdrawal from the official labor organizations and the establishment of autonomous committees that would campaign on behalf of workers' interests.[59]

In May 1988 the first independent labor union since the 1956 Revolution was formed in Budapest—the Democratic Union of Scientific and Academic Workers.[60] Its 1,000 founding members included scientists, technicians, and university staff. The organizers had repeatedly criticized the existing union for failing to oppose cuts in academic research funds or restrictions on scientific research and teaching. Strong political overtones were avoided in the founding declaration, even though the union refused to join the government sponsored SZOT trade union federation. The 59-member steering committee announced that it hoped to set an example for other groups. To counter such initiatives, Budapest formed an official Union of Scientific Workers, and denounced attempts to break up the "unity of (official) trade unions" for "politically motivated" reasons. Several other proposals for autonomous white-collar unions will test the limits of government tolerance at a time of pronounced belt-tightening and growing popular perceptions that official unions fail to defend properly the interests of employees.

During the 1968 Czechoslovak Prague Spring several attempts were made to establish autonomous unions. For instance, the Federation of Railroad Engineers declared its independence from the Central Council of Trade Unions; twelve other large unions split into smaller bodies, demanded freedom from central control, and granted internal independence to their subordinate sections. The free union episode was cut short by the "normalization" process after March 1969.[61] Independent labor activism remained largely dormant throughout Husák's rule until June 1981, when a clandestine Preparatory Committee of Free Labor Unions in Czechoslovakia was secretly founded.[62] Clearly inspired by the Solidarity experiment in Poland, its avowed aim was to "democratize the trade union movement from within"; and if this failed it intended to initiate independent unionization among blue-collar workers, claiming it had support in "many factories." The Committee's achievements to date have been negligible, and further notable campaigns for free labor organizations have not materialized in Czechoslovakia this decade.

The Free Labor Union of Working People in Romania (SLOMR) declared its existence in February 1979.[63] It reportedly included members of the dissident Bucharest intelligentsia as well as workers in the cities of Tirgu-Mures and Turnu Severin. The Union's objective was to defend workers against excessive production quotas and poor wages. At its peak SLOMR claimed between 1,600 and 2,500 members in three industrial centers, including members of the clandestine Unofficial Trade Union of Workers, Peasants, and Soldiers of Mures County, evidently set up during 1978. By April 1979 most of the union's activists had been arrested or terrorized into desisting from further organizational work.[64] Since mid-1979 little has been heard of SLOMR; after the Solidarity scare in Poland, the Romanian regime tightened union discipline and cracked down harshly on any independent worker initiatives. Free union activism has also been extremely subdued in the GDR and Bulgaria. Collective initiatives have quickly been quashed by the authorities. However, some reports did filter through about arrests in several East German plants in the summer of 1981 when small groups of workers called for independent committees along Solidarity lines. In 1982 an autonomous workers' association, Solidarity of Work, was reportedly formed in Bulgaria. It is difficult to gauge how much support it mustered before Sofia silenced the movement.[65]

In Poland the campaign for free labor unions in both industry and agriculture has continued in the aftermath of martial law. Between November 1986 and the summer of 1988, well over one hundred efforts have been made by factory Solidarity activists to obtain legal registration for union founding committees in state enterprises.[66] This campaign was initially opposed by Solidarity leaders because it implicitly accepted Jaruzelski's abolition of free unions. Solidarity officials began to back the initiative once they realized its scope and potential significance. The registration drive has tested the ground for union pluralism in an essentially legalistic way. Founding committee activists argue that covert union activity has very limited abilities to properly defend the workforce, whereas overt attempts to rebuild autonomous councils may provide a viable outlet for frustrated workers and help overcome widespread inertia.

After the wave of strikes in 1988, and increasing Solidarity pressures for formal recognition, applications for union registration were submitted in dozens of Polish cities. All these have been rejected by district courts and the Supreme Court, even though some committees deliberately dropped the "Solidarity" label in an effort to gain legal status. Warsaw is anxious about lifting the ban on union pluralism, and charges that the founding committees are a cover for "anti-state activities." Repressive measures have been applied against the most active union members, though the degree of harassment has varied between enterprises. Despite official intimidation many of the embryonic Polish unions have continued to function as advisory bodies that workers can approach with their problems. They have also backed independent candidates for factory self-management councils. The registration campaign itself is viewed as a valuable forum for independent activism in a repressive political climate. Some groups also publish information about their initiatives, collect data about factory conditions, petition management for changes in policy, and try to steer through loopholes in official regulations and prohibitions. In addition to blue-collar workers, other groups have also applied for registration, including professionals, students, white-collar staff, and private farmers.

During Solidarity's legal existence three major unions were formed by Poland's independent farmers. They were united in Rural Solidarity in March 1981; the union obtained legal status in May 1981 after substantial government obstruction. Rural Solidarity claimed a membership before martial law of about 2.5 million, or 70% of all private farmers. It demanded an end to the regime's irrational pricing structure, which discriminated against the peasantry; greater supplies of credits, machinery, feed, and fertilizer; and the rebuilding of the badly neglected rural infrastructure. Rural Solidarity's first national congress was scheduled for January 1982, but it was cut short by the "state of war." The union structure was practically obliterated by the regime and formally outlawed in October 1982. Since that time various independent farmers' committees have worked secretively to try and revive the union, but these are small, fractured movements exerting little effective pressure on the authorities.[67] Nevertheless, farmer activists continue to evade state supervision, particularly in parish groups engaged in self-education and cultural endeavors. Some independent peasant leaders have become more openly active since late 1986; for example, a Rzeszow-Ustrzyki Commission has been established to monitor the fulfillment of the February 1981 accords between state and farmers. The Commission has submitted various documents dealing with numerous peasant grievances. Some unofficial farmers' groups have favored the expansion of economic initiatives in the countryside, including a growth in direct trade between urban and rural residents to bypass state procurement and distribution networks.

There are diverging conceptions between government and opposition over the form and aim of workers' self-management, as well as differing emphases between states.[68] In general, Communist regimes concerned with decentralizing, streamlining, and modernizing the economic planning system view self-management as a useful means for stimulating worker motivation and boosting production. Workers' representatives on such councils are to serve as consultants for plant directors with some decision-making input in enterprise policy, but with little ultimate control or power sharing. In the age of *perestroika*, increased emphasis has been placed on self-management even among governments which have been lukewarm about economic reform. For example, statements to this effect have been issued by Prague and Sofia as an element of supposedly greater enterprise independence.

Dissident calls for independent worker self-management in Poland underscore the involvement of freely elected employee representatives in major enterprise decisions, such as investment policy, production schedules, and the selection of plant directors. This would need to be accompanied by a curtailment of Party interference in the enterprise and a more circumscribed role for central planners. Independent self-management initiatives have only been successful for short spells. Their agendas have frequently overlapped with the objectives of free labor unions—in protecting workers against unfavorable government and management policies—rather than aiming to boost factory productivity.

Self-governing workers' councils were established in several plants in Hungary and Poland during their respective 1956 rebellions against Communist rule. Independent councils also sprang up in Czechoslovakia in 1968, when attempts were made to create a national network of such bodies. All these efforts were diluted or extinguished by the state, and any remaining councils were reduced to a largely advisory position. In Pravda's estimation:

> The short life of genuine workers' councils and their general coincidence with periods of political turmoil reinforces the conclusion that they are not viable in the economic and political conditions prevailing in Eastern Europe.[69]

One may also add that, according to official reformist programs, Communist regimes may attempt to encourage and manipulate self-management bodies to improve the efficiency of state enterprises and pacify the workforce during potentially disruptive economic conditions.

In Solidarity's economic blueprints large plants would need to be divided into separate self-managing units responsible for maintaining productivity and raising profits. Workers could exercise extensive powers within the plant by controlling the appointment and dismissal of plant managers. At the national level Solidarity's economic experts advocate the involvement of independent self-management representatives with government agencies in economic policy-setting. The unofficial Network of Leading Enterprises, established in mid-1981, campaigned for a direct form of self-management in the larger enterprises, in which elected workers would have a role in making economic decisions. The Network claimed to represent over 3,000 enterprises on the eve of martial law. Predictably, its initiative was opposed by the regime, which feared any diminution of Party control in the factory. During and after Jaruzelski's "state of emergency," the initial state-Solidarity agreements on self-management were watered down by officials and some three million workers in the large, key plants were completely excluded from participation. Some five million state employees were permitted to form self-management councils under the watchful eyes of directors, official labor unions, and local Party functionaries. The government has encouraged participation without devolving any significant powers to the workforce. Horizontal links between self-management bodies were proscribed, plant managers remained state appointees, and directors and Party cells retained their decisive role in decision-making. At best, workers' representatives have been assigned a consultative role.[70]

Since 1982, efforts have been made by worker activists to strengthen the role of self-management in several dozen Polish plants, though attempts to reinstate the Network have borne little fruit.[71] In some instances, employees have elected Solidarity activists to self-management committees. By operating as surrogate free trade unions, the committees have clashed with the official labor, and undermined the credibility of the latter. Some observers note that the authorities may also deliberately foster or tolerate conflicts between self-management organs and labor unions in a "divide and conquer" strategy against workforce unity.[72] Solidarity leaders have expressed ambivalence about the officially permitted self-management bodies. Though initially dismissive of such ventures as "collaborationist," they have increasingly supported attempts to pressure the regime and revive flagging worker activism on the shop floor. Most of the councils, however, remain largely passive and exercise little real influence on management. Warsaw hopes they will function as safety valves for workers' frustrations, channel workers' energies into "constructive" pursuits, and help enforce labor discipline throughout industry by underlining the need for austerity and higher productivity.

Conclusion

Communist rule in Eastern Europe embraces all important decisions pertaining to economic planning, and involves centralized administrative control over material resources and economic privileges. Political and economic controls are closely intertwined in these countries. The authorities are wary of losing their grip on either, but seek to rectify serious market imbalances and neutralize public discontent by various admixtures of economic and political liberalization. Each Party-state fears that far-reaching economic decentralization could undermine the existing political arrangements, jeopardize its extensive social controls, and spur autonomous public initiatives. To differing degrees, Soviet bloc regimes will permit some measured independence in economic, cultural, and other pursuits, as long as "individuals or groups do not engage in activities designed to weaken or replace the political system or the socio-economic development program devised and executed by the political elite."[73] But there is no guarantee that official tolerance of partial economic privatization will lead automatically or irresistably toward genuine, institutionalized political pluralism.[74]

For the Leninist establishment, maintaining the political *status quo*, even if it is beset by economic difficulties, is preferable to an expanding, efficient private sector that buttresses independent social activism and seriously decreases state control. Periodic or prolonged liberalization, and the easing of various restrictions on private economic initiatives, has been motivated by potentially destabilizing shortages in the state sector that could breed social unrest. The authorities attempt to benefit from both legalized and unregistered private ventures, and try to steer independent initiatives into purely apolitical directions.

Aslund points out that the current tolerance or even limited encouragement of free enterprise in the East bloc "should not be seen as a radical change, because similar attempts were made in several countries in the mid-1950s and in the mid-1960s. The measures taken have never been far-reaching."[75] It would be grossly misleading to postulate the imminent emergence of capitalism or the "liberation" of market forces in the Communist economies. The process of market expansion and economic liberalization since Stalin's death has been uneven at best; it continues to be susceptible to sudden reversals and is hamstrung by severe bureaucratic constraints. Any leeway for private enterprise or quasi-autonomous cooperatives, as well as worker self-management, will be primarily used to alleviate bottlenecks and malfunctions in the socialist sector, while preserving the essential features of Communist Party dominance. The outcome of such a strategy in any country afflicted by profound economic problems and threatened by extensive social conflict cannot be easily predicted.

7

Social and Cultural Campaigns

In the Soviet bloc, official social and cultural policies aim above all at preserving Party-state control over the population. A network of Party-sponsored organs channels social behavior and interaction so as to neutralize potentially disruptive activity and minimize spontaneous self-expression or public self-organization. Those who benefit from this system have usually been co-opted or enticed by promised material or career advantages. Official social and cultural policies are implemented by Party-run youth and student organizations, peace movements, environmental protection agencies, ethnic minority associations, folklore groups, and artistic unions. During the 1980s, the ideological basis of Communist legitimacy has been significantly eroded. Party-created institutions have been discounted by sizeable sectors of the populace or criticized as being strictly ceremonial showcases or mouthpieces for government policies. Reflecting such popular dissatisfaction, numerous independent social and cultural campaigns have emerged throughout Eastern Europe. Because they threaten the regime's cherished monopoly of social control, independent activists have generally been subject to official reprisals. In this chapter, we shall focus on such initiatives and evaluate their origins and developments.

Peace and Disarmament Movements

The emergence of independent peace activists in the Soviet bloc is chiefly a phenomenon of the 1980s, when the cause of nuclear disarmament also attracted millions of campaigners throughout Western Europe and North America. The impetus for this development came largely from the scheduled deployment in Europe of new Warsaw Pact and NATO nuclear missiles. Eastern peace activists have welcomed contacts with sympathizers in the West, but there are major philosophical, political, and tactical differences between proponents on each side. The chief point of disagreement concerns unilateral nuclear disarmament, which many Western peaceniks support enthusiastically. Most Easterners reject this scenario as an abandonment of their countries to unchallenged Soviet hegemony. Instead, they emphasize the linkage between peace and freedom, a concept first articulated by Charter 77 in Czechoslovakia. Clearly, peace activists in Warsaw Pact countries also diverge radically from the Moscow-directed policies of official peace organizations. They disdain such organs' one-sided blame for the global arms build-up solely on the capitalist West.

The peace activism that has surged in the region is generally not "underground" in nature. Members of Poland's Freedom and Peace group (WiP), Charter 77's working group on peace, East Germany's pacifist youth, Hungary's democratic opposition or the Hungarian Peace Group for Dialogue, and conscientious objectors throughout the region who refuse military service on religious or moral grounds—all participate in overt demonstrations of their political and ethical principles. However, it is important to emphasize that a significant proportion of peace activism takes place spontaneously and independently, outside the framework of organized dissent. This has manifested itself in isolated cases of refusal of compulsory military service, usually among members of religious sects such as the Jehovah's Witnesses or the Nazarenes. The penalties for outright refusal can be severe, involving up to five years' imprisonment. It was estimated in 1986 that in Hungary alone, as many as 150 conscientious objectors were incarcerated in Baracska prison.[1]

Much of the animus behind conscientious objection has traditionally been religious. In the GDR, peace activists have been supported and sheltered by the Evangelical-Lutheran Church, which was instrumental in pressuring the state in the 1960s to introduce the *Bausoldat*, or construction soldier, option for inductees who did not wish to serve under arms. Approximately 500 young men a year currently choose this option.[2] However, in recent years there has been mounting pressure for an alternative service completely divorced from the military, as in health care or social work. The prospects for this remain dim, and each year there are approximately 200 *Totalverweigerer* who refuse both military and construction service; about half are Jehovah's Witnesses.[3]

Eastern peace activism first made an appearance on a wide scale in East Germany. An independent manifesto, entitled the "Berlin Appeal," was released on January 25, 1982, and eventually more than 2,000 signatures were appended to it. Drafted by the late dissident Robert Havemann and East Berlin Pastor Rainer Eppelmann, the unprecedented document raised questions about war toys, peace studies, alternative military service, civil defense, military parades, and non-military aid for the Third World. In addition, the Berlin Appeal demanded that "free expression" be tolerated in the public debate on peace issues, and called for the withdrawal of former Allied troops from the soil of the divided German nation. It began with an appeal for a nuclear-free Europe. This action was thought to be a response to the Krefeld Appeal, a single-issue petition protesting the NATO decision to install Cruise and Pershing II missiles in West Germany, for which three million signatures were gathered. The mass disarmament movement in the FRG, monitored and publicized by the West German media and closely followed by East Germans, clearly served as a catalyst for autonomous peace activity in East Berlin and other East German cities.

In February 1982, a "Peace Forum" was organized in Dresden to commemorate the 37th anniversary of the fire bombing of the city. Approximately 5,000 young people tried to organize an anti-war demonstration outside the Church of Our Lady in Dresden, but Church officials, fearing a showdown with the authorities, transformed the protest into a controlled discussion forum. One gripe aired there concerned government harassment of youths who wore the peace movement's symbol, the "Swords into Ploughshares" badge. A reproduction of the Soviet sculpture outside the United Nations building in New York, the symbol had been forcibly ripped off clothing by police, and those who wore it were threatened with expulsion from colleges and apprenticeships. The Church, wary of increased state pressure, counselled youths not to display the symbol in public. However, numerous clerics allowed the symbol to be worn and emblazoned on banners inside Church premises.

A series of public actions undertaken by peace activists in East Germany included an hour-long demonstration in an East Berlin square against the deployment of nuclear weapons by NATO and the Warsaw Pact in the fall of 1983. In the same year, on the same theme, protest leaflets were widely distributed and slogans were sprayed on city walls in Weimar; groups in Potsdam demonstrated in the Square of Nations; marches were organized in Leipzig; and women peaceniks demonstrated in East Berlin. In a particularly severe crackdown on dissent, East German authorities expelled twenty young peace activists to West Germany from the burgeoning pacifist community in Jena. Similar actions were taken against protestors in other cities, and Western peaceniks expressed outrage at the wave of arrests, expulsions, and forced emigrations of leading activists in the GDR. By late 1983, when it became clear that the Western disarmers had already lost the deployment battle and their influence had waned, East German authorities paid little heed to distant protests against their repression at home. With few exceptions, official acts of retribution worked to quieten and scale down acts of public protest. In recent years, East German groups have tended to organize and voice protest on peace issues solely under the umbrella of Church-sponsored forums, such as the "peace decades," or ten-day peace symposia.

In 1985 the independent peace movement in the GDR helped to spawn a new civil rights campaign—the Peace and Human Rights Initiative—under the leadership of pacifist spokesmen such as Rainer Eppelmann, Ralf Hirsch, and Wolfgang Templin.[4] Their first appeal in January 1985, signed by more than 300 people, called for full implementation of the UN Universal Declaration of Human Rights. Addressed to GDR leader Honecker, the document demanded a lifting of restrictions on travel, free expression and assembly. These same points of contention were reiterated in later appeals to government organizations and officials in July and May of that year. All petitions and open letters were signed by three spokespersons who gave their actual names and addresses. Members of the Initiative have produced a monthly *samizdat* publication since June 1986, devoted chiefly to peace, ecology and human rights issues. Another noteworthy sidelight to the GDR's peace movement was the formation in October 1982 of Women for Peace.[5] The group was created in response to new legislation that would enable women to be drafted in a national emergency. Over 300 women signed a letter of protest to Head of State Honecker, in which they declared that they would refuse military service if called up. Branches of Women for Peace were established in East Berlin, Dresden, Halle, and other cities. In December 1983, two members of the group were arrested in Berlin for contacting foreign journalists. International protest campaigns were largely responsible for the release of both women within the month.[6]

An independent peace movement, though small-scale and short-lived, made its appearance in Hungary in September 1982. Called the Peace Group for Dialogue, or "Dialogus," it was composed primarily of students and recent graduates at Budapest University, and it was led by a 25 year-old student of Hungarian literature, Ferenc Koszegi, and his wife. The group's badge, which has been widely displayed by Western peace groups, depicted two hands clasped around a flower on a background in the colors of the Hungarian flag. Dialogue held its first public meeting in November 1982 on the premises of the official Hungarian Peace Council; an estimated 350 young people attended. Speakers called for a nuclear-free Europe and an end to the Cold War, and expressed their commitment to terminate the "arms race" regardless of who bore responsibility for starting it. Proposals were voiced for a barrier to the deployment of NATO missiles; non-aggression pacts with Austria and Yugoslavia; and simultaneous withdrawals of NATO and Warsaw Pact forces from Europe.

Throughout its uneasy ten-month existence, the Peace Group for Dialogue struggled to maintain a formal distance from both the official Peace Council and the democratic opposition.[7] By doing so, the group hoped to win mass appeal while avoiding government sanctions. Nevertheless, group members did gradually find themselves persecuted and harassed by the authorities, who repeatedly denied them permission to publish a newsletter or to open their own offices. Dialogue leaders such as Ferenc Rusza were denied visas to attend peace conferences organized by West Europeans, and during the Prague Peace Assembly held in June 1983, Dialogue members were forced to leave the official "youth village." Government reprisals against the group mounted: a "peace camp" that opened on the outskirts of Budapest was broken up by police in July 1983, and foreign guests on the site were deported. Another camp to be opened near Debrecen was obstructed at the last minute by the National Peace Council, which invoked a series of zoning laws and age barriers. Twenty Dialogue members were detained for questioning and warned against taking part in "anti-state" activities after they went to greet Western delegates to a five-day international peace seminar. The Western visitors—from Great Britain, the Netherlands, Sweden, Austria, and the U.S.—were expelled from the country after being detained by police. Soon after, Rusza was called to the Ministry of the Interior and asked why the group had adopted an opposition stance toward the government—an allegation he adamantly denied.

In an "emotional" meeting on July 9, 1983, the Peace Group for Dialogue met and decided to disband in order to avoid further persecution. Rusza vowed at the group's final meeting that its supporters would not cease to campaign for disarmament. On July 27, former Dialogue members mounted a nationwide protest drive, calling for symbolic peace demonstrations. Hundreds of paper banners and posters were distributed in a Budapest park, and an open letter, deploring the police action taken against Dialogue members and their Western friends, was sent to members of the Hungarian National Assembly, Communist Party leaders, the Hungarian media, and leading intellectuals. In response, three in the group were detained by the authorities. Plainclothes police searched the homes of others, confiscating literature calling for a nuclear-free Hungary. In an unprecedented move, two peace activists from Szeged—Istvan Gonda and Janos Toth—were arrested and charged with violating the press law for distributing leaflets protesting the installation of Soviet SS-20 missiles—an offense punishable with a maximun fine of 180,000 forints or six months in prison.

Though former Dialogue members continued to meet in Budapest under the leadership of Rusza, the formal dissolution of the group was a defeat for independent activism in Hungary. Koszegi founded a Peace Club under the auspices of the official Peace Council, which attracted a docile and limited membership. One former member of the Peace Group for Dialogue, a Rabbi Csenyi, formed an independent peace group comprised of young Jewish intellectuals. Called "Shalom," which means "peace" in Hebrew, the group began to meet informally in the early 1980s.[8] Though Rabbi Csenyi had previously served a prison sentence for advocating conscientious objection, "Shalom's" activities were not strictly pacifist in nature. In an open letter issued in 1984, the group called for the recognition of Hungarian Jews as a cultural minority with the right to associate freely and cultivate links with Jews outside Hungary, including those in Israel. In its founding manifesto, "Shalom" also protested the support that Hungarian Jewish leaders accorded the Soviet Union, accusing them of insensitivity to threats against Israel's existence. In March 1984, Rabbi Csenyi and several "Shalom" members were briefly arrested. Reportedly, the group continues to be active, though its ranks are small.

An account of pacifist activity in Hungary would be incomplete without mention of the "basis communities"—small fundamentalist Christian groups under the general leadership of the Piarist Father Gyorgy Bulanyi. Young members of the basis communities advocate conscientious objection and have been persecuted for their refusal to consent to compulsory military service. According to Keston College, more than twenty basis community members have been imprisoned for conscientious objection since 1979.[9] In February 1987, Hungary's first political (as distinct from religious) conscientious objector was arrested under Article 336 of the country's penal code. Zsolt Keszthelyi, a dissident magazine editor, was sentenced to three years in prison in April, reduced a month later to two and one-half years on appeal. He sent his draft papers back to the recruitment center with a statement that left no doubt as to his motivation:

> I . . . hereby declare that I wish to refuse military service because of political motives. I am not inclined to put my trust in a "people's democratic" army which is not placed under the control of a government elected by universal suffrage involving competing political programs. I think that by this action, just like by my struggle for a free press, I can contribute to the creation of a society which is free of fear and in which the management of social affairs is determined by the responsibility and conscience of individuals and not by unquestioning faith and fear. If there is no other way, I am ready to throw in my lot with those conscientious objectors who, due to their decision of conscience, have been sentenced to prison during the "people's democratic" periods of the past forty years having penalties designed to deny true constitutionalism.[10]

Keszthelyi also dispatched a letter along similar lines about his case to the Helsinki Review Conference in Vienna.

Though political dissidence is still not officially accepted as grounds for conscientious objection in Hungary, religious pacifism has been reconsidered.[11] In February 1988, State Secretary Imre Miklos publicly conceded that existing regulations on conscientious objection needed amendment; a month later, Prime Minister Karoly Grosz confirmed that negotiations on this issue were under way. At a meeting of the National Peace Council in June 1988, officials agreed that civilian alternatives to military service would be offered in 1989. The shift in regime posture can be attributed partly to national and international campaigns in recent years by well-known oppositionists. Perhaps most significant was a change in Hungarian Catholic Church policy, which had previously been indisposed toward conscientious objectors from the basis communities. In March 1988 Primate Laszlo Paskai expressed support for an alternative form of service for young believers who could not bear arms in good conscience.

Poland can claim to have one of the most influential independent peace groups in Eastern Europe, as measured by the government concessions made recently in response to grassroots pressures. In May 1988, a government spokesman announced that Warsaw had approved a new military oath that omits a previous reference of allegiance to the Soviet Red Army—wording that had caused scores of young draftees to refuse military service in the past.[12] Jacek Szymanderski, a spokesman for Freedom and Peace (WiP), said that the change was "remarkable" and represented a "symbolic victory" for the opposition. The new oath, pending ratification by the Polish Parliament, does indeed represent a triumph of dissent in the post-Solidarity era. In the summer of 1988, the Polish government also passed legislation that introduced a non-military alternative service for conscientious objectors. And dozens of CO's were released from Polish prisons in July 1988 when the Jaruzelski regime suddenly announced a national amnesty.[13]

WiP is not, strictly speaking, a by-product of the banned Solidarity trade union movement. Nevertheless, Polish peace activists have received gestures of support from a few of Solidarity's erstwhile advisors, such as Michnik and Kurón. Even Solidarity leader Lech Wałesa has publicly appealed for the release of an imprisoned WiP member. And pacifist spokesmen have indicated that they drew vital inspiration from the unfulfilled promise of Solidarity during its brief above-ground existence.[14] Freedom and Peace was founded in April 1985 to protest the imprisonment of Marek Adamkiewicz, a young Pole who received a two and a half year sentence for refusing to take the military oath pledging loyalty to the Soviet Union. Unlike other recruits who had refused to take the oath, 21 year-old Adamkiewicz was the first to be imprisoned for the offense and treated like a common criminal. A hunger strike was mounted to support him, a peace and human rights seminar was held, and a protest petition with more than 1,000 signatures was sent to the Polish authorities. Eventually, by 1988, WiP had evolved into a loose federation of groups in some eleven cities, principally Warsaw, Cracow, Gdansk, and Wrocław.[15] There are an estimated 200 WiP activists in Poland who represent the core of the movement; however, WiP has held demonstrations in which over 2,000 people participated, and its petitions have borne as many as 10,000 signatures. The group eschews clandestine activity, preferring to operate openly as far as possible. Those who sign WiP documents use their real names and usually include their addresses. In a 1986 article, WiP leader Jacek Czaputowicz commented: "Open action is also the safest action. We are doing nothing illegal, only demanding the right of every citizen to be free of political coercion in matters of personal/ethical decisions, such as military service."[16]

As implied by its name, Freedom and Peace strongly underscores the interrelationship of peace and human rights. This tenet has governed WiP activism, not only in the areas of conscientious objection and nuclear disarmament, but also in the realms of ecology, religious freedom, and the political oppression of Third World people and citizens of other East European countries. The philosophy of nonviolence has been adopted by the movement as "the most appropriate means for social struggle for human rights." WiP members and sympathizers have been predominantly young people espousing a broad range of political and religious beliefs. The group's activities are similarly varied. In the first three months of 1987, for example, WiP organized actions against torture in Afghanistan; the arrest of peace and human rights activists in Czechoslovakia, Hungary and Yugoslavia; and the construction of a nuclear power plant in Zarnowiec, Poland.

Czechoslovakia's Charter 77 was the first dissident group in the region to articulate the "indivisibility of peace and freedom"[17] and to expatiate upon this theme eloquently in its documents and statements. After six years of fostering friendly contacts with Western pacifists, Charter 77 organized a "working group on peace" in June 1987, following an international seminar sponsored in May by Freedom and Peace in Warsaw. Though the working group has yet to issue an in-depth study or definitive statement, Charter 77 has already gone on record with respect to key concerns in the peace debate. In March 1986, for instance, the group issued a document calling for a reduction of compulsory military service from twenty-four to eighteen months, and an introduction of the right to conscientious objection.[18] Charter 77 was also active in fostering communication and cooperation with peace groups in the East; hence, in July 1984 there was a joint statement with Hungarian peace activists, and four months later a declaration signed jointly with East German peace activists, protesting the stationing of Soviet SS-20s in their countries and expressing solidarity with Western pacifists.[19]

In April 1988, Charter 77 issued an open invitation to an international seminar on human rights and peace, to be held in Prague in June 1988. Representatives from fifteen countries attended, including East Europeans from Hungary, Yugoslavia, and Czechoslovakia. In a decisive official crackdown, thirty-two foreign participants were expelled from the country and several members of Charter 77 were detained by police.[20] Also taken into custody were members of the Independent Peace Council, a little known Czechoslovak anti-war group. The seminar was the fourth in a series of independent peace conferences held in the East bloc during 1988. Earlier gatherings had taken place in Budapest, Warsaw and Moscow. The conference in Prague was the first of the four to be disrupted by government agents.

Outside the Charter 77 umbrella, there have been noteworthy manifestations of autonomous and spontaneous pacifism in Czechoslovakia. Much of this activity occurred in 1983, when Soviet missiles were about to be deployed in the country. Protest petitions, organized chiefly by workers in Moravia, attracted some 2,000 signatures. University students launched an anti-deployment campaign using the sun as a symbol. And in Prague, a group of youthful peace campaigners tagged on to an official peace march, much to the consternation of the authorities. In May 1986, a student group appealed to the Ministry of the Interior for permission to set up a peace and disarmament organization. Provisionally called "Young Art for Peace," the group proposed to work within the framework of the National Front rather than in opposition. Approximately 600 youths signed a petition supporting this concept. Security police, however, initiated an intimidation campaign which culminated in July with a retraction of the request by would-be members. Though some of them had been in contact with Charter signatories, there was no formal link between the two bodies, as police alleged.

Young pacifists in Czechoslovakia have also staged spontaneous peace demonstrations on each anniversary of John Lennon's death since the singer was murdered in December 1980.[21] Hundreds congregate in his memory, singing anti-war songs and chanting peace slogans at the "Lennon Wall" on Kampa island in Prague.[22] After yearly clashes with police from 1982 to 1984, the protestors again gathered in 1985, forming a procession that meandered throughout the capital. Demonstrators chanted: "We want freedom, we want peace," "Do away with the SS-20s," and "Do away with the army." Eventually, police dispersed the crowd and hauled off one of the organizers for questioning. In April 1988, an Independent Peace Association was established in Czechoslovakia by a small group of citizens who had not previously participated in dissident activities.[23] Emphasizing its thoroughly independent status, the Association's founding declaration contained five points, including a call for greater *glasnost,* even on military issues; an end to warmongering propaganda; and recognition of the right of conscientious objection. In addition, the group issued a letter calling for a "general reduction of military service." The letter also demanded public discussion of peace issues, and its five signatories asked that their names and full addresses be broadcast by foreign radio stations in order to enable people outside the country to contact them and cooperate with the Peace Association.

East bloc dissidents have recently launched a unified campaign to guarantee the right of conscientious objection, whether for religious or political reasons. In March 1988, a joint appeal issued by members of Hungary's democratic opposition was signed by 438 East European and Soviet activists. The appeal, which was submitted to the 35 delegations at the Helsinki follow-up conference in Vienna, urged that the right to conscientious objection and an alternative form of service be recognized in a CSCE document. Presenting the appeal at a Vienna press conference, Hungarian dissident Miklos Haraszti claimed that it was the largest joint action undertaken thus far by civil rights campaigners in the Soviet bloc. In a *New York Times* article in August 1987, Haraszti had appealed for independent activists working to make conscientious objection a legal right in the East bloc. The international publicity generated for this cause has indeed helped to wrest some concessions in the region, notably in Hungary and Poland.

Ecological Campaigns

Eastern Europe faces ecological disaster, with air and water pollution reaching increasingly threatening proportions. Decades of rapid industrialization have passed with little official concern for environmental protection.[24] Among other perils are dangerous levels of soil contamination, and health problems in the worst affected areas such as abnormally high infant mortality, birth defects, reduced life expectancy, respiratory ailments and a wide variety of cancers. In addition, in the Chernobyl era, as East European states slowly make a transition from coal and oil to nuclear energy, popular awareness of potential environmental hazards has surged, resulting in isolated instances of protest. The degradation of the natural environment in Eastern Europe[25] ranks, in several respects, among the worst in the hemisphere, even when one judges the situation by use of patchy official statistics, which may well be doctored to conceal the extent of the problem from the populace. It is not surprising, therefore, that independent ecological initiatives have been mounted in several East European states in the 1980s.

The first organized manifestation of independent ecological activism occurred in Poland, when the Polish Ecology Club was founded in

Cracow in September 1980. One of the country's most polluted cities, Cracow was also a meeting ground for some of Poland's leading environmental scientists and naturalists, who inaugurated their organization with an open letter to the Polish Sejm on the need for stricter environmental protection legislation.[26] Buoyed by the enlightened activism of the Solidarity movement, the group opened fourteen branches nationwide and swelled to 20,000 members by July 1981. By then, it had scored some stunning successes, notably the closure of the highly polluting Skawina Aluminum Smelter near Cracow in early 1981. The preliminary findings of a special government commission there were that every worker with over twenty years' seniority was suffering from some ailment. It was recommended that most of the plant's 2,400 employees should retire on pensions because they were too sick to work elsewhere.

Solidarity was also active in the field of environmental protection. In May 1981, its Interfactory Workers' Committee asked that work be stopped at an oil extraction area near Szczecin until extensive local environmental damage could be addressed. Air pollution in the area was also a concern of the trade union, whose activists had measured hydrogen sulfide in the atmosphere at twenty-nine times the acceptable level. The region's health service had also noticed signs of physical malaise in the local populace and Solidarity was instrumental in bringing these facts before the general public. Such revelations took place in many other regions of the country.

With the dismantling of legal Solidarity, ecological activism in Poland was for a time quelled. It re-emerged under the auspices of WiP, the Freedom and Peace group, which has mounted some important environmental initiatives, especially in the aftermath of the Chernobyl disaster in the Soviet Ukraine. WiP organized demonstrations in May 1986 to protest the lack of information being provided about the Chernobyl accident; an estimated 2,000 people participated in the Cracow march.[27] Another cause that has attracted WiP activism is the planned construction of Poland's first nuclear reactor at Zarnowiec, about forty kilometers from Gdansk. In Bialystok, an area particularly exposed to Chernobyl, about 3,000 people signed a petition calling for suspension of construction at Zarnowiec, nicknamed "Zarnobyl." Other demonstrations have been organized to protest construction of a second nuclear reactor near Poznan. In conjunction with efforts by journalists and scientists, WiP has been influential in pressuring the Polish authorities to close the Siechnice steel mill near Wrocław, which pollutes water in the area with ferrochromium composites. Three demonstrations against the foundry were organized by WiP activists in late 1986 and early 1987; they were disrupted by the police and fines were levied against the participants. In January 1987—nineteen days after WiP's third demonstration—the

Provincial People's Council in Wrocław announced that the Siechnice foundry would be closed before the end of 1992. Similar WiP demonstrations have been targeted against the Nowa Huta Steelworks near Cracow; some 500 other industrial enterprises have been identified by the group as serious polluters.

Since 1978, Charter 77 in Czechoslovakia has made ecological concerns a high priority with the aid of well-informed members of the country's scientific community. In July 1983, the human rights monitoring group issued a detailed document which warned the authorities of a serious, worsening environmental crisis in northern Bohemia.[28] The document was indirectly an indictment of the Prague regime's plan to contain ecological damage in the region, which had apparently been far from successful. In February 1984, Charter 77 created an international sensation when it obtained and reprinted a secret government report that revealed in depth the disastrous state of the country's ecology and resultant health problems.[29] Produced by the Czechoslovak Academy of Sciences in 1983, the report indicated that, since 1960, there had been a fifty percent increase in the incapacity of workers due to ill health. In polluted industrial regions, there are significantly higher rates of lung disease, infant mortality, and early deaths. Correspondingly, animal and plant life have been adversely affected by acid rain, air and water pollution, and the widespread chemicalization of agriculture.

Perceived environmental threats have drawn together independent activists in the East bloc, particularly those from Czechoslovakia and Hungary. Hence, the Danube Circle, a non-official Hungarian ecology group, appealed to Charter 77 in 1985 to advise the Czechoslovak public of the environmental dangers of the planned Gabcikovo-Nagymaros hydroelectric dam, a joint Czechoslovak-Hungarian project. In September 1985, Charter 77 issued an appeal to Prague to reconsider its commitment to the project; it also released the text of the Danube Circle's direct address to the Hungarian public:

> The hysterical industrialization of the 1950s and the continuous plundering of the economy have caused irreversible damage in many regions of Bohemia, Moravia, Slovakia and Hungary. The construction of the planned hydroelectric barrage system at Gabcikovo-Nagymaros is likely to have irreversible consequences which will affect all the nations living along the Danube . . . We appeal to the Czechoslovak public to join us in our fight to defend ecological values and the Danube region.[30]

In May 1986, Charter 77 issued a document deploring the government's inadequate response to the Chernobyl crisis. Addressed to the Federal Assembly, the document demanded that officials publish "as soon as possible" full information on increased radioactivity in Czechoslovakia. It also asked that the public receive expert opinion as to lingering health risks and how to deal with them, both immediately and in the future. In the first half of 1987, Charter 77 issued two noteworthy documents dealing with Czechoslovakia's ecological crisis. In its New Year's Day statement, the group called for an open public discussion of "catastrophic" environmental problems. In April, it issued a twelve-page document, poignantly entitled "Let the People Breathe."[31] Sent to several government agencies, the paper concentrated on the problems caused by severe industrial air pollution. It demanded the installation of air filters by plants burning low-grade coal, recommended the implementation of energy-saving technology, and warned of the potential dangers posed by greater reliance on nuclear power. Short-term and long-term solutions were enumerated. Predictably, no official response was forthcoming, although copies were sent to federal and national councils, as well as to the Czechoslovak Academy of Sciences.

Hungary's Danube Circle is an active independent environmental protection group that has campaigned energetically to stop construction of the Gabcikovo-Nagymaros hydroelectric dam project. Founded in 1984 by journalist and biologist Janos Vargha, the Danube Circle has concentrated exclusively on the proposed dam and the negative impact it would allegedly have on the environment. In May 1984, the group sent a protest letter both to the National Assembly and the Council of Ministers, signed by 4,000 to 6,000 people, including fifty prominent Hungarians in the cultural and scientific spheres.[32] At first, the Danube Circle distanced itself from the Hungarian opposition, by purporting to be a group concerned exclusively with ecological rather than political issues. By choosing this path, its members apparently hoped to minimize official displeasure. Nevertheless, the authorities effectively blocked an attempt by the group to register formally as the Association for the Protection of the Danube, by creating pretexts for interminable paperwork. They warned and intimidated group members and refused to engage seriously the issues raised by the Danube Circle, whether on or off the public record. Indeed, an official counter-offensive was mounted in the press, vaunting the benefits of the project. By late 1985, the Danube Circle appeared to have lost its cause, as Budapest reaffirmed and strengthened its commitment to build the dam.

The Danube Circle was revitalized in September 1985, when it was awarded one of the "alternative" Nobel Prizes during a ceremony in Stockholm at the Swedish Parliament. The privately donated "Right Livelihood" awards, worth the equivalent of about $95,000, are meant to complement the real Nobel Prizes. In 1987, eleven representatives of the Danube Circle received the prize money in Hungarian currency.

This transaction took two years to complete, due largely to the obstructions of the rankled Hungarian government, which did not permit the award to be collected in hard currency.[33] The recipients used their award to create in May 1987 the Danube Foundation, which pledged to "assist private citizens or movements who wish to perform acts towards the preservation of ecology, environment, or nature with particular regard to the Danube." A competition was organized by the Foundation in July, with project sponsorship, scholarships and loans offered as prizes. By November, eight competition entries had been received[34] and awards were under consideration. The Danube Circle has taken other steps to mobilize the public and change government policy. Calling for a referendum on the dam project, the group organized a petition and collected 2,655 signatures,[35] but the proposal was rejected by the authorities who continued to harass the Circle. In April 1986, thirty Hungarian intellectuals (including prominent members of the cultural and scientific communities) published a full-page advertisement in the Viennese newspaper *Die Presse*, intended to alert the Austrian public to widespread popular opposition in Hungary to the dam project. The Danube Circle was particularly interested in reaching the Austrian public because the Nagymaros project is to be financed largely by credits from Vienna; these are to be paid back over twenty years by the free provision of hydroelectric power from the dam. In addition, seventy percent of the construction will be subcontracted to Austrian firms. The advertisement declared: "A democratic society—and we regard Austria as such—must not allow itself to exploit the lack of democracy in another country for its own material advantage."[36] Some Austrian environmentalists and politicians have responded sympathetically to appeals by the Danube Circle; in fact, the *Die Presse* advertisement was reportedly paid for by Austrians. In July 1986, nineteen members of the Danube Circle addressed a petition to the Viennese parliament, urging a last-minute review of the dam agreement package.

Other independent environmentalist groups have surfaced in Hungary. In 1987, several attempts were made to organize a Danube Protection Society, but authorities would not extend recognition and, although meetings were held on a small scale, the group's organizers faced insurmountable obstacles to expansion.[37] More successful have been the independent "Blues," so named to underline concern with pure water and to recall the West European Greens. Founded in 1985, the Blues are younger and more militant than members of the Danube Circle, and have engaged in a public education campaign, notably about the protection of the Danube. The Blues lack formal membership and do not publish regularly. However, they have adopted a leafleting strategy to reach the Hungarian public. In September 1985, in its first and best known initiative, the group distributed 10,000 leaflets across the country, protesting the Gabcikovo-Nagymaros dam. In addition, the Blues sent letters to parliamentarians and members of the intelligentsia living in the Danube region. The letters listed damaging aspects of the project that had been overlooked in the mass media; they also discussed the financial and environmental problems entailed, and urged the public to pursue the matter with members of parliament and in other forums. In a 1986 interview in a Hungarian *samizdat* journal, a Blues member commented on the long-term, far-reaching objectives of the group:

> Our aims in fact extend beyond environmental protection, for we want to stimulate independent thinking in all aspects of life and to encourage greater autonomy in the way people live and act. We would like to see cooperation in matters that affect us all, in order to stop the fragmenting of society.[38]

Representatives of thirteen independent ecology groups, meeting in Budapest, formed a common coordinating committee in March 1988.[39] Called the Alternative and Environmentalist Groups' Information Network, the coalition launched a magazine entitled *Tuleles* (Survival), which is to appear biweekly. Among the organizations represented in the Network are the Danube Circle, the Danube Foundation, the Eotvos Lorand University Ecology Club, the Kal Basin Friendship Circle, the Petofi Alliance and the 4-6-0 Peace group. Most of these groups surfaced in the 1980s in response to rising concerns about Hungary's ecological crisis. They have cooperated to some extent with official agencies such as KISZ (the Communist Youth League) and the Ministry of the Environment. The Kadar and Grosz regimes have taken a cautious but increasingly tolerant stance toward these public-spirited ventures in a bid to contain popular pressure.

East German environmentalists, like peace activists, have in many instances sheltered behind the Evangelical-Lutheran Church. Clergymen have encouraged frank discussion of ecological issues at Church seminars, workshops, and on parish grounds; some have sponsored unofficial events such as auto-free days when urban drivers were urged to use non-polluting bicycles. Independent national ecology seminars have been held annually in East Berlin since 1983. Under heavy security surveillance, the third session took place in late November 1986, attended reportedly by one hundred people from no less than thirty-six environmental groups in the GDR.[40] Even before the Chernobyl debacle in the USSR, East Germany experienced isolated rumblings of anti-nuclear sentiment. Afterward, however, anti-nuclear protest intensified, fueled largely by the responses of the West German Greens movement and the uncensored information received in the GDR from the West German media. Seven months after the Chernobyl accident, East German security police arrested two environmentalists in Karl Marx Stadt for distributing home-made cassettes on the effects of the disaster.[41] Evidently, ecological activists believe that the East German public is largely ignorant of the risks of their country's nuclear energy program, which has been engineered largely according to the Soviet model.

A seven-page antinuclear petition, eventually signed by several hundred people, was sent to East Germany's People's Chamber and Council of Ministers in May 1986.[42] Entitled "Chernobyl Is Everywhere," the petition was self-described as an "appeal by the independent peace and ecology movement and other concerned citizens." Though little was known in the West about the signatories, they are believed to have been drawn from the small environmentalist groups that have sprung up in the 1980s under the aegis of the Evangelical-Lutheran Church. The petition's demands recall those of Western ecology groups, particularly the West German Greens. It called on the GDR authorities to eliminate the use of nuclear energy by 1990, to publish accurate measurements of radio-activity, and to allocate funds for the development of alternative energy sources. In addition, an appeal for a referendum on the use of nuclear energy was circulated in the summer of 1986 at a Church-sponsored "peace workshop" in East Berlin. The appeal was drafted by four members of the independent peace movement and was to be presented to the People's Chamber, which is empowered under East German law to call a referendum.

In late November 1987, security police in East Berlin raided a Church-supported environmentalist library and detained a number of dissidents.[43] This action was seen as the first large-scale repression of independent activists in recent years. Five people were detained after the raid on Zion Church, where police confiscated documents, *samizdat* journals and copying machines. At least another twelve people were arrested at a Church vigil being held to demand the release of the five activists. Moreover, an undisclosed number of other dissidents in East Berlin had their apartments searched, or were placed under house arrest. Simultaneous crackdowns were reportedly staged in Dresden and Rostock. Zion Church's environmental library was founded in late 1986 and had become a meeting place for independent peace and environmental activists. In fact two days after the raid, a three-day unofficial ecological congress with participants from other East European countries was to be held at Zion Church. Its library was also a printing center for one of the GDR's leading *samizdat* journals, the ecological *Umweltblaetter* (Environmental Pages).

Cross-border pollution has become a problem of increasing severity in Eastern Europe, spurring protest demonstrations on occasion. Such is the case in the Bulgarian city of Ruse on the Danube, where air pollution has been caused by chlorine gas emitted from a chemical combine in the Romanian city of Giurgiu across the river.[44] In September 1987, when the poisonous smog over the city grew unusually thick, many of Ruse's 185,000 inhabitants gathered in the central square, calling out: "Give us fresh air!", "No to the chlorine!" and "We want healthy children!" Sofia's concern has apparently grown as the pollution continues, resulting in high-level consultations with Romanian representatives and the provision to the Bulgarian public of revealing statistics on pollution-related health problems in Ruse and the surrounding region. In 1988 the Romanian Democratic Action group produced a twenty-two-page report on Romania's worsening environmental crisis.[45] The clandestine group sent copies of its findings to the Austrian Foreign Minister Alois Mock and the Green factions in the Austrian and West German parliaments. The report, highly critical of Romania's current "economic disaster" and "sociopolitical sclerosis," indicted the Ceausescu administration for the continuing deterioration and squandering of Romania's natural resources. Numerous results of pollution were noted, such as the "huge, red-colored cloud (that) hangs day and night over the town of Tirgoviste." Specific industrial polluters were named, as were "catastrophic explosions" and other accidents that have compromised environmental safety. Officially sanctioned practices such as toxic waste dumping were deplored in the report, as well as the regime's program of urban and rural reorganization, denounced as "planned aggression against the environment." A plea was made for comprehensive education about environmental protection "from earliest childhood." Furthermore, a number of legal and technological reforms were proposed.

National and Ethnic Minorities

The multiplicity of national and ethnic minorities in Eastern Europe has given rise in recent years to a limited range of activists campaigning for minority rights and the preservation of minority cultures.[46] Two of these groups, representing ethnic Hungarians and ethnic Germans living in Romania, have been particularly active in *samizdat* publishing. Both share grievances against assimilationist policies pursued by the Ceausescu regime. Both constitute the largest ethnic minority groups in the country, with 1.8 million Romanian citizens of Hungarian origin representing eight percent of the total population, and 400,000 of German origin representing two percent.[47] Ethnic Hungarians in Romania are concentrated in Transylvania, and their treatment by the Bucharest government has increasingly become a source of friction between officials at the highest levels in Hungary and Romania.

A small network of ethnic Hungarian intellectuals in several Transylvanian cities has produced the only known *samizdat* journals in Romania: the magazine *Ellenpontok* (Counterpoints) and its successor *Erdelyi Magyar Hirugynokseg* (The Hungarian Press of Transylvania). *Ellenpontok,* published in Hungarian, made its first appearance in December 1981, but ceased to be received in the West after January 1983. During that period, ten mimeographed issues were produced, dealing primarily with Romania's minority policies and their impact on ethnic Hungarians.[48] In September 1982, the editors sent a Memorandum to the Madrid Conference on Security and Cooperation in Europe, which called for the creation of an independent international commission to investigate the plight of Romania's Magyar minority. Their demands included full cultural autonomy and equal employment rights. *Ellenpontok's* editors published other memoranda on similar themes, as well as reports on repression against them and their staff. One issue dealt with the negative stereotypes of Hungarians propagated by the Ceausescu regime, and distortions in the official version of Romanian-Hungarian history. *Ellenpontok* writers, editors and publishers remained anonymous by choice until November 1982, when the authorities cracked down on dissident Hungarian intellectuals, allegedly treating them brutally in custody. Under duress, three admitted to being editors of the journal: philosopher Attila Ara-Kovacs, high school teacher Karoly Toth, and poet Geza Szocs.[49] Persecution of the journal's known or suspected staff members continued, eventually forcing emigrations and the discontinuation of publication.

The Hungarian Press of Transylvania continued, with important differences, from the point where *Ellenpontok* left off.[50] A mimeographed news bulletin that exceeded 200 pages in 1986, the publication reports primarily on discrimination against the Hungarian minority. But it also monitors the declining social and economic conditions that affect the Romanian majority and the ethnic minorities alike, producing occasional joint actions such as the protests and strikes that erupted in Transylvania in November 1986. The *samizdat* news bulletin, which generally reaches the West through Vienna, was the chief source of information about the unrest.

Individual Romanians of Hungarian origin have taken public stands in protest against Bucharest's forcible assimilation policies. Among them, perhaps the best known is Karoly Kiraly, a former RCP Central Committee member who resigned from his official duties in the early 1970s when discriminatory measures against the ethnic Hungarians were sharpened.[51] In August 1987, Kiraly sent a protest letter to Ceausescu, with whom he was once closely acquainted.[52] In his letter, Kiraly discussed anti-Hungarian propaganda circulating in Romania and commented: "We must stop producing scapegoats. Because of past sins, mistaken policies should not create scapegoats today." A brief but sympathetic reply was received from Ion Georghe Maurer, former Romanian head of state and premier, who wrote: "I agree with everything outlined in your letter . . . except . . . that things can be redressed." Soon afterward he was dismissed from office.

The plight of Romania's Hungarian minority has had a deep resonance in Hungary proper. On June 27, 1988, 30,000 to 50,000 Hungarians in Budapest marched to the Romanian embassy to protest "land reform" plans by Ceausescu to destroy more than half of the villages in Romania, many populated by ethnic Hungarians. It was by far the largest unofficial demonstration since the 1956 uprising. Also critical of the Ceausescu regime has been a small group of dissident Romanian refugees based since 1987 in Budapest. Calling themselves the Free Romania Group[53], these activists produced in 1988 the first known Romanian-language *samizdat* periodical, entitled *Romania Libera*. Meant for distribution in Romania, it was published with the assistance of Hungary's "democratic opposition." This effort marked the first time in Warsaw Pact history that an opposition group from one country openly undertook activism within the boundaries of another. The first two issues of the magazine expressed support for democratic reforms within socialism and for political reform as a means of ensuring Romania's observance of its human rights obligations under international covenants. Forced ethnic assimilation was deplored; Hungarian and Romanian reformers were urged to formulate a joint approach to the nationality problem as a contribution to a new "privileged" relationship between the two nations in the post-Ceausescu era.

Swabian German writers from Romania's northwestern Banat region have in recent years mounted protests against official cultural policies. A group known as the Aktionsgruppe Banat, comprising some ten young German-language writers, protested restrictions on ethnic German cultural life and the general condition of writers in the Communist state.[54] Their statements were characterized by a libertarian attitude and a tolerant view of minority coexistence in their ethnically mixed region. Though a stimulating presence on Romania's cultural scene, their influence was limited, as they found few allies among other German writers in Transylvania or among Romanian writers generally. Nevertheless, the authorities apparently perceived them as a potential threat and attempted to absorb them. When that failed, repression was stepped up, sometimes brutally. Most of the group's members were arrested and many were interrogated by the Securitate. Since 1986, they have been forced one by one into emigrating, primarily to West Germany.[55]

A small but active group of ethnic Hungarians in Slovakia has organized a minority rights coalition in recent years, called the Committee for the Protection of Hungarian Minority Rights in Czechoslovakia. Primarily it has expressed concerns about preserving the "living culture" of the 580,000-strong Hungarian minority in Slovakia. This has involved protests against acts of vandalism or arson that have been perpetrated in ethnic Hungarian communities. For example, in March 1987, one of the group's leaders, Miklos Duray, addressed a letter to the General Prosecutor of Slovakia, urging apprehension of those responsible for damaging four Hungarian cultural institutions in Bratislava in a single night.[56] Later that month, Charter 77 sent a letter to the Federal Government and Federal Assembly of Czechoslovakia, asking for an official investigation into these "acts of terrorism" and demanding that the public be informed "about these violent acts and the course of their investigation."[57] In a communique expressing support to the rights committee, Charter 77 condemned "previous acts of anti-Hungarian hatred," "cases of bullying," and "manifestations of stark intolerance."[58] The group affirmed its opposition to "cultural discrimination" against Czechoslovakia's Hungarian minority, citing the narrowing of educational facilities in the Hungarian language and limited job opportunities for ethnic Magyars. The Committee for the Protection of Hungarian Minority Rights in Czechoslovakia has also addressed wider minority concerns in Europe. In late 1987, the group sent eight proposals for improving minority rights on the continent to the Czechoslovak government.[59] It also asked the authorities to support the cause of minority rights at the Helsinki follow-up conference in Vienna and elsewhere; Charter 77 endorsed the request.

Youth and Student Currents

Independent youth-centered movements are often referred to as components of an incipient subculture or counterculture. Two primary aspects of this phenomenon are music-oriented youth groups[60] and independent student associations.[61] These will be surveyed against a backdrop of apathy and alienation characteristic of wide sections of the younger generation in Eastern Europe. Related problems such as drug and alcohol abuse, social deviance, and criminal activity are also on the rise in several states, according to official studies. A severe crisis may be looming for Communist elites in their attempts to secure a pliant, productive, and reliable future workforce. The symptoms of this malaise have been multiplying and deepening since the start of the decade, and there are numerous indications that the trend will continue.

Since the early 1980s, Communist regimes in Eastern Europe have been grappling—mostly unsuccessfully—with the punk rock invasion from the West. Along with punk music, "new wave" and heavy metal have gained widespread popularity among the young, as demonstrated by the proliferation of bands, concerts, "basement" tapes and records, and outlandish Western fashions in dress and hairstyles. But punk rock with its aggressively anti-establishment outpourings and appearances has posed a particular challenge to Soviet bloc regimes. With reckless abandon, Eastern punk musicians have publicly ridiculed Party leaders, condemned Communist ideology, and protested Soviet domination in Eastern Europe.[62] The official responses have fallen into two categories: suppression or co-optation. Bulgaria, Romania, and Czechoslovakia have chosen the first option, while Hungary, Poland, and East Germany have tried the latter with limited success.

Hungary was the first country to experience the burgeoning of a widespread punk movement. In the late 1970s, officials attempted to suppress the punk band Beatrice, which had gained notoriety for unruly public concerts.[63] This measure sparked off heightened interest in the musicians, so the government, in an effort to neutralize the band's popularity, reversed its tactics. Beatrice members were given extensive exposure in the official media. Rather than undercutting the movement, this led to an unprecedented proliferation of punk bands throughout the country. By the early 1980s, Hungary's music scene boasted entertainers such as The Cocaine Shock Brigade, The Cadaver Eaters, and The Galloping Coroners. At a concert in February 1983, Hungarian punk rockers scathingly attacked Soviet, Hungarian, and Romanian leaders. One song mocked the recently deceased Soviet leader Leonid Brezhnev: "The schemer has died/ the beast has died/ the dictator can now become an idol." Another song characterized Hungary's leadership as a "rotten, stinking, Communist gang," and asked, "Why hasn't anyone hanged them yet?" Reportedly, one band tore apart a live chicken on stage and a singer slashed his own face with a razor blade. Official tolerance strained to breaking point; in September 1983, several punk band members were arrested and imprisoned.

Budapest did not completely abandon its attempts to channel youthful energies into officially approved channels. After years of unsuccessful efforts to attract more participation in KISZ, the Communist Youth League, the government announced the creation of a new National Council of Hungarian Youth (MIOT), to be established in October 1988.[64] The founding agencies include official organizations and two unofficial groups, the Catholic Youth Movement and Circle 405. The latter was formed in 1980 by students and teachers at Budapest's Technological University who met in Room 405 of a student hostel. Bertalan Diczhazy, the leader of Circle 405, said in an interview with the Party daily *Magyar Hirlap* that MIOT was being established because KISZ had "lost the confidence of young people as the sole representative of their interests."

Poland also tried to cope permissively with the punk explosion. After imposing martial law and banning Solidarity, the Jaruzelski regime sought to gain acceptance from young Poles, and provide them with a recreational safety valve. However, Polish punks reviled the authorities to such an extent that the regime resorted to censoring, disbanding, and imprisoning some of Poland's leading rock groups. The band Deserter (originally named SS-20) was banned from major Polish cities after its members appeared on stage shredding the Party newspaper while screaming: "Propaganda!" In the fall of 1982, a concert by the rock group Perfect was broken up by riot police using tear gas and percussion bombs. Perfect was banned from appearing in Warsaw and other Polish cities. The group Lady Pank won a large following for its anti-government songs "December Evening" and "Disturbing the Peace" until it was outlawed in 1986. In June of the same year, Polish rock star Jan Borysewicz was arrested and imprisoned for screaming obscenities and performing a striptease before an audience of 40,000 at a "children's festival" in Wroclaw.[65]

Perhaps the best known rock group in Eastern Europe was The Plastic People of the Universe. This Czechoslovak band was put on trial in 1976 after releasing an album entitled "Egon Bundy's Happy Hearts Club Banned" (inspired by the Beatles' album "Sergeant Pepper's Lonely Hearts Club Band"). The record, banned by the authorities, came with a sixty-page softcover booklet called "The Merry Ghetto." The well-publicized persecution of the Plastic People, and other rock musicians, meant to serve as a disincentive to other would-be rock musicians, had an unintended effect in the country, creating a vast underground or "alternative" rock scene. Official constraints on rock music continued[66], but there was a notable easing in the summer of 1986, when the authorities permitted a large rock festival to take place in Prague. By then, the regime had reconsidered its policy of censorship and prosecution, which had obviously fanned the flames of independent musical activity. This change toward greater liberalism was demanded by Charter 77 in August 1983, when the group issued a lengthy document entitled "On Popular Music."[67] In that communique, Charter 77 also traced the development of alternative music in the country, mentioning that the creation of Charter 77 was originally an outgrowth of the public campaign on behalf of the hounded members of The Plastic People of the Universe.

East Germany has in recent years relied on a policy of co-optation with regard to rebellious rock musicians, though in the past it resorted to outright repression.[68] In October 1965, a rare public demonstration was held by several hundred young people in Leipzig to protest the official banning of an iconoclastic band called The Butlers. Police responded with attack dogs, truncheons, and water cannon. That same year, the GDR government also banned the protest singer Wolf Biermann, denouncing his lyrics as "toilet stall poetry." Defying the ban, Biermann continued to write and perform music in his East Berlin apartment. After gaining popularity countrywide and in West Germany, he signed a recording contract with CBS Records; for over a decade, he wrote, performed, and recorded songs criticizing the Honecker regime. Then, in November 1976, Biermann, having travelled to West Germany, was barred from returning to East Berlin. Though prominent East German writers, actors, and musicians protested the government's action, this failed to bring about a change of decision. Instead, a flow of artistic talent out of the country became common, as politically undesirable artists were forced or pressured to leave. More recently, the protest singer Stefan Krawczyk emigrated to West Germany in January 1988. In September 1975, East Germany's most dynamic rock group, The Renft Combo, was disbanded by the government. Founded by former members of The Butlers, Renft achieved tremendous popularity despite the withholding of official patronage. The band was politically daring, with songs such as "The Ballad of Otto," which told of an attempted escape to West Germany. The song "Glaubensfragen" (Questions of Belief) criticized the country's military and prison system. Eventually, two group members were imprisoned; under pressure, other band members either recanted or emigrated to the West.[69]

Punk counterculture arrived on schedule in East Germany in the early 1980s and was met by regime hostility. Security police broke up mass gatherings of several hundred punks in Leipzig in March 1981 and July 1982.[70] Students who come to school with multicolored hair and punk clothing have been punished by having critical entries made in their permanent academic files; these are likely to impede future professional advancement. Nevertheless, the typical East German punk is not committed to a particular political program; more often she or he seeks to make a nihilistic or "drop-out" statement. The East Berlin authorities have had to grapple in recent years with an upsurge of neofascism among urban youths who call themselves "skinheads";[71] their presence has also been noted in Hungary. In the GDR, their actions have often been violent and anti-Semitic; sporting Nazi insignia and shouting Nazi salutes, they have attacked passers-by, raided churches and defaced Jewish graveyards. The state began handing out stiff prison sentences of up to six years as the phenomenon spread in 1987. In East Berlin, official estimates put the number of skinheads at 150, but other towns have also been plagued by them. The term skinheads, used in English in the East German press, refers to young people who shave their heads and wear black leather jackets and paratroop boots. In East Berlin, they come primarily from the new housing developments in Marzahn, Kaulsdorf, and Hellersdorf, but they are also active elsewhere.

Romanian officials have had no known rock subculture to contend with, but in Bulgaria, a John Lennon cult and heavy metal music have caused some disquiet.[72] Ten fourteen year-olds staged an illegal commemoration of John Lennon's death in central Sofia in December 1986. Subsequently arrested and interrogated by police, they were put on probation like common criminals, their families were fined, and their parents' workplaces were informed of the case. Surprisingly, a journalist for the official weekly *Pogled* commented critically on the heavy-handed way the incident had been dealt with by the authorities. She called for "an honest and open dialogue" with the young and exposed a growing generation gap in the country. A later article in the same journal pleaded tolerance for "alienated" Bulgarian youths, particularly heavy-metal fans and punks. Though no precise estimates of the number of these youths was given, the article disclosed that a "heavy metal temperament" occasionally led to "public disturbances." Punks, rockers, break dancers, disco fans, and "neohippies," who also exist in the country, were said to value "freer personal relationships, a less structured way of life, and a less stereotyped educational curriculum."

Students in Eastern Europe have often organized or supported independent political campaigns, from peace groups in Hungary and the GDR to workers' trade union rights in Poland. Throughout the Soviet bloc, students are encouraged to join official youth groups and participate in regime-supervised activities. However, there has been a general disaffection and disillusionment among youths in these countries, which has occasionally found expression in independent political activities, much to the consternation of the authorities. A noteworthy demonstration of student activism occurred in Romania in November 1987, when several hundred students at Brasov Polytechnic held a campus meeting of solidarity with striking workers.[73] It was the largest manifestation of independent youth activity in that country since the Communist seizure of power.

An outstanding and possibly unique example of student self-organization occurred originally in Poland during the legal Solidarity era. In February 1981, the Independent Students' Association (NZS) was registered by the authorities, and within fourteen months the organization claimed a membership of twenty-five percent of Polish university students, exceeding the membership in the official students association. During martial law scores of NZS leaders were interned and a vicious propaganda campaign was initiated against the organization, forcing a diehard core of members underground. The NZS was banned in January 1982. Many of its activists subsequently joined other independent groups, such as the Freedom and Peace Movement. In January 1987, the NZS re-emerged at a congress in Warsaw; it was supported by representatives from nineteen higher education institutions.[74] The congress issued a statement outlining the organization's aims and principles, primarily the defense of academic freedom and university autonomy, the protection of students' social and material interests, and the propagation of democratic values. The NZS declared its supreme objective to be "an independent and democratic Poland," and stated its commitment to "preparing the young Polish intelligentsia for participation in the rebuilding of an independent state." In February 1988, approximately 1,500 students demonstrated in Cracow, demanding the legalization of the NZS. Another 1,500 students held a demonstration at Warsaw University, presenting the same demand to university officials, along with a petition signed by 700 students. These events were coordinated to mark the seventh anniversary of the founding of the NZS. Until recently, no concessions have come from the Polish authorities; the Education Law of 1982 was amended in 1985 to make authentic student self-government a serious offense. Despite such measures, student activism has shown signs of resurgence in Poland. Thousands of students from several major universities organized campus protests in support of striking workers in May 1988.

Alternative Education and Independent Publishing

With few exceptions,[75] education in Eastern Europe is tendered through officially run institutions from kindergartens and primary schools to universities. Communist political values permeate officially approved and supported scholarship, and teachers are generally constrained to adhere to Marxist-Leninist interpretations of history and the social sciences. Understandably, Communist regimes see their monopoly over learning instruments as a crucial control over the socialization and political indoctrination of the young. Self-censorship is a well-known feature of teaching and scholarly writing throughout the Soviet bloc, perniciously reinforcing official versions of truth. In the 1970s and 1980s, a movement challenging the Party stranglehold on education began to surface in Eastern Europe. Calling themselves proponents of "alternative education," activists in this area have been most successful in Poland, Hungary, and Czechoslovakia. In general, they have attempted to fill gaps in what is taught in schools and universities, rather than to set up a completely alternative system of education.

In October 1977, a group of Warsaw intellectuals began an independent series of lectures devoted primarily to the social sciences and history.[76] The lectures took place in private apartments and were attended mainly by college students. The initiative, known colloquially as "The Flying University," proved to be so popular that it soon led to the creation of a governing organization. In January 1978, some sixty prominent intellectuals and academics signed a declaration calling into being the Society for Academic Courses "with the intention of helping all those who want to enrich their knowledge through self-education." A list of thirteen courses was approved and publicized, with noted lecturers such as the dissident Michnik, whose Polish history course attracted a capacity crowd of 180. In its first year, 120 lectures were offered by the Flying University to at least 5,000 people in major towns countrywide.[77] The intellectual standards of the Society for Academic Courses were high; of the sixty signatories of its founding declaration, nineteen were full professors, including six members of the Polish Academy of Sciences. The authorities responded obstructively to the foundation of the Flying University. Lecturers were detained for short periods immediately before lectures. Police invaded private homes where lectures were being held, harassing those present. Later, owners of apartments where lectures took place were detained and heavily fined; sometimes they were imprisoned for short periods on trumped-up charges of disturbing the peace or hooliganism. In 1979, anonymous gangs stormed into lectures in private homes and violently disrupted the proceedings, assaulting the lecturers and participants. During martial law, about eighty percent of active Flying University lecturers were sent to internment camps, centers or jails, serving terms ranging from a few months to years.[78]

During the legal Solidarity era alternative education filtered down to the general public. Courses were organized for union activists, but demand grew to the point where requests from factory committees for lecturers and teaching materials flooded Solidarity cells in universities.[79] Specialists on subjects ranging from self-management and union organization to economics and modern history lectured to packed factory assembly halls. Demand for Polish history courses was most intense. After the imposition of martial law, hundreds of independent study circles were organized countrywide by workers, peasants, students, and even schoolchildren. Many were set up with help from underground Solidarity activists, but others were arranged on a neighborhood basis or among friends.

In the early 1980s, several formal bodies were organized in Poland to promote alternative education. Best known of these is the Team for

Independent Education (TIE), established in March 1982, which comprises an underground network covering most major cities.[80] TIE's aim is to provide advice and support for study circles or self-styled "independent universities." To this end it publishes educational pamphlets in seven academic disciplines, and produces a widely read monthly paper—*Tu, Teraz* (Here, Now)—that deals with educational matters. In the 1982–83 academic year, TIE received requests for lecturers from some 120 self-education groups in Warsaw alone.[81] Some of the groups, particularly those based in rural areas, are organized by local parish priests around secular subjects. Students of independent education are aided in many areas by clandestine collections of uncensored books and periodicals known as "underground libraries." The *samizdat* press in Poland has advertised their existence and published guidelines explaining how they should be run. Tape recordings are another popular vehicle for disseminating alternative educational material. Many lectures, as well as historical and economic programs broadcast by Radio Free Europe are taped and circulated in cassette form. The underground publishing house NOWA began issuing cassettes in 1983; the first in its series of historical compilations was a 90-minute audio documentary about the prewar Polish leader Józef Piłsudski.

In 1988, a group of parents began to clamor for the establishment of private secular schools in Poland, initially for the first three grades.[82] The lobbyists proposed to keep the syllabus in the private schools exactly the same as that under the state system; however, children whose parents could afford to pay for private education would be offered smaller classes and better teachers. The controversial proposal was seen as a reflection of the growing public dissatisfaction with overcrowding and administrative restrictions in Polish public schools. Official consent was not forthcoming.

In 1977, Hungarian intellectuals in Budapest founded the Free University, modelled after the Flying University in Poland and sometimes called the Flying Kindergarten (*Repulo Ovoda*) to acknowledge its Polish inspiration.[83] The Free University sponsored lectures and courses in private homes on subjects banned from official institutions. The dissident philosopher Gaspar Miklos Tamas, for instance, has used it as a forum to discuss the plight of the Hungarian minority in neighboring countries. In October 1981, dissident Gyorgy Krasso organized a special session of the Free University to commemorate the twenty-fifth anniversary of the 1956 Hungarian Revolution.

Although modest in scope compared to Poland's Flying University, the Czechoslovak counterpart scored its own successes.[84] Familiarly known as the Patocka University, or the "anti-university," it was started in the autumn of 1977. The concept behind it was to provide an educational program for young people excluded from higher education, using the talents of scholars barred from their professional work. Fairly regular seminar courses were taught in Prague and Brno by noted intellectuals, although lecturers and students were subject to police persecution. In 1978, the uncensored philosophy seminar of Julius Tomin became the focus of particularly severe police action and received international publicity. In response to an invitation by the philosopher, several Oxford scholars regularly visited Prague and participated in the seminar, which was usually held in Tomin's apartment. Several visiting Western academics were apprehended during the seminar and forcibly expelled from the country. Seeking a respite from mounting persecution, Tomin won permission to leave the country temporarily and accepted an invitation from Oxford University. In June 1981, he and his wife were deprived of their Czechoslovak citizenship and prevented from returning home.

Poland surpasses all other Soviet bloc countries in the variety and abundance of its *samizdat*. Since the imposition of martial law, independent publishing has grown precipitously throughout the country. The fuse of this literary explosion was lit by mounting dissident activity during the late 1970s; between 1977 and 1980, an estimated 300 illegal titles circulated in Poland.[85] Most of these were homemade products, forged on the precursors of today's far more sophisticated technology. Under the aegis of KOR, several noted intellectual periodicals were created. The most successful of KOR's publishing ventures was NOWA, the Independent Publishing House, which celebrated its tenth anniversary in 1987.[86] Under the stewardship of Mirosław Chojecki, a chemist and founding KOR member, NOWA won international renown; in the first three years of its existence, it produced no less than eighty-seven books, featuring poetry, novels, plays, and nonfiction. By 1988, NOWA had published more than 300 books, including works in translation by Bertrand Russell, Gunter Grass, Osip Mandelstam, Arthur Koestler, George Orwell, Milan Kundera, Bertolt Brecht, Andrei Sakharov, Alexander Solzhenitsyn, and Kurt Vonnegut. Leading Polish authors were also published, including emigres such as Nobel Prize winner Czesław Miłosz and Leszek Ko- łakowski. Uncensored literature swamped Poland during the legal Solidarity era. About 300 unofficial information bulletins and newspapers appeared in those eighteen months, enjoying a circulation of about 1.5 million.[87] The main union weekly *Tygodnik Solidarność*, with a national readership of about 500,000, was the most popular newspaper in the country. In addition, Solidarity staffed its own news agency, BIPS (Biuro Informacyjne Prasowe Solidarnosci). During this period, a major new publishing house called "Krag" appeared. While NOWA elected to concentrate on literature, politics and economics, "Krag" concerned itself mainly with history.

Since martial law, independent publishing has flourished, often with a strong regional character. According to underground Solidarity sources, unofficial newspapers and periodicals currently number between 500 and 1,000.[88] Problems of distribution exist, but have not stemmed the creation of new publications at an astounding rate.[89] The expense of paper, printing equipment and other graphic materials has been passed on to the reader and is reflected in substantially higher prices for uncensored books and periodicals.[90] Nevertheless, large sell-out print runs are not uncommon, with the popular Warsaw weekly *Tygodnik Mazowsze* publishing 40,000 to 80,000 copies per week.[91] Approximately 100,000 Poles are involved in printing and distributing the fruit of the underground press. More than twenty underground publishing houses exist; some of the best known are NOWA, "Krag," CDN, KOS, "Przedswit," "Feniks," "Unia," "Glos," and ABC.[92] On average, 3,000 to 4,000 copies of each book are printed, often in a tiny economical print that can be difficult to read. Offset machines are sometimes used, but often far more modest equipment is employed, such as mimeograph and silk-screen machines. Despite the poor material quality of much of the literature thus produced, opposition and government sources both estimate that about three million people regularly read uncensored literature.[93] Youth magazines comprise one area of independent publishing that has experienced rapid growth in recent years. And associated with the wide distribution of *samizdat* in Poland is the independent production of audio cassettes, stamps, postcards, calendars, and, most recently, videos.[94]

Early in 1986, representatives of the largest independent publishing houses in Poland established the Foundation for Independent Publishing. The clandestine body was created primarily to subsidize existing publishers and offer financial help to translators. A small advisory body, calling itself The Social Council for Independent Publishers, works in conjunction with the Foundation, attending to four main areas: the appraisal of published material; coordination of individual publishers' publishing plans; evaluation of how Foundation allocations are spent by publishers; and oversight of professional ethics in transactions between publishers and authors, and between publishers themselves.[95]

Inspired by the uncensored publishing fervor in Poland during Solidarity's heyday, Hungarian dissidents began to venture into *samizdat* with duplicating machines rather than mere typewriters. The first major step in this direction came with the founding in 1981 of AB: Independent Publishers, run by the sociologist Gabor Demszky.[96] Using a handmade silk-screen press, AB has issued well over 300 titles, including literary classics and social analyses. The works of Gyorgy Konrad, Gyorgy Petri, Miklos Haraszti, Arthur Koestler, Alexander Solzhenitsyn, and Mahatma Gandhi feature among its list, and Demszky claims to have reached between 10,000 and 20,000 readers, despite constant police harassment.[97] In addition to book publishing, AB produces the *samizdat* journals *Beszelo* (The Talker), *Tajekoztato* (Information Bulletin), and *Hirmondo* (The Messenger). This and other unofficial literature was at one time available for sale in Budapest at the "Samizdat Boutique."[98] Run by Laszlo Rajk, son of the Communist leader executed after a Stalinist show-trial in 1949, this served for two years as a bookshop and library until raided by police and finally closed in 1983.[99] The Samizdat Boutique was situated in Rajk's apartment, and was open to visitors every Tuesday evening.

The quarterly *Beszelo* was the first major *samizdat* publication to appear in a sizeable edition in Hungary.[100] Founded in October 1981, its issues usually surpass 100 pages and it is printed on a duplicating machine in copies of approximately 1,000. *Beszelo's* numerous editors publish their names and addresses; most are prominent dissident intellectuals. Subjects covered by the publication include censorship, strikes, independent religious groups, student organizations, pacifism, and ethnic Hungarians in neighboring countries. Approximately twenty issues have already reached the West. *Tajekoztato* was a short-lived but ambitious newsletter that first appeared in the spring of 1983; three issues were published before being stopped by the authorities. The newsletter carried bulletins about police raids, seizures, and house searches, as well as the latest courses offered at the non-state Free University.[101] After the closure of *Tajekoztato*, a new *samizdat* publication filled the gap. *Hirmondo's* first issue came out in November 1983 and declared as its aim the publication of information that cannot appear in the official press.[102] The monthly embraces news about dissident activity in Hungary and other East European states. A prime concern is the fate of ethnic Hungarians outside the country. But it has also entered into discussions of controversial political and economic reforms in Hungary.

The most recent *samizdat* publication to surface in Hungary is *Demokrata* (The Democrat). Five issues appeared in the first five months of 1987, despite police raids on the home of Jeno Nagy, one of its editors who is also affiliated with AB: Independent Publishers.[103] *Demokrata* has published a number of articles supporting political reform and democratization in Hungary. It has covered such topics as the Danube Circle environmentalist group, commemorations of the 1956 Revolution, and rising tensions between Hungary and Romania over the issue of the ethnic Hungarian minority in Transylvania.[104] The fifth issue included a special section on Raoul Wallenberg, the Swedish diplomat who saved thousands of Hungarian Jews from the Nazi holocaust.

Czechoslovakian dissident intellectuals have relied largely on typewriters to disseminate uncensored material.[105] In 1973, blacklisted Czech writers founded the *samizdat* Petlice (Padlock) publishing house, which issued over 250 typed volumes with Ludvik Vaculik serving as general editor. In 1982, Petlice announced that it was closing its operations. During its existence, it produced original poetry, plays, novels, short stories, literary criticism, and historical and philosophical essays.[106] Many of the books were beautifully handbound and appeared in editions of several hundred copies each. The list of authors thus "published" included such luminaries as Nobel Prize laureate Jaroslav Seifert, Ivan Klima, Bohumil Hrabal, Vaclav Havel, and Ludvik Vaculik. There are smaller scale and lesser known publishing efforts in Czechoslovakia. The 1980s has also seen a significant number of *samizdat* journals published in Slovakia, often but not exclusively devoted to religious themes.[107]

Politics and Art

Throughout the East bloc, uncompromising political statements have been made by independent-minded artists in defiance of censorship and other subtle pressures to conform. Political cartoonists from Romania and East Germany, graphic designers from Poland, playwrights and poets from Czechoslovakia have won a measure of recognition in the West, even if they have been denied official acceptance in their own countries. By refusing to bow to Party-sanctioned aesthetic guidelines, these artists have often displayed an inarguable courage and conviction; unfortunately, this has often isolated them in their native countries and inevitably limits their public exposure.[108]

Organized expressions of dissent by activist artists are not unknown in the region. In May 1978, the independent art group INCONNU (Unknown) was formed in Szolnok, Hungary. Ten years later, the three-member group, still active, issued a declaration that condemned the collaboration of Hungarian intellectuals with the authorities who quelled the 1956 Revolution.[109] Based since 1983 in Budapest, INCONNU has sponsored numerous cultural events addressing political themes in the face of police harassment.[110] In May 1987, members of INCONNU were instrumental in opening an "alternative cultural center" in Budapest at the home of graphic artist Gabor Zrinyifalvi.[111] Open to the public every Sunday afternoon, the center's main goal is to provide exposure for independent artists excluded from the nation's official cultural life. The invitation cards announcing the opening of the center stated:

> A peculiarity of East European societies is the state monopoly of culture. This [opening] contradicts the essence of the concept; it means its dis-memberment. The free flow and contest of ideas and information is the only possible means of the free self-construction of the culture and society.

By founding our alternative cultural center we would like to assure such a forum free of coercion, opposing restrictions, in support of independent intellectual manifestations.[112]

INCONNU sponsored a "Stalin" exhibition of satirical works by two Russian emigre artists.[113] It also organized an international graphics competition called "The Fighting City," commemorating the 1956 Revolution. In January 1987, Hungarian police confiscated all thirty-nine pieces of art donated to the dissident exhibition by artists from Hungary, Britain, the United States, the Netherlands, and Yugoslavia.[114] An open letter protesting the "illegal police action" was sent by INCONNU members—Peter Bokros, Tamas Molnar, and Robert Palinkas—to the HSWP Central Committee a month later.[115]

An unofficial three-day cultural symposium was held in Budapest in October 1985. Entitled "The Writer and His Integrity," it was organized by the International Helsinki Federation for Human Rights to coincide with the opening of the inter-governmental European Cultural Forum, held in Budapest as part of the Helsinki consultation process. Convened in a film director's private apartment, the "alternative" symposium was attended by noted writers from the West, and East Europeans such as the Hungarian novelist Gyorgy Konrad, exiled Czech poet Jiri Grusa and emigre Czech dramatist Pavel Kohout. Among the subjects under consideration were "Censorship and Self-Censorship" and "Writing in Exile."[116]

In Czechoslovakia, independent culture was until the late 1980s supported and spread notably by the Jazz Section of the Union of Musicians. Founded in October 1971, the Jazz Section's official membership was limited by the authorities to 3,000 members and 2,000 candidate members. Although it had official status until June 1983, it was able to publish its uncensored internal *Bulletin* for its members. Copies of this popular publication are believed to have regularly reached 70,000 to 80,000 readers.[117] Information provided by the *Bulletin* comprised a wide range of cultural topics from modern music to experimental theatre, abstract painting, and Western films and poetry; in addition, it covered such subjects as youth in Poland and life in Nazi concentration camps in Bohemia and Moravia. Between 1974 and 1979, the Jazz Section organized nine musical events called "Prague Jazz Days," in which tens of thousands of young people and hundreds of bands participated. Though the festivals were banned in 1980, the Section continued to encourage non-conformist amateur and semi-professional musicians who had little opportunity to perform before the broader public. In 1980, the Jazz Section joined the London-based International Jazz Federation and the Stockholm-based International Association for the Research of Popular Music.

Official tolerance, long strained, reached its limit in June 1983, when the Jazz Section was dissolved by the Union of Musicians. Immediately, the Prague branch of the union established a new Prague Jazz Section—with the same officers and statutes as the banned body. Pressure was exerted on the Union of Musicians to force the dissolution of the Prague Jazz Section; the latter, in a battle for its life, distributed a newsletter to its members describing its struggle. More than a thousand expressions of support were received in response to a questionnaire sent out by the Section.[118] Several thousand signatures were appended to a protest petition demanding the continuation of the Jazz Section.[119] Among the most popular of the Section's publications was *Situace*, a series of monographs on nonconformist artists. Equally in demand were editions of the *jazzpetit* series of books on music, literature, and art; twenty-three volumes appeared between 1979 and 1986, among them a pioneering *History of Czech Rock 'n Roll* and a three-volume encyclopedia, *Rock 2000*.[120] Top-notch fiction and non-fiction that could not pass the censor also appeared in the *jazzpetit* series.

Harassment of Jazz Section officers mounted in the mid-1980s. House searches and confiscation of membership files, passports, and *samizdat* were carried out. Police action culminated in the September 1986 arrest of seven Jazz Section officers: Karel Srp, Josef Skalnik, Vladimir Kouril, Tomas Krivanek, Cestmir Hunat, Milos Drda, and Vladimir Drda. They were charged under Article 118 of the criminal code for running an "unauthorized business enterprise." The house used as the Section's offices, library and art gallery was padlocked by the authorities. A joint statement by Charter 77 and VONS, issued two weeks after the Jazz Section arrests, defended and applauded the endeavors of the jailed men.[121] Despite an international outcry and widespread speculation that the authorities would relent in the emerging climate of *glasnost*, the trial of the Jazz Section took place as scheduled over two days in March 1987.[122] Srp, chairman of the group, was sentenced to sixteen months' imprisonment; Kouril, the secretary, received a ten-month sentence; three others received suspended prison sentences—Skalnik ten months, Hunat and Krivanek eight months each. The Drdas, too ill to attend the trial, were to be tried at a later date. Amnesty International subsequently adopted Srp and Kouril as prisoners of conscience.

One of the most unusual forms of dissent in the bloc has been embraced by the "Orange Alternative" in Poland.[123] Based since 1983 in Wrocław, the group has attracted thousands of youths to iconoclastic political "happenings."[124] In essence, these are street theatre performances that obliquely make a mockery of Communist society. The movement's aim, according to its leader, art historian Waldemar Frydrych (alias "The Major"), is "to treat the political system of Poland as a work of art."[125] Dadaism has strongly influenced the satirical cultural politics of the Orange Alternative, whose manifesto subscribes to a new aesthetics called "socialist surrealism."

In Wrocław and Warsaw, several thousand students participating in Orange Alternative "happenings" dressed as red dwarfs and paraded through the streets in a good-natured spoof of Poland's Children's Day.[126] In the capital, more than 500 young people distributed sweets and toilet paper and called for a "red dwarf revolution." They paraded behind a portrait of Feliks Dzierzynski, the Polish nobleman who founded the Soviet secret police. "Feliks for Kids" read the caption under the picture of the bearded Dzierzynski, who was adorned with a red dwarf's cap. In Wroclaw, shortly before elections to local councils, Orange Alternative members shouted veiled political slogans such as "Dwarfs of the World Unite" and "Vote for Us." In March 1988, to mark International Women's Day, Orange Alternative members paraded with large sandwich boards resembling sanitary napkins, a scarce commodity in Poland.[127] The signs read: "In the Spirit of Peace. Pershings, No. Sanitary Pads, Yes." Police arrested Frydrych; he was freed only after dozens of Polish artists and intellectuals, including the film director Andrzej Wajda, appealed for his release. The appeal of this antic and imaginative group has also reportedly spread to Poznan, Gdansk, and Cracow.

Conclusion

Independent social activism burgeoned in Eastern Europe during the 1980s. Peace and disarmament movements have grown significantly, spurred initially by the perceived arms build-up by Warsaw Pact and NATO forces. Single-issue campaigns have been mounted, such as the drive to ensure the right of conscientious objection in some countries. A factor in the growth of Eastern peace movements has been the development of an outspoken peace campaign in the West; though major differences in outlook between the two movements persist, cooperation has been fostered. Increased reliance on nuclear energy and its potential hazards—demonstrated by the Chernobyl disaster, which severely impacted on the region—has spawned active environmental protection campaigns. Industrial pollution has also reached alarming proportions, bringing health dangers that have stimulated a public outcry. And ambitious cross-border projects such as the Gabcikovo-Nagymaros dam, to be built by Czechoslovakia and Hungary, have raised questions of ecological safety.

A perceptible upsurge of interest in the preservation of minority culture has characterized transnational campaigns for ethnic and national minorities in some states. This has been fuelled, in the case of ethnic Hungarians in Transylvania, by rising tensions between Budapest and Bucharest. Youth and student movements, marked often by stark disillusionment with the Communist system, have also been a feature of the decade. To the dismay of the authorities, youthful rebellion throughout the area, particularly in matters of fashion, music, and lifestyles continues to be strongly influenced by Western trends. Meanwhile, in Poland especially, large groups of students continue to press for their own independent organizations. Young people have also been involved in a whole gamut of social and cultural campaigns in the region.

Alternative education programs and independent publishing have flourished in some countries. These activities are often bold expressions of political opposition, defying official reprisals such as censorship, harassment or imprisonment. *Samizdat* publishing has matured significantly in terms of mechanical sophistication, as offset printers have replaced typewriters and duplicating machines in some locales. Art as a form of political protest has gained ground too, and independent cultural activism has spread. From street theatre to "living room theater," from independent art exhibitions to progressive music concerts, this realm of experimentation has not been routed despite frequent official intervention.

8

Emerging Prospects

The Communist Party-states of Eastern Europe will require strong doses of de-Leninization if they are to overcome their acute domestic problems.[1] Sustained economic recovery, technological innovation, industrial modernization, and prolonged social stability will necessitate major political surgery that could imperil the traditional principles of single-party rule and centralized planning. A continuation of the stifling Communist monopoly over the most essential arenas of public life, and piecemeal "restructuring," will simply postpone important change and aggravate long-term decline throughout the East bloc.

Warsaw Pact leaders are generally cautious when introducing reforms that could destabilize their political systems and mechanisms of social control. They are also conscious of previous attempts at structural alterations that spurred popular demands for democratic freedoms in several countries, and ended in massive repression. Nevertheless, the ripple effects of Soviet *perestroika* (economic restructuring), combined with diverse domestic currents of reform, resistance to reform, and mounting public discontent, may engender severe emergencies during the next decade. Prevention, stabilization, and crisis management are only temporary solutions; conversely, any durable cure for economic decline could prove politically disruptive. Such a scenario also presents opportunities and pitfalls for dissent, opposition, and independent social activism in each country. The response of largely alienated populations to adverse or deteriorating socio-economic conditions could surpass the programs and strategies of experienced political dissenters who seek to gain benefits from the current round of Communist reformism. The ingredients of any emerging turmoil must also be scrutinized by the West, if it hopes to understand developments in Eastern Europe and have some positive influence on the outcome.

Recent Developments

Moscow's imperial priorities in the East bloc revolve around three key prerequisites: the maintenance of overall Kremlin control; the assurance of internal stability through the preservation of Communist Party rule; and smooth leadership transitions where aging leaders are nearing the end of their tenure. Superimposed on these central issues is a steady drive to stimulate economic growth, and tighter CMEA integration to bolster the Soviet economy and lessen its international burden.[2] Moscow intends to further scale down its subsidies in the region which have steadily decreased since 1981.[3] The rising cost of Soviet raw materials and energy supplies, and large indebtedness to the West, have increased pressures on the Party-states to produce more efficiently than in the past. Each regime will need to decrease its trade deficit and ensure that domestic reforms reduce energy consumption and improve the quantity and quality of exports to the USSR.[4] The strengthening of bilateral and multilateral economic ties in the CMEA is geared toward these objectives. Long-term intra-bloc agreements are designed to enhance technological cooperation and economic integration. Plans have been advanced for a renewed effort at national economic specialization facilitating an international division of labor in the 1990s. The Kremlin has laid stress on joint ventures and other "direct links" between CMEA enterprises; and a reform of the financial system envisages some form of currency convertability. The Gorbachev leadership is seeking to surmount the traditional economic stumbling blocks to closer economic coordination, such as governmental opposition, the discrepancies in industrial development between states, and the weak condition of bilateral economic ties.[5]

However, with numerous more compelling internal and international concerns, Gorbachev clearly seeks to avoid destabilizing any East bloc government through unrealistic demands, hasty pressures, or mismanaged reforms.[6] Domestic changes will need to "renew" or "strengthen socialism," and not endanger Communist control. Some market-oriented elements may be tolerated if they assist "socialist regeneration" and do not undermine the political structure. The Communist elite is seeking guarantees that any spur to public economic initiative does not unwittingly spill over into the political arena and threaten Party supremacy. Moscow also wants assurances that local reforms will be closely supervised to prevent them mushrooming into threatening social upheavals. In all its East European variants, the *glasnost* campaign is primarily a public relations device engineered to clarify Party objectives, signal the authorities' determination to rejuvenate socialism by eliminating "distortions," systemic malfunctions, and individual shortcomings, and to enlist and mobilize the support of wide sectors of the populace for the official program.[7]

With varying degrees of enthusiasm, most East bloc leaders are aiming for a "streamlined communism" steered by a leaner economic bureaucracy.[8] This may involve some separation of responsibilities between the

Party, government, and economic management at lower administrative levels, but no major structural overhaul or political democratization is envisaged. Machala points out that "technocrats" and "rational economists" in Communist states are far from being budding democrats. On the contrary, they may present a major barrier to political reform and are primarily predisposed toward efficient production where "the most efficient means to these ends are frequently in opposition to the forces of liberalization."[9] But the prospects for economic success do not appear very encouraging either. Each economy is severely hampered by glaring inefficiencies, technological backwardness, and feeble competitiveness on the world market. Gorbachev's pronouncements and policies may have injected some optimism among local technocrats and reformist elements, but this has been tinged with sober realism about prospects for rapid economic improvement. Mindful of the Khrushchev episode, East bloc leaders remain equally wary of sudden reversals in Kremlin policies and any anti-reformist counter-attacks which could leave them out in the cold. They also seek to prevent any disruptive inner-Party factionalism that could provoke social turbulence and direct Soviet intercession.

Notwithstanding the hesitancy of Moscow's satellites, some East European Parties could become emboldened in the Gorbachev era to explore the frontiers of diversity. The Soviets may be willing to tolerate various local initiatives to stimulate productivity in exchange for closer economic assimilation.[10] However, the Kremlin continues to reaffirm the parameters of national autonomy and internal democracy which if overstepped could hasten direct intervention with or without the "Brezhnev Doctrine."[11] Moscow prefers indirect levers to keep East bloc leaders in line but is not averse to exerting more forceful pressures where necessary. The CPSU considers it imperative to maintain overall control in Eastern Europe for strategic, military, and political reasons; any policy differences among Soviet leaders have primarily revolved around "what steps are either compatible with or necessary to fulfill that requirement, not over whether that requirement might some day be abandoned."[12]

A brief survey of the balance sheet of reform in each state helps to pinpoint conditions and prospects in the region.[13] Poland's economy remains in a dire predicament, with its Western debt now exceeding $39 billion, and suffers from sagging industrial output, poor investment potential, galloping inflation, persistent shortages, and declining living standards. The country's Domestic Net Material Product grew by only 2% in 1987, one-third lower than planned and half the growth rate recorded in 1986. Economic reforms are subordinate to persistent bureaucratic obstruction and the inbuilt political limitations on decentralization. The Jaruzelski regime is closely linked with the enforced "normalization" of Polish society. Although the most visible repressions have been eased in recent years, the interlocking administrative, political, juridical, and police controls preclude any organized counterweight to one-party rule. The "second stage" of Poland's reform program has displayed little sign of rationalizing production or motivating workers to raise output. Warsaw faces a daunting task of trying to muster any popular credibility for a reform policy that excludes the active involvement of independent social organizations. The much touted "democratization" program is widely perceived as little more than a publicity device to entice respected national figures under the government umbrella; very few have succumbed to such tactics. The "public referendum" on economic reforms in November 1987 and the local elections in June 1988 failed to elicit public trust, enthuse the workforce, or even pacify public hostility during the renewed austerity drive.

Like Hungary, Poland entered the *glasnost* era well ahead of the USSR, as Gierek's "propaganda of success" turned into admissions of failure. The "legal" Solidarity period witnessed the wholesale exposure of Party corruption, ineptitude, and gross economic mismanagement. Jaruzelski's administration usurped much of Solidarity's criticisms and incorporated them in its own propaganda campaigns against various political scape-goats while rebuilding the Communist apparatus. Serious conflict could again erupt in Poland if economic reforms are widely perceived to consist of continuous public belt-tightening. Since the imposition of martial law, price increases have been largely offset by sizeable wage rises, especially for workers in the large key industries. The regime periodically signals its determination to curb inflationary pay demands while constricting its enormous consumer subsidies. But a stringent adherence to such a strategy, especially in the absence of material incentives, political liberties, and government legitimacy, could again recharge worker opposition as they did in May and August 1988.

After Poland, Hungary appears to be the most likely candidate for internal upheaval. Despite Budapest's longer experiences with *perestroika* than other bloc states, the economy continues to slide. Hungary's hard currency debt to the West is the highest per capita in the region—exceeding $11 billion at the end of 1987—while growth in the Gross Domestic Product has consistently fallen short of modest planned targets. Gorbachev's policies may reinforce the position of Magyar reformers, but the regime seems incapable of accelerating the reforms enacted since 1968. The interference of central planners in the functioning of enterprises has simply become less visible and direct under the reform program. But the Party's overall control in the economy has not been substantially restricted, and all decentralizing measures and market elements are subject to contradictory pressures and inconsistent implementation.

Hungarian officials have warned about a potential economic catastrophe as financial reserves dwindle, productivity declines, living standards fall, and social tensions escalate. The Kádárist "social contract," which promised material well-being in return for political passivity, could rapidly unravel in the coming years. Turmoil is possible if sizeable sections of the working class refuse to swallow the bitter pill of incessant price hikes, increased income tax, and growing unemployment resulting from the closure of unprofitable enterprises. Budapest's current reform package amounts to a prudent "stabilization" program in which state subsidies to industry will be reduced, and prices raised on many consumer items; but no widescale marketization and privatization is envisaged. In May 1988 Prime Minister Karoly Grosz succeeded Kádár as Party General-Secretary, in a move designed to rejuvenate the reforms. Though Grosz may trim the economic *nomenklatura* and loosen some restraints on private enterprise, the Party shows mixed signs of relinquishing its powers to any independent public associations or tolerating any meaningful political pluralism.

Bulgaria has incorporated the least troublesome economic reforms but has not tampered significantly with central planning. Sofia's "restructuring" program has reshuffled the bureaucracy without tackling the economic malaise; the GNP growth rate is steadily decreasing each year. The "second stage" of economic reform largely consists of alterations in pricing and taxation, with a limited degree of autonomy for some industries. Formidable problems will remain even in implementing modest reforms, because of managerial hindrance, apprehensions about free enterprise, and chronic shortages of technology, energy, skilled labor, and capital investment. Bulgarian leader Todor Zhivkov may soon be edged into an honorific position by a younger *apparatchik*, but having scaled down his initial "reform package" after "fraternal consultations" in Moscow, the prospects for marketization and liberalization look decidedly bleak.

The Czechoslovak economy has steadily deteriorated during the 1980s, with growth in GNP regularly slipping below state plans. The projected "streamlining" measures are intended to eliminate wastage and raise productivity without significantly weakening Party controls over economic management or political decision-making. Prague is fearful of introducing any major market elements and will concentrate instead on maximizing the output of the existing command model. Some conflict between the more pragmatist and dogmatist Party leaders could emerge, but a broad "middle line" will probably be adopted which safeguards bureaucratic privileges. Official references to the Prague Spring should not be misconstrued. Such rhetoric is not intended to resuscitate extensive socioeconomic reform and political pluralism, but to recapture some popular legitimacy and set clear parameters to any forthcoming economic adjustments. In mid-December 1987 Gustáv Husák was replaced as Party chief by Milos Jakeš, who evidently hopes to neutralize any major pressures for extensive reform.

The GDR regime has displayed little enthusiasm for reform, and regularly underlines the relative success of its economic performance. Even Moscow has applauded East Berlin's industrial policies, rationalization measures, and impressive productivity—by Communist standards. But the country's economic triumphs should not be exaggerated; they have been aided and abetted by markedly favorable trading relations with West Germany. The GDR benefits from duty-free exports, preferential tax treatment, favorably priced raw materials, and large government-guaranteed loans from Bonn. East Germany's "special status" and outside assistance has enabled it to cope more effectively than other CMEA states with economic shortcomings. However, even in the "showcase of communism," an extensive modernization program is long overdue if economic expansion is to be sustained. The ruling Party admits to a gradual slowdown in economic growth, shrinking hard currency earnings, falling industrial output, delays in investment, and general shortages of consumer goods. The GDR is increasingly unable to rejuvenate its outdated factories, machinery, and capital stock, and its products are becoming less competitive internationally. Despite these mounting liabilities, the government is disinclined to introduce any politically unsettling restructuring programs. It seems that any successor to Party head Honecker will not deviate substantially from the country's distinctly non-reformist course.

Romania remains the most staunchly anti-reformist state. The regime of Nicolae Ceausescu legitimizes itself domestically by a quasi-independent posture toward Moscow. This has helped to camouflage somewhat its severe domestic repression and increasingly disastrous economic policies in which the annual growth is nearly half of the planned targets. Anxious about measures that could loosen Party controls, Bucharest concentrates on a stringent austerity drive to keep the economy afloat. It exports essential agricultural products and other goods in an effort to repay rapidly its Western debts; as a result, workers' living standards have dropped sharply this decade and will continue to decline. After the Brasov riots in November 1987, the possibility of more serious public protests looms over the horizon. Even high-ranking government officials have warned that the "cup of privation" may overflow during the next round of belt-tightening. *Glasnost* is practically absent in Romania. Instead of broadening the range of issues for public airing and trying to obtain popular support, Bucharest extols Ceausescu's unswerving allegiance to "scientific socialism" in which the introduction of any capitalist elements will be prohibited. Given such a posture, Moscow is inclined to use economic leverage to nudge Romania into a closer Soviet orbit, rather than risk provoking instability through blatant political interference. Ceausescu is reportedly grooming his son as a successor to ensure dynastic continuity, but a post-Ceausescu power struggle cannot be discounted, or the eventuality that a new Romanian leader may be more receptive to reformist currents.

During the last decade Eastern Europe has experienced the shock waves of Western recession, shrinking world markets, growth in import costs, and a steady rise in Soviet energy prices. However, the region's problems are more deeply rooted in the structure and function of Communist command economies, irrespective of any partial streamlining. Without reforms across the board, involving comprehensive marketization, privatization, decentralized production, a rational pricing system, and minimal government interference in economic processes, long-term economic decline looks inevitable. Instead of mere administrative reorganization and piecemeal incentive schemes, Party-state control over political and economic life will need to be substantially curbed. The danger also remains that any major structural reforms could cause short-term economic dislocation, fuel popular expectations, aggravate political conflicts, and provoke severe domestic unrest. With or without far-reaching reforms, Eastern Europe seems set for a decade of mounting crisis and severe national turbulence.

Dissident Responses

The reformist moves "from above" initiated by the Soviet leadership since the mid-1980s have generated various responses among East Europe's dissident circles. In general, seasoned Soviet bloc dissidents have grown accustomed to periodic government relaxations and officially sponsored reforms. As a result, many remain understandably suspicious of Gorbachev's *glasnost* and *perestroika* campaigns, and their repercussions on conditions within the bloc. Indeed a double fear seems to have materialized. First, there is some apprehension that any reforms initiated by the ruling Party elites could prove cosmetic, ineffectual, or a cunning substitute for authentic and far-reaching economic and political concessions. Second, dissidents have pointed out that without safeguarded and institutionalized changes, in which the governments concerned surrender some of their powers and privileges, the current thaw could eventually turn into another freeze. They are clearly fearful that *glasnost* may be merely a temporary respite preceding another repressive clampdown on independent social activism.

One can detect the emergence of three broad interpretations among East Europe's political opposition regarding Gorbachev's impact in the bloc. These diagnoses and prescriptions can be characterized in turn as "positivist," "negativist," and "potentialist." The differences between these positions can be partially accounted for by national peculiarities, specific historical experiences with reform, particular dissident programs and political orientations, and more personalized individual inclinations. Nevertheless, each strand of opinion crosscuts several states, and all three tendencies can be found to varying degrees in most Soviet bloc countries. Though such responses and expectations may overlap and shift over time, in relation to positive or negative developments in one or more states, they could increasingly set the tempo for the policies and strategies adopted by dissident groups in any future confrontations with the authorities.

A renewed optimism is evident among East Europe's "positivists," with variable degrees of prudence, particularly among former Communist reformers, Marxist revisionists, and assorted "democratic socialists." "Positivists" believe Gorbachev provides an important opportunity for resurrecting aborted or stalled economic and political reforms within and outside the ruling Parties. Such reformist-oriented oppositionists believe that Moscow should be given more sympathy and active support by all East bloc dissenters. In their view, Gorbachev's possible defeat by anti-reformist elements within the Soviet bureaucracy would presage a severe setback for all democratic forces and reformist currents in Eastern Europe. A number of "ex-communist" Charter 77 signatories in Czechoslovakia, who were active in the Prague Spring reform movement, consider Gorbachev's current course to be a vindication of their own endeavors at democratic restructuring during the late 1960s.[14] Czechoslovakia may be unique in this respect, in that reformist currents are still in evidence among sectors of the half million strong "Party of the expelled" twenty years after the Soviet invasion. The Prague Spring remains a cogent symbol of the potentials of "democratic communism" irrespective of the serious setbacks it sustained. In Poland by contrast, reliance on inner-Party liberalization has few supporters and many critics. Most Polish dissident work since the late 1970s has focused on stretching the parameters of independent social activism outside Party supervision. Inner-Party reformism has some backers among Hungary's intellectual "semi-legal" opposition, but their numbers are generally small, their proposals enjoy little public resonance, and until recently they have not spawned any wider social movements.

In January 1988, 43 ex-CPCS members expelled in the aftermath of the 1968 Soviet invasion issued an appeal to their countrymen. In it they asked that activists more forcefully demand political rehabilitation for all purged Communists.[15] They also called for sweeping political and economic reforms instead of the "half-hearted steps" pursued by the Husák and Jakeš regimes. Communism, they believe, can and must be democratized in order to end twenty years of "bureaucratic stagnation." Former CPCS cadres have dispatched letters to the official Party daily *Rude Pravo* asserting that what they had hoped to accomplish during the "Prague Spring" was basically identical to what Gorbachev is now attempting in the USSR.[16] A number of reform Communists who have been politically inactive during the past two decades and who eschewed involvement in Charter 77's human rights campaigns, may now increasingly look toward Moscow to rejuvenate their reformist platform both within and outside the CPCS.

Several Charter 77 signatories—particularly the "ex-communists" and socialists, but also some of the "independents" and Christians within the movement—have directed messages to the Soviet leader and publicly endorsed his policies. However, their support has contained some salient provisions and reservations. Charter 77 statements have repeatedly called for the removal of Red Army troops and Soviet nuclear missiles from Czechoslovakia as a "positive symbol" of Russian intentions to restore "normality" between the two states.[17] The withdrawal of Soviet forces, they contend, would "constitute a practical step towards convincing the Czechs and Slovaks that *glasnost*, democracy, respect for human rights, and the desire for peace, are not mere slogans." In the words of Charter 77 spokespersons addressed to Gorbachev in March 1987:

> Freedom, democracy, and the universal values you spoke of recently are indivisible and therefore cannot be fully and lastingly enjoyed by those who deny them to others. Were the Soviet Union to lift the main barrier which it itself once placed in the way of progress towards democracy in Czechoslovakia, it would give impetus to its own process of democratization, while at the same time strengthening the trust among nations and states without which even the best intentioned peace initiatives must founder.[18]

Some Charter 77 representatives have reported that since Gorbachev's consolidation of power more Czechoslovak citizens have taken an active interest in politics, in the hope that Moscow's policies may produce some beneficial changes throughout the region.[19] However, the majority of human rights activists also concur that East European populations are fully cognizant that they cannot simply depend on outside factors to introduce reforms. The Czechoslovak opposition therefore continues to underscore the role of independent social forces in various public domains as a crucial source of pressure on the Party leadership to institute reform.

The voluminous underground press in Poland has increasingly covered Soviet events since Gorbachev's rise to power. It now more regularly engages in debates over the significance of *glasnost* and *perestroika* for Eastern Europe in general, and Poland in particular.[20] Opinions have ranged from a positive approval of Gorbachev's measures as a fairly genuine attempt to democratize the Soviet system, to a highly critical evaluation of Moscow's ulterior motives and maneuvers. Solidarity advisor Adam Michnik, who is not easy to pigeonhole in any single category and who is consistently critical of Soviet behavior, nevertheless thinks that evolving Kremlin policies may open up new possibilities by creating opportunities for political compromises that would lessen domestic social conflicts.[21] For example, Moscow may give East bloc states a freer hand to introduce much needed reforms, including those initially proposed by the Solidarity movement—such as workers self-management, local self-government, labor union pluralism, and more tolerance for political diversity. Furthermore, attempts at economic restructuring to enhance output may produce irresistable internal pressures for politically oriented reforms. Michnik and other like-minded dissidents consider it essential that any economic reform or "streamlining" be accompanied by full-scale "political reconstruction." They feel that continuing progress in the USSR may indeed provide such opportunities, but remain concerned that the present Warsaw leadership will try to contain any reforms within the framework of the system without significantly remodelling political relations. Poland's cautious "positivists" contend that public pressures should be stepped up on each regime to encourage it to transcend "bureaucratic constraints" and neutralize or remove all "regressive" elements from the administration.

A section of Hungary's dissident intelligentsia has issued tentatively positive evaluations of East European prospects under Gorbachev. In June 1987, the leading *samizdat* journal *Beszelo* published detailed "prerequisites for resolving the political crisis" that were evidently agreed upon by different groupings in the "democratic opposition."[22] In addition to specific reform proposals in the economic, cultural, legal, and political spheres, one section of the document notes that Moscow has become more tolerant of East European reforms thus presenting "an opportunity for the satellite countries to increase their relative independence of the Soviet Union." Gorbachev has purportedly recognized the need for "changes in mutual relations" and is more amenable to tolerate local political reform. External conditions have apparently "never before been so favorable as now," and *Beszelo* called upon Magyar dissidents, and all reformist forces within the ruling Party, to avail themselves of current opportunities to push for major changes, including the gradual separation of Party from government:

The more we are able to get the Soviet leadership to accept today, the more we would be able to defend later, during a possible backlash. And when we are weighing the force of the possible backlash, we have to take into account the long-term trends of the changes that are weakening Soviet control over the region.[23]

Degrees of optimism over Gorbachev may also be found among the small dissident community in particularly repressive states such as Romania and the GDR. These individuals may not necessarily view the Kremlin leader as a uniquely democratic force, but they perceive that his programs compare favorably with those of their own regimes; they thereby aspire to a modicum of Soviet-type liberalization. Some may indeed see Gorbachev as a potential "ally" in their struggles with the entrenched domestic Communist *apparat*, and an important external lever for internal change. About the time of Gorbachev's visit to Bucharest in May 1987, dissident Romanian intellectuals sent two letters to the Soviet embassy proposing various political reforms in the country, in the hope of obtaining Moscow's support and protection against Ceausescu's rigid dogmatism.[24] Rather than propounding a comprehensive program of democratization in their documents, Romanian dissidents have petitioned for a resuscitation of "socialism" and the termination of Ceausescu's "cult of personality," considered to be a throwback to the worst features of Stalinism and involving numerous abuses of power. The prominent oppositionist figure Mihai Botez has reported that a growing number of Romanian intellectuals, both within and outside the Party, are looking towards Moscow to apply pressure on Bucharest to ease its repressions and introduce a "technocratic and rational approach to policy."[25] Botez believes that mounting public discontent in the country could assist Moscow in pushing for appropriate adjustments in the Romanian Communist Party.

Dissidents in the GDR have initiated campaigns for *glasnost*, but have tended to avoid calls for *perestroika* given East Berlin's seemingly immovable opposition to economic reform. For instance, members of the unofficial Peace and Human Rights group have issued statements demanding greater openness in the mass media. In their estimation, an independent press is "an essential prerequisite for the development of a country's democracy."[26] They have complained that even in other Communist countries journalists experience more opportunity to engage in factual commentary, whereas in East Germany "mendacious reporting" and "linguistic barbarism" are still prevalent. More broadly based expressions of protest against the government's restrictive cultural and information policies have also been displayed by crowds of East German youth chanting Gorbachev's name during several public demonstrations.[27]

Such actions are also designed to taunt and mock the regime. Ironically therefore, some GDR dissidents seem to be using Gorbachev's rhetoric as a weapon against their own intransigent regime, in the hope of spurring wider human rights campaigns.

A sizeable body of independently monitored public opinion about Gorbachev can best be described as "negativist." This term encompasses the majority of "non-engaged" or "apolitical" people who do not actively participate either in government directed or dissident sponsored activities. It also includes some former reformers now fully disillusioned with prospects for democracy in Leninist systems, as well as potential revolutionists who believe that only a government collapse or an armed insurrection will transform or dislodge the system. The latter concede that the prospects for violent revolution are extremely remote at present.

Ideas expressed in one Polish *samizdat* publication early in 1987 may indeed be more widely based in East European societies. According to the authors, many if not most Poles believe that "everything Gorbachev says and does is mere propaganda . . . directed primarily at the West," in order to gain credits, markets, and technology, and to throw Western powers "off their guard."[28] The underlying assumption among "negativists" is that "the nature of Communism will never change; the only thing that does change is its tactics."[29] Such critics do not envisage any meaningful reforms under Gorbachev's rule, irrespective of Moscow's actual intentions. Economic and social problems are so deeply rooted, they feel, that only radical measures by non-Communists with no ultimate stake in the system could prove decisive. In the existing state of "lawlessness" and political arbitrariness, any reforms or innovations introduced in economic, cultural, or political life can be swiftly revoked if it suits the whims and goals of the Party leadership. In the final reckoning, "negativists" contend, democratic pluralism and the rule of law can only be institutionalized and protected by independent checks and balances fully outside Communist Party control.

Several Polish oppositionists have cautioned against invoking Gorbachev's policies to buttress their own demands for domestic reform. During a discussion between leading dissidents under the auspices of Solidarity's Temporary Council, Konrad Bieliński and Andrzej Celinski stressed that positive evaluations of Gorbachev by the political opposition could result in their "loss of credibility and social authority" among wide sectors of the Polish public.[30] In the opinion of the respected dissident intellectual Jacek Kuroń, "such misgivings cannot be underestimated" as Poles apparently harbor little faith or trust in Kremlin programs, whatever the avowed goals. Widespread public skepticism about Moscow's current policies was confirmed during Gorbachev's visit to Poland in July 1988 when small crowds displayed little evident enthusiasm for his presence.[31] One of Wałesa's advisers, Bronisław Geremek, has complained about the "widespread attitude of ignoring events in the USSR in the belief that nothing good can come out of them for Poland." The depth of popular suspicion was echoed by Solidarity activist Celinski, who estimated that: "The question of whether anything is to be gained from changes in the Soviet Union is based on an illusion, (as) any Communist cadre will think entirely in terms of hanging on to power for another six months or a year. . ."[32]

The third broad category of dissident opinion concerning Gorbachev may be termed "potentialist." It can be detected particularly among independent worker activists, self-proclaimed nationalists, and anti-Communist democrats of various political persuasions. "Potentialists" perceive the Gorbachev phenomenon as a potentially valuable—though unintentional—spark for far-reaching political change that could ultimately elude Party control. However, *glasnost* and *perestroika* are not viewed as instrumental factors in bringing about genuine democratization. Indeed, the Soviet General-Secretary and his "faction" are seen principally as Communist "realists" or "problem solvers" who understand the system's failures and the urgent need to revitalize seriously flagging socialist economies. But far from promoting the development of a "post-totalitarian" society, the CPSU leaders purportedly aim to salvage and strengthen the Leninist system by boosting economic performance under overall Party supervision.

In fact, some "potentialists" see in the attempted rejuvenation of Communism an inherent danger; thereby each ruling Party may increase its controls by streamlining a more efficient and stable economy. During the process, repression may be eased, criticism may be tolerated, and some tentative gestures may be made toward organizational pluralism. But these measures are primarily means to an end. They are liable to sharp reversal once the state's economic base is consolidated and some political momentum is regained. Dissenting elements can then be brought under tighter rein and genuine pluralism outlawed or forcefully co-opted. Tadeusz Jedynak, the former Solidarity underground leader in Upper Silesia, has warned that "at a certain point it may turn out that *perestroika* is just a maneuver which will turn against us."[33] In his view, nothing has yet happened in the USSR that cannot be undone practically overnight. Despite their pronounced skepticism, "potentialists" believe that in the process of "restructuring," Gorbachev's policies could well provoke political instability in the Soviet Union by energizing nationalist forces and democratic movements that Moscow may find increasingly difficult to contain. This scenario in turn could help rekindle and reignite popular pressure, manifested in mass anti-government campaigns throughout Eastern Europe. At the very least, political confusion and a loosening of central controls could stimulate the creation of rival political groupings and independent public organizations. The "potentialists" are evidently calculating that the unintended consequences of *glasnost* will sooner or later surface, releasing latent pressures within each subjugated society.

According to Vaclav Havel, the key to change in the Soviet bloc does not rest exclusively with Gorbachev or any other Communist leaders. Much depends on social dynamics and the mood of the masses in interpreting and acting upon perceptions of political change. Havel seems to adopt a "potentialist" stance *vis-à-vis* Moscow; he neither dismisses the Gorbachev phenomenon outright as a mere tactical ploy, nor does he concur with the positive reformist observations of some of his dissident colleagues. The point he believes is to test the system by expanding public initiatives and not simply relying on the power apparatus to introduce democratic measures. He concedes that:

> Admittedly, Gorbachev is a more enlightened ruler than his predecessors, and Jakeš imitates Gorbachev verbally when he goes on about purported restructuring and democratization in our country; but both of these facts have so far had precious little influence in our lives. If they have an influence at all, then it is perhaps mainly in the way and the degree to which society accepts them as terms of reference . . . to the extent that they can be played back into their originators' court.[34]

Though "potentialists" can be found within most of the major dissident movements, their standpoint has perhaps crystallized most forcefully in the Polish opposition, particularly among some of the non-Solidarity political groupings that have sprouted since martial law. Organizations such as the clandestine Fighting Solidarity campaign for a complete political transformation, reject "illusory compromises" with the regime, and dismiss reformism in all its guises as a cosmetic exercise that simply helps to preserve Communist rule. But despite their pronounced skepticism about any Communist Party initiatives, Fighting Solidarity spokesmen have stressed the potentially opportune side-effects of Gorbachev's search for economic improvement throughout the East bloc. This could unwittingly motivate numerous autonomous movements "from below" which the Party *apparatchiki* may eventually prove unable to keep at bay.[35] According to such "potentialist" observers in Poland:

> We should not invest too much hope in the Kremlin's new course. . . . Our efforts ought to concentrate on sustaining the advantage in the field of democratization and liberalization that we have achieved in the forty years of our resistance and struggle. . . . We see our greatest hopes not

in Gorbachev's intentions but in the process that his actions may set in motion.[36]

In "potentialist" estimations the public should prepare itself by all possible means to exploit fully any emerging opportunities Gorbachev's policies may offer, or which any easing of repression could encourage. Pressures should be exerted on the Party by purposively increasing the scope of autonomous private and public initiatives, particularly in the political and economic realms.

Several statements have been issued by dissident groups in Poland, Czechoslovakia, and Hungary in an attempt to formulate some common international stance toward Gorbachev's reforms. Following a meeting on the Polish-Czechoslovak border in August 1987, 21 opposition activists distributed a communique stressing that it still remained to be seen whether Moscow's program would create more favorable conditions for "self-liberation" in the bloc. Though their assessment was cautiously optimistic, they concluded that the Kremlin's officially proclaimed policy of democratization "cannot evoke credibility if it is not translated into concrete actions"—including "a more intense and deeper respect for the independent interests, traditions, and hopes of other countries."[37] Participants at the Czech-Polish meeting stated their intention to launch a more comprehensive debate about Gorbachev's policies, objectives, and effects among independent groupings throughout Eastern Europe. In order to improve coordination and help forge a coherent joint response to Gorbachev's policies among Soviet bloc dissidents, Michnik and others have called for a "common platform" reflecting the position of Polish, Czechoslovak, and Hungarian oppositionist strands.[38] The precise contours of this venture have still to be specified, but occasional joint meetings continue to be held. The July 1988 Polish-Czechoslovak border gathering was the largest in over ten years. The 26 participants, including members of the Polish Socialist Party and Charter 77 signatories, called on each government to allow independent social groups to contribute to the current reform process.[39]

Available evidence indicates that most East European dissidents maintain a reasonably sober and realistic assessment of Gorbachev's tenure and the possibilities for lasting improvements. Their opinions are likely to alter or further crystallize as developments unfold in Moscow and elsewhere in the region. The majority seem to consider it premature to draw any final conclusions, whatever their individual aspirations and approaches. Not surprisingly, some have voiced dismay that Western observers may be allured by the symbols rather than the substance of Soviet policy. In the words of Vaclav Havel:

As far as Gorbachev is concerned, I am neither an optimist nor a pessimist. . . . Concerning his popularity in the West I am rather shocked to find that the "realist" politicians who mock us for our lack of realism allow themselves to be charmed by a few seductive glances in their direction. . . . The fact that all those worldly-wise, long-serving "realist" politicians, who mock us naive dreamers fighting for human rights in Eastern Europe, are unable to see through it is something I find alarming.[40]

Western Policies

Since the late 1950s, the West has pursued a cautious policy of "peaceful engagement" and "bridge building" with Soviet bloc states in order to involve them in closer economic, cultural, and political ties, and promote their evolution toward greater national autonomy and internal pluralism.[41] This approach has been maintained by all U.S. administrations whatever the precise terminology applied, and whatever the state of U.S.-Soviet relations at any particular juncture. Through a program of "differentiation" it was hoped to draw at least some countries into mutually beneficial relationships with the West. During the 1970s, a rank order of Soviet bloc regimes was adopted, whereby rewards obtained from the West became contingent upon "progressive" domestic policies, such as respect for human rights, political and cultural liberalization, and expressions of national sovereignty. By devising a flexible sliding scale of rank, reward, and punishment it was hoped that diversity would be encouraged, Soviet interference peacefully reduced, and Western influences correspondingly increased.

The period of East-West *detente* in the 1970s formalized relationships with Eastern Europe on the assumption that the reduction of international tensions would help to liberalize Communism. *Detente* maintained a linkage between internal human rights conditions and the content of external cooperation with Western countries. This "carrot and stick" approach was demonstrated in attempts to link trade and credits to the internal politics of Communist states. For example, the U.S. Jackson-Vanik Amendment to the 1974 East-West Trade Act avowedly coupled trading relations with domestic civil rights; if the latter were deemed adequate by Congress then the state in question could obtain favorable tariff and trading treatment. From the outset, however, a number of problems arose. There were disagreements among Western powers as to the actual performance of specific East bloc states in the human rights arena; the "linkage" policy was hampered by imprecision; and the "carrot and stick" approach was inconsistently and often half-heartedly applied. Rewards for reasonably positive, neutral, or even poor behavior soon outpaced any effective punishment for blatantly bad behavior. Furthermore, the Communist regimes manipulated *detente* to their own advantage, both economically and politically, without implementing any significant or lasting domestic relaxations. Though some of the most extreme forms of repression against political dissenters may have been eased or avoided, this was principally a matter of altering the methods of social control and not its premises, objectives, or consequences. The anti-democratic principles of the Party-state systems remained essentially intact.

By the late 1970s, the West had discovered that there was no direct correlation between international *detente* and Communist "liberalization." "Eurodetente" neither destabilized East European governments nor stimulated far-reaching democratization, though some of its features, such as the Helsinki Final Act, evidently encouraged several dissident groups to campaign against official human rights violations. Nevertheless, each ruling Party was primarily concerned with devising a workable balance between domestic repression and overt tolerance in order to maintain favorable economic arrangements with the West and to seal its international legitimacy, without relinquishing its monopolistic controls. Kovrig considers that through its *detente* policies, Western governments in effect *de jure* recognized the Communist status of Eastern Europe and "abandoned all pretense at revisionism," while ratifying "the political consequences of World War II."[42]

Soviet bloc governments are seeking the obvious advantages of capitalist-type democracies—high productivity, technological modernity, and individual motivation—without incurring the "costs" of political pluralism. But they confront a growing contradiction between the necessity for economic development and the regressive constraints of the traditional command system; a conflict in its essence between liberty and coercion. East European contradictions will require active and skillful exploitation by the West if it hopes to influence events, even if it cannot ensure that these estranged countries will transform into democratic and sovereign states. Only a steady evolution in this direction will preclude recurring regional emergencies that expose the West to improvised and largely ineffectual short-term responses. East bloc reforms in the direction of pluralism, diversification, and greater national autonomy are clearly to the West's advantage, particularly if they help to loosen somewhat the Soviet stranglehold over the region. Without such reforms economic conditions will degenerate and increase the chances of major social conflict, aggravate East-West tensions, and threaten Europe with destabilization. Active Western involvement from the outset may not insure maximum influence over internal developments, but diplomatic and economic levers could at least assure some input into reformist programs and government decisions. Western inactivity could prove counter-productive; it would preclude all forms of pressure and persuasion, and send a message of indifference to Communist rulers and their subordinate populations.

The Western allies could pursue four parallel strategies to help sustain the erosion of Europe's antiquated totalitarian systems: encourage reform, pressurize Moscow, support independent social activism, and exploit economic leverage. Though past experience has shown that a joint Western approach is difficult to uphold, there is enormous room for improvement.[43] Regular consultations and some complementary division of labor *vis-à-vis* the East could focus on concrete policy instruments such as export controls, stipulations for trade and credits, the coordination of sanctions, and the application of political levers against specific regimes.[44] EEC governments, which have a high stake in the performance of Soviet bloc economies, are unlikely to oppose a program which links increased cooperation with market-oriented reforms, political decentralization, and long-term internally generated economic development. Each Western state could more effectively use its particular strengths and points of contact with East bloc regimes to help push forward the reform process.

First, the West could provide economic and political support to reform minded individuals and factions within each ruling Party. Such support would need to be flexible and conditional on verified results. In addition to essential economic reforms, any meaningful political relaxation in these states would have to entail the legalization of independent occupational and social organizations, guarantees of judicial impartiality, genuine multi-candidate local and regional elections, industrial self-management, and the participation of freely elected intellectual and worker representatives in shaping domestic policies. The criteria on which the U.S. policy of "differentiation" is based need to be re-evaluated so that rewards more accurately reflect Communist performance in both the democratic-reformist and national-independence arenas. Steps which institutionalize and protect liberalization in various public spheres have to be distinguished from cosmetic palliatives aimed at gaining Western economic assistance. Regional ties between East and West European nations should be fostered to promote internal reform. An assortment of cross-bloc economic, scientific, cultural, and educational exchanges could be enhanced to help permeate democratic ideas and practices to societies which have been deprived of free debate and association for over four decades. This should involve the freer flow of information and the means of communication, including radio and television broadcasts, published material, personal computers, video recorders and audio equipment, whether through open or clandestine channels.

The consequences of such East-West contacts on domestic conditions will need to be gauged more meticulously to assure that they involve ordinary citizens and are not merely state-controlled charades. The relevant governments should be pressed to expand their reformist agendas, and not renege on promises of liberalization once the limelight has dimmed. Definitions of human rights must be broadened, so that the international spotlight is not simply focused on the most glaring abuses. Such definitions must incorporate fundamental political, cultural, religious, economic, and civil liberties to nurture the emergence of democratic societies. East bloc regimes oppose any close scrutiny of their human rights record as this undermines the legitimacy of their existing political arrangements.[45] The West could combine a longer term program for supporting the development of democratic institutions with more intense short-term pressures against specific human rights violations.[46]

Secondly, the West could motivate Moscow to reconsider the burdens of maintaining an unwilling and increasingly costly empire. Through pressure, persuasion, and example, the Kremlin needs to be shown the advantages to be gained from tolerating greater local diversity and national autonomy in the bloc—especially in terms of improved economic performance and enhanced social stability. Conversely, the immediate and long-term economic and political costs of forcefully subduing democratic reforms would have to be specified well in advance of any potential domestic unrest. A sounder mix of economic restrictions and political penalties could at least increase the perceived costs of a military intervention or an internal crackdown. Early signals about Western reactions to crisis could prove more influential and effective. They are more likely to be included in Soviet calculations at that stage than after a crisis spins out of control.[47] A united Western front may not be easy to maintain, but at the very least political signals from Western governments should not be contradictory and conflicting. Long-range planning and regular high-level consultations could prevent the worst pitfalls of inconsistency, divergence, and perceived weakness in comparison with Soviet bloc "uniformity."

The contradictions between Soviet internal reforms, *a la glasnost* and *perestroika*, and external repression constitute valuable political capital for the West. Moscow's self-proclaimed sincerity in allowing democratization and self-determination throughout the bloc should be raised on summit agendas, openly tested by international tribunals, and the results widely publicized. Inter-governmental pressure and international public opinion, which Gorbachev is so studiously cultivating, should be redirected by Western agencies to influence Kremlin behavior without threatening its strategic security concerns.[48] Any renewed *detente* must be constructed around substantive progress in Soviet bloc reform, as the West has an important economic and political stake in the region's stability and development.

The extent to which Moscow would allow reforms to proceed in Eastern Europe remains a moot point, particularly if such reforms seriously undermine the political structure and erode the distribution of power. However, under Gorbachev the limits of Soviet tolerance could become broader than at any time since the death of Stalin. Moscow has realized the urgent need for economic improvement throughout the region, and there is even a recognition that some political reform will have to accompany economic restructuring if public incentives are to be stimulated and bureaucratic interference curtailed. Communist leaders appear to understand that the West may provide invaluable economic assistance but is unlikely to mount a comprehensive and continuous rescue operation. Moreover, new technology can only be profitably absorbed in Eastern Europe through appropriate structural reforms in administration, management, and public participation. In the final reckoning, there is no certainty at what point the balance of economic and political reform will tip over in any state to provoke direct Soviet intervention. History has shown that two prohibitions will not be lifted—a unilateral withdrawal from the Warsaw Pact and a disintegration of the ruling Communist Parties. However, there is a very wide area between immobility and revolution which Moscow should be encouraged to tolerate.

In the third instance, Western support for independent social forces, including dissident and oppositionist movements in Eastern Europe, could be enlarged. This would embrace all religious movements and associations, social and cultural initiatives, self-publishing, educational and artistic ventures, the expansive youth counter-culture, and numerous single issue campaigns seeking to curtail state control. All manner of autonomous professional and labor unions should be supported financially, and the corresponding organizations in the West encouraged to campaign on behalf of organizational pluralism. A whole spectrum of independent social activism, which we have discussed in previous chapters, must be sustained if democratization is to take root in the East bloc. Small concessions "from above" are much less impressive than local initiative and public emancipation "from below." Various forms of individual or collective economic enterprise could be bolstered, whether among workers, intellectuals, farmers, students, and entrepreneurs. The long term political implications of an expanding non-state sector must not be underestimated.

Fourth, on the economic front, there is no valid reason to suppose that a stringent regulation of economic benefits to Eastern Europe will push the region into a tighter Soviet grip. The need for Western technology, credits, and trade is paramount in these states. Gorbachev's integrationist plans for the CMEA do not signify economic isolation from the West. On the contrary, Western resources and knowhow will be eagerly sought to modernize economies that Moscow cannot rescue but which act as conduits for capitalist technology to the USSR. The relationship between West-East economic ties and CMEA integration may be either competitive or complementary. Increasing trade and cooperation with the West could indeed foster greater Comecon assimilation, rather than simply "opening up" these states to global market mechanisms. As some governments seek economic contacts more eagerly than others, thus converging or conflicting with Soviet interests, the effects of any bilateral cooperative agreements with the West have to be shrewdly evaluated in line with long term economic objectives.[49] Comecon difficulties and needs must be properly measured and engaged, to gain tangible political benefits.

There is an unfortunate Western propensity to assume that simply exporting capital to Leninist states is synonymous with exporting capitalism. But despite the promises of *detente* in the 1970s, there has been no correspondence between internal reform and the degree of Western economic aid.[50] The unrestrained pumping of finances into the Eastern bloc has not liberalized Communism or enhanced national independence. Likewise, there are no guarantees that future economic generosity will result in internal liberalization or national autonomy. In fact, such benevolence may have the opposite effect. All too often economic rescues and liberal credits have merely allowed Warsaw Pact governments to postpone rather than introduce durable reforms.[51] The West's "carrot and stick" approach has lacked precision and consistency in the past. The "stick" has not been sufficiently powerful to inflict lasting pain on these regimes, while too many juicy "carrots" have been devoured without any meaningful reciprocal response. The accumulation of a combined $70 billion debt to the West, and the staggering waste of resources by Soviet bloc rulers, should have convinced Western policymakers that economic packages without specific reformist objectives have little practical value.[52] Sound business sense is called for by the West and must be encouraged in the East. Each Communist regime has to be shown that only real economic competitiveness will be rewarded with markets, technology and credits. Such competitiveness can in turn only be achieved by extensive, institutionalized and irreversible economic and political liberalization.

There are indications that compared to the 1970s, Western creditors and companies are increasingly concerned to link aid and trade with proof of structural change, including tax and labor reforms, fiscal discipline, and decentralization of managerial decision making. This has been the case with the World Bank and IMF in their dealings with Warsaw since the lifting of martial law.[53] New loans throughout the bloc should be earmarked for specific investments and productive civilian industries once a state has displayed its growing creditworthiness. Specific reforms could be matched by specific forms of assistance, while particular benefits should be denied if conditions agreed to are not met. In addition, Western support could also help to cushion each society against the transitory socioeconomic dislocations brought about by initial steps toward some form of "mixed economy."

Conclusion

East Europe's Communist states face a dangerous spiral of economic decline, political instability, and social turbulence. Serious economic stagnation could result in a further loss of government credibility, and a shrinking ability to control fully the discontented populations. Party control and public passivity depend on overall economic satisfaction, signs of material improvement, and maintenance of the instruments of coercion and social control. If economic recovery is to be fostered, "restructuring" will need to be accompanied by substantial political reform and liberalization. This in turn could stimulate organized opposition and public activism which may well escape Party supervision and galvanize more demanding political movements. While the supply of tangible material benefits to the population will prove increasingly difficult without sweeping structural reforms, any intensified repression could prove counterproductive if economic modernization is to be accomplished and workers motivated to spur productivity. A regression to more coercive methods may subdue or postpone major social upheaval, but could in turn worsen economic conditions and insure that future unrest is more widespread and explosive.

Previous political conflicts in the region have been confined to individual states at particular times, thus making it easier for Moscow and local Party leaders to isolate and eliminate popular opposition. However, future collisions between state and society may prove less constricted and containable. It remains to be seen whether any forthcoming crises will be major emergencies or minor irritants, enabling the regimes to muddle through and prevent damaging social eruptions. In such unstable conditions, the West may be ill-prepared to influence fruitfully the process of change, or to ensure that East Europe's fault lines do not develop into severe internal tremors and international earthquakes.

Conclusion

Political dissenters, opposition activists, and independent public groups in several East European countries are on the front line of the struggle against monopolistic Communist Party rule. They may also be on the verge of a renewed offensive, by amplifying the pressures on Soviet bloc regimes to implement substantive domestic reforms in the post-Brezhnev era. More strident campaigns could emerge in the foreseeable future, aiming to enlarge the autonomous "civil society," as each Leninist state becomes increasingly vulnerable to economic decline, political instability, and public disquiet. It seems apparent, however, that East bloc regimes aim to place effective limits on any independent social actors, by maintaining comprehensive controls over the populace while neutralizing or co-opting selected critics into Party-supervised institutions and activities. In addition, some leeway may be allowed for quasi-autonomous pursuits in the cultural and economic realms; such tentative official experiments have already been evident in a number of states. These measures are unlikely to appease the majority of dissenters, or actively involve the masses in any genuinely representational public interest lobbies. In the absence of a multi-party system, free national elections, and a democratic parliamentary system, political checks and balances on government powers will remain illusory.

Given these important constraints, are dissent and organized opposition likely to increase or decrease during the next decade, will they be confined to present levels, or will they expand in some fields and contract in others? Though developments, reactions, and outcomes will differ substantially between states, the overall trend may be characterised by intensified political and economic pressure on each government to grant more than cosmetic concessions, to tolerate more extensive private and public domains, and to decrease state control over a gamut of social activities. Opposition activists in Poland, Czechoslovakia, and Hungary have asserted that dissidents should strive to be more forceful in formulating and promulgating viable economic policies and political programs. East German, Romanian, and Bulgarian critics of the government have also become more active of late; many perceive a more opportune period for reformist or non-state initiatives as the authorities grapple with severe internal problems.

The numbing effects of Solidarity's martial law downfall and massive Communist repression could wear off in the next few years, and not only in Poland. Indeed, the escalation of social tensions fuelled by serious economic imbalances may have revolutionary implications if the system is unable to satisfy, contain, divert, or constructively channel public pressures for major change. If they occur, popular explosions are likely to be spontaneous, unorganized, and unpredictable. But the more plausible scenario will not involve any mass insurrection or a frontal oppositionist challenge to the state by a large, organized movement. Unless mass repression is again revived to eradicate dissent, we are likely to witness a gradually expanding panorama of initiatives outside Party-state control, involving an assortment of social groups. Inbuilt political, economic, cultural, religious, and national fault lines in Eastern Europe could widen and deepen despite official attempts to contain the opposition, keep protests within certain bounds, and conduct a controlled "thaw" to elicit public trust and credibility. Ironically, any creeping liberalization may not extinguish but merely rekindle public dissent. Party leaders will find it increasingly difficult to uphold a workable balance between repression and relaxation while trying to "re-negotiate" a post-Brezhnev "social contract" with the population.

In such circumstances, dissident strategists will undoubtedly seek to expand the range of overt, independent public ventures. Some activists may explore possible common ground with reformist elements within the ruling Parties or on its peripheries. They may plan to take advantage of the limited legislative concessions proposed by the regime in the hope of spurring further political emancipation. Other activists are more likely to exploit the authorities' inability to control a number of budding public initiatives, in order to facilitate the growth of an "alternative society" free of state control. Numerous independent activities may deliberately or unintentionally acquire a stronger political flavor in the campaign for popular representation and organizational pluralism. What public initiatives could Communist regimes reasonably tolerate without undermining their overall mechanisms of social control? Conversely, which fault lines could be most profitably exploited by the opposition without provoking destructive official retaliation? Credible answers to these pressing dilemmas may be offered by separating and assessing several distinct areas of public life.

In the economic realm, state officials throughout the region have underscored that "restructuring," "renewal," or "reform" does not signify any far-reaching tolerance of rival power centers or the untrammelled growth of social independence. Economic privatization has its limitations;

even those regimes which seem willing to permit an expansion of free enterprise and the non-state economic sector arm themselves with guarantees that the Party's "commanding heights" over the means of production and distribution will not be scaled. The most crucial political and economic privileges of the Communist establishment will be protected from any concerted challenges by autonomous interest groups with their own agendas for development. Though independent farmers, craftsmen, manufacturers, and other entrepreneurs may be allowed or even encouraged to operate, with a view to buttressing the inefficient "socialist sector," official fears of resurgent capitalism and full marketization remain pronounced. Likewise, any economic emancipation of the workforce, through genuine factory self-management, independent labor unionism, and free collective bargaining will be opposed and combatted by state employers. In all probability, the Party apparatus will obstruct and stifle any large-scale de-nationalization, and will enforce numerous administrative and legalistic restrictions on free enterprise.

From the public angle, growing economic autonomy for private business brings a mixed blessing in an overall Communist framework. It is likely to mean further enrichment for a minority having access to scarce resources, and stagnation or relative pauperization for the majority, especially if the state system remains mismanaged and underproductive. Nevertheless, the economic arena could be increasingly utilized by oppositionist groups to extend the scope of public and private enterprise. It could strengthen the self-organization of various professional and occupational groups, far surpassing what the regime had originally anticipated. Economic ventures could also stimulate non-economic initiatives by funnelling more substantial funds to independent social and political campaigns.

In the political sphere, the credibility of any embryonic opposition movements should not be dismissed prematurely. Some nascent pluralism could emerge through a combination of Party-directed reforms "from above" and sustained public resilience "from below." Overt political organizations could expand and gain wider public backing while testing the limits of "socialist pluralism." Covert political movements could equally enlarge their base of support if official policy continues to frustrate popular expectations. Evidently, Communist governments will not countenance the formation of truly independent and influential political parties, but some regimes may be willing to sponsor or permit semi-autonomous political associations that remain within the overall purview of the state. The latter may be permitted a "consultative" role, with outlets for criticizing specific policies, as long as they do not challenge the tenets of Communist hegemony.

Restrained concessions and full or partial co-optation may prove altogether insufficient to satisfy dissenters or pacify the popular mood. However, such government maneuvers may be tentatively accepted by some groups favoring a gradualist approach to change within and outside the prevailing political system. Some political dissidents contend that peaceful, piecemeal compromises could in the long run erode the resistance of state organs and enlarge the scope of authentic public representation in political decision making. A few regimes have already embarked on circumscribed forms of political experimentation, but without evoking any noticeable public enthusiasm for what are generally perceived as paltry and deceptive concessions. Nevertheless, one should not disdain the possibility that further government attempts to broaden its legitimacy, regain some economic momentum, motivate the workforce, and appease important sectors of society in order to enhance productivity may provide greater opportunities for all manner of independent political activism.

Growing public restlessness and popular awareness of the possibilities for self-organization could increase the number and size of various social campaigns. East European regimes may prove unable to fully control or suppress these initiatives without resorting to ultimately counter-productive police persecution. Some of these "single issue" movements, for example for environmental protection and cultural rights, could have a positive effect on the authorities, by applying pressure on officials to adjust their policies and take some stock of public opinion. Other social campaigns may prove more difficult to contain or defuse. The visibly growing disillusionment and discontent among large sections of the younger generation, including college students and working class youths, could prove particularly menacing. The Communist system is clearly failing to meet their material demands or reward their non-material aspirations. Youth protests may remain unstructured, dispersed, camouflaged, and spontaneous, but they could also take the form of destructive local revolts or evolve into more durable opposition movements that the regime could find increasingly problematic to ignore or dispel. The authorities evidently perceive such dangers but may lack the necessary economic resources to neutralize all public pressures. They are also wary that public perceptions of official weakness could energize further social campaigns for various popular causes.

Religious practices are reportedly on the rise throughout the Soviet bloc. A growing portion of the populace appears to be seeking spiritual meaning, moral values, credible belief systems, reassuring ritual practices, and public participation outside Party-state control. The authorities could well tolerate stronger, well organized, independent Churches in return for the clergy's political neutrality, and a public religious life that is primarily confined to theological, scriptural, moral, and ethical issues.

Officials will remain on guard, however, against Church incursions into the political arena, either through direct support for oppositionist campaigns, or through indirect sanctuary for "anti-state" activities. Furthermore, with more pronounced economic decline and social blight on the horizon, the authorities may encourage the Churches to help alleviate chronic social problems, as long as charitable programs do not sustain independent pressure groups that politically challenge the regime.

In the ideological and cultural domains, official Marxism-Leninism as a system of beliefs and exhortations is practically in its death throes and will be increasingly unable to sustain itself by manipulating national and historical symbols. The field of independent cultural activity, unencumbered with Communist dogma, is undergoing a renaissance in several states. It may in fact contain an irresistible dynamic which government ideologues and watchdogs will find increasingly difficult to suppress or manipulate. Indeed, Communist officials may be prepared to allow for a wider-ranging cultural liberalization in exchange for guaranteed political acquiescence. But such assurances could prove elusive, as autonomous cultural activities help to formulate and strengthen values, norms, and behavioral patterns that question and undermine the premises and institutions of single Party rule. They are also a potent stimulant for numerous independent public initiatives that contribute toward eroding the bedrock of Communist control in Eastern Europe.

Postscript

Since we completed this manuscript in August 1988, political developments in some parts of Eastern Europe have raced ahead of earlier expectations. The past few months have witnessed an increasing diversification of government responses to economic stagnation and the Soviet domestic reform process. A division has emerged between states which oppose both economic restructuring and political liberalization (the GDR and Romania) and those which seek to enhance economic decentralization with alterations in the structure and composition of political institutions (Poland and Hungary). Between these two poles lie regimes which support some economic reform and rationalization but wish to avoid introducing any disruptive political changes (Czechoslovakia and Bulgaria). It seems likely that creeping economic decline, a further loosening of Kremlin definitions of acceptable "roads to socialism" for Warsaw Pact states, and growing public restiveness and self-assertion will fuel pressures for more substantive social, political, and economic reform throughout the East bloc. Indeed, a quantitative leap in the scale of popular opposition and social activism has been evident, particularly in Hungary and Poland which stand at the forefront of the current wave of economic and political *perestroika*.

Warsaw and Budapest have been forced to cope with a widening spectrum of dissident activity and independent public initiatives. Calculating that outright repression would be counterproductive by undermining an economic reform program which necessitates entrepreneurial expansion, public involvement, and Western material assistance, the two regimes have opted for greater political relaxation. Poland's plans for reinstating Solidarity, establishing a freely contested upper chamber of parliament, and granting a minority block to the opposition in the lower house, and Hungary's impending law on free associations and eventual multi-party elections, are a response to severe social discontent. Such liberalization is intended to defuse popular unrest and enlist the Communist Party's political opponents in the economic reform program. However, the gap between the theory and application of economic restructuring in Eastern Europe must not be overlooked when assessing the fortunes of political reform. It remains to be seen how such measures will be implemented, what bureaucratic obstacles they will face, and how Party officials will seek to restrict the impact of legalized independent organizations and the prerogatives of partially democratized governmental institutions. Both ruling Parties will reserve the right to outlaw associations which are deemed to be acting contrary to the constitution and threatening the security of the state. Moreover, it is not at all clear that piecemeal democratization will be sufficient to assure political stability and social acquiescence, or whether it will serve to stimulate further political demands. Budapest and Warsaw aim to register and incorporate some political groups and opposition activists within their reformist agenda in order to set and supervise the pace of change, to split "moderates" from "radicals," and to acquire greater popular legitimacy. Compromise and co-existence are now offered in exchange for dissident support in neutralizing mass disquiet which will be fanned by the deleterious effects of economic reform on living standards. But both governments remain wary that liberalization may bring unintended consequences by galvanizing social activism which could snowball out of official control and precipitate an avalanche of the entire Leninist edifice.

In recent months, several new public initiatives have materialized, while other already existing autonomous movements have been strengthened. In Poland, after two waves of industrial strikes during 1988 and the threat of more extensive protest actions against deteriorating economic conditions, the Jaruzelski regime has pledged to restore Solidarity and other independent groups in return for the union's support of painful economic reforms and a restructured parliamentary system. But Lech Wałęsa and his Citizens Committee advisers have faced substantial public opposition to any long range compromises with the authorities. Some Solidarity officials, including members of the Working Group of Solidarity's National Commission, numerous shop floor activists, and increasingly militant youth groups remain deeply skeptical about any meaningful or lasting concessions from the Party, and in some cases favor more forthright confrontation with the regime. The Independent Students Union has become more active on Poland's campuses in anticipation of re-legalization, and several new student associations have been registered, including the Young Poland Academic Union and the Association of Catholic Student Youth. The Rural Solidarity movement is also preparing for legal operations, and some farmers activists are planning to revive a full-fledged independent Polish Peasants Party. Among the dozens of political groups recently launched in the country it is worth mentioning the resuscitated Polish Labor Party and the newly formed Polish Ecological Party.

The Grosz regime is preparing to legalize diverse political currents which will operate in accordance with a proposed new law on associations. But the Hungarian Party itself appears to be divided on how to handle the growing number of autonomous groups; pro-reformist forces are urging greater liberalization while more traditionalist forces warn about the specter of anarchy. Some reformists have established a New March Front to try and channel domestic discontent away from overt opposition to the Communist state and to build a "national consensus" which preserves the Party's leading role. More orthodox Leninists have set up a new Party of Hungarian Communists and a Ferenc Munnich Society. Official tolerance has buttressed political pluralism in the country as witnessed in the formal inauguration of the populist Hungarian Democratic Forum in September 1988. The Forum is in the process of evolving from a loosely knit intellectual movement into a more structured political organization with local branches open to all Hungarians. Its leaders seek to benefit from the political thaw by participating in national and local elections while promoting the gradual emergence of a multiparty system. The Federation of Young Democrats has continued to develop into a more coherent political movement with cells in universities and work enterprises throughout the country, and a number of traditional political parties have resumed operations, including the independent Smallholders Party, the Christian Democratic Party, and the Social Democratic Party. Numerous other oppositionist groups have surfaced in Hungary; prominent among them is the populist Szarszo Front, consisting of representatives from over thirty unofficial groupings which advocate the dismantling of single-party rule. At least three alternative lawyers groups have been established to press for sweeping reforms of the legal system. The Magyar free trade union movement has also expanded with the formation of the Democratic League of Independent Unions, designed to assist workers in establishing autonomous labor bodies, and the founding of Workers Solidarity, the first independent union of manual workers.

Despite persistent repression in Czechoslovakia, the frequency and size of public protests has visibly increased and several new informal groups have been formed. These include the Initiative for Social Defense, the Movement for Civil Liberties, the Independent Ecological Group, the youth-oriented Children of Bohemia, the Masaryk Society, and the T.G. Masaryk Association. The Movement for Civil Liberties, acting as an umbrella body for the new opposition, has issued a political manifesto calling for the formation and coordination of political groups to apply pressure on the anti-reformist administration. In the GDR, youth protests have steadily swelled and over two hundred small, autonomous Basis Groups pressing for greater religious, cultural and political freedoms, have blossomed in a number of cities sheltered by the Evangelical Church. Further dissident stirrings have also been manifest in Bulgaria, centered around the Independent Association for the Defense of Human Rights. The group has petitioned for freedom of movement and emigration, as well as for liberalization in the mass media, but its members continue to be subjected to persistent repression. Other independent groupings have also surfaced of late, including the environmentalist Committee for the Defense of Ruse and the Party of the Green Masses, the Discussion Club for the Support of Perestroika and Glasnost, and several informal youth associations based at the nation's universities.

The groundswell of opposition and public activism in Eastern Europe shows every sign of continuing and expanding into the 1990s, presenting fresh challenges to the increasingly vulnerable Communist systems.

Notes and References

Chapter 1: Historical Dimensions

1. The "peoples' democracies" established in the Soviet bloc were designed as a transition stage between capitalism and socialism. They involved a domestic struggle against the remnants of the "old order" without necessitating an identical replication of the Soviet system. Several East European states eventually declared themselves "socialist republics" once the groundwork for state socialism was considered completed.

2. For a useful summation of the Communist takeover process in Eastern Europe see Hubert Ripka, *Eastern Europe in the Post-War World* (New York: Praeger, 1961).

3. A valuable background to Stalin's East European policies can be found in Malcolm Mackintosh, "Stalin's Policies Toward Eastern Europe, 1939–1948: The General Picture," in Thomas J. Hammond (Ed), *The Anatomy of Communist Takeovers* (New Haven: Yale University Press, 1975), pp. 229–42.

4. Hugh Seton-Watson, *The New Imperialism* (London: The Bodley Head, 1961), p. 81.

5. An excellent historical synopsis of each Communist regime and its political structure can be located in Richard F. Staar, *The Communist Regimes in Eastern Europe*, Fourth Revised Edition (Stanford: Hoover Institution, 1982).

6. For an invaluable analysis of the stages of Communist Party consolidation in Eastern Europe see Zbigniew K. Brzezinski, *The Soviet Bloc: Unity and Conflict*, Revised and Enlarged Edition (Cambridge: Harvard University Press, 1967).

7. Tokes posits the question whether the postwar systems were compatible with the prewar political cultures of Eastern Europe. See Rudolf L. Tokes, "Human Rights and Political Change in Eastern Europe," in Rudolf L. Tokes (Ed), *Opposition in Eastern Europe* (London: Macmillan, 1979), pp. 1–25. Whatever the similarities between the prewar authoritarian and postwar totalitarian regimes, the differences are more striking, particularly with regard to the all-pervasiveness of Communist political, social, and economic control, and Soviet imperial domination. The enduring tensions between each nation's traditional political culture and the Leninist systems imposed essentially from outside have been evident during the past four decades.

8. The "Muscovites" benefited from Stalin's trust largely because they had spent the war years in the USSR under direct Soviet guidance, or had belonged to the Comintern or NKVD *apparat*. These carefully selected Stalin loyalists understood that any rupture with the Kremlin would endanger their own leadership positions as they were fully dependent on Moscow's support.

9. The list of "nationalist" or "rightist" victims included the following Party-state leaders: László Rajk in Hungary, Traicho Kostov in Bulgaria, Vladimir Clementis in Czechoslovakia, Lucretiu Patrascanu in Romania, and Władysław Gomułka in Poland; all except Gomułka were executed.

10. Consult Jonathan R. Adelman (Ed), *Terror and Communist Politics: The Role of the Secret Police in Communist States* (Boulder: Westview Press, 1984).

11. An important history of the Bulgarian Communist Party can be found in John Bell, *The Bulgarian Communist Party from Blagoev to Zhivkov* (Stanford: Hoover Institution Press, 1986).

12. For an excellent summary of postwar Bulgarian history see Robert R. King, "Bulgaria," in Teresa Rakowska-Harmstone and Andrew Gyorgy (Eds), *Communism in Eastern Europe* (Bloomington: Indiana University Press, 1979), pp. 168–88.

13. According to official statistics issued in 1945, 2,138 opponents of the Sofia regime were executed at this time, and several thousand received long prison terms; a total of 11,667 people were processed by the courts. See Stanley George Evans, *A Short History of Bulgaria* (London: Lawrence and Wishart, 1960), p. 189.

14. For a thorough history of the Czechoslovak Communist Party see Zdenek Suda, *Zealots and Rebels: A History of the Ruling Communist Party of Czechoslovakia* (Stanford: Hoover Institution Press, 1980).

15. A discussion of the 1948 coup in Czechoslovakia can be found in Pavel Tigrid, "The Prague Coup in 1948: The Elegant Takeover," in Hammond (Ed), *op. cit.*

16. A synopsis of the German Democratic Republic is contained in Arthur M. Hanhardt, Jr., "German Democratic Republic," in Rakowska-Harmstone and Gyorgy (Eds), *op. cit.*, pp. 121–44. For a fuller study see Mike Dennis, *German Democratic Republic: Politics, Economics and Society* (London: Frances Pinter, 1988).

17. For a valuable summary of the East German Communist campaign against rival political groupings see Hans W. Schoenberg, "The Partition of Germany and the Neutralization of Austria," in Hammond (Ed), *op. cit.*, pp. 368–98.

18. See Bennett Kovrig, "Hungary," in Rakowska-Harmstone and Gyorgy (Eds), *op. cit.*, pp. 71–99.

19. Details of the Communist takeover and consolidation of power can also be found in Paul Ignatius, "The First Two Communist Takeovers of Hungary, 1919 and 1948," in Hammond (Ed), *op. cit.*, pp. 385–98.

20. An essential history of the Hungarian Communist Party can be found in Bennett Kovrig, *Communism in Hungary: From Kun to Kádár* (Stanford: Hoover Institution Press, 1979). Also see Hans-Georg Heinrich, *Hungary: Politics, Economics and Society* (Boulder: Lynne Rienner, 1986).

21. For a useful summary of the key elements of the Communist seizure of power in Poland see Marian K. Dziewanowski, *The Communist Party of Poland: An Outline History* (Cambridge: Harvard University Press, 1976), pp. 183–207. An excellent history of the Polish Communists can be found in Jan B. de Weydenthal, *The Communists of Poland: An Historical Outline* (Stanford: Hoover Institution Press, 1978).

22. See in particular Susanne S. Lotarski, "The Communist Takeover in Poland," in Hammond (Ed), *op. cit.*, pp. 339–67. The Home Army had sustained enormous losses during the failed 1944 Warsaw Uprising against the Germans, and the later Soviet arrests, deportations, and executions.

23. The main underground forces in the armed struggle against Communization between 1945 and 1948 included the Freedom and Independence (WIN) movement, and the National Armed Forces (NSZ).

24. Gomułka was imprisoned in 1951 as a "Titoist" and thereby gained some of his reputation as being more independent from Moscow than his predecessors and colleagues; this served him in good stead during the transfer of power in Poland after Stalin's death.

25. A history of the Romanian Communist Party can be found in Robert R. King, *History of the Romanian Communist Party* (Stanford: Hoover Institution Press, 1980), and Michael Shafir, *Romania: Politics, Economics and Society* (London: Frances Pinter, 1985).

26. For a synopsis of post-war Romania see Robert R. King, "Romania," in Rakowska-Harmstone and Gyorgy (Eds), *op. cit.*, pp. 146–67.

27. For details see Stephen Fischer-Galati, *The New Rumania: From People's Democracy to Socialist Republic* (Cambridge: MIT Press, 1967).

28. A helpful guide to the organization and structure of Communist political systems in the Soviet bloc can be found in Ivan Volgyes, *Politics in Eastern Europe* (Chicago: Dorsey Press, 1986); Stephen White, John Gardner and George Schopflin, *Communist Political Systems: An Introduction* (New York: St. Martin's Press, 1987); and Ota Sik, *The Communist Power System* (New York: Praeger, 1981).

29. For an analysis of political control mechanisms in Communist directed mass organizations see Trond Gilberg, "The Political Order," in Stephen Fischer-Galati (Ed), *Eastern Europe in the 1980's* (Boulder: Westview Press, 1981), pp. 121–68.

30. An excellent survey and analysis of the de-Stalinization process and its repercussions in Eastern Europe between 1953 and 1968 is contained in Francis Fejto, *A History of the People's Democracies* (Middlesex, England: Penguin, 1977).

31. William Griffith, "The Decline and Fall of Revisionism in Eastern Europe," in Leopold Labedz (Ed), *Revisionism: Essays on the History of Marxist Ideas* (New York: Praeger, 1962), pp. 223–38.

32. Brzezinski, *op. cit.*, p. 225.

33. For a chronology of the Hungarian Revolution refer to Vojtech Mastny, *East European Dissent: Volume 1* (New York: Facts on File, 1972), pp. 99–140. See also William Lomax, *Hungary 1956* (London: Allen and Busby, 1976).

34. Hubert Ripka, *Eastern Europe in the Post-War World* (New York: Praeger, 1961). For some details on the course of the uprising based on eyewitness reports see Neal V. Buhler, "The Hungarian Revolution," in Ernst C. Helmreich (Ed), *Hungary* (Westbrook, Connecticut: Greenwood Press, 1956), pp. 352–89. Some sources estimate that about 46,000 Hungarians were sent to Soviet labor camps after the Revolution was extinguished.

35. For details see Mastny, *op. cit.*, pp. 79–99. Anti-government riots and protests were also reported in at least seven other Polish cities, including Cracow

and Chorzow. They were also forcefully suppressed, and price reductions on some food items were quickly implemented to forestall further unrest.

36. Among the active dissident intellectuals were those associated with *Po Prostu* magazine and the *Krzywe Koło* discussion clubs. A number of pro-reformist working class centers of debate were also formed in several major cities during 1956.

37. After 1956 only 2,000 out of 10,000 collective farms remained in Poland, though the ultimate Communist Party objective of a dominant "socialist agriculture" was never formally abandoned.

38. For a discussion of the complex mixture of "dogmatists," "evolutionists," and "reformers" in the PUWP refer to Brzezinski, *op. cit.*, pp. 248–52.

39. For some details on the East German workers' revolt see Mastny, *op. cit.*, pp. 10–27, and Arnulf Baring, *Uprising in East Germany: June 17, 1953* (Ithaca: Cornell University Press, 1972).

40. About 5.8 million Soviet bloc refugees fled to the West between 1945 and 1961, largely through West Berlin; about 2.6 million of these escaped after 1949 when the GDR was formally established.

41. Refer to Suda, *op. cit.*, pp. 252–76.

42. Fejto, *op. cit.*, p. 46. In April 1965 an army conspiracy to seize power was reportedly uncovered by Zhivkov. The plotters were tried and imprisoned, and Sofia accused "liberals" within the armed forces of seeking to break Bulgaria's alliance with the Soviet Union; further details were not forthcoming.

43. Refer to Fischer-Galati, *op. cit.*, p. 60.

44. Djilas argues that Soviet leaders utilize economic and other differences among the East European states to deepen their dependence on Moscow. See Milovan Djilas, "Eastern Europe Within the Soviet Empire," in Robert Conquest (Ed), *The Last Empire: Nationality and the Soviet Future* (Stanford: Hoover Institution Press, 1987), pp. 369–80.

45. See Donald E. Schulz, "On the Nature and Function of Participation in Communist Systems: A Development Analysis," in Donald E. Schulz and Jan S. Adams (Eds), *Political Participation in Communist Systems* (New York: Pergamon Press, 1981).

46. For a useful overview see John F. N. Bradley, "Prague Spring 1968 in Historical Perspective," in *East European Quarterly*, Vol. XVI, No. 3, September 1982, pp. 257–76.

47. One must also be mindful of the skepticism surrounding the Prague Spring. Many advances toward democracy at this time were not the result of a coherent Communist Party reform program, but due to the dynamics of criticism and experimentation released both within and outside the Party during the process of liberalization in 1968. For some discussion of these issues see Mark Wright, "Ideology and Power in the Czechoslovak Political System," in Paul Lewis (Ed), *Eastern Europe: Political Crisis and Legitimation* (New York: St. Martin's Press, 1984), pp. 111–53.

48. Among several valuable books on the Prague Spring see: Ivan Svitak, *The Czechoslovak Experiment, 1968–1969* (New York: Columbia University Press, 1971); H. Gordon Skilling, *Czechoslovakia's Interrupted Revolution* (Princeton:

Princeton University Press, 1976); and Karen Dawisha, *The Kremlin and the Prague Spring* (Berkeley: University of California Press, 1984).

49. Some demonstrations in support of the Prague Spring were also staged in neighboring states. These and subsequent post-invasion protests were promptly liquidated even though they did not generally extend beyond the intellectual and student communities.

50. An insightful summary of the external and internal circumstances surrounding the 1968 Soviet invasion can be found in Karen Dawisha, "The 1968 Invasion of Czechoslovakia: Causes, Consequences, and Lessons for the Future," in Karen Dawisha and Philip Hansen (Eds), *Soviet-East European Dilemmas: Coercion, Competition, and Consent* (New York: Holmes and Meier, 1981), pp. 9–25.

51. Even though there was no significant armed resistance, the Soviet intervention claimed 186 lives; 362 people were wounded, and several thousand arrested. About 25,000 citizens fled to the West. See Vojtech Mastny, *East European Dissent, Volume 2* (New York: Facts on File, 1972), pp. 73–102.

52. Some observers and participants in the Prague Spring maintain that Soviet pressure on Prague helped to unite disparate political forces within the country, and even contributed to bridging the gap between CPCS members and anti-Communists in "patriotic anti-Sovietism." But as a result of widespread repression, such unity did not forge any significant movement or program of opposition even while destroying "whatever base of mass support the ruling Communist Party had enjoyed in the past." See Otto Ulc, "Czechoslovakia," in Rakowska-Harmstone and Gyorgy (Eds), *op. cit.,* pp. 100–120.

53. For an analysis of the "normalization" process in Czechoslovakia see: Vladimir Kusin, *From Dubček to Charter 77* (Edinburgh: Q Press, 1978); Zdenek Mlynar, "Normalization in Czechoslovakia after 1968," *Crises in Soviet-Type Systems, Study No. 1* (Koln: Index, 1982); and Otto Ulc, "The Normalization of Post-Invasion Czechoslovakia," in *Survey,* No. 24, Summer 1979, pp. 201–13.

54. The only Czechoslovak reform that actually survived the "normalization" process was the constitutional amendment of October 1968 making the country a "federal state," comprised of the Czech and Slovak socialist republics. But even in this instance, federalization did not involve Communist decentralization or democratization; the CPCS simply acquired a subsidiary "territorial organization," the Slovak Communist Party.

55. A succinct account of regular workers' protests in postwar Poland can be found in Jakub Karpinski, *Countdown: The Polish Upheavals of 1956, 1968, 1970, 1976, 1980. . .* (New York: Karz-Cohl, 1982).

56. For a useful overview of Gierek's Poland see Andrzej Korbonski, "Poland," in Rakowska-Harmstone and Gyorgy (Eds), *op. cit.,* pp. 37–70.

57. Among several helpful volumes on the "legal" Solidarity movement, it is worthwhile to consult: Jadwiga Staniszkis, *Poland's Self-Limiting Revolution* (Princeton: Princeton University Press, 1984); Kevin Ruane, *The Polish Challenge* (London: British Broadcasting Corporation, 1982); Abraham Brumberg (Ed), *Poland: Genesis of a Revolution* (New York: Random House, 1983); and Timothy Garton Ash, *The Polish Revolution, 1980–1982* (London: Jonathan Cape, 1983).

58. Helpful books on the martial law operation include: George Sanford, *Military Rule in Poland: The Rebuilding of Communist Power, 1981–1983* (New York: St. Martin's Press, 1986); and *Poland Under Martial Law: A Report on Human Rights by the Polish Helsinki Watch Committee* (New York: Helsinki Watch Committee, 1983).

Chapter 2: Dissident Strategies I

1. According to H. Gordon Skilling, "the crucial difference between the communist and the democratic regimes has been the absence of an institutionalized opposition, expressed and guaranteed in constitutional principles or in political custom." See "Background to the Study of Opposition in Communist Eastern Europe," in Leonard Schapiro (Ed), *Political Opposition in One-Party States* (London: Macmillan, 1972), p. 73.

2. See Donald E. Schulz, "On the Nature and Function of Participation in Communist Systems: A Developmental Analysis," in Donald E. Schulz and Jan S. Adams (Eds), *Political Participation in Communist Systems* (New York: Pergamon Press, 1981), pp. 34–35.

3. Two prominent Hungarian dissidents argue that from the mid-1950s onwards a process began in Eastern Europe, though it was not uniform, consisting of "a regular alternation of easing, tightening, and easing restrictions," whereby the ruling Party elites granted some concessions to various groups of technocrats. See George Konrad and Ivan Szelenyi, *The Intellectual on the Road to Class Power* (New York: Harcourt Brace Jovanovich, 1979), p. 189.

4. For a useful discussion of the post-1953 crises in East Europe, with special reference to the position of Communist elites, legitimation difficulties, and crisis management, refer to Paul G. Lewis, "Legitimation and Political Crises: East European Developments in the Post-Stalin Period," in Paul Lewis (Ed), *Eastern Europe: Political Crisis and Legitimation* (New York: St. Martin's Press, 1984).

5. Some observers have posited the relative industrial underdevelopment of the Balkan Communist states as a major reason for the lack of political dissent and sustained opposition. The industrial working class in these countries is fairly new, and has little or no tradition of concerted action. In addition, the ruling Parties have been more "traditionalist" in Romania and Bulgaria, less prone to experimentation, and still predominantly reliant on Stalinist-type coercive methods.

6. For a useful account of the sources and manifestations of conflict in "oppositionless states" see Ghita Ionescu and Isabel de Madariaga, *Opposition: Past and Present of a Political Institution* (London: C. A. Watts, 1968).

7. See Leonard Schapiro's discussion in the "Introduction" to Schapiro, *op. cit.*, pp. 1–12.

8. *Ibid.*

9. Conflicts based on ethnic, religious, or linguistic cleavages play a smaller role in the largely homogeneous states of the "northern tier" than they do in Romania or Bulgaria which contain more sizeable national minorities.

Notes and References 273

10. Much of the reform-oriented debate centered around informal "discussion clubs" and quasi-independent publications linked to the larger universities. Budapest's dissident Petofi Circle included scholars and students exchanging ideas about the shape of post-Stalinist Hungary, while in Poland the *Po Prostu* journal germinated independent thought and helped sow the seeds of future political dissent.

11. For a useful analysis of Soviet bloc intellectuals as an emerging class see Konrad and Szelenyi, *op. cit.*

12. For some insights into the struggle between dissident and Communist Party intellectuals see Rudolf L. Tokes (Ed), *Opposition in Eastern Europe* (London: Macmillan, 1979), pp. 21–22. According to Tokes, East European dissident intellectuals often give the impression that they see themselves as "putative members of an alternative leadership." (*ibid.*, p. 21)

13. Since the late 1960s, critical intellectuals in various parts of the East bloc have sought new ways of linking up with the working class. During the 1960s and 1970s, members of the alienated intelligentsia increasingly considered it their obligation to present a seemingly attainable vision of a "new order" for the population.

14. According to Konrad and Szelenyi, *op. cit.*, pp. 237, 247.

15. Several observers have argued that intellectual dissenters may either accelerate or constrain working class protest. Their efforts to influence workers often coincide with personal ideological precepts and tactical ploys *vis-à-vis* the regime. Indeed, the "democratic opposition" in Poland since 1980 has periodically been criticized for placing limits on popular resistance by defusing working class radicalism and obstructing the politicization of the Solidarity underground movement.

16. Nevertheless, during strikes and other forms of protest, workers evidently display their "class consciousness" or "national consciousness," particularly as they realize that much of their "economistic" grievances are rooted in political injustice and foreign domination.

17. See J.M. Montias, "Observations on Strikes, Riots, and Other Disturbances," in Jan F. Triska and Charles Gati (Eds), *Blue Collar Workers in Eastern Europe* (London: George Allen & Unwin, 1981), p. 177.

18. For a thorough analysis of economic factors spurring workers' strikes see Alex Pravda, "Industrial Workers: Patterns of Dissent, Opposition and Accommodation," in Tokes (Ed), *op. cit.*, pp. 209–61. Pravda, however, tends to minimize the numerous non-economic interests and conditions that inspire strikers.

19. For an assessment of conflict between workers and the Party organization as a source of potential opposition to the Romanian regime, consult Daniel N. Nelson, "Worker-Party Conflict in Romania," in *Problems of Communism*, Vol. 29, No. 5, September–October 1980, pp. 40–49.

20. Pravda assesses some of the values and attitudes of workers which underlie dissident behavior, and identifies several spheres of discontent based on inadequate material conditions. See Pravda in Tokes (Ed), *op. cit.*, pp. 209–61.

21. Second-generation workers in the Soviet bloc generally have higher aspirations than their parents, with regard to occupational satisfaction and

remuneration, access to consumer goods, and better opportunities for their children. Such aspirations have been reinforced by rising educational levels.

22. For a valuable summary of workers' participation and non-participation in a range of official organizations, and for useful statistics on strikes and other protests during the period from 1947–1967, see Richard C. Gripp, "Workers Participation in Communist Polities," in Schulz and Adams (Eds), *op. cit.*

23. Jean Woodall, "New Social Factors in the Unrest in Poland," in *Government and Opposition*, Vol. 16, No. 1, London, 1981, pp. 53–4.

24. In surveys conducted in Poland during a 25-year spell, worker respondents stressed their high regard for equality of opportunity rather than stringent socio-economic egalitarianism. For some details on the survey see David W. Paul and Maurice D. Simon, "Poland Today and Czechoslovakia 1968," in *Problems of Communism*, Vol. 30, No. 5, September–October 1981, pp. 25–39.

25. Poland presents a poignant example where working class leaders have emerged since the late 1970s and have remained prominent political dissenters and strategists despite government attempts to silence them. This can be partly explained by the size, durability, popularity, visibility, and symbolic importance of Solidarity as a national movement that the regime has been unable to fully eradicate.

26. For an extremely valuable account of the political position of East Europe's peasantry see Paul G. Lewis, "Potential Sources of Opposition in the East European Peasantry," in Tokes, *op. cit.*, pp. 263–91.

27. A perceptive overview of these issues can be found in Walter D. Connor, "Social Change and Stability in Eastern Europe," in *Problems of Communism*, Vol. 26, No. 6, November–December 1977, pp. 16–32.

28. Lewis speculates about the possibilities for a future "worker-peasant" oppositionist alliance in certain East European countries. See Lewis in Lewis (Ed), *op. cit.*, p. 288.

29. For some details refer to Walter D. Connor, "Dissent in Eastern Europe: A New Coalition?," in *Problems of Communism*, Vol. 29, No. 1, January–February 1980, pp. 1–17.

30. Consult John Starrels, "Political Development in the German Democratic Republic," in *Government and Opposition*, Vol. 16, No. 2, London, 1981, and Wolfgang Mleczkowski, "In Search of the Forbidden Nation: Opposition by the Young Generation in the GDR," in *Government and Opposition*, Vol. 18, No. 2, London, 1983.

31. The impact of each of these political tendencies is explored in Chapter 4.

32. In particular, see Jiri Pelikan, *Socialist Opposition in Eastern Europe—The Czechoslovak Example* (New York: St. Martin's Press, 1973), pp. 93–103, and Ivan Szelenyi, "Socialist Opposition in Eastern Europe: Dilemmas and Prospects," in Tokes, *op. cit.*, pp. 187–207.

33. In a similar vein, Communist revisionists within the ruling establishment have at certain junctures proposed the possibility of "partnership and cooperation" between the Party and other "workers' parties."

34. Pelikan, *op. cit.*, p. 95. Some of the Marxist "socialist oppositionists" have in the past made rather grandiose claims about the ideal nature of "socialist

democracy." According to Pelikan, the "socialist opposition" is avowedly the best warranty that upheavals in Eastern Europe will not turn into "nationalist outbursts" or even into "counter-revolution" (Pelikan, *op. cit.*, p. 102). The tendency to visualize personal political preferences as the only realistic or justifiable alternative to the existing system is of course not confined to members of the "socialist opposition."

35. Szelenyi in Tokes (Ed), *op. cit.*, p. 201.

36. See Chapter 5 for a discussion of relations between Church and state in each East European country, and the implications for religious-based political opposition.

37. For an examination of Church-state relations in Poland during martial law see Janusz Bugajski, "Poland's Anti-Clergy Campaign," in *The Washington Quarterly*, Vol. 8, No. 4, Fall 1985, pp. 157–68.

38. Adam Michnik, "On Resistance," in *Letters from Prison and Other Essays* (Berkeley: University of California Press, 1986), p. 46.

39. The Church-sponsored weekly publication *Tygodnik Powszechny*, and its Catholic intelligentsia milieu, has taken an active role during the last three decades, especially in cultural and educational affairs, while renouncing blatantly political activities. Catholic intellectuals have set themselves the task of preserving fundamental Christian values bombarded by Communist policy since World War II.

40. Michnik, *op. cit.*, p. 59.

41. The Catholic Intelligentsia Clubs (KIKs), which were established in several Polish cities since the late 1950s, preserve free discussion and independent ideas, and arrange seminar courses on a multitude of religious and non-religious issues.

42. See Michael J. Sodaro, "Limits to Dissent in the GDR: Fragmentation, Cooptation, and Repression," in Jane Leftwich Curry (Ed), *Dissent in Eastern Europe* (New York: Praeger, 1983), pp. 82–116.

43. For a worthwhile summary of recent religious trends in Eastern Europe see *Radio Free Europe Research*, Background Report/139, 1 October 1986. Also see Chapter 5.

44. In addition, the autonomous "Committee for the Defense of Freedom of Religion and Conscience" (ALRC) was established in the late 1970s. See Emil Freund, "Nascent Dissent in Romania," and Vlad Georgescu, "Romanian Dissent: Its Ideas," in Curry (Ed), *op. cit.* The outlawed "Lord's Army," a mass movement of evangelical rebirth among some of the Orthodox peasantry, has also become more active of late in several regions of Romania.

45. See in particular, Adam Michnik, *Kosciol, Lewica, Dialog* (Paris: Instytut Literacki, 1977).

46. These factors may help to answer Connor's evident surprise in asserting that "the remarkable thing is not that riots occurred or that they were suppressed, but that so few have taken place." See Walter D. Connor, "Social Change and Stability in Eastern Europe," in *Problems of Communism*, Vol. 26, No. 6, November–December 1977, pp. 16–32.

47. The Communists have often used uprooted and disaffected groups—ex-peasants, ethnic minorities, and young ambitious people—to assist in establishing

and preserving their rule, particularly through recruitment into the police and security service apparatus.

48. Konrad and Szelenyi, op. cit., p. 217.

49. Paul Lewis, "Legitimation and Political Crises: East European Developments in the Post-Stalin Period," in Paul Lewis (Ed), Eastern Europe: Political Crisis and Legitimation (New York: St. Martin's Press, 1984), p. 14.

50. Ionescu and Madariaga, op. cit., p. 163.

51. Robert A. Dahl, "Introduction," in Regimes and Oppositions (New Haven: Yale University Press, 1973), p. 13.

52. For an analysis of how such paranoia is manifest among the Party leadership in post-martial law Poland consult Janusz Bugajski, "Poland's Political Scapegoats," in Political Communication and Persuasion, Vol. 3, No. 2, 1985, Crane Russack, New York.

53. Robert Sharlet, "Varieties of Dissent and Regularities of Repression in the European Communist States: An Overview," in Curry, op. cit., p. 10.

54. Since 1976, the GDR government has cracked down severely on any manifestations of dissent, to preclude a Polish or Czechoslovak-type opposition from taking root. East Berlin has also broadened and sharpened the laws defining intolerable criticism, and hardened the penalties correspondingly. Details on this are provided by Sodaro, in Curry (Ed), op. cit. The GDR's special position vis-à-vis the West has also tended to limit the opportunities for dissent, because oppositionist figures are easily exiled to the German Federal Republic, and the chronically dissatisfied have an available "escape hatch."

55. Details on government measures against Czechoslovak dissidents since the birth of Charter 77 can be found in Janusz Bugajski, Czechoslovakia: Charter 77's Decade of Dissent, The Washington Papers, CSIS/ Praeger, 1987, pp. 78–92.

56. A useful account of how Budapest deals with its domestic critics is contained in George Schopflin, "Opposition in Hungary: 1956 and Beyond," in Curry (Ed), op. cit., pp. 69–81.

57. For some discussion of "normalized" Poland and official restraints on independent social activism refer to Andrzej Swidlicki, "Mechanisms of Repression in Poland During Martial Law," in Polish Review, Vol. XXIV, No. 1/2, 1984, pp. 97–126.

58. Official social organisations and labor unions are primarily transmission belts to and from the Party leaders, channeling policy directives down to the masses, and passing upward information on local conditions and workers' attitudes.

59. For a useful discussion of this issue see Tadeusz Szafar, "The Political Opposition in Poland," in Polish Review, Vol. XXIV, No. 1, 1979, p. 79.

60. Consult Werner Volkner, "East Germany: Critical Voices," in Survey, Vol. 23(3), London, 1978, pp. 208–17.

61. For the text of the "manifesto" see Frantisek Silnitsky, Larisa Silnitsky, and Karl Reyman (Eds), Communism and Eastern Europe: A Collection of Essays (New York: Karz Publishers, 1979), pp. 233–42. Also consult Werner Volkmer, "East Germany: Dissenting Views During the Last Decade," in Tokes (Ed), op. cit., pp. 113–41.

62. This point is made by Alexander J. Matejko, "The Structural Roots of Polish Opposition," in *Polish Review*, Vol. XXVII, No. 1/2, 1982, pp. 112–39.

63. Szelenyi in Tokes (Ed), *op. cit.*, p. 203.

64. Quoted in Leopold Labedz (Ed), *Revisionism: Essays on the History of Marxist Ideas* (New York: Praeger, 1962), p. 18.

65. For a discussion of these issues see William E. Griffith, "The Decline and Fall of Revisionism in Eastern Europe," in Labedz (Ed), *ibid.*, pp. 223–38.

66. V.I. Lenin, *Against Revisionism*, Second Revised Edition (Moscow: Progress Publishers, 1966), pp. 110–18.

67. In Lenin's time "social democratic distortions" referred to "Bernsteinism." After the Bolshevik seizure of power this epithet has been used to characterize various socialist, laborite, and social democratic political parties in the Western democracies.

68. Lenin, *op. cit.*, pp. 162–65.

69. Michnik, *op. cit.*, p. 47. Michnik also believes that the "role of revisionism was to coach the Party for its confrontation with the explosions of social anger that followed Stalin's death."

70. For a valuable discussion of the meaning of reform in Communist parlance, and its development in postwar Eastern Europe see Vladimir Kusin, "An Overview of East European Reformism," in *Soviet Studies*, Vol. XXVIII, No. 3, July 1986, pp. 338–61.

71. A pertinent example of Soviet bloc denunciations of the Czechoslovak reform movement can be found in I. M. Mrachkovskaya, *From Revisionism to Betrayal: A Criticism of Ota Sik's Economic Views* (Moscow: Progress Publishers, 1972).

72. According to the Husák regime, the establishment of workers' councils in Czechoslovak enterprises was apparently only a camouflage adopted by "rightist opportunists" to disguise their "anti-socialist" actions, weaken the Party, and create a "socio-economic breeding ground for counter-revolutionary elements." The reintroduction of private enterprise was purportedly intended to provide the foreign bourgeoisie with an economic base to restore capitalism in Czechoslovakia.

73. Though inner-Party revisionism constitutes one form of factionalism, not all forms of factionalism are necessarily revisionist or reformist. They may simply consist of internal struggles for power or resources between contending interest groups in the Communist establishment.

74. One prevalent idea among revisionist Communists is that genuine socialism can only be attained once a certain level of industrialization and economic development has been attained. An anti-Russian trend is also present in some of the neo-revisionist writings, with an underlying assumption that Moscow has stifled the "development of productive forces" throughout Eastern Europe; hence, some long overdue changes are necessary to further "develop socialism."

75. See for instance the blistering attack on present-day revisionism by the official Bulgarian propagandist Georgi Karasimeonov, *Marxism-Leninism and Modern Revisionism* (Sofia: Sofia Press, 1983).

76. Consult for example Ota Sik, *The Third Way: Marxist-Leninist Theory and Modern Industrial Society* (London: Wildwood House, 1976).

77. Michnik, *op. cit.*, p. 47.

78. According to a prominent Czechoslovak "socialist oppositionist" now in exile, Jiri Pelikan, a movement of popular discontent which lacks support from any elements within the Party cannot as a rule bring about fundamental changes in the political system. See Pelikan, *op. cit.*, pp. 101–2. Such propositions have been disputed by dissidents attempting to transform the system "from without." Pelikan's assumptions were also outpaced by events in Poland between August 1980 and December 1981.

79. In his discussion of the Prague Spring, Kusin notes that "Party functionaries are not averse to capitalize on reformist issues if it suits them to do so, and they are of course prone to abandon ship as soon as their 'pragmatic' aims are satisfied, or when the counter-currents begin to predominate." Nevertheless, "the participation of non-reformist functionaries in reformist moves can be of key importance, as shown by the temporary alliance between genuine reformers and some 'pragmatic' opponents of Novotny in the autumn and winter of 1967." See Kusin, *op. cit.*, p. 359.

80. For instance see Sik, *op. cit.*

81. Many of these disillusioned former Party activists still considered themselves "socialists" and tended to base their political programs on "democratic socialist" concepts. The two most prominent "ex-revisionist" Polish socialists, Jacek Kuroń and Karol Modzelewski, asserted in the mid-1960s that "in practice a workers' multi-party system means the right of every political group that has its base in the working class to publish its own paper, to propagate its own program through the mass media, to organize cadres of activists and agitators—that is, to form a party. A workers' multi-party system requires freedom of speech, press, and association, the abolition of preventive censorship, full freedom of scholarly research, and of literary and artistic creativity." See Jacek Kuroń and Karol Modzelewski, "The General Crisis of the System," in Tariq Ali (Ed), *The New Revolutionaries* (New York: William Morrow, 1969), p. 149.

82. See Michnik, *op. cit.*, p. 32.

83. For some information on the Polish "horizontalist" movement during 1980–81, see Nicolas G. Andrews, *Poland 1980–81: Solidarity Versus the Party* (Washington, DC: National Defense University Press, 1985), pp. 151, 155, 158.

84. George Konrad, *Antipolitics* (London: Harcourt Brace Jovanovich, 1984), p. 128.

85. *Ibid.*, p. 165.

86. Szelenyi considers that this essentially "socialist opposition" has to base its criticisms and programs on a pro-reformist stance, since "economic reforms challenge the system of expropriation which dominates the contemporary state socialist economies." See Szelenyi in Tokes (Ed), *op. cit.*, p. 200.

87. Konrad, *op. cit.*, p. 69.

88. *Ibid.*, p. 126.

89. *Ibid.*, p. 79.

90. They have included notable figures such as Rudolf Bahro, Wolf Biermann and Robert Havemann, who proposed the introduction of "genuine democracy" into East Germany's Communist Party.

91. Robert Havemann, a revisionist Communist, has been called the grand old man of East German political dissent. His designs for what amounts to a communist utopian alternative to capitalism and "actual socialism" are contained in *Ein Deutscher Kommunist: Rueckblicke und Perspektiven aus der Isolation* (A German Communist: Reflections and Perspectives of an Isolated Life) (Reinbeck: Rowohlt Verlag, 1978). Like Bahro, Havemann's Communist future has evidently exhibited little appeal to the younger generation in the GDR.

92. See in particular Rudolf Bahro, *The Alternative in Eastern Europe* (London: New Left Books, 1977).

93. *Ibid.*, p. 11.

94. For Bahro and other Marxist revisionists the "state-party bureaucratic apparatus" and its isolation within national frontiers is incompatible with the original conceptions of Marx and Engels. Instead of the often espoused absorption of the state by society, the opposite has apparently occurred in Eastern Europe, with the state absorbing society.

95. Bahro, *op. cit.*, p. 259.

96. *Ibid.*, p. 305.

97. *Ibid.*, pp. 325–26.

98. *Ibid.*, p. 274.

99. Statements such as "we must realize how intensely our society, purged of capitalism, is waiting for a renovated Communist Party" (Bahro, *op. cit.*, p. 373) convey the somewhat misleading neo-Marxist interpretations of East European societies. Descriptions of a communistic future that entails an "association of communes into a national society . . . (and) . . . an association of nations in a contentedly cooperating world," (*Ibid.*, p. 453) display the inherent utopianism of much of the literature.

100. Any potential sympathizers of Bahro's prescriptions within the SED apparatus are effectively silenced and display little sign of constituting a "core of the movement for socialist renewal" as propounded by the author.

101. For some details on the political ideas of East German Communist dissidents see Sodaro, in Curry (Ed), *op. cit.* Their characteristic and almost puritanical anti-consumerism, and a thinly veiled despotic egalitarianism, evidently exert precious little appeal in the country, especially among young people.

102. See Stephen White, John Gardner, and George Schopflin, *Communist Political Systems* (New York: St. Martin's Press, 1982), p. 243.

103. According to Georgescu, *op. cit.*, pp. 182–94.

Chapter 3: Dissident Strategies II

1. Some miniscule revolutionary nationalist conspiracies were evidently uncovered after the Communist seizures of power, particularly in the mid to late-1940s, but they were methodically liquidated by the security forces. Some of the purported attempts at "armed conspiracy" were officially planned provocations assisting in the elimination of rival sources of power.

2. One must of course bear in mind that calls for a "revolutionary transformation" of the political system, such as those voiced by the GDR's Rudolf

Bahro, are not necessarily concomitant with support for violence and bloodshed. Indeed, Bahro seems to exclude specifically any violent rebellion from his scenario of the forthcoming "communist reformation." See Rudolf Bahro, *The Alternative in Eastern Europe* (London: New Left Books, 1977).

3. Quoted in Adam Bromke, "The Opposition in Poland," in *Problems of Communism*, Vol. 27, No. 5, September–October 1978, p. 46.

4. Kuroń and Modzelewski were initially inspired by Trotsky's theories of a "permanent revolution" to counter the Stalinist "corruption of socialist society." See Ivan Szelenyi, "Socialist Opposition in Eastern Europe: Dilemmas and Prospects," in Rudolf Tokes (Ed), *Opposition in Eastern Europe* (London: Macmillan Press, 1979), p. 191.

5. Gyorgy Konrad, *Antipolitics* (London, New York: Harcourt Brace Jovanovich, 1984), p. 114.

6. Tokes, *op. cit.*, p. xviii.

7. In some cases, the "internal opposition" or rival factions within the ruling Communist Party have also adopted clandestine models of operation in their struggle for power.

8. For a pertinent statement about the Polish situation by the anonymous PPN and its criticisms of government policy check *Dokumenty: Ruch Oporu* (Paris: Instytut Literacki, 1977), pp. 187–93.

9. See Adam Michnik, *Letters from Prison and Other Essays* (Berkeley: University of California Press, 1986), pp. 53–54.

10. For useful accounts about the development of the Polish Solidarity underground movement consult Maciej Lopinski, Marcin Moskit and Mariusz Wilk, *Konspira: Rzecz o Podziemnej Solidarnośći* (Paris: Editions Spotkania, 1984) and "Poland Under Jaruzelski: Part II," in *Survey*, Vol. 26, No. 4 (117), Autumn 1982.

11. For more details on the varieties of non-violent protest action see the section "Unorganized Dissent and Non-Violence" below.

12. After the comprehensive amnesty for political prisoners in the summer of 1986, some Solidarity activists began to establish above-ground groupings. In October 1987 Solidarity established an overt national coordinating center—the National Executive Commission. However, much of the Solidarity movement especially at the local level has continued to operate in clandestine conditions to protect activists, material, and communications networks. For more details check Chapters 4 and 6.

13. For an invaluable list of the various political organizations in the Polish underground see Teresa Hanicka, "Political Groups in the Polish Underground," *Radio Free Europe Research*, Background Report/118 (Poland), 14 October 1985, and Francis Michalski, "The Rise of Political Opposition in Poland," Poland Watch, No. 8, Washington, DC, 1986, pp. 87–107. The programs and significance of these groupings are discussed in Chapter 4.

14. For some details on the Revolutionary Action Group (SRA) and other Czechoslovak oppositionist groups refer to Janusz Bugajski, *Czechoslovakia: Charter 77's Decade of Dissent*, The Washington Papers/125 (New York: Praeger/CSIS, 1987).

15. There is a constant danger of police provocation against underground movements, as witnessed in Poland in recent years. The SB security services have attempted to penetrate the Solidarity movement and manipulate it for their own purposes. In the process they have: issued extremist statements to discredit the union and thereby assist government propaganda attacks; captured underground activists and pressurized them to testify against Solidarity; and planted informers in underground cells to keep the police abreast of the organization's members, plans, and activities. For details on these and other police measures see Janusz Bugajski, "Polish Security Operations Against the Solidarity Underground," *Radio Free Europe Research*, Background Report/57 (Poland), 10 April 1984.

16. Jan B. de Weydenthal, "The Character of East European Dissent During the Late 1970s," in Jane Leftwich Curry (Ed), *Dissent In Eastern Europe* (New York: Praeger, 1983), p. 150.

17. A valuable overall assessment of Polish "new evolutionism" is contained in Jane Leftwich Curry, "Polish Dissent and Establishment Criticism: The New Evolutionism," in Curry (Ed), *op. cit.*, pp. 153–72. For an original statement of purpose see Adam Michnik, "The New Evolutionism," *Survey*, No. 100–101, Summer–Autumn 1976. A parallel Czechoslovak dissident treatise along "new evolutionist" lines was authored by Charter 77 activist Vaclav Benda in May 1978, entitled "The Parallel Polis," and circulated in *samizdat* form.

18. For an informative discussion see the Hungarian dissidents Gyorgy Bence and Janos Kis, "After the Break," in Frantisek Silnitsky, Larise Silnitsky, and Karl Reyman (Eds), *Communism in Eastern Europe: A Collection of Essays* (New York: Karz Publishers, 1979), pp. 133–40. In their estimation "only the external pressure of independent social movements can exert a serious, lasting effect on the government."

19. Konrad, *op. cit.*, p. 116. In the Hungarian case the application of the "neo-evolutionist" strategy is particularly slow and cautious, because many dissidents still tend to place their faith in the cumulative effect of Party-initiated reforms and seem fearful of provoking the regime into a repressive reaction.

20. For a more substantive discussion of the process of "social self-determination" see the section on "Social Movements" below.

21. Alex Pravda, "Industrial Workers: Patterns of Dissent, Opposition, and Accommodation," in Tokes (Ed), *op. cit.*, p. 250.

22. For a useful summary of the Warsaw "positivists" in the wake of the unsuccessful January 1863 insurrection see Stanislaus A. Blejwas, "Warsaw Positivism—Patriotism Misunderstood," in *Polish Review*, Vol. XXVII, No. 1–2, pp. 47–54.

23. Moreover, contrary to the 19th century "organic workers," many of today's "positivists" pin little hope on lasting government concessions. They are evidently not direct political descendants of the conciliatory and loyalist-conservative strand of "positivism" that veered toward accepting the permanent dismemberment of Poland. Many of the contemporary "neo-evolutionists" stand closer to the democratically minded liberal "positivists" who did not reject eventual national independence but calculated that it would have to be postponed until more promising circumstances materialized.

24. Jiri Pelikan, *Socialist Opposition in Eastern Europe—The Czechoslovak Example* (New York: St. Martin's Press, 1973), p. 98.

25. *Ibid.*, p. 101.

26. For an insightful discussion of the dichotomy between Marxist reformism and the post-1968 political opposition movement in Poland refer to Tadeusz Szafar, "The Political Opposition in Poland," in *Polish Review*, Vol. XXIV, No. 1, 1970, pp. 70–81.

27. In the case of Poland, "neo-evolutionism" and the Solidarity movement evidently helped to stimulate the activities of inner-Party "horizontalists" and other assorted Communist reformers during 1981.

28. Both tendencies appear to have largely excluded any individuals or groupings espousing totalitarian or xenophobic authoritarian sentiments and platforms.

29. For the political evolutionist program of the Confederation for an Independent Poland (KPN) see Leszek Moczulski, "Rewolucja Bez Rewolucji," in *Droga*, No. 7, 1979, Warsaw.

30. A useful history of KOR can be found in Jan Józef Lipski, *KOR: A History of the Workers Defense Committee in Poland, 1976–1981* (Berkeley: University of California Press, 1984).

31. The mutual antagonisms between some KPN and KOR-KSS activists were also exploited by the Warsaw regime in its efforts to split Solidarity and the political opposition. KOR's influence and avoidance of overt political activities is considered by some Polish activists to be partly responsible for the political vacuum among the opposition during and after the legal Solidarity period—in terms of political authority and leadership, programs, organizational structures, and effective long-term strategies for resisting Communist "normalization."

32. For a valuable early history of Charter 77 see H. Gordon Skilling, *Charter 77 and Human Rights in Czechoslovakia* (London: Allen & Unwin, 1981).

33. Some information about the various Charter 77-related independent activities in Czechoslovakia can be found in Bugajski, *op. cit.*, pp. 52–77.

34. For a landmark essay on non-conformism in Eastern Europe, and its political ramifications, see Vaclav Václav, "The Power of the Powerless," in Václav, et al., *The Power of the Powerless: Citizens Against the State in Central-Eastern Europe* (New York: M.E. Sharpe, 1985), pp. 23–96.

35. See Robert Sharlet, "Varieties of Dissent and Regularities of Repression in the European Communist States: An Overview," in Curry (Ed), *op. cit.*, p. 11.

36. Some observers have speculated that the Polish government in its post-martial law guise even "tolerates" a certain amount of *samizdat* literature to channel dissident energies into the relatively "safe" pursuit of independent writing and publishing. Others maintain that the authorities are simply trying to put on a brave face against a nationwide phenomenon that they are incapable of eliminating.

37. Refer to Chapter 7 for a fuller discussion of independent cultural initiatives in Eastern Europe.

38. Since the onset of martial law with its comprehensive ZOMO "pacification" drives, the Jaruzelski regime has taken numerous steps to prevent spontaneous

mass protests. Apart from selective wage rises and other incentives for workers in critical large industries, the government has created various bodies to assess the public mood, sponsored official labor unions to channel discontent, and placed agents and informers in state enterprises to locate and weed out "troublemakers."

39. Among the more notable East German dissenters during the past decade, one can mention the prominent poet and singer Wolf Biermann; the actor and folk singer Manfred Krug; the eminent Marxist professor Robert Havemann (who died in 1981); and the former journalist and economist Rudolf Bahro. For details on these and other oppositionist intellectuals in the GDR check Werner Volkmer, "East Germany: Dissenting Views During the Last Decade," in Tokes (Ed), *op. cit.*, pp. 113–41.

40. For a discussion of intellectual opposition in the GDR during the 1970s see Werner Volkmer, "East Germany: Critical Voices," in *Survey*, Vol. 23, No. 3, 1978, pp. 208–17.

41. Some details on East Berlin's persecution of dissidents can be found in Michael J. Sodero, "Limits to Dissent in the GDR: Fragmentation, Cooptation, and Repression," in Curry (Ed), *op. cit.*, pp. 82–116.

42. Over two and a half million East German citizens left the country before the Berlin Wall was erected in August 1961. Thousands more have applied for visas—many of which have been granted—to emigrate to the West since that time.

43. The sums amounted to about $25,000 per prisoner. During the period 1963–78 the West Germans paid approximately $500 million to secure the release of over 13,000 individuals held in East German jails. This figure is cited in Michel Meyer, *Freikauf: Menschenhandel in Deutschland* (Vienna: Paul Zsdnay, 1978), pp. 37, 196–97. Despite the sale of political prisoners, observers concur that the number incarcerated has remained substantial and is replenished each year with new arrests. In 1982 there were about 4,000 detainees; in 1985 the number reportedly totalled somewhere near 9,000. (See *DPA*, 14 June 1985.)

44. In the Romanian context one should mention the writer Paul Goma, Professor Mihai Botez, Victor Frunza, and Constantin Dumitrescu. Goma, his wife, and six other protestors issued an appeal to Bucharest in 1977 for Ceausescu to honor the Helsinki Final Act human rights stipulations. The total number of signatories of this appeal reached about 200 by the close of 1977. The Bucharest regime, like its GDR counterpart, subsequently pressurized a number of dissident intellectuals to emigrate permanently.

45. See Vlad Georgescu, "Romanian Dissent: Its Ideas," in Curry (Ed) *op. cit.*, pp. 183–84.

46. It has been argued that displays of only sporadic and individualistic protests in markedly repressive systems, such as Romania, do not indicate the attainment of a high level of "social peace." On the contrary, they may actually represent a pronounced degree of public discontent in a situation where dissidents have to be willing to take enormous personal risks by going public.

47. A discussion of the East European "social compact" can be found in Antonin J. Liehm, "The New Social Contract and the Parallel Polity," in Curry (Ed), *op. cit.*, pp. 173–81.

48. Indeed, some have argued that Hungary's "semi-legal" intellectuals have more in common with the critical intelligentsia in other Soviet bloc states than with the indigenous working class.

49. See George Schopflin, "Opposition in Hungary: 1956 and Beyond," in Curry (Ed), *op. cit.*, pp. 69–81.

50. See Liehm in Curry (Ed), *op. cit.*, p. 181.

51. Jan Zielonka, "Strengths and Weaknesses of Nonviolent Action," in *Orbis*, Spring 1986, pp. 91–110.

52. *Ibid.*, p. 109.

53. Konrad concedes that "It is a great misfortune to have to fire on occupiers. We would become murderers ourselves in so doing, but it may happen that we will decide we have to be murderers." (Konrad, *op. cit.*, p. 233)

54. Václav, *op. cit.*, p. 71.

55. For a helpful account on the outbreak of strikes in Eastern Europe see S. M. Montias, "Observations on Strikes, Riots, and Other Disturbances," in Jan F. Triska and Charles Gati (Eds), *Blue Collar Workers in Eastern Europe* (London: George Allen & Unwin, 1981), pp. 173–86.

56. Poland's Solidarity also developed the "working strike" during 1981. The idea was to keep the plant operating during a prolonged protest action without causing any material damage while neutralizing or eliminating Party and management control from the enterprise.

57. "Hunger marches" were organized in several Polish cities during the summer of 1981 to express growing public anger with inadequate food supplies, rationing, and the high cost of food staples and other products.

58. In Poland, "hunger strikes" have most frequently been staged either in prisons, churches, or other buildings that provide sanctuary from police intervention.

59. Both the membership of the "new" labor unions and the extent of public participation in the Sejm and Peoples' Councils elections have been monitored by non-government observers at the behest of the Solidarity underground. The idea was to provide more accurate statistics on workers participation, voting participation, and the extent of official manipulation. For details see *Radio Free Europe Research*, Polish Situation Report/13, 13 July 1984, item 1, and Polish Situation Report/18, 8 November 1985, items 1 and 2.

60. Much has been written about the pros and cons of pressuring ostensibly "neutral" individuals to partake in anti-government activities, particularly in Poland's underground press. Some have argued that applying undue pressure on basically decent but uninvolved people too closely resembles Communist tactics and should be avoided. The assumption here is that ends and means in the political struggle are basically congruent.

61. See Gene Sharp, *The Politics of Non-Violent Action, Extending Horizons Books* (Boston: Porter Sergent, 1973), pp. 117–82.

62. Konrad, *op. cit.*, p. 227. For Konrad, "antipolitics" in the Communist setting principally means "the rejection of the power monopoly of the political class." (p. 231)

63. For a comprehensive survey of self-defense and self-help groups that arose in Poland during the late 1970s see Peter Raina, *Independent Social Movements in Poland* (London: Poets and Painters Press, 1981).

64. Social self-defense activities in Poland can be traced back to 1975 when proposed amendments to the Polish constitution, eternalizing Poland's links with the Soviet Union, provoked an initial protest by 45 intellectuals. About 40,000 signatures were eventually gathered to help "defend the nation's independence"; the constitutional amendments were later modified by Party leader Edward Gierek to appease public opinion.

65. As Bromke points out, one of the chief objectives of Polish dissident intellectuals was to apply pressure on writers, scholars, and artists to improve their political performance by not conforming or submitting to either official or self-censorship. See Adam Bromke, *op. cit.*, p. 48.

66. During the most repressive period of Poland's martial law, a network of aid to political prisoners and their families was established. It channelled material, financial, and medical assistance both from around the country and from abroad; much of it was organized under the auspices of the Catholic Church.

67. For an examination of human rights issues as a source of tension in Communist states see Rudolf L. Tokes, "Human Rights and Political Change in Eastern Europe," in Tokes, *op. cit.*, pp. 1–25.

68. *Ibid.*, pp. 2–3.

69. See the Charter 77 founding Declaration, issued in Prague on 1 January 1977. The document lists numerous areas in which international and national laws are violated by the regime. They include: discrimination in employment and education; government control over the communications media, publishing, and culture; the curtailment of religious freedoms; and systematic Party interference in all aspects of private life.

70. Many of the Polish Helsinki Committee reports have been translated and made available in the West, particularly by the Helsinki Watch Committee in New York.

71. Some observers have argued that this approach not only conflicts with the interests of the Communist power system during the past forty years, but also with the political traditions of Central-East European states. For instance, during the brief interwar interlude of national independence, democracy remained a scarce commodity, and respect for individual rights over "national interests" had little opportunity to establish firm roots outside of Czechoslovakia.

72. Walter D. Connor, "Dissent in Eastern Europe: A New Coalition?" in *Problems of Communism*, Vol. 29, No. 1, January–February 1980, p. 12.

73. De Weydenthal in Curry (Ed), *op. cit.*, p. 150.

74. Bence and Kis, *op. cit.*, p. 139.

75. Ghita Ionescu and Isabel de Madriaga, *Opposition: Past and Present of a Political Institution* (London: C.A. Watts, 1968), p. 172.

76. The various autonomous single-issue campaigns are discussed comprehensively in Chapter 7.

77. For some details see Schopflin in Curry (Ed), *op. cit.*, pp. 77–78.

78. Refer to *AFL-CIO Free Trade Union News*, Vol. 34, May 1979, Washington, DC.

79. According to Michnik and other Polish dissidents, the sudden politicization of millions of people produced a potentially explosive combination of populism and nationalism that the Solidarity leadership found increasingly difficult to control.

80. Krzeminski divides the internal factions within pre-martial law Solidarity into two main tendencies—the "academic" and the "populist." The former supported social and political pluralism and professed liberal-positivist views; they were weary of mass movements and their potential threat to individual liberty. The "populists" by contrast sought to guarantee full workers' independence from the Party, and supported "collectivist" principles over "individualistic" ones. Some "populist fundamentalists" embraced more "radical" positions, contending that no genuine democratization was possible without the destruction of the Communist system. See Ireneusz Krzeminski, "Solidarity—The Meaning of the Experience: A Sociological Survey," in *Religion in Communist Lands*, Vol. 14, No. 1, Spring 1986, pp. 4–15.

81. See Curry in Curry (Ed), *op. cit.*, pp. 166–67.

82. An informative discussion of proposals for an emerging "alternative society" can be found in Jack Bielasiak, "Solidarity and the State: Strategies of Social Reconstruction," in Bronisław Misztal (Ed), *Poland After Solidarity: Social Movements Versus the State* (New Brunswick: Transaction, 1985), pp. 19–38.

83. The most far-reaching goal of the "alternative society" was endorsed at Solidarity's first and only national congress, held in September and October 1981. This called for the eventual creation of a "self-governing republic" without the necessity of seizing power or overthrowing the Communist dictatorship, but simply diluting state control to its bare minimum through extensive social activism in independent institutions. The "Self-Governing Republic" thesis is discussed in Timothy Garton Ash, *The Polish Revolution, 1980–1982* (London: Jonathan Cape, 1983), pp. 222–31.

84. Wiktor Kulerski, "The Third Possibility," *Solidarność Information Bulletin*, Paris, No. 17, 27 April 1982, reprinted in *Survey*, Vol. 26, No. 3, Summer 1982, pp. 158–59.

85. For a useful summary of Poland's underground movement and the organizational skeleton of the "independent society" see Roman Dumas, "Poland's Independent Society," in *Poland Watch*, No. 8, Washington, DC, 1986, pp. 64–86.

86. Konrad, *op. cit.*, p. 175. Such a proposal is obviously not presently feasible even in the "liberal" Hungarian setting. The state maintains a monopoly over the publication and dissemination of information and stages periodic crackdowns against any alternative media outlets. For an important discussion of Party control over communications consult Paul Lendvai, *The Bureaucracy of Truth: How Communist Governments Manage the News* (London: Burnett Books, 1981).

87. Part of the reason for the limited development of independent publishing in the GDR may be linked with the comparatively easy access to the West German media by the majority of the population. This reportedly deflates demand for home-produced unofficial texts.

88. Apart from the "illegal" importation, production, and circulation of leaflets, pamphlets, newspapers, journals, and books, audio and video cassettes and

records provide an additional medium for gaining and spreading uncensored information. For a fuller discussion see Chapter 7.

89. Alexander J. Matejko, "The Structural Roots of Polish Opposition," in *Polish Review*, Vol. XXVII, No. 1–2, 1982, pp. 112–40.

90. For an assessment of these issues, with examples of autonomous economic initiatives in Eastern Europe, see Chapter 6.

91. These "revisionist hopes" of transforming Party institutions were seriously dashed in Poland during the reign of Władysław Gomułka, and were dealt a severe blow in Czechoslovakia after the quelling of the Prague Spring. Nevertheless, reformist proposals continue to surface periodically, particularly during officially directed relaxations when hopes for genuine change appear to increase.

92. In many instances, the political and ideological convictions of some dissident thinkers tend to impinge on their international equations. Several pro-socialists subscribe to or veer toward the "moral equivalence" theory between the United States and the Soviet Union. See, for example, Konrad, *op. cit.*, pp. 11–24. But even those who draw a sharp distinction between Soviet and American "imperialism" propose that an increasingly independent Eastern Europe should enter into dialogue and eventual alliance with an equally independent Western Europe, leading to "mutual withdrawal" from the Warsaw Pact and NATO.

93. For some details on the August 1987 meeting see *AFP*, 20 August 1987, and the Joint Communique issued on 21 August 1987, available from the "Committee for the Support of Human Rights in Czechoslovakia," Washington, DC.

94. For example, consult the letter from a Soviet "Group of Sympathizers of Fighting Solidarity," published in *Solidarność Walczaca*, No. 13 (157), 21 June– 5 July 1987, Wrocław. Some contacts have also been maintained in recent years between Polish and Czechoslovak dissidents and the independent pacifist "Moscow Trust Group"; more details on peace campaigners are provided in Chapter 7.

95. For details see Western news agency reports on 2 and 3 February 1988. For a useful summary of recent developments see Jackson Diehl, "East Bloc Dissidents Coordinate Protest," *Washington Post*, 2 February 1988, and Vladimir Socor, "Independent Groups in Eastern Europe Urge Support for People of Romania," *Radio Free Europe Research*, Background Report/30 (Eastern Europe), 25 February 1988. Emigre support groups were also mobilized to stage protests outside Romanian embassies in London, Paris, Rome, Bonn, and the Hague on 1 February 1988.

96. The significance of such communiques should not be exaggerated however. In themselves they pose no immediate danger to the authorities, and are unlikely to lead swiftly to more meaningful and active contacts between dissident groups. For the contents of the Hungarian Revolution anniversary document see *Voice of Solidarity*, No. 122, October 1986, London.

97. Schopflin in Curry (Ed), *op. cit.*, pp. 72–73.

98. East European dissidents in the mid-1970s were also encouraged by the emergence of an indigenous Soviet human rights movement.

99. Konrad, *op. cit.*, p. 212.

100. A Czechoslovak dissident in exile, Pelikan, who has represented one current of thought among East Europe's "socialist opposition," speaks of the "mutual interests of the Soviet and American establishments . . . to maintain the political status quo in the world." See Jiri Pelikan, *Socialist Opposition in Eastern Europe—The Czechoslovak Example* (New York: St. Martin's Press, 1973), p. 99.

101. For some discussion of these issues see Karl Reyman and Herman Singer, "The Origins and Significance of East European Revisionism," in Leopold Labedz (Ed), *Revisionism: Essays on the History of Marxist Ideas* (New York: Praeger, 1962), pp. 215–22.

102. In scanning Western media reports on East European dissidents, it is noticeable that the views of reformists and self-proclaimed socialists and social democrats tend to predominate. There are two mutually reinforcing explanations for this phenomenon: more effective cultivation of contacts with Western visitors by such dissidents, and the propensity of Western journalists to give more credence to oppositionists espousing gradualism and accommodation with Communist governments than to "extremist" dissidents who dismiss any compromises with the regime as illusory exercises.

103. The silence of many Western socialist intellectuals is especially conspicuous when it concerns non-socialist and "non-proletarian" opposition to Soviet-bloc Communism, such as that displayed by religious believers, private farmers, and radical youth groups. But even in the case of mass working class movements such as Solidarity, Western socialist backing has been patchy at best. Support from many non-socialist political organizations in the West has also consistently fallen short of East European expectations.

104. Details about the uneven record of support shown by Western trade unions can be obtained from the Solidarity Coordinating Office Abroad, Brussels, Belgium, and from the various pro-Solidarity committees based in Western capitals since 1981.

105. This support has been especially important in the case of Poland and Czechoslovakia. Politically active emigre organizations have helped to transmit various materials to dissident groups—including printing equipment, books, journals, cassettes, and substantial financial aid.

106. The capacity of Western governments to influence developments in the Soviet bloc, and their prospects during the Gorbachev era, are explored more fully in Chapter 8.

107. Vladimir Kusin, "An Overview of East European Reformism," in *Soviet Studies*, Vol. XXVIII, No. 3, July 1976, p. 348.

108. Konrad, *op. cit.*, p. 117.

Chapter 4: Political and Human Rights Movements

1. Pedro Ramet, "Disaffection and Dissent in East Germany," *World Politics*, Vol. XXVII, October 1984, No. 1, pp. 85–111.

2. An indispensable account of the founding of Solidarity can be found in *August 1980: The Strikes in Poland* (Munich: Radio Free Europe, October 1980).

3. For a useful account of the "legal" Solidarity period see Jadwiga Staniszkis, *Poland's Self-Limiting Revolution* (Princeton: Princeton University Press, 1984), and Alain Touraine, *Solidarity: The Analysis of a Social Movement, Poland 1980–1981* (New York: Cambridge University Press, 1983).

4. A helpful overview of underground Solidarity is contained in Roman Dumas, "Poland's 'Independent Society'," *Poland Watch*, No. 8, 1986, pp. 64–86.

5. For details on the reconstruction of Solidarity since the imposition of martial law refer to Michal Kołodziej, "The Underground Structure of Solidarity," *Radio Free Europe Research*, Background Report/30 (Poland), 11 April 1985.

6. For a useful summary of Solidarity developments after the 1986 amnesty see *Radio Free Europe Research*, Polish Situation Report/17, 18 November 1986, item 1. Among the more important regional executive committees to surface or undertake some open activities alongside their clandestine operations were: Mazowsze, Lublin, Upper Silesia, Szczecin, and Łódź. Other major regions, such as Lower Silesia, refrained from resuming overt activities for fear of police retaliation.

7. See Chapter 6 for a fuller discussion of the reactivation of free labor unionism in Poland. Inter-factory committees also exist in some regions to enhance cooperation between nearby plants, to act as intermediaries between region and enterprise, and to provide channels of material support.

8. For a full account of the April-May 1988 strikes consult *Radio Free Europe Research*, Polish Situation Reports/7, 8, and 9; 6 May, 13 May, and 7 June 1988, respectively.

9. For some details on post-martial law Rural Solidarity see *Radio Free Europe Research*, Polish Situation Report/4, 5 March 1985, item 4.

10. In January 1988 the formation of a Polish Peasant Party was announced in Warsaw, together with a "provisional leadership." The size and influence of the group does not appear to be substantial. See *Uncensored Poland News Bulletin* (London), No. 3, 4 February 1988, p. 11.

11. For a useful collection of KOR documents consult Peter Raina, *Independent Social Movements in Poland* (London: London School of Economics, 1981), pp. 183–310.

12. Valuable material on ROPCiO is contained in *Ibid.*, pp. 311–25.

13. For a brief history of Poland's Helsinki committees see *Radio Free Europe Research*, Polish Situation Report/13, 16 August 1985, item 4.

14. Details on these committees can be found in Janusz Bugajski, "Poland's Human Rights Committees," *Radio Free Europe Research*, Background Report/32 (Poland), 17 April 1985. Each committee adopted a different name to minimize the government campaign against them as a single network. The most active groups have been evident in Wrocław, Cracow, Warsaw, Walbrzych, Szczecin, and Toruń.

15. For detailed information on the KOS movement, together with numerous translated documents, including articles by the prominent KOS publicist Dawid Warszawski, consult *Voice of Solidarity*, published by the Solidarity Information Office in London since 1983.

16. A discussion of these issues is contained in Francis Michalski, "The Rise of a Political Opposition," in *Poland Watch*, No. 8, 1986, pp. 87–107.

17. An excellent review and analysis of oppositionist currents in the wake of martial law, and their differing stress on "legalism," "realism," or "radicalism" can be found in an unpublished paper by Aleksander Smolar (Ecole des Hautes Etudes En Sciences Sociales, Paris), entitled *The Polish Opposition*, completed in early 1988.

18. Important details on Poland's autonomous political trends are contained in Teresa Hanicka, "Political Groups in the Polish Underground," *Radio Free Europe Research*, Background Report/118 (Poland), 14 October 1985.

19. For the initial KPN proposal for transforming Poland's political system refer to *Gazeta Polska*, No. 3, 10 September 1979.

20. The "Ideological and Programmatical Principles" of Fighting Solidarity were published by the SW agency in Wrocław in June 1987.

21. For the first draft of the LDP'N' program see *Niepodleglosc* (Warsaw), No. 21–22, September–October 1983.

22. See Hanicka, *op. cit.*, pp. 14–15.

23. See the "KSN Declaration, Easter 1984," in *Polska Jutra* (Warsaw), No. 1, Spring 1984.

24. Consult the *Biuletyn Informacyjny Polskiej Socialistycznej Partii Pracy*, which has appeared in Szczecin since May 1983.

25. Check *Wyzwolenie* (Warsaw), No. 1 (10), I–II, 1986, Warsaw, and *Robotnik* (Warsaw), No. 51, 12 March 1984.

26. Some details on "Wyzwolenie" are provided in Michalski, *op. cit.*, pp. 101–102, and Hanicka, *op. cit.*, pp. 15–17.

27. For the text of the PPN program issued on 3 May 1987 see *Uncensored Poland News Bulletin* (London), No. 3, 4 February 1988, pp. 11–12.

28. Several "radical" clandestine youth groups have also appeared in Poland in recent years; they include the Federation of Fighting Youth (FMW) and the Democratic Youth Movement "Freedom" (RMD'W').

29. Consult *Kultura* (Paris), No. 9, 1987.

30. Details on the founding of the PPS can be found in *Radio Free Europe Research*, Situation Report/16, 24 November 1987, item 8.

31. For the GP'W' founding statement see *Wola* (Warsaw), No. 15 (98), 16 April 1984, as well as the "program theses" in *Naprzod* (Warsaw), No. 1, 1986.

32. A useful review of the group's platform is contained in *Głos* (Warsaw), No. 3 (49), December 1986.

33. For the group's political statement see *Polityka Polska*, No. 1, Autumn 1982.

34. See *13 Grudnia* (Cracow), No. 10 (25), 24 October 1983.

35. Consult *Przeglad Wiadomosci Agencyjnych* (Warsaw), No. 40, 7 December 1986.

36. For an overview of the "Dziekania" club, which is seeking official registration, see *Tydzien Polski* (London), 13 February 1988.

37. See the Polish government daily *Rzeczpospolita*, 30 September 1987.

38. For a history of Charter 77, its members, activities, and influences see Janusz Bugajski, *Czechoslovakia: Charter 77's Decade of Dissent* (New York: Praeger/ CSIS, 1987).

39. Charter 77 Declaration (Prague), 1 January 1977.

40. *Ibid.*

41. *Ibid.*

42. A small segment of Charter 77 "independents" has consisted of self-styled revolutionary Marxists, led principally by Petr Uhl. They wanted the movement to assume a more radical political stance—for example, by agitating among workers and young people, and by openly declaring a revolutionary program of action. Revolutionary Marxists have gained little support among the Charter signatories or among society at large.

43. Most texts relating to the work of Charter 77 have been reproduced in Czech and Slovak emigre publications, including *Listy* (Rome), *Studie* (Rome), and *Svedectvi* (Paris). For all translated Charter documents consult the Palach Press Ltd. in London.

44. For an account of VONS activities see VONS Statement No. 400: Summary of Cases Monitored by VONS (Prague), 8 November 1984.

45. Cited by the Palach Press Ltd (London), 15 December 1981.

46. *Ibid.*, 24 April 1982.

47. For some details on the group check *Radio Free Europe Research*, Czechoslovak Situation Report/4, 12 March 1988, item 4.

48. See Charter 77 Document No. 20/86: "The Publication of the Almanac on Responsibility in Politics and for Politics," (Prague), June 1986.

49. Refer to Charter 77's statement on its tenth anniversary, entitled "A Word to Fellow Citizens" (Prague), 1 January 1987, Prague.

50. An insightful discussion of Hungarian intellectual dissent during the 1960s and 1970s is contained in George Schopflin, "Opposition and Para-Opposition: Critical Currents in Hungary 1968–1978," in Rudolf Tokes (Ed), *Opposition in Eastern Europe* (New York: Macmillan, 1979), pp. 142–85.

51. The statements and documents of Hungary's various oppositionist strains and a chronicle of their activities can be obtained from the Hungarian October Freepress Information Centre, London.

52. An Independent Legal Aid service was also established in Budapest in April 1988 by four prominent members of the "democratic opposition," to document injustices and provide legal counsel to victims of repression.

53. For example, check the interview with Gabor Demszky, "The Opposition in Hungary," published in the Warsaw *samizdat* weekly *Tygodnik Mazowsze*, No. 155, 23 January 1986.

54. See the *East European Reporter* (London), Vol. 2, No. 1, Spring 1986. *Demokrata* (The Democrat) was launched by Jeno Nagy who set up the independent publishing house AB in the early 1980s.

55. The complete document appeared in *Beszelo*, No. 20, June 1987, and was republished in English in the *Hungarian October Freepress Information Centre*, No. 6/1987, 1 October 1987.

56. For some details see *Radio Free Europe Research*, Hungarian Situation Report/6, 19 May 1988, item 3, and the *Hungarian October Freepress Information Centre* 110/1988, 1 May 1988.

57. Check the *Hungarian October Freepress Information Centre* 73/1988, 2 April 1988, and *Radio Free Europe Research*, Hungarian Situation Report/6, 19 May 1988, item 3. An initial petition by the founders of the Network was issued in March 1988; it was signed by several hundred people and called for the formation of a multiparty democracy and for "Hungarian national autonomy."

58. As in other East European states, a section of the Communist establishment has sympathized with some aspects of populism, drawing in particular on its patriotic elements as a source of legitimacy. See Schopflin, in Tokes (Ed), *op. cit.* Vice versa some nationalist elements have also supported the ruling Party, particularly when this has seemingly enhanced "national unity."

59. See the Hungarian Socialist Workers Party report on "The Political Tasks Connected with the Activities of Opposition-Enemy Groups," discussed at a Politburo meeting on 1 July 1986, and published in the *Hungarian October Freepress Information Centre*, 12 March 1987.

60. Pozsgay was subsequently criticized by Prime Minister Grosz for publicly condoning populist demands for greater political freedoms, which included calls for clear limitations on the Party's "leading role." See *AP* (Budapest), 5 December 1987.

61. For the text of the Democratic Forum's founding statement consult the *Hungarian October Freepress Information Centre* 21/1988, 6 February 1988.

62. For a valuable overview of dissent in the GDR read Roger Woods, *Opposition in the GDR under Honecker, 1971–1985: An Introduction and Documentation* (New York: St. Martin's Press, 1986).

63. An assessment of this phenomenon can be found in Roger Woods, "East German Intellectuals in Opposition," in *Survey*, Vol. 28(3), 1984. Bierman's expulsion from the country in 1976 led to a protest by about one hundred leading intellectuals who were later subjected to official intimidation.

64. *UPI*, 2 August 1981, Hamburg, and *Der Spiegel*, 3 August 1981.

65. For some details refer to Laurie Wiseberg (Ed), *Human Rights Internet Directory: Eastern Europe and the USSR* (Cambridge, Mass.: Harvard Law School, 1987), p. 215. Previous East German human rights movements have been persecuted and terminated. This was the case with the Riesa Petition Movement launched in October 1976 with its "Petition for the Full Implementation of Human Rights," signed by 110 people in Riesa and Karl Marx Stadt.

66. *UPI*, 23 August 1981, Hamburg.

67. For fuller reports on the protests and later repressions see *Reuter*, 1 February 1988, and *The Washington Times*, 8 February 1988.

68. An analysis of this official campaign can be found in Barbara Donovan, "Crackdown on Dissidents in the GDR," *Radio Free Europe Research*, Background Report/22 (GDR), 17 February 1988.

69. For a partial list of Romania's political prisoners see Vladimir Socor, "Known Prisoners of Conscience in Romania: An Annotated Checklist," *Radio Free Europe Research*, Background Report/134 (Romania), 7 August 1987, and

the International Helsinki Federation for Human Rights, *Violations of the Helsinki Accords: Romania*, a report prepared for the Helsinki Review Conference, Vienna, November 1986.

70. See Brucan's book *World Socialism at the Crossroads* (New York: Praeger, 1987), and his article "Political Reform in the Socialist System," in *World Policy Journal*, Summer 1987.

71. Filipescu was sentenced to ten years' imprisonment, adopted Amnesty International Prisoner of the Month, and released in April 1986.

72. Check Vladimir Socor, "The Workers' Protest in Brasov: Assessment and Aftermath," *Radio Free Europe Research*, Background Report/231 (Romania), 4 December 1987.

73. For details see Vladimir Socor, "Dissent in Romania: The Diversity of Voices," *Radio Free Europe Research*, Background Report/94 (Romania), 5 June 1987.

74. See Vladimir Socor, "Are the Old Political Parties Stirring in Romania?" *Radio Free Europe Research*, Background Report/69 (Romania), 22 July 1985. A number of veterans of Communist prisons have been freed in recent years, including former members of the Liberal Party and the National Peasants Party.

75. Three leading members of the National Peasants Party signed the East European dissident declaration on the 30th anniversary of the Hungarian revolution, in support of sweeping democratization in the Soviet bloc. See Chapter 3 for some discussion of international oppositionist solidarity.

76. See *Liberation* (Paris), 19 January 1987, and Vladimir Socor, "Romanian Democratic Action," *Radio Free Europe Research*, Background Report/34 (Romania), 2 March 1988.

77. For an example of the regime admitting to the existence of internal dissent consult J.L. Kerr, "Dissidence in Bulgaria," *Radio Free Europe Research*, Background Report/156 (Bulgaria), 10 July 1978. In February 1977 over a dozen intellectuals were detained by police for expressing solidarity with Charter 77.

78. These include the doctor Nikolai Popov, who was forced to leave Bulgaria in February 1983; the mathematician Peter Boyadjiev, who spent ten years in prison; and Dimitar Pentcher, a building worker who was persecuted for seeking to emigrate to the West.

79. Amnesty International has reported that Bulgarian political prisoners have suffered severe psychological and physical pressure. For some individual cases on which data is available see *Voice of Solidarity*, January–February 1987, No. 125, pp. 26–28.

80. For the text of the "Declaration 78" see *Die Presse* (Vienna), 3 April 1978. The "ABD" group was reportedly quashed by the regime who revealed next to nothing about its size or composition.

81. *AP*, 28 September 1983, Sofia.

82. Discussed in *Radio Free Europe Research*, Bulgarian Situation Report/3, 20 May 1987, item 6. The protestors demanded freedom of movement and information, and the right freely to change one's job. Previous attempts were also made to lobby the CSCE conferences in Belgrade and Madrid, but the relevant letters and documents were intercepted by the police. Bulgarian dissidents

and exiles complain that the lack of Western interest in Sofia's repressive policies plays into Zhivkov's hands and makes it easier for the regime to outlaw and eradicate dissent.

83. Consult *Radio Free Europe Research*, Bulgarian Situation Report/6, 14 July 1988, item 4.

84. See *The New York Times*, 1 September 1982.

85. For details on the text and context refer to *Radio Free Europe Research*, Bulgarian Situation Report/5, 27 May 1986, item 1.

Chapter 5: Religious Activities

1. For an excellent analysis of the Marxist theory of religion, see Delos B. McKown, *The Classical Marxist Critiques of Religion: Marx, Engels, Lenin, Kautsky* (The Hague: Martinus Nijhoff, 1975).

2. An informative Polish biography of Wyszynski, now available in an English translation, is Andrzej Micewski, *Cardinal Wyszynski: A Biography* (New York: Harcourt Brace Jovanovich, 1984).

3. Trevor Beeson, *Discretion and Valor* (Philadelphia: Fortress Press, 1982), p. 156.

4. *Ibid.*, p. 155.

5. Eric Hanson, *The Catholic Church in World Politics* (Princeton, N.J.: Princeton University Press, 1987), p. 199.

6. *Ibid.*

7. Jan Nowak, "The Church in Poland," *Problems of Communism*, No. 1, Vol. 31, 1982, p. 13.

8. *Ibid.*, p. 14.

9. For a detailed discussion of Warsaw's war of attrition against the Catholic clergy in the Solidarity and martial law eras, see Janusz Bugajski, "Poland's Anti-Clergy Campaign," in *The Washington Quarterly*, Fall 1985, Vol. 8, No. 4, pp. 157–68.

10. A useful encapsulated history of the patriotic priests movement and other developments in postwar Church-state relations is provided in Nowak, *op. cit.*, pp. 1–10.

11. Beeson, *op. cit.*, pp. 166–67.

12. *Ibid.*

13. For an informed analysis of recent talks between Polish Catholics in KIKs and the Polish authorities, see J.B. de Weydenthal, *Radio Free Europe Research*, Background Report/118 (Poland), 14 July 1987. The report also gives a brief history of the KIK movement.

14. Details of a KIK cultural symposium are provided in Bugajski, "A Glimpse of Poland's 'Alternative Society,'" *Soviet/East European Survey, 1985–1986* (Durham: Duke University Press, 1987), pp. 286–88.

15. For background information on the Popiełuszko murder, see *Radio Free Europe Research*, Polish Situation Reports in October and November 1984. Accounts of the murder trial are provided in *Radio Free Europe Research*, Polish Situation Reports in January and February 1985.

16. Bugajski, "Poland's Anti-Clergy Campaign," *op. cit.*, p. 161.

17. Jerzy Urban's statements at the press conference were reprinted in the government daily *Rzeczpospolita* on 4 September 1984.

18. An instructive account of the "war of the crosses" and other popular religious movements in Poland is given by Szymon Chodak, "People and the Church Versus the State: The Case of the Roman Catholic Church in Poland," in Richard L. Rubenstein (Ed), *Spirit Matters: The Worldwide Impact of Religion on Contemporary Politics* (New York: Paragon House, 1987), pp. 280–307.

19. For an excellent encapsuled history of the Hungarian Roman Catholic Church, see Beeson, *op. cit.*, pp. 256–87.

20. An informative account of the historic rivalry between the Roman Catholic and Protestant Churches in Hungary can be found in Leslie László, "Religion and Nationality in Hungary," in Pedro Ramet (Ed), *Religion and Nationalism in Soviet and East European Politics* (Durham: Duke Press Policy Studies, 1984).

21. For an evaluation of the Uniate Church in Eastern Europe see the last section in this chapter.

22. A notable analysis of the basis communities can be found in *Radio Free Europe Research*, Hungarian Situation Report/2, 6 February 1984, item 7.

23. A thorough analysis of Bulanyi and his followers is given by Steven Polgar in "A Summary of the Situation of the Hungarian Catholic Church," *Religion in Communist Lands*, Vol. 12, No. 1, 1984.

24. See Pedro Ramet, *Cross and Commissar: The Politics of Religion in Eastern Europe and the USSR* (Bloomington: Indiana University Press, 1987), pp. 145–46, 166.

25. *Reuter* and *AP*, 9 January 1984. The original press law required court hearings for press violation cases and could lead to prison sentences or fines. Under the amended version, fines of up to 10,000 forints can be imposed without a court hearing.

26. László Cardinal Lekai, who died in June 1986, was inextricably associated with the Hungarian Catholic Church's "small steps" policy.

27. The statements were made in an interview in an official Budapest weekly published in German and sold mainly to foreigners. See the *Budapester Rundschau*, 27 December 1983.

28. *AFP*, 2 November 1983; *AP*, 3 November 1983.

29. *Kathpress* (Vienna), 27 September 1983.

30. *Radio Free Europe Research*, Hungarian Situation Report/4, 30 March 1988, item 4.

31. For an invaluable summary of the persecution of religious orders in Czechoslovakia, see Charter 77, Document No. 31/84, December 12, 1984. A useful account of the Prague government's recent anti-religious measures is also contained in the US Department of State, 19th Semiannual Report on the Implementation of the Helsinki Final Act, April 1, 1985–October 1, 1985, pp. 13–14.

32. Among the outlawed religious sects are the Jehovah's Witnesses. Several members have been incarcerated for various periods because of "illegal religious activity."

33. The lack of qualified clergymen is also painfully apparent at the highest echelons of the Catholic hierarchy, where, as of 1988, 10 of the country's 13 bishoprics remain vacant.

34. See Antonin Kratochvil, "The Church in Czechoslovakia," *Radio Free Europe Research*, Background Report/78, 30 March 1982. VONS, the dissident Committee for the Defense of the Unjustly Prosecuted, regularly chronicles official persecution of religious believers in various parts of the country and makes this information available in its documents.

35. An irregular Slovak religious periodical, *Nabozenstvo a Sucastnost* (Religion and the Present), has also appeared since 1985. At least four issues have been published by an unknown dissident group purportedly based in Bratislava.

36. See H. Gordon Skilling, "Independent Currents in Czechoslovakia," *Problems of Communism*, Vol. 34, No. 1, January–February 1985, pp. 43–45.

37. See *Reuter* from Vienna, January 14, 1988 ("Czechoslovak Catholic Church Appeals for Religious Freedom"). The appeal was subsequently supported by Charter 77 spokesmen. See also *Radio Free Europe Research*, Czechoslovak Situation Report/1, 21 January 1988, item 11.

38. For an account of this police operation, see *Radio Free Europe Research*, Czechoslovak Situation Report/11, 24 June 1983, item 4.

39. Amnesty International Report 1985 (London: Amnesty International Publications, 1985), pp. 281–82.

40. Velehrad celebrations were described in *Radio Free Europe Research*, Czechoslovak Situation Report/12, 15 July 1985, items 1 and 2. Among the positive repercussions of the event was the publication in March 1986 of a new *samizdat* periodical entitled *Velehrad* that features articles by theologians and philosophers.

41. For some details on the campaign, see *Radio Free Europe Research*, Czechoslovak Situation Report/9, 18 June 1986, item 3.

42. As reported by *Studie*, No. 71 (Rome, 1980), pp. 482–85.

43. *Radio Free Europe Research*, Czechoslovak Situation Report/17, 27 November 1987, item 5.

44. *Radio Free Europe Research*, Czechoslovak Situation Report/8, 3 June 1988, item 3.

45. Beeson, *op. cit.*, pp. 355–56.

46. *Ibid.*, p. 366.

47. *Ibid.*, p. 377.

48. *Ibid.*

49. See Barbara Donovan, "East German Catholics Meet in Dresden," *Radio Free Europe Research*, Background Report/120 (German Democratic Republic), 15 July 1987.

50. Beeson, *op. cit.*, pp. 196–97.

51. *Ibid.*, pp. 206–07.

52. *Ibid.*, p. 208.

53. *Ibid.*, p. 210.

54. Donovan, *op. cit.*, p. 3.

55. Stephen Ashley, "The Vatican Seeks to Aid the Catholic Church in Bulgaria," *Radio Free Europe Research*, Bulgarian Situation Report/5, 8 July 1987, item 4.

56. Beeson, *op. cit.*, p. 347.

57. Ashley, *op. cit.*, pp. 17–18.

58. Beeson, *op. cit.*, p. 347.

59. Janice Broun, "Catholics in Bulgaria," *Religion in Communist Lands*, Winter 1983, p. 314.

60. Otto Luchterhandt, *Die Gegenwartslage der Evangelischen Kirche in der DDR* (Tubigen: J.C.B. Mohr, 1982), p. 3.

61. *Archiv der Gegenwart* (June 29, 1983), p. 26770.

62. Ramet, *op. cit.*, pp. 80–81.

63. Beeson, *op. cit.*, p. 201.

64. *Ibid.*, pp. 202–03.

65. *Ibid.*

66. *Ibid.*, pp. 205–06. An estimated forty percent of the Evangelical Church's general costs are met by its companion Churches in West Germany. Building restoration is often funded by Western donations, and clergymen transport themselves in automobiles paid for by the West. Accordingly, the Church is able to maintain upkeep of its properties, pay salaries to clerics, and finance its extensive administration.

67. Barbara Donovan, "Church Groups Call for Democratic Reforms," *Radio Free Europe Research*, Background Report/105 (German Democratic Republic), 10 June 1988.

68. Quoted in Barbara Donovan, "Fear of Change: The East German Dilemma," *Radio Free Europe Research*, Background Report/117 (German Democratic Republic), 28 June 1988. See also Barbara Donovan, "Church-State Relations in the GDR Continue to Deteriorate," *Radio Free Europe Research*, Background Report/135 (German Democratic Republic), 15 July 1988.

69. *Frankfurter Allgemeine Zeitung*, 27 June 1988.

70. For an informative discussion of this phenomenon as it impinges on Protestants and other denominations, see László in Ramet (Ed), *op. cit.*, pp. 140–48.

71. George Cushing, "Protestantism in Hungary," *Religion in Communist Lands*, Vol. 10, No. 2, 1982, p. 125.

72. This brief overview of the Reformed Church of Hungary and the Hungarian Evangelical Lutheran Church is heavily indebted to the research of Beeson, *op. cit.*, especially pp. 262–63.

73. *Ibid.*

74. *Ibid.*, p. 279.

75. For an excellent encapsulated history of the vicissitudes of the Czech Protestant Church, see Ramet, *op. cit.*, pp. 73–78.

76. See *Radio Free Europe Research*, Czechoslovak Situation Report/4, 10 March 1986, item 2. The estimate of 1,300,000 non-Catholic believers in Czechoslovakia is confirmed by statistics on "adult Church members" (over 15 years old) published in *The World Christian Encyclopedia* (Oxford: Oxford University Press, 1982).

77. Lutherans are, however, outnumbered by Hussites, who claim 475,000 members and 650,000 affiliates. Created at the end of World War I, the Czechoslovak Hussite Church is a non-Roman Catholic Church and considers itself to be a reformed Catholic rather than a Protestant faith.

78. Data on the Protestants in Czechoslovakia comes from *Radio Free Europe Research*, Background Report/93 (Czechoslovakia), 10 July 1986.

79. *Ibid.*, p. 5.

80. *Glaube in Der Zweiten Welt*, No. 6, 1983. Quoted in *ibid.*

81. *Radio Free Europe Research*, Czechoslovak Situation Report/31, 17 August 1977, item 2.

82. See Ramet, *op. cit.*, p. 145.

83. "Eastern Europe: Toward a 'Religious Revival'?," *Radio Free Europe Research*, Background Report/88, 23 May 1984.

84. *Era Socialista* (Bucharest), No. 7, April 10, 1984, translated in Joint Publications Research Service, *East Europe Report* No. EPS 84-063 (May 17, 1984), p. 40. Quoted by Ramet, *op. cit.*, p. 161.

85. A lengthy document compiled by the ALRC can be read in "Truths Which Cannot Be Hidden," *Religion in Communist Lands*, Vol. 10, No. 2, 1982, pp. 218–26. It gives numerous details of persecution of Protestant activists in Romania.

86. Joseph Ton, "Persecution of the Neo-Protestants in Romania," paper presented at the RCDA Conference on Religion in the Balkans, Marymount College, Arlington, Va., May 21–23, 1986, p. 2.

87. See "Repressive Measures Against Evangelical Christians," *Radio Free Europe Research*, Romanian Situation Report/8, 17 July 1986, item 9. Also see Vladimir Socor, "Mounting Religious Repression in Romania," *Radio Free Europe Research*, Background Report/95 (Romania), 30 August 1985.

88. A brief but useful list of repressive actions against Protestant clergymen is given by Ramet, *op. cit.*, pp. 161–62.

89. *Keston News Service*, No. 208, September 13, 1984, p. 3.

90. Statistics here on Poland's Protestant minorities are taken from Beeson, *op. cit.*, p. 158.

91. *Ibid.*, p. 168.

92. *Ibid.*, p. 350.

93. For an informative account of Calciu's activities and a biography, see Vladimir Socor, "Gheorghe Calciu, Defender of Religious Rights," in *Radio Free Europe Research*, Romanian Situation Report/13, 20 September 1984, item 8.

94. *Keston News Service*, No. 249 (May 1, 1986), p. 9.

95. *Buletin de Informatie Pentru Romani in Exil* (Paris, December 1, 1981), p. 10. Translated in Joint Publications Research Service, *East Europe Report* No. 79864 (January 15, 1982), p. 51.

96. See "The 'Lord's Army' Movement in the Romanian Orthodox Church," *Religion in Communist Lands*, Vol. 8, No. 4, 1980, pp. 314–17.

97. *Ibid.*, p. 315.

98. For a detailed account, see Marin Pundeff, "Church-State Relations in Bulgaria under Communism," in Bohdan R. Bociurkiw and John W. Strong (Eds),

Religion and Atheism in the USSR and Eastern Europe (Toronto: University of Toronto Press, 1975), pp. 328–50.

99. Janice A. Broun, "Religious Survival in Bulgaria," *America*, November 16, 1985, p. 324.

100. For this insight, we are indebted to the original research of Ramet, *op. cit.*, pp. 117–22.

101. See Gerhard Simon, "The Catholic Church and the Communist State in the Soviet Union and Eastern Europe," in Bociurkiw and Strong (Eds), *op. cit.*, p. 202; Rudolf Grulich, "Unierte Glaubige in Kommunistisch Regierten Landern," in *Digest des Osten* (1980), No. 11, pp. 1–51; *Keston News Service* No. 155 (September 1, 1982), p. 10.

102. Michael Bourdeaux, "Roman Catholics and Uniates," in George Schopflin (Ed), *The Soviet Union and Eastern Europe: A Handbook* (New York: Praeger, 1970), p. 476.

103. Ramet, *op. cit.*, p. 17.

104. "Zwischen Anpassung und Unterdruckung," in *Herder Korrespondenz*, Vol. 32, No. 8 (August 1978), p. 414.

105. Ramet, *op. cit.*, p. 18.

106. "Die Lage der griechisch-katholischen Ukrainer in Rumanien," *Glaube in der 2. Welt*, Vol. 5, Nos. 7-8 (July–August 1977), p. D54.

107. Ramet, *op. cit.*, pp. 19–20.

108. Official statistics are available for Bulgaria, though the estimates are considerably lower than those given by church or sect leaders in the country. See *Churches and Religions in the People's Republic of Bulgaria* (published in English), (Sofia: Synodal Publishing House, 1975), p. 68. According to this source, there are 6,000 Pentecostals; 5,000 Congregationalists; 3,000 Adventists; 1,300 Methodists; and 650 Baptists.

109. *From Below: Independent Peace and Environmental Movements in Eastern Europe and the USSR* (New York: Helsinki Watch Committee, October 1987), p. 39. A larger Protestant sect in East Germany is the Mormons, with an estimated 5,000 members of the Church of Jesus Christ of Latter-Day Saints. The Mormons do not, however, typically protest against compulsory military service.

110. Amnesty International, Report 1986.

111. *From Below, op. cit.*, p. 55.

112. *Ibid.*, p. 87.

113. Lindsey Davies, "Pentecostals in Bulgaria," *Religion in Communist Lands*, Vol. 8, No. 4, 1980, p. 299.

114. Case No. 145, Turnovo People's Court, 3rd District; in *Protestantskite sekti v Bulgaria* (Sofia: Partizdat, 1972), p. 202.

115. Ramet, *op. cit.*, p. 35. All are 1971 figures, as reported in Smail Balic, "Eastern Europe: The Islamic Dimensions," in *Journal of the Institute of Muslim Minority Affairs*, Vol. 1, No. 1 (Summer 1979), p. 31.

116. Maxine Pollack, "Official Policy Abolishes a People," *Insight Magazine*, September 4, 1987, p. 34.

117. See Arch Puddington, "The Real Bulgaria . . . in which Turks vanish," *The American Spectator*, May 1987, p. 19. Also *Bulgaria: Continuing Human Rights Abuses Against Ethnic Turks*, Amnesty International, July 1987.

118. Hopes for a revival of East Berlin's small Jewish community of 200 were dashed in May 1988, when visiting American rabbi Isaac Neumann announced that he would cut short his stay after only eight months in the GDR. He was the country's first rabbi in twenty-two years. For more details, see Barbara Donovan, "American Rabbi to Leave the GDR," *Radio Free Europe Research*, Background Report/78 (German Democratic Republic), 9 May 1988.

119. Beeson, *op. cit.*, p. 266. Some analysts would contend that Beeson's estimate is too great. Evidently, it is based on a count of Hungarians of Jewish descent, defined extremely broadly.

120. *Ibid.*, p. 266.

121. *Radio Free Europe Research*, Hungarian Situation Report/1, 11 January 1988, item 6.

122. Maxine Pollack, "Anti-Semitism in Poland," *The Tablet*, January 30, 1982, pp. 99–100.

Chapter 6: Economic Initiatives

1. See Wlodzimierz Brus, "Economic Reform as an Issue in Soviet-East European Relations," in Karen Dawisha and Philip Hansen (Eds), *Soviet-East European Dilemmas: Coercion, Competition, and Consent* (New York: Holmes and Meier, 1981), pp. 84–89.

2. Horst Brezinski, "The Second Economy in the GDR—Pragmatism is Gaining Ground," *Studies in Comparative Communism*, Vol. XX, No. 1, Spring 1987, p. 98.

3. For an important analysis of East Europe's command economies, and the various reformist modifications since the installation of the "classic Stalinplan," see Jan Prybyla, *Market and Plan Under Socialism: The Bird in the Cage* (Stanford: Hoover Institution Press, 1987).

4. Jan Drewnowski, "The Anatomy of Economic Failure in Soviet-type Systems," in Jan Drewnowski (Ed), *Crisis in the East European Economy: The Spread of the Polish Disease* (London: Croom Helm, 1982), p. 82. According to the author, the causes of persistent economic failure are embedded in a political system which suppresses truth, eradicates dissent, and repudiates fairness or meritorious competition.

5. Bruce McFarlane, "Political Crisis and East European Economic Reforms," in Paul Lewis (Ed), *Eastern Europe: Political Crisis and Legitimation* (New York: St. Martin's Press, 1984), p. 184.

6. A valuable overview of Budapest's reform process can be found in Rudolf L. Tokes, "Hungarian Reform Imperatives," *Problems of Communism*, Vol. XXXIII, No. 5, September–October 1984, pp. 1–23.

7. For details see *Radio Free Europe Research*, Hungarian Situation Report/5, 2 May 1988, item 5, and Hungarian Situation Report/8, 10 June 1988, item 3.

8. Refer to Jan Adams, "Regulation of Labour Supply in Poland, Czechoslovakia, and Hungary," *Soviet Studies*, Vol. XXXVI, No. 1, January 1984, pp. 69–86.

9. For an insightful comparative study see Anders Aslund, *Private Enterprise in Eastern Europe: The Non-Agricultural Private Sector in Poland and the GDR, 1945–1983* (New York: St. Martin's Press, 1985).

10. For the Solidarity position on economic reform check *Tygodnik Mazowsze* (Warsaw), No. 207, 22 April 1987.

11. See for example the program published by *Demokrata* (Budapest), and reprinted in *East European Reporter* (London), Vol. 2, No. 1, Spring 1986.

12. For some details consult *Radio Free Europe Research*, Hungarian Situation Report/4, 18 May 1987, item 3.

13. A survey of the bureaucratic entanglements involved in establishing small private enterprises in Poland can be located in "A 'Green Light' for Private Enterprise?" *Uncensored Poland News Bulletin* (London), No. 3, 4 February 1988, p. 19.

14. For an essential historical and economic analysis of East European agriculture under Communist rule see Karl Eugen Wadekin, *Agrarian Policies in Communist Europe: A Critical Introduction* (The Hague: Martinus Nijhoff, 1982). Agriculture in general was neglected in the first decade after World War Two because of the high priority given to heavy industrialization and urbanization.

15. *Ibid.*, p. 258.

16. For example, the private sector contribution to agricultural output in Hungary reached 34% in 1985. Though very few private farms remain in the GDR, barely employing 1.5% of the agricultural population, in 1985 they contributed 3.7% to net agricultural output. Their actual share is likely to be much higher if account is taken of the numerous household plots worked by cooperative farm members. See Brezinski, *op. cit.*, p. 87.

17. For a useful analysis see Nancy J. Cochrane, "The Private Sector in East European Agriculture," *Problems of Communism*, Vol. XXXVII, No. 2, March–April 1988, pp. 47–53. Cochrane points out that there is a "persistent suspicion" of the "rich kulak" among the Party elites. Ironically, if economic conditions were to improve in Eastern Europe, government support for private farming might again diminish.

18. Ivan Volgyes, "Social Deviance in Hungary: The Case of the Private Economy," in Ivan Volgyes (Ed), *Social Deviance in Eastern Europe* (Boulder: Westview Press, 1978), pp. 65–87.

19. The rest of Polish agriculture consists of state farms or government controlled cooperatives. For some details and statistics see Wadekin, *op. cit.*, pp. 63–101.

20. See *Radio Free Europe Research*, Polish Situation Report/17, 18 December 1987, item 3. The fund will be entitled to use donations obtained from the West in order to purchase farm equipment. Private farmers will then be entitled to buy this machinery with local currency, and the latter is to be invested in a much needed water supply system for chronically deprived villages.

21. In February 1988 Warsaw established the Foundation for the Development of Polish Agriculture, which is to channel Western assistance to private farmers, initially in the Poznań area. The fund is to be run by a mixed Western-Polish board of directors, but the Ministry of Agriculture will maintain the right to

veto any projects deemed unsuitable by the state. Warsaw is clearly desperate for Western funding, but seeks to maintain as much control over investments as possible without frightening off Western donors. Details on the Foundation are available in *Radio Free Europe Research*, Polish Situation Report/3, 25 February 1988, item 3.

22. See *Radio Free Europe Research*, Polish Situation Report/7, 25 April 1986, item 4.

23. According to *Nepszabadsag* (Budapest), 7 October 1987.

24. Check *Radio Free Europe Research*, Hungarian Situation Report/5, 2 May 1988, item 5. However, the National Association of Entrepreneurs still belongs to the Hungarian Economic Chamber through which it has to deal with the government.

25. The travails of Warsaw's Economic Society in seeking official registration are summarized in the "Statement of the Provisional Board of the Economic Society, December 1987," in *Uncensored Poland News Bulletin* (London), No. 24, 16 December 1987.

26. Check *ADN, International Service* (East Berlin), 11 April 1988, cited in *FBIS-EEU-88-073*, 15 April 1988.

27. See *Rude Pravo* (Prague), 21 January 1988, for the recent Czechoslovak government decree on private enterprise.

28. See *BTA* (Sofia), in English, reproduced in *FBIS-87-217*, 10 November 1987, and *Rabotnichesko Delo* (Sofia), 15 June 1987.

29. *Nepszabadsag* (Budapest), 17 September 1986.

30. For one helpful discussion of the scope and significance of the non-state sector in Hungary and Poland see Alec Nove, "Reform Models: Hungary, Yugoslavia, Poland, China," in Alec Nove, *The Economics of Feasible Socialism* (London: Allen and Unwin, 1983).

31. A full account of Hungary's "semi-private" businesses operating within the constraints of the command economy can be found in Kalman Rupp, *Entrepreneurs in Red: Structure and Organizational Innovation in the Centrally Planned Economy* (Albany: State University of New York Press, 1983).

32. See "Private Sector—Has it a Future?" in *East European Reporter* (London), Vol. 1, No. 1, Spring 1985, pp. 54–58.

33. Consult Andrzej J. Bloch, "The Private Sector in Poland," *Telos: A Quarterly Journal of Critical Thought*, No. 66, Winter 1985–1986, pp. 128–33.

34. For example, see *Radio Warsaw*, 15 May 1988.

35. For a thorough evaluation of the available literature on the "parallel economy," with some statistics, see Steven L. Sampson, "The Second Economy of the Soviet Union and Eastern Europe," in Richard Lambert (Ed), *Annals of the American Academy of Political and Social Science*, Vol. 493, September 1987, pp. 120–36.

36. A comprehensive survey of unofficial economic activity in Hungary, which is to some extent reflected in other Soviet bloc states, can be found in Istvan Kermeny, "The Unregistered Economy in Hungary," *Soviet Studies*, Vol. XXXIV, No. 3, July 1982, pp. 349–66.

37. George Schopflin, "The Political Structure of Eastern Europe as a Factor in Intra-Bloc Relations," in Dawisha and Hanson (Eds), *op. cit.*, p. 79.

38. Andrzej Korbonski, "The 'Second Economy' in Poland," *Journal of International Affairs*, Vol. 35, No. 1, Spring–Summer 1981, p. 9.

39. There is also a criminal underworld throughout Eastern Europe, with which we are not concerned here, dealing in illicit products such as narcotics. The "second economy" in our assessment primarily embraces goods and services which are legally transacted in market economies, or those which are unrecorded and evade taxation but which are not in themselves criminal or illegal.

40. See Brezinski, *op. cit.*, p. 91.

41. Aslund, *op. cit.*, p. 209.

42. Such stores bring in large amounts of Western currency for the government. Warsaw also encourages citizens to establish bank accounts in foreign currency in order to discourage hoarding and gain precious revenues for the state.

43. In Czechoslovakia about one-third of all apartments are built through "individual construction" with people enlisting the help of family, neighbors and "moonlighters." In Hungary and Poland the ratio is believed to be even higher. See the *Frankfurter Allgemeine Zeitung*, 19 January 1987.

44. See *Radio Free Europe Research*, Romanian Situation Report/1, 7 January 1984, item 1.

45. An excellent synopsis of illegal, private, cross border trade can be found in "'Merchant Tourism' in Eastern Europe," *The World Today*, Vol. 44, No. 1, January 1988, pp. 16–18, and *Radio Free Europe Research*, Polish Situation Report/10, 20 August 1987, item 5.

46. Sampson points out that in the West informal economic networks are a supplement to the "formal system of market relations and welfare bureaucracy." By contrast, because consumer items are constantly in short supply in the Soviet bloc, informal channels and social networks become crucial for large segments of society for much of the time. See Steven Sampson, "The Informal Sector in Eastern Europe," *Telos: A Quarterly Journal of Critical Thought*, No. 66, Winter 1985–1986, pp. 49–50.

47. Read Janos Kenedi, *Do It Yourself: Hungary's Hidden Economy* (London: Pluto Press, 1981).

48. See Janine Wedel, *The Private Poland* (New York: Facts on File, 1986).

49. After Stalin's death the Party apparat gained a greater security of tenure and readier access to personal privileges. It also obtained new opportunities for corruption, bribery, and the abuse of administrative positions for personal material gain.

50. For an invaluable evaluation of official corruption in Gierek's Poland, as an extreme example of Communist corruption see Maria Hirszowicz, *Coercion and Control in Communist Society: The Visible Hand in a Command Economy* (New York: St. Martin's Press, 1986), pp. 127–46. Much of the *nomenklatura* enjoys benefits normally inaccessible to ordinary citizens, including travel allowances, easy access to hard currency, special shops, better apartments, superior medical and vacation facilities, and educational opportunities for offspring. The quality and volume of benefits often correspond with the individual's position in the establishment hierarchy.

51. For some details on the Church's charitable work both prior to and during martial law consult *Radio Free Europe Research*, Polish Situation Report/11, 1

July 1982, item 3. Since the Communist takeover over 1,000 charitable and educational institutions of various sizes have been removed from Church control.

52. Warsaw banned "Caritas" in 1950, and since then has operated an official charitable body, the Association of Catholic Caritas. It usurped both the name and the funds of the traditional Catholic organization but lacks either Church backing or public trust.

53. For the founding statement of the Solidarity Social Foundation see *Uncensored Poland News Bulletin* (London), No. 20/87, 14 October 1987.

54. Some details on SZETA can be found in Laurie S. Wiseberg (Ed), *Human Rights Internet Directory: Eastern Europe and the USSR* (Cambridge, Mass.: Harvard Law School, 1987), p. 200. SZETA's most prominent spokesperson has been Otilia Solt.

55. For a useful discussion of the "samizdat market" refer to the "Statement of the Social Council for Independent Publishing," in *Tygodnik Mazowsze* (Warsaw), No. 213, reprinted in *Uncensored Poland News Bulletin* (London), No. 16, 12 August 1987.

56. A helpful account of trade union policy in Leninist states can be found in Adrian Karatnycky, Alexander J. Motyl, and Adolph Sturmthal, *Workers' Rights, East and West* (New Brunswick: Transaction Books and League for Industrial Democracy, 1980).

57. For an overview of the officially sponsored OPZZ unions see *Radio Free Europe Research*, Polish Situation Report/5, 22 March 1985, item 1, and Jerzy M. Kolankiewicz, "Polish Trade Unions 'Normalized'," *Problems of Communism*, Vol. XXXVI, No. 6, November–December 1987, pp. 57–68.

58. Though the official unions claimed about 5.5 million members nationwide by late 1986, many workers have joined for practical reasons to obtain welfare and vacation benefits dispensed by the unions, and to avoid potential discrimination or blacklisting. The Solidarity sponsored boycott has had some effect, as the free trade union itself claimed some 10 million members in 1981.

59. Consult in particular the *Hungarian October Freepress Information Centre* (London), 6/1988, 10 January 1988.

60. For some details on the new union check *Radio Free Europe Research*, Hungarian Situation Report/6, 19 May 1988, items 3 and 4, and the *Hungarian October Freepress Information Centre* (London), 62/1988, 23 March 1988.

61. For a valuable account of worker participation in a range of official organizations, and incidents of free unionism and independent workers' self-management since the death of Stalin see Richard C. Gripp, "Workers' Participation in Communist Polities," in Donald E. Schulz and Jan S. Adams (Eds), *Political Participation in Communist Systems* (New York: Pergamon Press, 1981), pp. 137–62.

62. The Preparatory Committee's statements are available from Palach Press Ltd., London.

63. Some details on Romania's SLOMR can be obtained in Wiseberg (Ed), *op. cit.*, pp. 169–70, and Karatnycky, Motyl, and Sturmthal, *op. cit.*, pp. 78–81.

64. They included Vasile Paraschiv, who had first emerged as a dissident worker in 1971, when he complained about infringements of workers' rights and proposed the creation of an independent labor union.

65. Some information on the initiative can be found in *Radio Free Europe Research*, Bulgarian Situation Report/5, 27 May 1986, item 1.

66. See *Tygodnik Mazowsze* (Warsaw), No. 226, 4 November 1987, and *Radio Free Europe Research*, Polish Independent Press Review/4, 18 May 1988, items 3 and 4.

67. Check *Radio Free Europe Research*, Polish Situation Report/4, 17 September 1986, item 3. For the political aspects of rural self-organization consult Chapter 4.

68. For a useful collection of theoretical essays and case studies on self-management see Jaroslav Vanek (Ed), *Self-Management: Economic Liberation of Man* (Middlesex: Penguin, 1975).

69. Alex Pravda, "Industrial Workers: Patterns of Dissent, Opposition, and Accommodation," in Rudolf Tokes (Ed), *Opposition in Eastern Europe* (New York: Macmillan, 1979), p. 239.

70. For a valuable analysis of post-martial law self-management see Wlodzimierz Pankow and Michal Federowicz, "Samorzad w Gospodarce Polskiej, 1981–1985," *Kontakt* (Paris), No. 11, November 1986, pp. 38–52.

71. Refer to *Radio Free Europe Research*, Polish Situation Report/12, 5 August 1985, item 3.

72. Check Kolankiewicz, *op. cit.*, p. 64.

73. Trond Gilberg, "The Political Order," in Stephen Fischer-Galati (Ed), *Eastern Europe in the 1980s* (Boulder: Westview Press, 1981), p. 140.

74. Frence Feher and Agnes Heller, *Eastern Left, Western Left* (Cambridge: Polity Press, 1986), p. 37.

75. Anders Aslund, "The Functioning of Private Enterprise in Poland," *Soviet Studies*, Vol. XXXVI, No. 3, July 1984, p. 427.

Chapter 7: Social and Cultural Campaigns

1. *Amnesty International Report 1986* (London: Amnesty International, 1987).

2. Helsinki Watch Committee, *From Below: Independent Peace and Environmental Movements in Eastern Europe & the USSR* (New York: Helsinki Watch Committee, October 1987), p. 39.

3. John Sandford, *The Sword and the Ploughshare: Autonomous Peace Initiatives in East Germany* (London: Merlin Press, 1983), p. 30.

4. *From Below, op. cit.*, pp. 34–36.

5. Laurie Wiseberg (Ed), *Human Rights Internet Directory: Eastern Europe and the USSR* (Cambridge: Harvard Law School, 1987), p. 218.

6. Though feminist movements in the Western sense have not taken root in Eastern Europe, a dynamic and controversial women's literature has emerged in East Germany. On this, see Christiane Lemke, "New Issues in the Politics of the German Democratic Republic: A Question of Political Culture?" in *The Journal of Communist Studies*, Vol. 2, December 1986, No. 4, pp. 350–52. For general sociological insights, see Sharon L. Wolchik and Alfred G. Meyer (Eds), *Women, State, and Party in Eastern Europe* (Durham: Duke University Press, 1985).

7. For a detailed account of the troubled relationship of the group with the authorities, particularly in its final months, see Maxine Pollack, "Hungary: Monologues Again?" in *Index on Censorship* (London), January 1984, pp. 37–38.

8. Wiseberg (Ed), *op. cit.*, p. 202.

9. John Eibner, "'The Hope of the Church': Basis Groups in Hungary," *Frontier*, Keston College, March–April 1987.

10. *Hungarian October Freepress Information Centre* (London), 23 February 1987.

11. *Radio Free Europe Research*, Hungarian Situation Report/9, 8 July 1988, item 5.

12. Radio Free Europe/Radio Liberty *Daily Report*, No. 98, 25 May 1988.

13. Michael Dobbs, "Peace Groups Gaining Influence in East Bloc," *The Washington Post*, 24 July 1988.

14. In an interview with the Hungarian *samizdat* journal *Hirmondo*, WiP activist Piotr Niemczyk said: "We are the children of Solidarity, our views have their roots in the Solidarity program. But Solidarity is a trade union and a trade union has tasks other than the concern for conscientious objection. Freedom and peace is very close to Solidarity as far as its principles are concerned, but its sphere of activities differs." See "Freedom and Peace: A Conversation With Piotr Niemczyk On The Day After His Release From Prison," *East European Reporter* (London), Vol. 2, No. 3, 1987.

15. *From Below, op. cit.*, p. 77. The other cities are Szczecin, Gorzow, Katowice, Bydgoszcz, Czestochowa, Kołobrzeg, and Poznań.

16. Campaign for Peace and Democracy East/West (New York), *Peace and Democracy News*, Fall 1986.

17. This phrase was used as early as November 1981 in Charter 77's "Statement on West European Peace Movements." Reprinted in Jan Kavan and Zdena Tomin (Eds), *Voices from Prague: Documents on Czechoslovakia and the Peace Movement* (London: Palach Press Ltd., 1983).

18. "Charter 77 Demands Space for Czechoslovak Youth," *East European Reporter* (London), Vol. 2, No. 1, Spring 1986.

19. For the text of this declaration, see *Summary of Available Documents*, No. 25 (London: Palach Press), December 1984, p. 37.

20. John Tagliabue, "Prague Steps Up Hard Rights Stand," *The New York Times*, 23 June 1988.

21. *Radio Free Europe Research*, Czechoslovak Situation Report/5, 25 March 1988, item 6.

22. For an account of one such gathering, see Jan Kavan, "Spontaneous Peace Demonstration in Prague," *East European Reporter* (London), Vol. 1, No. 4, Winter 1986.

23. *Radio Free Europe Research*, Czechoslovak Situation Report/8, 3 June 1988, item 2.

24. For a concise overview of the problem, see Vladimir Sobell, "The Ecological Crisis in Eastern Europe," *Radio Free Europe Research*, Background Report (Eastern Europe), 20 January 1988; John Tagliabue, "Industrialized Eastern Bloc Faces Pollution Crisis," *The New York Times*, 25 October 1987; Christine L. Zvosec,

"Environmental Deterioration in Eastern Europe," *World Affairs*, Vol. 147, No. 2, Fall 1984; and Fred Singleton, "Eastern Europe: Do the Greens Threaten the Reds," *The World Today*, August–September 1986.

25. Degradation of the manmade environment is also a problem in Eastern Europe, although the subject lies outside the scope of our present study. In Romania, where scores of architectural treasures have been unceremonially razed by urban developers, there has been some popular outcry, but to no avail. In Poland, the preservation of historic monuments and buildings has become a public concern; for example, groups in several cities have taken independent action to preserve and rejuvenate Jewish cemeteries from the prewar era.

26. Zvosec, *op. cit.*, pp. 116–17.

27. *From Below, op. cit.*, pp. 92–93.

28. Zvosec, *op. cit.*, p. 117.

29. Singleton, *op. cit.*, p. 161.

30. *Summary of Available Documents*, Palach Press (London), October 1985.

31. *Radio Free Europe Research*, Czechoslovak Situation Report/6, 4 June 1987, item 9.

32. Wiseberg (Ed), *op. cit.*, p. 202. See also "Unfinished Past: The Gabcikovo-Nagymaros Project: 1953 and Now," *East European Reporter*, Vol. 1, No. 3 (1985), pp. 25–28.

33. "Danube Foundation has been Established in Hungary," *Hungarian October Freepress Information Centre* (London), 4 June 1987.

34. "Environmental Meeting in Budapest," *Hungarian October Freepress Information Centre* (London), 6 November 1987.

35. Wiseberg (Ed), *op. cit.*, p. 203.

36. Herbert Reed, "Hungarian 'Greens' Petition Austrian Parliament," *Radio Free Europe Research*, Background Report/96 (East-West Relations), 11 July 1986.

37. "Environmental Meeting in Budapest," *Hungarian October Freepress Information Centre* (London), 6 November 1987. See also "Organisers of the illegal National Nature Conservation Society call a meeting," *ibid.*, 31 October 1987; "Application for License to Establish a National Environmentalist Association," *ibid.*, 9 May 1987.

38. The interview appeared in *Hirmondo* (Budapest), No. 2, April–June 1986. Quoted in Wiseberg (Ed), *op. cit.*, p. 203.

39. *Hungarian October Freepress Information Centre* (London), 68/1988, 29 March 1988; and 34/1988, 2 March 1988.

40. Wolfgang Ruddenklau, "Nuclear Power in the GDR—Chipping Away a Cornerstone," *East European Reporter* (London), Vol. 2, No. 4 (1987), p. 55.

41. *AP* (Berlin), December 21, 1986. Twenty-two East Germans from a Church-based environmentalist group sent a letter to Honecker appealing for release of the two activists.

42. The following information on the petition is drawn from B.V. Flow, "The Nuclear Debate Opens in the GDR," *Radio Free Europe Research*, Background Report/102 (German Democratic Republic), 21 July 1986.

43. Barbara Donovan, "East German Police Raid Offices of Church-Based Dissidents," *Radio Free Europe Research* (RAD/Donovan), 27 November 1987.

44. *Radio Free Europe Research,* Bulgarian Situation Report/10, 4 November 1987, item 2. See also Bulgarian Situation Report/2, 11 February 1988, item 6.

45. *Radio Free Europe Research,* Romanian Situation Report/8, 23 June 1988, item 10. Background information about this group can be found in Chapter 4.

46. There are several other national or ethnic minority groups in Eastern Europe which have experienced persecution or discrimination. They include the Gypsies throughout the region; the Ukrainians, Belorussians, Slovaks, and Lithuanians in Poland; the Sorbs in the GDR; and the Turks in Bulgaria (see Chapter 5). In some instances, protests, self-defense campaigns, and organized resistance have been registered by them or on their behalf in the country in question. However, we have focused in this section on those minorities that seem to have displayed higher degrees of independent self-organization and about whose activities information is readily available.

47. *Radio Free Europe Research,* Romanian Situation Report/16, 14 November 1985, item 5.

48. Wiseberg (Ed), *op. cit.,* p. 171.

49. Ara-Kovacs and Toth were expelled from Romania to Hungary in May 1983 and July 1984, respectively. Geza Szocs, later one of the principal editors of the Hungarian Press of Transylvania, was forced to emigrate in 1986.

50. Vladimir Socor, "Dissent in Romania: The Diversity of Voices," *Radio Free Europe Research,* Background Report/94 (Romania), 5 June 1987.

51. An interview with Kiraly appeared in *East European Reporter* (London), Vol. 2, No. 3 (1987), pp. 44–48.

52. "Karoly Kiraly's Letter to Ceausescu," *Hungarian October Freepress Information Centre* (London), 6 January 1988.

53. *Radio Free Europe Research,* Romanian Situation Report/9, 20 July 1988, item 4.

54. Vladimir Socor, "Dissent in Romania: The Diversity of Voices," *Radio Free Europe Research,* Background Report/94 (Romania), 5 June 1987.

55. *Radio Free Europe Research,* Romanian Situation Report/5, 18 April 1986, item 2. See also Romanian Situation Report/4, 25 March 1986, item 5.

56. For the full text of the letter, see *East European Reporter* (London), Vol. 2, No. 4 (1987), pp. 23–24.

57. Charter 77 Document No. 23/87. Published in English in *Palach Press Bulletin* No. 28 (London), 1987.

58. "Letter of Charter 77 to the Committee to Defend the Rights of the Hungarian Ethnic Minority in Czechoslovakia/Document No. 24/87," *Hungarian October Freepress Information Centre* (London), 28 April 1987.

59. *Radio Free Europe Research,* Czechoslovak Situation Report/2, 15 February 1988, item 11.

60. For a thoughtful consideration of the Eastern European music scene, see Pedro Ramet, "Rock Counter Culture in Eastern Europe and the Soviet Union," *Survey,* Summer 1985, Vol. 29, No. 2 (125).

61. An overview of student activism is provided by "Alienation and Protest: Students in Eastern Europe," *Radio Free Europe Research,* Background Report/ 119 (Eastern Europe), 28 June 1988.

62. An excellent analysis of this phenomenon is provided by T. Václav in "Soviet-Bloc Rock on the Offensive," *Radio Free Europe Research,* Background Report/121 (Eastern Europe), 5 September 1986. This discussion is largely indebted to Václav's report.

63. *Ibid.*

64. Radio Free Europe/Radio Liberty *Daily Report* No. 139, 26 July 1988.

65. Many of Poland's most popular rock bands have politically provocative names, such as Delirium Tremens, The Fifth Column, SS-20, Crisis, Shortage, Paralysis, and Protest.

66. No less than thirty-five punk rock groups were banned in Czechoslovakia in 1983 alone. See *Radio Free Europe Research,* Czechoslovak Situation Report/5, 26 March 1986, item 6; also Czechoslovak Situation Report/12, 5 September 1986, item 6.

67. Charter 77 Document No. 31/1983. Dated 30 August 1983.

68. T. Václav, "Will the Czech Rock Scene Adopt an East German Beat?," *Radio Free Europe Research,* Background Report/127 (Eastern Europe), 11 September 1986.

69. Two books providing detailed information about the underground rock scene in East Germany are: Wolfgang Buescher, *Null Block auf DDR* (Reinbek bei Hamburg: Rowohlt Verlag, 1984) and Olaf Leitner, *Rockszene DDR: Aspekte einer Massenkultur im Sozialismus* (Reinbek bei Hamburg: Rowohlt Verlag, 1983).

70. Pedro Ramet, "Disaffection and Dissent in East Germany," *World Politics,* Vol. XXXVII, October 1984, No. 1, p. 93.

71. A valuable analysis of this phenomenon is afforded by Barbara Donovan in "Skinheads and Neofascism in the GDR," *Radio Free Europe Research,* Background Report/96 (German Democratic Republic), 30 May 1988.

72. *Radio Free Europe Research,* Bulgarian Situation Report/3, 20 May 1987, item 7.

73. Vladimir Socor, "The Workers' Protest in Brasov: Assessment and Aftermath," *Radio Free Europe Research,* RAD Background Report/231 (Romania), 4 December 1987.

74. *Radio Free Europe Research,* Polish Situation Report/3, 25 February 1988, item 2.

75. Church-run educational establishments, constituting a major exception, are noted in Chapter 5.

76. For in-depth coverage, see Chris Pszenicki, "The Flying University," *Index on Censorship,* Vol. 8, No. 6, November–December 1979, pp. 19–22.

77. *Ibid.,* p. 20.

78. Wladyslaw Bartoszewski, "Flying Through the Fear Barrier," *Index on Censorship,* No. 2, 1985, p. 36.

79. Teresa Hanicka, "The Independent Education Movement in Poland," *Radio Free Europe Research,* Background Report/150 (Poland), 16 August 1984.

80. See "OKN: Organizing Underground Education, Culture and Science," *East European Reporter* (London), Vol. 1, No. 2, Summer 1985, pp. 12–14.

81. U.S. Helsinki Watch Committee, *Reinventing Civil Society: Poland's Quiet Revolution 1981–1986* (New York: U.S. Helsinki Watch Committee, December 1986), p. 33.

82. *Radio Free Europe Research,* Polish Situation Report/4, 17 March 1988, item 7.

83. Wiseberg (Ed), *op. cit.,* p. 200.

84. The endeavor was named in memory of Jan Patočka (1907–77), a professor of philosophy and Christian activist who was a founding member of Charter 77 and later a Charter 77 spokesman. He died of a heart attack in March 1977, after eleven hours of grueling police interrogation.

85. Ted Kaminski, "Underground Publishing in Poland," *Orbis,* Vol. 31, No. 3, Fall 1987, p. 315. This excellent article provided much of the background for this section.

86. "The Nowa Independent Publishing House's 10th Birthday," *Uncensored Poland News Bulletin* (London), No. 2, 22 January 1988. See also Konrad Bieliński and Mirosław Chojecki, "NOWA: Poland's Unofficial Publisher," *Index on Censorship,* Vol. 10, No. 1, February 1981.

87. Kaminski, *op. cit.,* pp. 315–19.

88. This wide margin in estimates may be due in part to the lack of continuity or short-lived nature of many independent publishing endeavors. For a sampling of underground articles that deal with the subject of clandestine publishing, see "Solidarność Clandestine Press," *Voice of Solidarity* (London), No. 115, March 1986.

89. "On the Independent Publishing," *Uncensored Poland News Bulletin* (London), No. 15, 30 July 1987.

90. "The State of the Independent Publishing Movement," *Uncensored Poland News Bulletin* (London), No. 16, 12 August 1987.

91. Stefan Bratkowski, "Explosion of Independent Journalism," *Index on Censorship,* Vol. 16, No. 4, April 1987, p. 18.

92. For a fuller list, see Wiseberg (Ed), *op. cit.,* p. 120.

93. Kaminski, *op. cit.,* p. 320.

94. Wiseberg (Ed), *op. cit.,* p. 121. See also "Poland's Flourishing Independent Culture," *Index on Censorship,* No. 6, 1986, pp. 24–26.

95. "The Independent Publishing in Poland," *Uncensored Poland News Bulletin* (London), No. 3/87, 3 February 1987.

96. See Anonymous, "AB: Hungary's Independent Publisher," *Index on Censorship,* Vol. 12, No. 2, April 1983, pp. 5–7.

97. Wiseberg (Ed), *op. cit.,* pp. 198–99.

98. Bill Lomax, "Independent Publishing in Hungary," *Index on Censorship,* Vol. 12, No. 2, April 1983, pp. 3–5.

99. *Radio Free Europe Research,* Hungarian Situation Report/3, 8 February 1983, item 2.

100. Stephan Polgar, "Samizdat in Hungary: A New Voice is Heard," *Radio Free Europe Research,* Background Report/104 (Hungary), 3 May 1982.

101. Wiseberg (Ed), *op. cit.,* p. 199.

102. *Radio Free Europe Research,* Hungarian Situation Report/5, 13 April 1984, item 1.

103. "Coordinated Police Actions Against 'The Democrat,'" *Hungarian October Freepress Information Centre* (London), 101/1987(E), 1 September 1987.

104. "Demokrata—Hungarian Samizdat," *Index on Censorship*, No. 9/87, p. 4.

105. Zdena Tomin, "The Typewriters Hold the Fort," *Index on Censorship*, Vol. 12, No. 2, April 1983, pp. 28–30.

106. Wiseberg (Ed), *op. cit.*, p. 185.

107. For example, see *Radio Free Europe Research*, Czechoslovak Situation Report/2, 15 February 1988, item 13.

108. Alternative theater has flourished, notably in Czechoslovakia. For an account of so-called "living room theatre," in which works of banned authors are performed by banned actors and actresses, see Karel Kyncl, "A Censored Life," *Index on Censorship*, No. 1, 1985, pp. 37–42. See also Barbara Day, "Theatre on a String," *Index on Censorship*, No. 1, 1985, pp. 34–36. For a description of comparable developments in Poland, see Agnieszka Wojcik, "Alternative Theatre," *Index on Censorship*, No. 1, 1985, pp. 11–14.

109. "The Independent Art Group INCONNU is Ten Years Old," *Hungarian October Free Press Information Centre* (London), 109/1988, 1 May 1988.

110. See, for example, "High Fine Imposed on Members of the INCONNU Group," *Hungarian October Freepress Information Centre* (London), 39/1987, 7 April 1987.

111. "'Alternative Cultural Centre' in Budapest Opened with Wallenberg Exhibition," *Hungarian October Freepress Information Centre* (London), 56/1987, 9 May 1987.

112. Quoted in "'Alternative Cultural Centre' Opened in Budapest," *Hungarian October Freepress Information Centre* (London), 55/1987, 8 May 1987.

113. "Stalin-Exhibition of the INCONNU Group," *Hungarian October Freepress Information Centre* (London), 67/87, 25 May 1987.

114. "Artworks Confiscated in Budapest by Hungarian Police," *Hungarian October Freepress Information Centre* (London), 6/1987, 28 January 1987.

115. "The INCONNU Group's Open Letter to the Central Committee of the Hungarian Socialist Workers' Party," *Hungarian October Freepress Information Centre* (London), 10/1987, 7 February 1987.

116. George Theiner, "Last Year in Budapest," *Index on Censorship*, 1/86, pp. 37–41.

117. "Beseiged Jazz Section," *East European Reporter* (London), Vol. 1, No. 3 (1985), pp. 33–35.

118. "Against Kitsch Culture," *East European Reporter* (London), Vol. 2, No. 3 (1987), pp. 2–6.

119. Wiseberg (Ed), *op. cit.*, p. 186.

120. Josef Skvorecky, "Jamming the Jazz Section," *The New York Review of Books*, 30 June 1988, p. 41.

121. "Non-Conformist Culture in the Dock," *East European Reporter* (London), Vol. 2, No. 2 (1986), pp. 17–20.

122. *Radio Free Europe Research*, Czechoslovak Situation Report/4, 6 April 1987, items 4 and 5. See also "Please Don't Give Up," *East European Reporter* (London), Vol. 2, No. 3 (1987), pp. 7–9; and "Victory or Compromise?," *East European Reporter* (London), Vol. 2, No. 4 (1987), pp. 9–12.

123. Accounts of this group from the Polish underground press are translated in "Gnomes, Revolution and Toilet Paper," and "More on 'Orange Alternative'" in *Uncensored Poland News Bulletin* (London), No. 2, 22 January 1988 and No. 6, 22 March 1988.

124. See "Statement by the Orange Alternative," *Uncensored Poland News Bulletin* (London), No. 7, 15 April 1988.

125. Quoted in "Alternatively, in Poland," *The Economist*, 21 May 1988, p. 54.

126. Radio Free Europe/Radio Liberty, *Daily Report* No. 104, 3 June 1988.

127. John Tagliabue, "Police Draw The Curtain, But The Farce Still Plays," *The New York Times*, 14 June 1988.

Chapter 8: Emerging Prospects

1. Earlier versions of sections of this chapter were previously published in the following: "East European Developments and U.S. Responses," *CSIS Contingencies Series*, October 1987, Washington, DC; "The Bird in Moscow's Cage: Eastern Europe and Perestroika," *National Interest*, No. 12, Summer 1988; "East European Dissent: Impasses and Opportunities," *Problems of Communism*, Vol. XXXVII, No. 2, March–April 1988; and "Liberating the Soviet Bloc," *The World and I*, Vol. 3, No. 8, August 1988.

2. Since the 1960s Eastern Europe has become an economic liability for Moscow. Some analysts estimate a net cost for the Soviets in the region of $50 billion per annum. The financial burden is likely to increase if military equipment is to be updated and local economies kept afloat. For a history of economic relations between the USSR and the East bloc consult Valerie Bunce, "The Empire Strikes Back: The Evolution of the Eastern Bloc from a Soviet Asset to a Soviet Liability," *International Organization*, Vol. 39, No. 1, Winter 1985, pp. 1–46.

3. For details see Charles Wolf, et al., *The Cost of the Soviet Empire* (Santa Monica: Rand Corporation, 1983).

4. See Carlotta Gall, "The Burden of Empire," *Radio Liberty Research Bulletin*, No. 512/87, 16 December 1987.

5. For a valuable analysis of the chief factors and constraints in CMEA integration see Paul Marer and John Michael Montias, "Theory and Measurement of East European Integration," in Paul Marer and John Michael Montias (Eds), *East European Integration and East-West Trade* (Bloomington: Indiana University Press, 1980), pp. 1–38. Among the problems enumerated are: constraints on producers to supply for foreign trade as enterprises operate in order to fulfill a predetermined plan, not to make a profit; little interfactory competition; and a coarse information system inhibiting proper international specialization.

6. Among several helpful recent histories and assessments of Soviet-East European relations see J.F. Brown, *Eastern Europe and Communist Rule* (Durham: Duke University Press, 1988); Robert L. Hutchings, *Soviet-East European Relations: Consolidation and Conflict* (Madison: University of Wisconsin Press, 1987); and

Karen Dawisha, *Eastern Europe, Gorbachev, and Reform: The Great Challenge* (Cambridge: Cambridge University Press, 1988).

7. For a discussion of these issues see Janusz Bugajski, "Soviet Bloc Propaganda: The Glasnost Factor," *Political Communication and Persuasion*, Vol. 4, No. 4, 1987.

8. Illuminating discussions of Soviet bloc "restructuring" objectives can be found in Vladimir Sobell, "Is 'Restructuring' a Fake Reform?" *Radio Free Europe Research*, Background Report/189 (Economics), 20 October 1987; and "CMEA Reforms and the East-West Technological Gap," *Radio Free Europe Research*, Background Report/181 (Economics), 9 October 1987. According to the author, *perestroika* "should be understood not as a quick move to a new Western-like system but as a process of removing piece by piece the most glaring irrationalities rooted in central planning."

9. Pavel Machala, "Eastern Europe, Eurocommunism, and the Problems of Detente," in Morton A. Kaplan (Ed), *The Many Faces of Communism* (New York: The Free Press, Macmillan, 1978), pp. 228–65.

10. An evaluation of the foreign policy components of Gorbachev's East European program can be found in Helene Carrere D'Encausse, *Big Brother: The Soviet Union and Eastern Europe* (New York: Holmes & Meier, 1987).

11. Moscow remains adamant about the inviolability of Red Army bases and troop deployments, the non-blockage of its military lines of communication across the region, and the maintenance of the Warsaw Pact "alliance." For an important study of how Moscow maintains its hegemony over Eastern Europe through the structures of the Warsaw Treaty Organization see Christopher D. Jones, *Soviet Influence in Eastern Europe: Political Autonomy and the Warsaw Pact* (New York: Praeger, 1981).

12. Harry Gelman, *East Europe and Soviet Leadership Contention: Implications for the West*, European American Institute for Security Research, Paper No. 10, Spring 1985, p. 16.

13. Facts and figures on the East European economies discussed in this section are largely gleaned from various Radio Free Europe reports which closely track statistics issued by the respective Communist states.

14. According to an interview with Jiri Hajek, the former Minister for Foreign Affairs and Charter 77 signatory, with *The New York Times* on 10 April 1987, during Gorbachev's visit to Prague.

15. *AP* (Prague), 14 January 1988.

16. Their letters have evidently not been published by the Czechoslovak Party daily; see *The New York Times*, 5 April 1987.

17. See *Charter 77 Document No. 20/87* (Prague), 23 March 1987. Numerous letters have also been sent by dissidents to the Prague regime to encourage it to initiate far-reaching reforms, to restore government respect for human rights, and to "develop democracy."

18. *Ibid*.

19. Based on comments by Charter 77 signatory Jiri Dienstbier to the *Christian Science Monitor*, 9 April 1987.

20. For a useful compilation of such debate in Poland consult *Radio Free Europe Research*, Polish Independent Press Review/4, 29 May 1987, item 3.

21. In an interview for *Der Spiegel*, 11 May 1987. Michnik has also suggested that Gorbachev may directly help to improve Polish-Soviet relations by more openly discussing burning historical controversies, such as the Katyn forest massacre of Polish officers during World War II, about which the two ruling Parties have remained silent or evasive.

22. See the "Social Contract" in *Beszelo*, No. 20, June 1987.

23. Among several Gorbachev-related phenomena within the Hungarian opposition, 200 journalists applied to the government in March 1988 to establish a "glasnost club." The aim is to provide the public with information about important issues in the reform movement that are sorely neglected by the official media, and to "follow up injustices against citizens." The journalists' application was carefully worded to stress the club's intention to work alongside rather than against the official Journalists Association. Budapest's reaction to the initiative was not sympathetic; pressures were placed on state media editors to impose sanctions against any staff signing the "glasnost club" application. See *Reuter*, 4 March 1988.

24. For details about the letters see *Radio Free Europe Research*, Romanian Situation Report/11, 15 October 1987, item 8.

25. See the interview in *L'Express*, Paris, 28 May 1987. Another prominent Romanian dissident, the veteran National Peasant Party leader Ion Puiu, was detained by the security police when found in possession of a memorandum intended for Gorbachev during the latter's visit to Bucharest.

26. *DPA* (Berlin), 28 August 1987.

27. For example, see *The New York Times*, 10 June 1987, *Reuter* (Berlin), 1 February 1988, and *The Washington Times*, 8 February 1988.

28. See the article by the underground political commentator Karol Grodkowski in *Tygodnik Mazowsze* (Warsaw), No. 202, 11 March 1987.

29. *Ibid.*

30. For a summary of the views expressed during the discussion refer to *Tygodnik Mazowsze* No. 218, translated and reprinted in *Uncensored Poland News Bulletin* (London), No. 18, 11 September 1987.

31. Check in particular reports from Poland in *The Washington Post* and *The New York Times* on 13, 14, and 15 July 1988.

32. *Tygodnik Mazowsze*, *op. cit.*

33. *Ibid.*

34. For the translated text of Václav's interview with a Czechoslovak *samizdat* publication, entitled "Reasons of Doubt and Sources of Hope," see Vladimir Kusin, "Vaclav Václav on Doubt and Hope," *Radio Free Europe Research*, Background Report/33 (Eastern Europe), 1 March 1988.

35. Refer for instance to *Solidarność Walczaca* (Wrocław), No. 13 (157), 21 June–5 July 1987.

36. Quoted in *Tygodnik Mazowsze* (Warsaw), No. 201, 4 March 1987.

37. The full text of the joint communique, issued on 21 August 1987, is available from the "Committee for the Support of Human Rights in Czechoslovakia," Washington, D.C.

38. *AFP* (Warsaw), 5 August 1987.

39. For information on the July 1988 meeting and the joint statement issued by Czechoslovak and Polish dissidents see *Radio Free Europe Research*, Czechoslovak Situation Report/10, 14 July 1988, item 4.

40. From an interview with the British Labour Party monthly in London, *New Socialist*, February 1987.

41. Consult J.F. Brown, "Eastern Europe's Western Connection," and Lincoln Gordon, "Interests and Policies in Eastern Europe: The View from Washington," in Lincoln Gordon (Ed), *Eroding Empire: Western Relations with Eastern Europe* (Washington, DC: Brookings Institution, 1987).

42. See Bennett Kovrig, "The United States: 'Peaceful Engagement' Revisited," in Charles Gati (Ed), *The International Politics of Eastern Europe* (New York: Praeger, 1976), pp. 131–53.

43. Some West European states have engaged in their own distinctive brand of "engagement" with Eastern Europe, sometimes at variance with other NATO allies. For a valuable account of the successes and failures of West Germany's Ostpolitik from the mid-1960s onwards see Andrew Gyorgy, "Ostpolitik and Eastern Europe," in Gati (Ed), *op. cit.*, pp. 154–72.

44. Specific guidelines for Western cooperation *vis-à-vis* the Soviet bloc are provided by Lincoln Gordon, "Convergence and Conflict: Lessons for the West," in Gordon (Ed), *op. cit.*, pp. 292–328.

45. A discussion of these issues can be found in Vratislav Pechota, "East European Dissent, the United States, and the Soviet Union," in Jane Leftwich Curry (Ed), *Dissent in Eastern Europe* (New York: Praeger, 1983), pp. 197–213.

46. An analysis of the provisions and consequences of the Conference on Security and Cooperation in Europe (CSCE), which produced the Helsinki Final Act, can be found in Vojtech Mastny (Ed), *Helsinki, Human Rights, and European Security: Analysis and Documentation* (Durham: Duke University Press, 1986).

47. Gelman thinks that the more forthright and united are Western positions, specifying the political and economic costs of military intervention, the more likely that these will be seriously considered by the Kremlin. They may also "help to encourage Soviet propensity toward discord and hesitation." See Gelman, *op. cit.*, p. 16.

48. In Brzezinski's estimation, though the West cannot easily undo the partition of Europe, steps can be taken in this direction without full-scale warfare or a Russian defeat: "A wider Europe can only emerge as a consequence of historical stealth so to speak, which can neither be quickly detected, nor easily resisted." Refer to Zbigniew Brzezinski, "The Future of Yalta," *Foreign Affairs*, Vol. 63, No. 2, Winter 1984/1985, p. 17.

49. According to Marer and Montias, "the expansion of East-West commerce has set in motion both centrifugal and centripetal forces in the CMEA; their strength and impact differ from time to time and from country to country." See Marer and Montias, *op. cit.*, p. 31.

50. Consult Philip Windsor, "Stability and Instability in Eastern Europe and their Implications for Western Policy," in Karen Dawisha and Philip Hansen (Eds), *Soviet-East European Dilemmas: Coercion, Competition and Consent* (New York: Holmes & Meier, 1981), pp. 195–211.

51. For a criticism of Western assumptions that increasing unconditional economic cooperation will lead to a "convergence" between capitalist and Communist systems see Jan Zielonka, "East-West Trade: Is There a Way Out of the Circle?" *The Washington Quarterly*, Vol. 11, No. 1, Winter 1988, pp. 131–49.

52. A major cause of Soviet bloc indebtedness is the unfavorable and worsening balance of trade, where Eastern imports from the West far exceed exports and compound the chronic shortage of hard currency necessary to purchase further imports. Communist regimes face a major business problem: an urgent need for Western capital and technology, where their capacity for importation ultimately depends on an ability to obtain hard currency through loans or exports. Western demand for CMEA products is low and falling, largely because of their poor quality, unmarketability, and uncompetitiveness. Inability to earn sufficient currency is aggravated by the obligation to service large debts to the West; these payments absorb a growing proportion of export earnings. For some assessment of East-West trade see Martin Sznitzel, *U.S. Business Involvement in Eastern Europe* (New York: Praeger, 1980).

53. One recent report on U.S. relations with Poland, which could be more widely applied to Western policy throughout Eastern Europe, recommends: "A policy of re-engagement on a basis of clear and prioritized political and economic conditionality . . . in which steps taken by Poland to implement reform are matched with steps by the United States. . . . This could be a process to reward favorable change or to deny benefits if conditions agreed to were not met." See *Poland's Renewal and U.S. Options: A Policy Reconnaissance*, report prepared for the Subcommittee on Europe and the Middle East of the Committee on Foreign Affairs, U.S. House of Representatives, by the Congressional Research Service, Library of Congress, 5 March 1987, p. 38.

Index